The Ruricolist

Essays & Caprices

Paul M. Rodriguez

New Orleans
Argiope
2019

BY THE SAME AUTHOR

The Endless City

ISBN 9781794566699

Contents

Year Two   95

Year Three   213

Year Four   299

Year Five   381

Nondefinitions

Preface

The Ruricolist is an essay series in the form of a blog. By the time you read this, the last sentence may be unintelligible. What is an essay series? What is a blog? But what the Ruricolist is will be recognizable as long as books last.

In writing fiction we do not hesitate to imagine ourselves as equals with the masters. But when we sit down to write prose we console ourselves with our limitations. The masters could rely on the interest and knowledge of their audience, could coin their own words and bend grammar to their needs without defying spell checkers and proofreaders, could write sentences that needed to be read twice to be understood. They could put as many ideas as they wanted in an essay – in a paragraph – in a sentence – in a very long sentence. For them, style was end and means.

If our work is lesser, if it does not endure, it is not our fault. We are creatures of our time. We have to draft query letters, appease editors, and calculate reading levels. We defer to specialists and hedge against character-limit assassins. We admit concentrated literary effects only on credit, as quotations. Our works are stepping stones, not bricks. We do not build on them; we use them to get ahead, and we leave them behind.

But there was a moment. A chance to meet an audience without editors, without marketing departments, without censors official or self-appointed. A chance to do what would never sell, what would never pay. To write without the need for permission or forgiveness. A moment the work could stand on its own. A moment we stood before an ocean not yet acidified, while our messages in bottles could reach another shore.

I saw other people using that freedom, admired what they were doing with it, and though I am not a joiner, I decided to join in. And I used that moment for all it was worth. I took it as far as it could go.

What would happen if one of us – someone from our century learned and ignorant, our century callow and sensitive, our century then hardly begun – what would happen if one of us assumed the same freedoms, the same scope, as the canon and the classics?

What would happen if a modern writer attempted the classical essay? Opened all the resources of the language? Took the synoptic view? Philosophy, psychology, history, literature – why not do everything at once? It would be hard; but it's not supposed to be easy. And none of it seemed worthwhile by itself.

That was me; that was the Ruricolist. I was bounded only by my idea of general interest. I never found a large audience; the audience I did find was composed mostly of other writers. I turned the writers I admired into readers.

There was a moment, but it ended. Crisis frightened us. We wanted nothing to identify us as dreamers or thinkers. We retreated from our freeholds into the shelters of social media, only to discover that what we thought was a shelter was, in fact, a barracks. That we were not guests, but conscripts.

There was a moment, but it ended. In the end, I looked up and saw I was alone. And now so many of the writers I admired are missing, gone silent or self-effaced.

The Ruricolist was never meant to be read from start to finish, but to draw in readers as it went. And unlike many of its contemporaries, it is not one of those projects that builds up its own idiosyncratic vocabulary over time. Start anywhere; start with what interests you, and I will try to earn your trust.

It has been eight years since the end of the Ruricolist. Naturally, some of my opinions and conclusions have changed. Only a fool never changes his mind; only a coward pretends his mind has never changed. But I have clarified arguments that could be misunderstood.

This is the point where I am supposed to self-deprecate. I was young, it was a different time, I was writing on a schedule. But the truth is I could never renounce what is here. What is here is who I am.

Year One

"This I had never thought, this came as a shock: reason could sleep. Reason could be asleep and helpless."

NOTICE

APRIL 14, 2007   I find writing to be its own reward. But there is something cowardly in spending time amassing what is not to be shared. I have therefore created this blog and mean here to expose, at intervals tending towards weekly, something worth reading – even re-reading.

The name, *The Ruricolist*, is meant to recall the essay series of old, when they could stand alone: *The Tatler*, *The Idler*, *The Rambler*, and others. I mean to be similarly eclectic and similarly to space out essays with other forms – what I call caprices. But my mark is Baconian concentration and brevity, not smooth Augustan prolixity.

It would be worse to hide my political and religious principles than not to have them, but my intentions are strictly literary. I do not mean to advance, join, or create a faction. I believe as others believe, but I wear no uniform.

I write not for myself, not for friends, not for an audience, not for posterity: this is my end of a conversation.

ON ESSAYS

APRIL 14, 2007   The essay cannot be usefully defined, because it is always subject to redefinition. Essays are the most individual form of writing, and the most governed by tradition. An essayist must be themselves, but they must also know the whole history of the essay. The essay is a language we learn, and only having mastered, employ fluently.

We call many compositions essays only for their length: for some purposes the essay is a unit of composition arranged from paragraphs, just as paragraphs are arranged from sentences. Or else it is the sump of literature, where everything ends up that has nowhere else to go. These definitions are true, but meaningless; two-legged without feathers.

The essay is a *via negativa*. The essay is not a treatise; it is not a tract; it is not a sermon. It does not begin from first principles, it deduces nothing. Like conversation, the essay can take interest, background, and good will for granted. It is not a tract; it does not line up points and facts to support them. The essayist does not expect to persuade. And it is not a sermon: the essay has no reproach, only sympathy and commiseration, for our failings.

The essay is the fruit of experience – but writing (and reading) essays is a particularly fruitful form of experience. Being untried, we think ourselves sound; being pure, we think ourselves incorruptible; being strong, we think ourselves able; having hope, we think ourselves destined. Until we learn better, until we are tried, nothing we write, however clever, can be an essay. But *essai* really means *trial* – *trial*, not *attempt* – and essays are one way we can try ourselves.

An essay may be fine, patient work, or swift swashbuckling, but the tool is the same: to be honest; to omit nothing and exaggerate nothing. Secondhand opinions, clichés and party lines, annul the essay in the beginning, or derail it in the end. An essayist dreads corroboration. You bring to an essay only what is your own: not the text of your philosophy, but its marginalia; your exceptions, not your rules.

A HOUSE IN THE COUNTRY

APRIL 20, 2007   City people's country houses are easy to recognize – not just by the signs of wealth. City people move to *the country* as if it were a place; to them it is all one green emptiness filling the spaces between cities. Formerly such people came fleeing the city; as many now profess a love for the country, founded in landscape paintings, movies, music, or sometimes even when an eye for beauty, lifted for a moment from the road or the screen, notices that there is more beside the highway or the trail than scrolling scenery.

But once they have their piece of the country, city people set about re-creating it. They re-make it in an image of *the country* from magazines and movies. They take a *place*, with its own character and private history, and cut and prune and saw and fertilize and plant and irrigate until they have turned it into a picture. It is all for the eye. Every leaf and blade and flower screams of the desperation to please critical visitors, also city people, making their visit to *the country*, not to *this place*. The sense of place vanishes. It goes untouched by its owners. Bare feet, a little light gardening, a little pruning; but it is the contractors, even the best of them strangers to this soil, these trees, who perform the grafts and amputations.

The wry tree and the curious outbuilding are sawn down, torn down, cut out to ensure that all is scenic and even; all ready for photographs; all up-to-date; unassertive prospects, like background music, with nothing to catch the eye or hold the fancy, nothing to draw off the trail, nothing to impress the memory except how impressed you were with the means and taste of your host – didn't we read that designer's name in a magazine somewhere; and pictures of this place will be appearing in the next issue; yes, that magazine, it's wonderful and we're so proud of this place, we'll send you a copy; of course you can have that number.

The magazine shows the designer's work, a dozen different places in a dozen different states – "We wanted to reflect the local idiom" – but the photographer didn't really capture the gingerbread curves impressed in the stucco of the northeastern house, or the smooth corners of the southwestern house. If you didn't know any better you might swear that every shot was of the same place: smooth grass you could play golf on, a touch of whimsy in that little statue, demure trees concealing the horizon in an anonymous rank, the three trees lined up by the house as an umbrella trimmed so they seem one tree with three trunks.

It is all country, not a car or a speck of concrete or asphalt, and look at that wooden wagon with the empty pots in it – but it is all city. It is neat, and tame; and it is hard to understand, and tragic, how your escape from the city brings the city with you, how your love of the country creates a virtual reality, seen but not touched, too eager to please for beauty. Do you keep the prints of those old paintings, watch those movies, listen to those songs; do you ever come outside from them and realize that no one will ever paint your house, that no stories will be born or live or come there?

In the city, in the suburbs, we dwell lightly. Others have been and gone as we are and must go. There is no connection except sequence. But a country house is not just a property. To have it is not merely to own something, but to become part of something, of the life which is there already – an ecology, a history, a place. It is proper to bring order to that life – it is yours, leave your mark – but you also have responsibilities: to nature, to the past, and to the future.

EVOLUTIONARY PSYCHOLOGY

APRIL 27, 2007   After the tawdriness of psychoanalysis, evolutionary psychology is an inspiring project. It is moving to contemplate, in those around us and in ourselves, the traces of the struggles of our immemorial ancestors. It satisfyingly draws together all the departments of human self-knowledge, the range of human accomplishment and failure. Its potential mass appeal is much greater than that of psychoanalysis, because it does not try to reduce that range to the result of a universal incest drama. Evolutionary psychology is romantic; in our irrationalities and stupidities it hears the echoes of the forest (or savanna) primeval. Given the choice, most human beings would prefer to ascribe their failings – their shortsightedness, their lust, their temper, their haste – to the habits of the hunters of antiquity, than to Adam's and Eve's sin, or to the unremembered sexual frustrations of childhood.

But evolutionary psychology presents the same central problem as psychoanalysis. It explains absolutely everything, and in several different ways, with nothing to falsify, and nothing to guide choice save taste, or loyalty to a particular hypothesizer. Natural selection, a principle similarly subject to speculative application, is constrained by the records of fossils, geology, and genetics. No such constraints prune evolutionary psychology. Its applications grow, not with the data to be understood, but with the problems to be explained,

Evolutionary psychology connects modern behaviors with the needs and living conditions of ancient hominids. We have their skeletons, which have much to say, but we have no living specimens. We generalize from primates; but that is an analogy more driven by the human habit of projecting our own traits onto animals – here especially tempting with so many real commonalities – than any actual resemblance in behavior between humans and our very distant cousins: we who organize like ants, sing like whales, laugh like nothing else.

But evolutionary psychologists do not work out, on practical grounds, what primitive humanity was like. *Our ancestors* as in *our ancestors needed this behavior* are not taken from anthropology, primatology, or zoology. What we are presented with in *our ancestors* is neither human nor animal; it is human wit, human intellect, without the danger of human error, uncivilized and therefore prelapsarian, illiterate yet storyless and with-

6

out self-consciousness, their behavior always to the animal's long-term optimum without an animal's forgetfulness. *Our ancestors* is not a theory, a model, or a guess; it is a myth.

Evolutionary psychologists note that hominids made tools and mastered fire; but they continue to treat these hominids as if their tools – and their increasingly invented and instrumental social order – were inert epiphenomena of the usual evolutionary interactions, with predators, competitors, and climate. But by rewarding the better knapper, kindler, imitator of vocalizations announcing prey or predator, marker of trails building up a symbolic instead of a kinesthetic map in memory, giver of orders, maker of allies – by rewarding them evolution simultaneously created clumsiness, carelessness, awkwardness, taciturnity, stupidity, uncertainty, servility, and domineering. Somewhere, far enough back, there was the animal that would be human; but in between there was no morning when optimally behaved hominids became human beings with their baggage of irrelevant reflexes and drives.

Where is history? Evolutionary psychologists take a parochial view of humanity, ignoring historical change and modern diversity, a view where the human animal is assumed irrelevant and obsolete. But we did not leave the savannas and start building skyscrapers. Somewhere in between was Heorot; there was the wolf, now there is the door, but once one scratched and snorted at the other. You can explain altruism? Good, now explain stylites.

In their offices and conferences the evolutionary psychologists do not always stop to check that the subject is dead before the autopsy. Not everyone gets through life without having to fight or fly. They do not notice primitives, peasants, refugees; nor the wilderness worse than jungle that follows famine, disaster, war; nor even the criminals, politicians, soldiers around them who live by instinct, against worse than saber teeth. It would be well to stop and remember that civilization did not drop down from heaven or occur by accident: it was made, made by human beings with animal strength.

The form of the answers evolutionary psychology gives is correct. The way we are is because of the way our ancestors were. But we do not how they were and, for the most part, we do not know how we are.

Evolutionary psychology is a worthy project; but so far the project has been ignored while the *idea* of an evolutionary psychology has been used to weight the clichés of cynicism and misanthropy. But swinging the blackjack, satisfying as it, is not science.

To mature, evolution psychology must ask its own questions. What was each species of hominid really like? What marked the transitions, how sudden were they, were they qualitative or quantitative? What was the role of population bottlenecks, or of population centers? How far did cohabitation produce sociability, how far did forced sociability produce cohabitation? Are aboriginal peoples and cultures, exhibiting perennial stability – are they where we started, or are they dead ends, diverging from a mainstream which shades from pre-agricultural villages into civilization? Are reason and language, once set in motion, self-perpetuating, or are they only a reflection of external pressures?

This should be the work of the infant science: not to yield new answers, not to reinforce old answers, but to ask new questions of its own.

THE BETTER MOUSETRAP

MAY 4, 2007   You are an entrepreneur and inventor of an all-around innovative product called the Better Mousetrap. Your competitor in this field is a new conglomerate, Universal Mousetrap, formed from the merger of American Mousetrap, Imperial Mousetrap (of England, with subsidiaries in all Commonwealth nations), and Anygrad Mousetrap (formerly the Anygrad Mousetrap Design Bureau). Universal Mousetrap also has a good relationship with the Mousetrap Company of Shanghai – once a subsidiary of Imperial Mousetrap, before Mao and the nationalization of foreign assets.

To start with, naturally, you need money. You make presentations to several venture capital firms, irrefutably demonstrating the technical superiority of the Better Mousetrap. You are nonetheless repeatedly turned down. This perplexes you until you realize, from certain cryptic comments and a long look through the hagiographies at Universal Mousetrap's website, that most of the Universal Mousetrap management, particularly the famous, dashing, well-tailored CEO, are graduates of a certain famous American university, which also supplies much of the management of these venture capital firms. You are asking them to betray their old friends and golf partners.

Very well, then. You will not be daunted. You seek out a smaller company, with management of less exalted background, and quickly obtain the funds you require. You build a factory in the Midwest, and start churning out samples of the Better Mousetrap to demonstrate to retailers.

Your first disappointment comes from your greatest hope: the ubiquitous retail chain, Tanto-Mart. Their handshakes are listless; they seem hardly to be listening to your presentation. They express doubts about your capacity to produce the volume they require. You produce charts, diagrams, ranks and files of facts and figures to show them they are wrong. You already have the whole chain worked out, from deactivated nuclear warheads to Tanto-Mart shelves. They are noncommittal, even after you show them independent studies demonstrating people's universal desire for a better mousetrap and their high opinion of yours. They contact you later to decline. Your mousetrap would have a shelf price ten cents higher than Universal's. If you were just willing to outsource production...

But the Better Mousetrap is a sophisticated product. Cryptography is involved which it would be illegal to export; and there is the fear of patent violation and piracy. The manufacturing process for the mus capacitor is a trade secret which might be difficult to keep overseas.

You keep trying. You make local presences for yourself, especially in the "global cities" where sophisticated buyers love the Better Mousetrap. You start getting into the smaller chains and franchises on regional levels. From local supply you are building global demand.

Then one day you are out shopping at your local Tanto-Mart, and you discover a product called the Gooder Mousetrap. You buy it, take it home, and discover that it is in clear violation of your own patent. It is manufactured, according to the box, by the Gooder Mousetrap Company of Frontville, Kansas. You decide to sue. As you prepare your lawyers find that the Gooder Mousetrap Company is in fact owned by Universal Mousetrap.

Your sales are already declining. Ad outlays actually seem to be decreasing your sales as the Gooder Mousetrap Company takes out competing ads putting its product forward as the cheaper alternative.

Universal's lawyers come into court and admit they have been in violation. They claim that they neglected to conduct a search for prior art before patenting the Gooder Mousetrap. They volunteer to withdraw the product from the market. They accept a fine and agree to destroy all stock of the Gooder Mousetrap.

You are elated. Gooder Mousetraps disappear from the shelves. Your Internet and mail-order sales increase dramatically, as publicity from the trial spreads the work about the Better Mousetrap. But outlet sales stay down. Why? You discover that the Gooder Mousetrap has reappeared in stores. You buy one and take it apart. It has all new workings; you are confident that it still violates your patents, just in a completely different way. You decide to go to court again.

You also decide that the time has come to capture the market you have always been aiming for: industrial mousetrapping, for grain storage and food warehousing. Only no one is interested. You discover why: Universal is selling the Gooder Mousetrap in bulk, below cost, to industry. You manage to get ahold of one of these mousetraps only to find: this is not the new model; it is the old model you have already won your case against, all stock of which was supposed to have been destroyed. This is not just a temporary setback: since the Better Mousetrap, and consequently the Gooder Mousetrap, uses lasers to vaporize the carcasses and runs on 30-year plutonium thermoelectric batteries, buying an order of mousetraps is not a continuing expense, but an infrastructural investment unlikely to be repeated for decades. You start another suit against Universal Mousetrap.

The court judgments go against you. A media campaign has cast Universal Mousetrap as the victim of your incessant, litigious persecution. Media campaigns, of course, should not influence court judgments. You know that. Judge and jury, apparently, do not.

Although the only byproduct is drinkable water, and clean disposal by microsingularity is as simple as pressing the self-destruct button, an environmentalist group, PAP – People Against Plutonium – forms to protest the Better Mousetrap. It is easy to trace PAP's funding back to Universal Mousetrap; but few bother. Fake websites, fake blogs, fake packaged news reports from fake reporters soon start attracting a real community of real activists. PAP attains special notoriety after staging an event, video of which circulates widely on the Internet, in which a Better Mousetrap, hacked to remove all of its extensive safety protocols, is swallowed by an elephant, which promptly explodes.

Universal Mousetrap offers a new product: the Saner Mousetrap. It differs from the Gooder Mousetrap in three respects: the box and case of the mousetrap are green in color; the words – true of all models – "Eco-

Friendly" appear on the box; and it is more expensive than the Better Mousetrap. Catalog sales plummet as the Saner Mousetrap becomes the connoisseur's choice.

The Shanghai Mousetrap Company begins churning out its own licensed version of the Gooder Mousetrap, the Mousetrap 3000. It looks, and is, crude; it would never sell on shelves; but it is choking your Internet sales.

With the cost of litigation to defray you cannot persevere. You put the Better Mousetrap Company up for sale. It is bought by Universal Mousetrap, which now offers the Better Mousetrap as one of its three lines: the Gooder Mousetrap, with a beige plastic case; the Better Mousetrap, with a white plastic case; and the Saner Mousetrap, with a green textured resin case.

Even as you buy a half-dozen Better Mousetraps from your former competitor to combat an infestation in you apartment you take a grim pleasure in the knot of PAP protesters outside – even now that their funding has lapsed, they have endured to annoy.

NEW WORLDS

MAY 11, 2008   We are trapped on this planet, among earthly problems without earthly solutions. Real change takes room to experiment. Think of the changes in the world over the past few centuries from the mutual discovery of new continents. I live in a country which was conceived and undertaken as an experiment, and has become the proof and example of democracy without mob rule or faction and of freedom without chaos.

Some conscientious voices say that before we look to the stars, we should fix our problems on earth. But if you had asked an educated Spaniard of the year 1491 what the principal problem facing Spanish society was – provided you could communicate what you meant by "problem" and "society" – the answer would be: "The Jews." 1492, the year of the discovery of America, was also the year that Ferdinand and Isabella expelled the last of the Jews of Spain. If our species survives, then our ideas of what the problems of society are, and how to solve them, will likely sound to our descendants as quaint, and as cruel, as the voice of Torquemada.

We cannot sit and reason out nature without experiment. The same is true of human nature and human possibilities. It must come to experiment. To colonize our sister planets or the stars is not to repeat the world we know on a larger scale: it is to discover new worlds, not in the sky or in the stars, but in ourselves.

I am stuck here in the earthly mud with all the rest of us. I cannot imagine what experiments are yet to be done. But I trust that what hope there is to better the human condition lies through them.

To see what we take for granted, to see unimagined alternatives, will take perspective broader than the narrow experience of Earth. We have come to the end of what continents can do; we need planets. If there is nothing new under the sun, we must have new suns.

MEDIOCRITY

MAY 18, 2008   Tyrants always first *burn the books and bury the scholars*. They have never gotten them all; but what the survivors have learned, whether alone with the hidden texts or forbidden books in their attics, or reciting them over and over to keep them straight in the attics of their brains; what they have learned while despised as wizards, witches, devil-traffickers, heretics, sentimentalists, reactionaries, pedants, or just as mad; what they have learned is that an age is not made dark or light by its luminaries, but by the lesser lights crowding around and beside them.

In an age of darkness an incandescent mind is an annoyance. At best it disorients, at worst it horrifies, those who live in darkness. Great lights are bearable only to those with eyes adapted to light, to those already aware, in themselves and in those around them, of the possibility and the worth of light. Those who have walked in darkness all their lives, who have given their whole trust and faith to one or another set of directions, committed to memory, that have guided them from falls and collisions without requiring them to be aware of where they are – they will hate light. They have been blind to the world, and worse, unmirrored, unknown to themselves. Light will pain them, and they will hide from it, shroud it, or put it out with slogans and proverbs, with laughter and mockery and shouting down; with exiling potsherds, with crosses, with the auto-de-fé and the pyre, with the breaking wheel, with guns, with imprisonment, with transportation, with impoverishing lawsuits.

Greatness requires audient mediocrity not for contrast, but for support. The opposition the great meet from the mediocre is like the resistance of the water to the swimmer. What holds them back also holds them up.

VICTORIAN HYPOCRISY

MAY 25, 2007   The hypocrisy of the Victorians is the spittoon of critics: everyone feels entitled to take a passing shot. But it was the Victorians who taught us how to hate them, who exposed and exhibited how far they fell short of their own standards. They did not know how to take things, the Victorians: when they found that the best of them fell short, they concluded not that their standards were unworkable, but that the ones who had seemed best were hypocrites.

Other ages took it for granted that to be born human was to be born weak, part of a fallen race. But with the Victorians, and with their real descendants among us, it was established that moral malfeasance was always positive evidence of the intent to deceive and manipulate; that high standards are high only to shadow the sins that lurk behind them.

We have inherited, not the Victorian standards, but the Victorian attitude, the double bind that the ultimate sin is sin concealed. So we have become catalogers of sins; we have named them all, from megalomaniacal delusions to the crannies of sexual perversion. In this sense only, we have gone farther than any other age in understanding human nature; but though we have all the data, we learn nothing from it.

We are ungenerous with the species that we study. We have descriptive lexicographers, but no descriptive psychologists; they all study us in order to instruct us; and by instruct, they do not mean illuminate or capacitate, but disillusion. The psychologist who writes to disabuse us of pride writes to recognition and admiration; the psychologist who writes to convince us that we have strengths as well as weaknesses is walled off into the ghetto of self-help and managerial platitude-peddling.

The Victorians thought we were born good. That is nothing new; ask Mencius. But where Mencius blamed the bad examples we set for one another, the Victorians blamed themselves for being bad examples. In the Victorian view, evil is powerless over us until we give it power, the way Ahriman was born from a doubting thought of Ormazd; except that our misstep is not doubt, but hypocrisy.

The ancients offered us proverbs and dark sayings to make us wise, that is, to give us regret and fear; not to purify us from temptation but to teach us to compensate for human frailty. The moderns invite us to the spectacle of the convicted hypocrite being thrown to the lions and expect us to cheer. Here is instruction enough in not trying, in not daring, in not sticking the neck out.

The Victorians did something terrible to us. They lacerated the continuity of history. They hid the wide, wild world from us for our own good, and when at last we found it again, tucked away in the attic, we thought we had discovered something new. They disinherited us; they denied us our birthright, our place in history. Even when we denied them, we had no ground to stand on but the one they left us: their hypocrisy.

We are all Victorians; and they are Victorians most who, like the Victorians themselves, pile on contempt for the hypocrisy of their contemporaries or their forerunners, for whom the instrument which seeks out the motes in others' eyes becomes the beam in their own.

ON BEAUTY

June 1, 2007   Beauty is, of course, subjective. Beauty is never proved, only recognized; never earned, only achieved. No one thing is beauty. Symmetry may be beauty or boredom. Ruins may thrill or disgust. In this sense only beauty is *in the eye of the beholder* — it has no table of recombining elements.

Beauty is subjective, but not a matter of taste. It is always recognized, if not always enjoyed. Beauty that is to your taste is sweet; beauty revolting or exceeding your taste is disgusting; but the phenomenon is something beside taste: something is *beautiful*, whether it appeals to you or not, not as something is *tasty*, but as something is *edible*.

Beauty is subjective, but not a matter of taste. The experience of beauty has two parts. What is beautiful has a certain power to provoke a reaction; and that power affects us, subjectively, as beauty — or as ugliness. Classical beauty may make harmony to the eye of one, or slip like a razor on the flesh of another. Romantic beauty may demand the enthusiasm of one, and bewilder another. But no one, who is not afflicted with inattention or arrogance, is insensible to beauty. They may be unmoved, but not untouched. What can be experienced as beautiful can be experienced as ugly; what can be experienced as ugly can be experienced as beautiful. The only thing that cannot be experienced as beautiful is not what is ugly, but what is indifferent.

And beauty is always individual. Things are beautiful only when each is beautiful in and of itself. Paintings flock in museums and churches; buildings are passed on tours or captured on postcards or in photostreams; faces succeed each other in crowds, on the big screen, on the small screen; and weak habit makes us think, "That is a beautiful painting, or building, or face." But it is only proper to say – when we trouble ourselves to mean what we say – "That painting, that building, that face, is beautiful."

Beauty is not a religion. Beauty is not obeyed, only found or made. There is no secret law in beauty, not of art, not of music, not of face, no secret truth. Truth is always ugly to some, because it comes to the table like a fish with eyes: it does not let you forget, or take for granted. Beauty may lie or be true, but beauty has no secrets; no sanctuaries; beauty is cheap and easy as a leaf, as the patina of a wall, as the elementally fragile yet powerful machinery of the hands before you. Finding beauty is only a habit, making beauty – or drawing the attention of others to the beauty you have discovered – is but a task.

Photography has made this obvious for vision, but it is true for the other senses. There are fine, subtle, beautiful sounds in the world, every day, which only compilers of sound libraries trouble to note. In nature's surfeit of visual beauty, in leaf or cloud, we may lose ourselves as long as we wish; but a single sound, whatever pleasure or interest it brings, does not last. It required the appearance of intelligence, the songbird's brain, to make sound another vision; and we who are born with speech, its tones and rhythms, have perfected melody with harmony and satisfied the ear with beauty not merely broad enough to become lost in, but actively transporting.

And the other senses? The chef and the perfumer concert smells and tastes (every strong smell has an element of taste). The sense of touch is more neglected, though certainly there are harmonies of physical sensation, and they are the strongest part of memory, though neglected in favor of smell because harder to recreate.

Truth may or may not be relative; honesty is absolute. Beauty is subject to confusion, has been fought over and abandoned as unwinnable, because there is no distinction in aesthetics parallel to that of *truth* and *honesty*. It is obvious that one may be honestly wrong; but our vocabulary only gives us a contradiction, not a distinction, when we say that something is beautifully ugly or ugly-beautiful.

Sometimes critics borrow the word and call a work of art *honest*. But they mean honest in the sense that has to do with truth. This confuses the question, by entangling aesthetics with concerns not its own. We hear the word *honest* and create a standard of judgment for art based on *truthfulness* – which, by subjecting beauty to truth, becomes the straight road to dishonesty in the aesthetic sense.

The honestly ugly, or the dishonestly ugly, does not correspond to the acquired taste or the personally distasteful. Guqin music, for example, is very beautiful and very hard on Western minds; gamelan music on Western ears. That is not what I mean; that is something outside my experience, a distant speciality, an unmapped land. I can no more *like* or *dislike* it, on the first encounter, than some newly discovered alien race or planet. My reaction to it is only the index of my attitude toward any novelty.

The eye for beauty, we discover in the training of the artist, is capable of indefinite refinement. With sufficient discrimination anything, it would appear, may be found beautiful; with sufficient skill anything may be presented so as to appear beautiful. Ruskin to the drawing student: "In general, everything that you think very ugly will be good for you to draw."

Still, we are revolted by the idea that *everything is beautiful*. The problem of aesthetics resembles the problem of theodicy. We are revolted by the idea of beauty everywhere as we are revolted by the idea that ours is the best of all possible worlds. Any serious venture in theodicy begins with Anselm's observation that given that all things are good, and pursue their own good, it is not therefore necessary that all the goods they pursue are compatible. It may be found likewise with beauty.

In experience not all beauty is compatible: city or wild wood or desert, sun or night. It is the same with taste. The slightest preference in taste, conceived innately, implanted by education, or arrived at arbitrarily, by placing one beauty before another, creates the perception and the fact of ugliness in the beauty it casts into shadow. To see beauty here is to see ugliness there; to love this beauty is to hate that ugliness. This is not naivety. We must choose among kinds of beauty, as we much choose among kinds of good. If we cannot choose which kinds of good are our own, and where we stand, if we cannot say that this kinds of good is more important than that one, we end as cowards. And there is a like quality, another courage, conditional to aesthetic experience. Everywhere, always, in everything – we must choose.

We sink; sinking, we enter the sea. The sea is the model and measure of all beauty. It would be no loss to take beauty as another name for the sea, beautiful for sea-like or sea-recalling. It is not that every beauty is first the sea's. Its waves' rhythm is not the origin of music. Its wave-jagged reflections are not the first images. Not everything is beautiful which comes from the sea, nor is everything made beautiful which goes into the sea. But the love of beauty is the same as the love of the sea. There is no love of or experience of beauty which does not begin in or come to sea – or at least, unknowing, to a space for the unmet sea. If beauty is the Creator's concern, the sea embodies it; if beauty is an adapted and adaptive instrument of life, the sea taught it. Aesthetics is not a subject for philosophical debate, sociobiological fantasy, or critical caviling or febrility. *The sea* is not the answer to every problem of aesthetics. But as there is a scientific method where the answer is not *nature* but the way to the answer is *go to nature* – so I would instore an aesthetic method: *go to the sea*.

FANFICTION

JUNE 8, 2007   Fanfiction is new. It is possible to find antecedents for it only by diluting the concept. The *Aeneid* is not fanfiction; *Hamlet* is not fanfiction; *Paradise Lost* is not fanfiction. Not even Sherlockian pastiche is fanfiction. Fanfiction has the form and the ethos of its environment, the fandom.

Why is the *Aeneid* not a fanfic? The gambit of raising a minor to a main character irresistibly recalls fanfiction. Aeneas is the Blaise Zabini of classical literature. But no one writes a fanfic to prove the power of their language or to glorify their sovereign. As the proof of Latin's equality in poetic power with Greek; as the scripture of Rome's world-conquering and law-giving destiny; as a renewal of the Roman spirit after the end of the Republic; Virgil achieved with the *Aeneid* what fanfiction would never dare to aim at – not because it is new, but because it is fanfiction. The Aeneid *mattered* to Virgil and Virgil's age, and it is written like it matters. Fanfiction, even the best fanfiction, does not try to matter. It always means less than its model. It is secondary entertainment, something to do between volumes or seasons.

It has been argued that Shakespeare was able to dispense with introductory exposition to Hamlet because the story's shape was already known to his audience. The story of Amlethus was old before Shakespeare, and had been dramatized before. But this was not fanfiction. Authors of fanfiction alter and re-invent as tribute and experiment, not judgment. *Hamlet* is *better* the story of Amlethus. Hamlet throws Amlethus into shadow, but a fanfic can never overtake its model.

I cannot see that *Paradise Lost* fulfills any instrumentally religious purpose. Whom has Milton converted to Christianity? To Protestantism? No one mines *Paradise Lost* for sermon texts. *Paradise Lost* proves the equal literary dignity of Christianity with Paganism, but no one was asking. Those who take Christianity seriously need not take literature seriously. Those who take literature seriously, but not Christianity, will not be moved to reconsider Christianity by its exposition along Homeric lines unless Homer moves them to Zeus-worship. To those who take both literature and Christianity seriously it is a delightful confirmation of their harmony, and of the worth of maintaining a balanced position. But it is after the fact.

What Milton produced was not an apology or a tract, but a statement of his own faith as a learned man, an (idiosyncratically) religious man, and a poet, who believed that these plainly good things went together and did each other good. Fanfiction makes no statements at all. It is as ephemeral as a mood; it is easily found and easily lost; and it always obeys the literary democracy of a fandom. To make statements a writer must be a despot. Nothing forbids such despotism over borrowed characters, but the result would not be fanfiction.

Sherlock Holmes is one of the first modern characters. A generation earlier his coolness and calculation would have made him a fine villain; he is modern because he is the hero. Why can't new adventures for Sherlock Holmes be fanfiction? Many are: stories of Holmes time-traveling or displaced through time, or slashed, or crossing over into Yog-Sothothery may be fanfiction. (I think that the first Mythos story I ever encountered was a Lovecraftian *Giant Rat of Sumatra*.) But *The Case of the Man Who was Wanted*, or Rathbone's World War II Holmes, or Edith Meiser's radio plays, are not fanfiction: not only because they were written for profit, but also because they were written to stand alone. You could, without prior knowledge of Sherlock Holmes, go see *Terror by Night* or tune into *Death is a Golden Arrow* and come away with a sense of Sherlock Holmes. But fanfiction is written to expect knowledge of the original work. The original is less a model than a shared vocabulary of allusions (as classical mythology has been to all Western literature).

Fanfiction is not folklore. Fanfiction is democratic; folklore is the people's. The changes of folklore are like the changes of unwritten languages and dialects. No one decrees or enforces them, but they do not express popular consent. They have their own laws which indifferently roll the masses along. Illiterate or isolated individuals cannot be truly creative because, having nothing to compare their stories to, they cannot know that they could have been different, and might be changed. There is an adventitious fanon for every fandom; but there is also a stand against plagiarism between authors of fanfiction. Writers of fanfiction observe the idea of authorship that printing formed.

The phenomenon of fanfiction says something good about the modern world. To me it seems to be rearing a generation of good readers, at once hungry and discriminating.

Most fanfiction is bad; but it is gainfully bad. It is badly constructed, badly thought out or not thought out at all. The characterization is flat or inconsistent. When the plot moves, you can see the strings. *Of course.* These are first attempts. These are young minds finding their legs, or old minds stretching atrophied limbs.

If they do no more than try, they still gain, and where there is a small gain for some there is gain for all. A mind that has failed in the rigor and endurance writing requires is superior to the untried but confident mind – "I could write, if I could just find the time" – because it respects what it cannot do.

But some succeed by rising steps. They begin to learn the art of writing, along with the practical, writerly side of criticism, not acquired from precepts but burned in by trial and error. This will not multiply masterpieces; they have their own law that keeps them rare. But even an apprentice or journeyman writer becomes, in literature at least, impatient with affectation and intolerant of bullshit.

Fanfiction shows that there is still blood in civilization. As it is a rude, raucous, lawless thing, as it is grotesque and rantipole, it proves that it grows in good soil. The roots it is growing may yet keep that untended soil from washing away.

THE SLEEP OF REASON

JUNE 22, 2007   Introspection is impossible. There is no geometry that lets the mind fold back on itself. We can know ourselves in only two ways. If we consciously re-create and re-make ourselves, then we know who we have become, because we know who we set out to be. And we can recognize ourselves, unchanged, in someone else, or in a work of art made by another. It cannot be be your own work: even after abstracting parts of yourself, you cannot get a good look at them. A song, a story, its subject or style, becomes the mirror in which you see yourself: it is assimilated and becomes part of the mental equipment, recalled or replayed as the mind's mirror.

In my case, it was a picture. No other image, and no other phrase, haunts me like Goya's *Capricho* no. 43, *El sueño de la razon produce monstruos* – "The sleep of reason produces monsters." I return to it over and over like a regretful lover to a hidden photograph. They run through my head, those words, over and over, like a strain of music, like a formula of prayer.

When I first saw it, it frightened me: I had a faith in watchful reason which I had never imagined might sleep. I was a child, so it was not me, but all I wished to be that I saw slumped on that table, and in the thronging night-gaunts overhead was all the barbarism I feared in and for the world, and all the weakness to be dragged along from without or swept away from within I feared in myself.

Very little surprised me growing up. I figured out for myself and thus cushioned with the pride of precocity that virtue could go unrewarded, merit unnoticed; good could lose to evil, books could be burned and libraries – darkness could win – love be in vain, hard work for nothing – but this I had never thought, this came as a shock: reason could sleep. Reason could be asleep and helpless.

I remember the first time I saw it, a little thing in the margin (the words illegible, the caption reproduced beneath it), and the feeling in my mind like a hand on a hot stove, and a compulsion to come to terms with it which I have yet to exhaust.

The roots of this picture have been sought in essays of Addison's – a sub-series of *The Spectator*, "The Pleasures of Imagination" – and in a frontispiece to an edition of Rousseau. But I am satisfied that there was nothing in Addison's polish or Rousseau's petulance capable of giving on to this depth. There was not enough rope in either of them to fathom this picture.

A contemporary glossed it: "Imagination abandoned by reason produces impossible monsters; united with her, she is the mother of the arts and the source of their wonders." It is tempting to think of reason as the directing principle which harnesses the energies of the wild unconscious. So, in many ways, it is: but you will not harness *these* monsters. You cannot master them; you cannot cage them; you can only wall them out, and pace the narrow streets of reason's city forever besieged.

As a rule, I balk at efforts to betray the overall impression of a picture by a tunneling attention to its details, but I must point out that the sleeper is not under attack. The cat poised on the back of his chair, the owl on his back screeching for his attention, indicate it; the great cat seated to his left, composed, even protective, confirms it; and the owl to his right explains it. It imperiously extends to him one of his own porta-crayons. The monsters are not the issue of the sleeper's diseased imagination; he is not their victim and not their source; they are emissaries, come to the sleeper to compel and to guide his work.

It was made as the introduction to *The Caprices*, but it could make for an introduction to *The Disasters of War*, itself an introduction to the age of nightmares to come: the trench and the machine gun, the tank and the bomber, propaganda and secret police, stage-managed orgies of hate, idols in uniforms or suits and their political cults, revolutions and purges, the atom bomb and the world for fifty years of cold war in the throne of Damocles, frenzied to forget itself.

What reason made by day – science, industry, democracy, mass culture

– became by night the instruments to realize the old nightmares of the world's ending – but worse, because the world would not end. Through the tides of blood and the overthrown cities and the sacrificed generations and the slaughterhouses of the speaking and through one anti-Christ after another – the world would not end. *The sleep of reason produces monsters.* And there are more dreams to come. We declared an age of reason; we left behind the dark woods; but the open sky has its own monsters our philosophy cannot name to warn us against – and what is worth watching for out here in the open is seen too late. *The sleep of reason produces monsters.* I do not know if it is a warning, or a curse, or a judgment.

URBAN EXPLORATION

JUNE 29, 2007   Cities do not grow; they have to be made. Somewhere, sometime, people made all this; they made all the machines that made all the artifacts and buildings that made all the cities. And somewhere, sometime, everything made has answered to a purpose. But try this: walk, or be driven through, any section of any city – the older the better, but new will do – under the aspect of an alien or an artist. Try, if you can, to notice everything – the strange knobs and wires and pipes, the bits of metal, the shapes of concrete, which make puzzles of every structure. Who knows what every knob and lever is for? There are devices on the old buildings that are remembered only by scholars. No one comes to fix them; no one comes to check them. They gather dust, rust, verdigris, character. In neglect they pass from function to form.

It must have been bewildering for those who were part of the great world-spanning, unsleepingly active age of dawning industry – that age, in its dreams and its nightmares, so wedded to the spirit of youth and youthful strength – it must have been bewildering for them to see that the world is not, in fact, remade with every generation; to see how time has carried forward their works, made in unquestioning faith in the future, into a faithless future where they have become all they were made to supplant: not just old-fashioned and obsolete, but curious and quaint; lingering through time, artifacts, shadowy relics brought out from the strange country, the alien planet, of the past.

And it has happened. Young people armed with flashlights and cameras crawl over and among the picked bones of Leviathan-industry. This is not the archaeology of labels and measurements and excavations; not the piracy of the past that sunk shafts and cut tunnels into the buried homes of Pompeii; not the romanticism that would bring young Englishmen to Italy to watch old marble until they could fancy that a statue might drop its staff and admit it had only been pretending. They make me think instead of some medieval Italian shepherd – for such there must have been – who fell into a lost grotto dedicated to a god he never knew, never would know; who shivered and wondered at such a place, sacred to his blood though unholy to his god; who withdrew and covered it again, only having marked its ceiling with the smoke of his fuming lamp. Such there must have been; such there are.

An urban explorer seeks context, not knowledge. Among the great machines on the factory floor they only want to know what each is for, not how they worked. They are satisfied to see the buttons and levers; they do not need to know which one does what. They are satisfied to know where to stand; they do not need to know what to do. They take the pictures for their walls or accounts; they do not need to know the names of what their pictures contain. They are not designers, planners, scientists, engineers, even artists – I do not think you could satisfactorily draw an abandonment. Only the affectless lens can capture the appeal.

I am not an urban explorer; I want to know everything. But that would be missing the point. It is not knowing, and it is not *not* knowing; it is not ghosts; it is not even the beauty of patination or of ruins; it is the sight, the memory of the sight, that the photograph stands in for. Our steel ruins do not reach the same part of the brain as the arts, or even the stone ruins of a farther past. They follow a different way, reach something deeper. We wander and delight in abandonments for the same reason we wander in the forest: the beauty of these gathering ruins is only the beauty of nature – another nature humanity made for itself. For the deepest part of the brain the old, abandoned factory and the dark, spooky wood have the same appeal.

When I was a child my father took me to see many old forts, too many to remember. They have run together in my mind; unilluminated tunnels branching from the lighted tourist-track; huge rooms with massive doors and the knowledge that were they to be closed you could starve or suffocate here unheard; condemned outbuildings of weather-striated concrete, darkened by late rains, overgrown and seen through screening leaves; that low fence (you know you could climb it) in front of the sight-passing vaulted tunnel, the paled and rusting sign bearing a long since indecipherable warning, the same leaves under your feet lining the floor of the tunnel – I know the urge. I was a boy, and did not climb. I am glad others have done it, grateful that they have let me share at lens distance.

THE SOCIETY OF TREES

JULY 6, 2007   Our remote ancestors lived on the plains; but our even more remote ancestors lived in the trees. It is hard to imagine the transition. Open spaces are not very long tolerable to our species: we must be shut in and canopied over to sleep or live at ease. The universal report of those who try sleeping under the star-laden skies of the desert dark: "It was like I was falling into the sky." Whoever left the trees first did not do it easily, or by choice. More likely the forest died and left them, than that they left the forest.

It is fitting that the same Roman minds that invented espaliering would invent crucifixion, would assume the conquest of the world as the duty fate had burdened them with. And it is fitting that a civilization careful to trap half-wild forests – *bois* or *Wald* or park – within the walls of its cities, would value freedom, discovery, and genius.

Sometimes the woods are like the sea, with swells and breakers of foam-foliage, as along green-walled Southern roads in summer; and sometimes the woods are like the library, and every tree as much an individual, as deep in itself, as much to be known, as a book. People, too, may be like the sea – as the crowd, the mob, the throng, or under uniforms (soldiers, suits, staff, and street people alike). But all of us are individuals, though we deny or try to hide it, while only some trees can distinguish themselves. To use a local (New Orleanian) metaphor, City Park is as full of remorseless individuals as is the French Quarter; but there is nothing humane in an orchard or a tree farm. Still, trees more often distinguish themselves than people, and are easier to get to know. Affectations aside, there are people I love more than any tree, but I have loved more trees than people.

BACON AND MONTAIGNE

JULY 13, 2007   Suppose yourself a child, and that two old men live near you.

One is Montaigne. He is delighted by your visits, stuffs you with cookies, asks after your interests, takes it graciously in stride when you tell him (being a child) that they have changed, offers up anecdotes and friendly advice that he will not be offended if you disregard.

The other is Bacon. When you visit, he sits you down, offers you wine – they do that where he comes from – and takes everything you say seriously. You have opinions; he treats them like theories. You have observations; he treats them like theses. You have tastes; he treats them like positions. You finish bewildered and afraid. Montaigne makes you feel grown up; Bacon lets you know that you are not even as grown up as you thought.

The *Essais* of Montaigne sum to an autobiography in topical cross-sections; the *Essayes* of Bacon are ventured as *Counsels Civill and Morall*. Montaigne was the first essayist, the inventor of the essay; he is the standard. There will never be a better essayist than Montaigne, because trying to write an essay is trying to write like Montaigne.

But I should not have to argue that Bacon's was the greater mind (though the two were more alike than goes acknowledged). Montaigne conceded to the world and posterity, "What do I know?"; Bacon, troubled that he knew nothing, determined to find something out. Read the *Apology for Raymond Sebond*; count how often Bacon's method has discovered what Montaigne thought we could never know.

Bacon's essays, and Bacon himself, have lost their once universal regard. Bacon has been expelled from the history of science. The very idea that an individual might be responsible for the project and phenomenon of science, and a philosopher at that, offends mathematicians who find a debt to the condemned practice of thinking in mere words distasteful, and would prefer an ancestry direct from Galileo to Newton. And it offends historians who conclude that, because science was supported by economic forces, science was therefore predestined by them – the role of individuals, and certainly of an instorer, being redundant; and any claim of originality or responsibility, naive.

Even as Bacon's achievement increases in importance, he and his age sink ever farther from us into the costumed past. His glory as the founder of science, already lost, is irrecoverable.

But Bacon's essays should not be forgotten. They are the model of strength in writing: swift, direct, and final. If Shakespeare's position in society had allowed writing essays, they would read like Bacon's – only natural in two contemporaneous, equipollent minds meeting the same challenge in Montaigne. They have that life in themselves, and that closeness to life as it is lived; lived not in passing, but in success or failure. Bacon's language is free from the texture and balance which batten Addison's meaning; free of Macaulay's fireworking showmanship; free of the diffidence (or, worse, the confidence) of the twentieth century essay.

Analogy is the proof of a writer's skill and character. Bacon and Shakespeare were both immune to the absurdity by which office workers pushing keys and paper under fluorescent lights *make hay while the sun shines*. Bacon's Idols (not in his essays, but still his) deserve a place in the analogical equipment of every mind besides Shakespeare's stage of life; or the winding stair, beside time and tide; or death and the dark, beside what dreams may come.

Still, I expect no literary renascence or restoration for Bacon. We still read Montaigne because he, himself, appeals to us; because his observations, centered on and conditioned by himself, are easy even for our suspicious sympathies to enter into.

But Bacon is a counselor; an adviser. We do not like to take advice at all; and the advice that is not accompanied by an exemplary life we not merely reject, but oppose unheard. Bacon's counsels are stern, harsh distillations. He was not a pitying man; he would not even pity himself. He knew his failure, and he measured it as clearly as he would any other's.

Bacon had a destination in mind for science, a New Atlantis, and sought the royal road to it. When geometry denied him, he denied geometry. Having found the right course, he took the easy way; as he did in politics, where he certainly practiced flattery (with the ease and excess of the arrogant and disingenuous) with his superiors, and was probably corrupt to his inferiors. These are the vices of politics, inescapable; but Bacon did not merely allow them, he perfected them – the easy way to power, and from power, he must have thought, to what we would call reforms, but he called instoration.

Bacon set himself apart from the world and from mankind so he could inspect them, make experiments on them, and recognize in and learn from them the accidental experiments conducted by nature. In this way, his two great failures – his failure to see the value of mathematics in science, and his failure to – I will not say, practice as he preached (for his essays are not secular sermons), but to act with patience or discretion – are the same failure. He sought, not (as some have) to know God's thoughts, but to have God's view. As his aim was too high, his fall was certain.

FABLE OF THE OLD MAN AND THE RAVENS

JULY 20, 2007   Once there was an old man, a farmer. Every day he drove his cart to market, and every day he stopped to throw seed to the ravens. Now, the old man did not load the cart, but paid his young nephew to do it. The old man, who had little use for words, had never spoken to him, except to hire him, and to promise that he would inherit the farm.

When the old man was late to rise one morning, the young man left in anger; and the ravens sent one of their number to check on the old man. Through the window, the chosen raven saw that the old man was dead. When he told the other ravens, they became fearful, for they had grown in numbers and depended on the old man for food.

"I have a plan," said the chosen raven. The ravens came in numbers to the deserted farm. They broke in a window with their beaks and gathered up the farmer's clothes: his hat, his gloves, his coat, his boots. They brought the farmer's old scarecrow, and dressed him in the farmer's garments. They tied the farmer's fishing line to the hands and feet and head of the scarecrow.

When the young man arrived the next day, he saw the ravens overhead and said to the old man, who was waiting for him: "Aren't they here a little early?" The farmer shrugged. "Guess they're hungry," continued the young man. The farmer nodded and climbed stiffly into the cart. "That fall chill bothering your joints already?" The farmer nodded, picked up and tugged the reins, and the cart rolled on.

Once the cart was out of sight, the ravens let the scarecrow fall and ate everything on the cart. In this way, day by day over months, the ravens grew many and fat.

One day his nephew said to the farmer: "Your fields are getting scraggly. You want me to handle it this year? This place'll be mine someday, and I might as well start getting to know it." The farmer nodded rhythmically. "Those ravens sure do follow you around." The uncle nodded sharply and climbed onto his cart.

It was so for years, the young man doing the farm work and loading up the cart for the market. Fortunately for the ravens, the old man, who had prospered in his last years, had become a miser. Whenever the young man needed money they only had to dig up coins where they had seen the farmer bury them.

One day the young man said: "It's time I leave here and go see the world. I've stored plenty of food for you, you'll be fine for a few years until I come back. I know *you'll* still be here. People keep saying you're bound to kick off, but you won't give them the pleasure, will you?"

What could the farmer do, but raise his arms and shrug?

What would feed an old man for years would last the many ravens only months. They became afraid and lamented; but the chosen raven, now the king of the unkindness, said: "I have a plan." At his order, many ravens came together and lifted the scarecrow high into the air, searching for the young man's night camp. When dark had come, while the young man tied his horse and lit his fire, there came much squawking of ravens out of the dark woods. "Damn ravens are everywhere these days."

The young man saw the farmer come slowly out of the wood. "Is – is that you? It can't be. How..." The farmer rose into the air unsupported, his arms waving. "Oh, no! You're dead. You're a ghost!" A raven lighted on the ground before the fire. The old man pointed to it. "The raven? The ravens. You want me to keep feeding the ravens. Of course I will. Don't worry about it. I'll keep feeding them. As many as show up."

The ghost rose up over the young man, arms outspread. "I swear I will!" At that, the ghost sank, lowered his arms, and drifted back into the forest and the dark.

The young man returned to the farm, only to find that his uncle's house had burned down – with him in it. The young man had only his dear uncle's bones to bury.

The young man soon regretted his oath, as ravens appeared in incredible numbers; but when he came out of his tent to feed them, they led him, leading him from before and behind, to where his his uncle had buried his wealth. With that money, the young man was able to build a new house, and he found a wife to keep it.

So as the young man became an old man, keeping his vow, he often told how the ravens, to whom his uncle had always been so kind, had shown their simple gratitude; and he always laughed at any who called ravens cunning.

Moral: *Silence is not Evidence of Wisdom.*

THE BOOK OF MISMATCHED LISTS: A FICTION

27 JULY, 2007   [Preface to the Edition of 1984]

Jacques Bourges, the author of what is known as *The Book of Mismatched Lists*, was born in 1645, the illegitimate son of the favorite mistress of George Blanc, the Abbé de Lamothe. The Abbé was a wealthy man, of diverse interests, but with a particular passion for philosophical languages which would later extend to the preparation of *Essai vers une Langue Philosophique*, printed in Rouen in 1688, a translation of Wilkins's *Essay towards a Real Character and a Philosophical Language*.

In 1655, the Abbé visited England along with his favorite mistress and his favorite bastard. During this time the Abbé, browsing (inattentively, as most do) a copy of Thomas Urquhart's *Logopandecteision*, discovered Urquhart's boast that his philosophical language could be taught to a boy of ten years in three months. Since the Abbé intended a long stay in England, he wrote to Urquhart to offer him a large sum of money to undertake that very task. The Abbé's own words (from his *Correspondence 1630–1687* – the Abbé employed several secretaries in the maintenance of folio letter-books) are worth repeating:

> It is my fondest wish and dearest hope that you, the illustrious author of this most wonderful plan for a fully developed philosophical language, would undertake the education of my son in your wonderful language of languages, Logopandecteision. My son is but ten years of age; if you will only come to us, we shall be pleased to receive you during those three months of invaluable instruction.

Urquhart, ready for comfort after his confinement to the Tower and hounded by his creditors, took the offer. Urquhart's stay lasted, in fact, only two months, until the Abbé discovered that this Urquhart was the same as the translator of Rabelais into English – to the Abbé, who wore his tonsure lightly, but took his faith seriously, the whole of Europe had never held anyone else half so despicable as that scoffer Rabelais.

No immediate change in young Jacques was observed, and the Abbé concluded that the lessons Urquhart had offered had been a fraud. This opinion changed quickly after their return to France. Jacques's restoration to his former tutors was only to their embarrassment; he had only (the Abbé gathered, from the accounts of the thinly enlightened tutors, who had resorted to accusations of sorcery) to work out the names of subjects and their leading ideas in a language unknown to any of those tutors – unknown, but singularly beautiful and fascinating, "more sung than spoken" (as the Abbé wrote, relating the events) – to be able to evince, with but minutes of reflection, a total mastery of the discipline, from its principles to its most arcane and abstruse results. This facility was not only intellectual; he could play any instrument as soon as handle it. He ruined the reputation of his fencing master by repeatedly disarming him before his students in his own sallé.

The Abbé wrote to Urquhart in the most grovelling terms, begging him to come to France (this letter, not collected with the rest of the Abbé's correspondence, belongs to the British Museum), but Urquhart had left Britain, vanishing into the Continent. The Abbé soon realized that the intellectual facility which the language Logopandecteision gave his son – the Abbé decided to call it Adamic, considering it the rediscovery of the language of Eden – was not altogether a good. Try as he might, the Abbé could not get Jacques to attempt to teach another the language – the boy claimed to have no systematic knowledge of the grammar, as that would have been the burden of the third month of Urquhart's instruction – or to explain or write out any of the marvelous discoveries the language had allowed him to reach. "He says that while anything that may be said or written in any other language may be said in Adamic," wrote the Abbé, "very little of what may be said in Adamic can be translated into the languages stemming from the confusion of Babel."

Young Jacques spent nearly all his time in the composition of poetry – "A sonnet of Adamic, he tells me, contains more than all the treatises of Aristotle and the Schoolmen" – and in one-sided conversation with animals and plants. The Abbé found one incident startling enough to record and send on:

> I went down to the orchard, which had fallen barren in my grandfather's time; those old trees, it seemed to me, would never fruit again. I discovered that without my knowledge, my son had preceded me, and was haranguing the trees in Adamic. I say haranguing, from the loudness of his voice; but his tones were those of a seducer. It was already autumn then. In the depth of that winter, I was riding through the village in my carriage, when an apple was thrown through my window. Astonished at seeing a fresh apple in winter in this remote place, far from the sea, I examined it by what light there was; and it seemed to me that something was familiar in its color. I bit into it; at first taste it was superbly sweet; but the sweetness grew on my tongue, until surpassing sweetness, the taste became painful and bitter, like Spanish licorice. I returned swiftly to my home, and walked through deep snow to the old orchard, where I found the withered trees with their branches obscured with apples, which frost had turned white. I ordered the apples distilled to a cider, to preserve their strange quality. This spring, the trees have all died.

The profit the Abbé made from selling that extraordinary cider to eagerly curious correspondents convinced him that here was a miracle of practical consequence; so he ordered the construction of a greenhouse. The extraordinary flowers which grew there under Jacques's persuasion – roses which required two hands to hold; orchids which could be worn, properly prepared, like hats – were harvested several times a year and transported to Paris and Versailles to adorn the ladies of fashion. But yet more profitable were certain plants of medicinal virtue which could not otherwise be grown in France, and for which apothecaries were willing to pay more than their weight in gold. The clever Abbé, looking to diversify, had several racing horses brought to his son; each of these won the first race it was entered in by an extraordinary margin, but thereafter could hardly walk. The Abbé entered a few undistinguished horses every year, whose remarkable victories made them, though useless for racing, valuable studs.

In 1669, Jacques fell from a horse and broke his leg. The leg would never heal properly, and Jacques was nearly dumb with fear and exhaustion for some months. The Abbé, alarmed at the prospect of an end to the marvel of Adamic, and optimistic that the language could be systematized along the lines of Wilkins's new work, again attempted to convince Jacques to try to teach him Adamic. Jacques again professed his inability. The Abbé resolved on an indirect tactic – to create a dictionary of Adamic. Jacques demurred that no writing system available was sufficient to record the subtle accents of Adamic; however, he agreed to begin writing out definitions, pledging to create a writing system later.

The Abbé left with Jacques his manuscript translation of Wilkins, and embarked on a prolonged absence to visit his nominal benefice. During this time, Jacques wrote out in Latin, in a series of octavo notebooks, nearly five thousand definitions. When the Abbé returned, he wished to see them; but they seemed to him only to be gibberish, so he grew angry with Jacques, whom he accused first to trying to trick him; then, in anger, of traffic with the devil.

The Abbé indignantly quoted certain of these gibberish definitions in his letters; to his surprise, his correspondents begged to hear more of them – even correspondents who had never returned his letters before. The Abbé realized that nonsense might still have much of poetry. Jacques, wounded by the Abbé's first reaction, refused to write any more definitions; but the Abbé took the existing notebooks and had them transcribed by his secretaries, then published as *Liber Nominandarum* (Rouen, 1670). The Abbé took charge of the whole stock, and shipped copies to his correspondents, keeping careful records of each. Of the original notebooks, history provides no further mention. The printer attempted another printing for sale, printed in Rouen but marked as if printed in Paris; these books, along with the transcription and possibly the notebooks, the Abbé had destroyed.

In 1672, the Abbé died. Jacques closed the greenhouse, gave his fortune into the hands of a firm of Rouen factors, and lived in seclusion until his own death in 1720. His only contact with the outside world was that necessary to secure publication of the Abbé's correspondence, and of his translation of Wilkins. After Jacques's death, his and his father's papers were confiscated by the *Intendant*; Jacques himself was posthumously convicted of witchcraft; and royal order commanded the utter destruction of the *Liber Nominandarum*.

The Abbé's careful records enabled the tracing of every copy; none survive. Three partial manuscript translations into French, and what the Abbé himself quoted in his letters, are all that remain. Between them, they number 612 distinct *appositions*, as each entry is known. One of these French manuscripts was in 1730 made the basis for an English translation, containing 285 appositions and published in London *The Complete Wonderfull Book of Mis-Matched Lists of the Abbot of Lamothy* — the printer apparently being confused as to its authorship. From the English edition, all the many other direct and indirect manuscript copies have been made — for the catalog, see Appendix A.

The influence of the Book, in France and England, is difficult to ascertain, as it was almost never quoted directly. The recipients of the Abbé's copies included nearly every significant figure of the period in French literature and philosophy — one copy, taken from the royal library, was burned in the presence of Louis XV. The French never named the book itself before the burning, because, everyone knowing it, they never had to; after the burning, they were afraid to; and the English, having learned from the French example, kept their copies uncatalogued and out of sight.

Nonetheless, it would be difficult to find an author of the eighteenth or nineteenth centuries who did not show, in some degree, the influence of the Book. Some of the appositions have even influenced popular language and sayings. Most notably, Ap. 128 (using the enumeration of Reicher's definitive 1870 edition): "Devils, the color blue, the deep sea, violins, vinegar, salt, fruits red within." One appears to be the basis of a common *non sequitur*: (Ap. 40) "Ravens, batons [or walking sticks], *escritoires*, night clouds, steeples, old songs." Some appear to derive from mythology: (Ap. 26), "A woman, an old man, a cane, a lion, a lord, a loss, graves." Some — and it should be remembered that they precede even Champollion — seem to allude to Egyptian mythology: (Ap. 23) "A heart, a feather, a butcher, a son, a river, scales," or Babylonian: "The sea, storms, a dragon, water under the earth, the river mouth, mountaintops." They vary in length, from the shortest (Ap. 7), "Wine, worms," to the longest (Ap. 90), "A king, a home, a bushel, a mirror, a knife, a god, long [finger]nails, steam, a labyrinth [or the Labyrinth], sand, marble, foreigners, comers, a door, madness, old crimes, hills, a tower, a whale, grass, memory, broken strings [musical], a pit, a torch, the green sea, a stylus, boards, rings, plaster, maps, lamps, a tiger, a plate, a height, a fall." Snatches of sense in these and other appositions (a king's home being a palace, knife and mirror both being reflective, and a height preceding a fall) have inspired interpretative efforts which have yet to succeed in making much more sense than the original. There were, it seems, some efforts at organization in the original; compare, for example, appositions 5 and 6, each with eight terms: (5) "Gold, sand, spit, a scythe, a [split] rail, a key, a flock, a [nun's] habit," and (6) "Silver, rain, blood, a staff, a post, a lock, a crook, skin." But each translator felt it worth their time to record only one member of each pair; such pairs as we do have come each from different manuscripts.

The obscurity of so influential a book is a problem of literature without a literary solution; but the human answer is as obvious as the existence of the book is repulsive. It invalidates at least all literature since it was created, and possibly all literature. A Jung could look for a collective unconscious in the mind; but in the Book we have one of paper, a shared universe of dreams which has been the artificial unconsciousness of the whole of romanticism and modernism, a false nature which has beguiled the world alike from classical worldliness and medieval religiosity. But the Book is more than a practical repudiation of the value of criticism and authorship. It debases the value of imagination, to find that all that can be imagined yields to interpretation by this single key, that every myth and story and work of art and piece of music is but a failed evocation and adumbration of a single word of the only true and perfect language. It blasphemes the idea of mystery, that there should ever have existed a Book such as this, in which all mysteries are potentially present. The Book is a rebuke to the intellect of humanity, to our provisional and grasping efforts, to what in the Book's light we can only mistake for creativity. The Book is a fragment of Divine design – incomprehensible as a fragment of a machine's design would be if we have but the plan of a valve or a seal; an echo of the confident and fearless thoughts of angels. The Book is as cruel as our vision and understanding is limited; it is as foul as the fact that we built our tower at Babel, and it fell. They were wise who tried to destroy it; and we are fools who have forever bound ourselves to it, by its study, and by this reprinting.

DEAD LANGUAGES

AUGUST 2, 2007   Linguistics fascinates me, but there is something about it that makes me uncomfortable: something that embarrasses me when linguists try to act as public intellectuals. It is the fence that linguistics draws around what count as linguistic phenomena. It seems to me that the distinction between descriptivism and prescriptivism is untenable; prescription too is a phenomenon of language, and one of the things that any honest description must describe.

As a corollary, the distinction between natural and artificial languages is untenable. Literate languages are part natural and part artificial, in varying proportions. Latin has become more artificial than natural, but it is not a dead language; its artificiality sustains it. Sumerian is all natural and all dead; no one reads it except to translate from it. No one writes in Sumerian – and what you wrote in Sumerian, if you had that whim, would be philological caprice, not real Sumerian. But with diligence anyone can learn to write Latin; and what they write is real Latin, because Latin has been immortalized by the prescriptions of its grammarians, who cut free their language from the Tiber by making it answerable only to written, explicit, portable, unowned rules.

The Latin model is not ideal for English. (It is not even ideal for Latin, whose grammar is modeled after Greek.) But our Latinate grammar is not a cage; it is a trellis. It supports the whole structure of English literature. It is not a limit on English, not a smothering weight. It is, itself, the English language. It has not prevented English from fracturing into dialects, but it has preserved over and above those dialects a true, nuclear English. I dare call it *true* because English as we know it is not the product of any natural development. English too is an artificial language; a consciously and self-consciously *made* hybrid of Englisc, French, and Latin. The great writers and translators into our English, Mallory, Browne, Bacon, Burton, Florio, North, Urquhart, Sidney, Spencer, Shakespeare, did not use the English they found: they created the English we know. I do not believe that anyone in their time, even they, spoke as they write. But we speak *their* language, not a descendant of the argot-pidgin-creole-cant-jargon-lingoes (likely closer to Chaucer) that would have been heard in the London of their time.

How can a language be both artificial and natural? There is an English-language literature, not several streams of British and American and Commonwealth literature, and English is fit to be the universal auxiliary language of commerce and science, only because of its rules and its models. The English language is still vital, and thus changeful on the tongue, particularly in its vocabulary; but most new words will die, becoming quaint or obsolete. While they live, they may serve probation to become part of the language; but likelier, they will never be cut free from their contexts, and if they come to be written at all it will be only for color.

Here is one way that linguists make themselves obnoxious – when they condescendingly insist that vogue words, obviously destined for rapid obsolescence, halfway to quaint even before they are current, represent the future of the language. The fact that linguistics has no such category as *fad* is one of its deficiencies. The successions of fashion are unlike the forces determining national costume or native dress; likewise, the changes of a written language belong not to the order of cultural change, but to the order of revolutions and discoveries – of change in worldview, where prescription is the necessary basis for consensus.

Dialects, whatever the charm they have to linguists, cannot be entered into by outsiders. They presume and enforce a shared background, a particular geographic, racial, cultural, and economic set of coordinates. Our dialects are all the seeds of potential languages, as the proto-Romance accents were to Latin. But they will not last. There will always be a new crop of dialects and jargons, a new harvest of what they have to offer English. But, once harvested, they wither to make way for the next crop.

Because English is immortal and universal as it is captured in books, English literature is being fed into by countries with nothing else but English in common, and by the best minds of these countries, who know that what they write in their mother languages is only for their brothers and sisters; but what they write in English is for the world and forever.

Latinizing missionaries who stretched native languages on the rack were able to give them Bibles in their own languages. Linguists produce accurate descriptive grammars which make beautiful epitaphs to those languages. Bahasa Indonesia has preserved Indonesian language at the cost of Indonesian languages; the French created France out of the possessions of the Bourbons by suppressing regional dialects; the Arabic world is a world only by its devotion to the language of the Koran.

All rules seem arbitrary until they are gone without; all systems of rules suffer rot, once useful provisions becoming shibboleths; but a language without rules is a house on fire. Fire is a kind of life, breathing and eating; but it is too much life, and it leaves only ashes. A language is not safe, not hospitable to literature, until it has been settled prescriptively, not by itself but by learning from the grammarians of, and translators from, older languages.

The great puzzle of linguistics – why are the oldest languages the most complex? Greek is more complex than Latin; Sanskrit is more complex than Greek. The great puzzle of prehistory – what were people doing in the millennia between the arrival of *Homo sapiens* and the dawn of civilization? If they had all the same impulses we do, for creation and invention, what did they create? What did they invent? These puzzles may be the same puzzle. Their inventions, their creations, were their languages, refined and restricted with the same joy in the possibilities of form that would later diversify poetry.

SO MANY BOOKS

AUGUST 8, 2007   We remember what we learn more by the incidents of its acquisition than by its place in a scheme of knowledge. The voice of your teacher, the table where you studied, the stage of your life when you learned them – these are the things that make memories stick. (We learn best when we are young, not just because the mind is plastic, but because those are the years – the years of our firsts – we will always remember.) A book, as an artifact, is full of such adhesive incidents: binding, paper, cover and fonts; the author's style and voice; its weight on or in your hand; how you marked it or took pains not to mark or mar it; who gave to you; where you bought it or took it out; who recommended it to you; how old it is – new, secondhand, antique.

A book is as mnemonically individual as a teacher and has the advantages of cheapness, reliable supply, permanence, and retainability – you cannot put a teacher on a shelf. Precisely because it is fixed and set, a book is not just a medium through which an item of data crosses from mind to mind; it is a thing in itself, fraught and sensuous, whose circumstances receive and bind, like spiders' silk, gossamer and flighty thought.

The ancients, who had only fragile scrolls, and the scholars and school-men of the Middle Ages, who owned few books, built dream palaces in their memories, labyrinthine, full of niches and ramifying halls and galleries mortared from shards of remembered or imagined buildings. These palaces were miscellaneous as pattern books, like the strange buildings which haunt Renaissance backgrounds, Dürer's rambling castles or the scenes where Poliphilo wandered; and which came as ruins to dominate Romantic landscapes, senseless conjunctions of towers and walls and columns; Piranesi's prisons of invention, Death's city in Poe, resembling *nothing which is ours*. These palaces housed only commodious niches, ranged along hall walls or between arcade columns, or grouped behind doors: and in each niche lived a vision, or a nightmare. Here is a fox-headed lady standing for a name beginning with V (*vulpus*); here is the goat with swollen testicles who was Cicero's *testator*.

Why did the memory palace go out of fashion? Because of the library. Not because the sudden plenty of books made memory obsolete; but because the true palace of memory is the library, with wings of shelves, corridors of volumes, pages as niches where memory is bound.

So many counted light-years will not suffice to hold universe enough to justify, let alone satiate, the appetites and powers of the human mind; but books brought together do not add, but multiply; to be among books you know well is to be lifted out of mortal span and reach.

THE RICH AND THE HEALTHY

AUGUST 17, 2007   The rich and the healthy misunderstand poverty and sickness. They see only a line to be crossed between too little and enough, between sickness and health. But there is poverty without imminent starvation, and sickness not prey for cancer or infection. The fear of death is easy to sympathize with; but the rich and the healthy never understand what it means to have to choose.

Torture is not about pain; it is about humiliation and violation. Those who succumb to torture do not succumb because of the pain, but because of the horror, because such things can really happen. Your mother never taught you that someday you might be given over naked and helpless into the hands of your enemies and left to their devices. Subject to torture, you cannot believe what is happening to you. It is never your will that breaks; it is always your mind.

Poverty also warps the mind. The lives of the rich and healthy branch out like trees or deltas. The world lies before them like a menu, where they choose not just what to do, but who to be. They are free to indulge or abstain. The poor and sick run on rails, along routes chosen by others. Where they are going depends on nothing but where they came from.

The old company store model is the extreme. But what is better about wages so low that you can survive only by shopping for food that destroys your health as it prolongs your life? To be poor, if not starving, is still to have to make such unbelievable choices: food or health, a safe home or crushing debts, enough hours for a decent wage or knowing your children on sight; and when you go to a doctor, or the hospital, or to beg from your insurer – your money or your life.

There is a syndrome of poverty that results from walking such mazes, like the lethargy of an animal punished repeatedly and capriciously. Hope is the leavening every mind requires to imagine, to try, to dare, to build; but it does not take very much poverty to crush hope out of a person. This living with eyes taped open, in vigilance as unsleeping as it is certain to be unavailing, in awaiting the disaster you know is coming but cannot stop, is known in the poor as *laziness*.

The poor must make do, when they can get them, with damaged or dying machines: old cars that fume and guzzle, a dishwasher that uses so much electricity you can only run it once a week, a chainsaw that spits chips and stutters, but whose blade you cannot afford to replace or have sharpened.

The same is true of their bodies. Even in the most enlightened societies it is the right of the poor, not to be healthy, but to be healthy enough for work, or at least not to draw attention. Even when medicine can do nothing for them, the rich and the sick may enjoy an excusing diagnosis, even if just a *syndrome* without treatment; they have *idiopathic* as a marker for the diseases we recognize but do not understand. But for the poor, what the first test does not show, does not exist. There are no follow-ups, no referrals. They cannot fight. It is in the autopsies of the rich and vocal in their sufferings that new diseases are discovered; it is therefore strange, but likely true, to think that there are afflictions only of the poor stemming from malnutrition, stress, or hard labor, which have never been and never will be named, for they silence their victims.

This is the way of the world; the alternatives known so far are worse. The disappearance of visible poverty from parts of the first world is partly the result of fitted blinders (not just a cowardly unwillingness to see the problem – the visibility of the poor only discourages investment, and worsens their plight), and partly the result of globalization, which segregates classes in their own countries.

My interest here is sociological, because all civilizations have the poor in common, and the poor of all civilizations are alike. Details of costume, language, and climate aside, all hovels are really one hovel, and all unskilled labor is really one vast project, now building a pyramid, now digging a canal; now sewing shirtwaists, now sewing jeans. In thinly populated hunter-gatherer societies, or in civilizations with money to hand, there is room for culture, room to work out what it means to be human; but the poor are always and everywhere worn down to the same nub: what we all are in the end, at the last, at the core.

FABLE OF THE WHALE AND THE DOLPHIN

AUGUST 24, 2007   It happened in a cold sea that a dolphin and a whale became friends. In the shallows they would breach and rise into sunlight together; and the whale would admire the dolphin's burnished, piercing swiftness, and regret his fell bulk. In the deep they would talk of deep things together; and the dolphin would admire the plangent voice of the whale and the patient subtlety of whale-speech, and regret the flightiness of the skipping, glittering speech of dolphins.

Now, once when both were near the surface, there rose a great storm, and each had to flee to his own shelter – the whale to his deep and the dolphin to his cove – without the chance to appoint another meeting. After the storm had passed, the whale sang a summoning song that carried in resonant echoes of sound deep through every sea to the ends of the world; and the dolphin appointed to all his dolphin-fellows to search the whole surface of the sea. But the dolphin did not hear the whale, and news of the whale did not reach the dolphin. So after a time, when the dolphin grew annoyed with the sleepless restlessness of his kind and the whale impatient with the memorious melancholy of his kind, they set out in search of one another.

The dolphin stretched his lungs as far as he could and dove straight down to seek the utter deep where the whales slide and the water rings forever with the thunder of their voices. He had sought that deep before, with his friend the whale. He had learned from the whale how to fill his lungs farther than he had thought possible, how to brace himself to bear the pressure of mountains on his every side. These terrors of the deep he knew; but he had never known how his great friend's nearness, how the heat of his blood, had sheltered him from the last terror of the deep – from its cold. Cold pierced him from every side; first he was full of needles, then hollow. Realizing his mistake, he tried to turn and rise, but the cold had locked his muscles. He floated for a time until his air was spent, then drifted down dead through the substance of darkness to the snaky floor of the deep.

The whale sought out the cove where he knew his friend would hide. There were no dolphins in it he could see from without, but he thought that his friend might be waiting for him within. The dolphin had warned him against the cove, but the whale saw that there was plenty of water. He entered the cove and searched and searched it, examining every crevice with great eyes which were not used to such prolonged brightness. Then he turned to go, but found that now the cove was cut off from the sea. This was the *tide* he had been warned against and forgotten – but he did not fear, even as his slick heaving side was dried out by the declining sun, for he knew the tide would come back.

But the moon was waning, and the tides were low. Through weeks the whale lay on his side heaving for breath, feeling the ungracious carrion birds that would not wait for his death. Hope became courage, courage gave way to despair, and the great heart, defeated without and within, burst and stilled.

Moral: *The Wise and the Happy mix at mutual Peril.*

CURIOSITIES

SEPTEMBER 7, 2007   Not all curiosities are of scientific use or value; but the habit of collecting curiosities, their gothic fascination, grows from the same ground as the scientific temperament. The philosopher may reject the aberrant as the spoiled ideal; but to the scientist, as to the poet, all things out of the ordinary – everything curious, bizarre, monstrous, abstruse, singular, marvelous – whatever it proves to be on examination, in the first instance and encounter it seems the token and promise of a new world.

It was not in their first reaction, but only in their later scrutiny, that scientist and magus diverged: the scientist applied Occam's razor, to find the place of the thing in the known world; the magus tried to find new worlds in the thing. Of course sometimes the scientist is wrong. It was difficult for scientists to accept the notion of meteors; now they journey to cold white wastes to find the iron traces of the occult commerce, not just of earth with sky, but of planet with planet.

What is vast inspires our wonder. The mountain! The sky! But there is equal inspiration in the glamour of the small and strange: in the jests of nature, in the freakish, inexplicable, puzzling, or inscrutable, even in the foreign banal exoticized by lack of context. (We are all foreigners to someone.) If explanation cannot dim the wonder of the vast, it should not dim the glamour of the curious.

MODERN LETTERS

SEPTEMBER 14, 2007   The idea of serious writing is increasingly a paradox, because what is considered serious in modern letters is what it is impossible to disagree with and take seriously. What we read from the best modern essayists and critics, and in the best modern venues, is assembled from parting and passing shots, from the revelations of the *esprit d'escalier*. Everything shows the guerrilla spirit of political pamphleteering; and if we view each camp from its opposite, the world seems made up of monsters and fools.

The pamphleteer is certainly among us, but it is not the spirit of the pamphleteer which haunts modern letters; it is the spirit of the missionary. In place of lessons from religion, our secular sermonists preach the historical revelation – some moving catastrophe which (like a sacred book) delimits the permissible range of serious controversy. Beyond lies irrelevance (or heresy).

WWI was such a revelation for Europe – a message of horror and futility Europe found more powerful than the Gospel. That revelation has been superseded for them by the Holocaust. Even of a Christian, one may ask which is the more meaningful image: the Man of Sorrows, or the men of Dachau? Until 9/11 the principle revelation of American history was Vietnam – either as a betrayal of the people by an overreaching government, or the betrayal of victory by a weak people.

Where religion has disappeared from state liturgy and private conscience, it has been replaced with the cults and rites of infamy. The world of letters, and the world at large, is divided into factions, each with some central atrocity for which it works to broaden the basis of outrage. Religious fanaticisms, nationalisms, and secular ideologies are secondary. It is faction which drives events. It is impossible to explain the world today in terms of beliefs and loyalties. Everyone sees the strange alliances behind the forces of our time; it is common outrage which brings and ties them together.

The religious can, in principle, extend tolerance and decent behavior to members of other religions. Worship, where it does not become fanaticism, leaves room in the mind for other feelings. But outrage is an uncontainable passion. It subordinates every other feeling, warps every observation, breaks every chain of thought. These factions are as mutually deaf and mute as the most extreme fanaticisms of religion.

Outrage drives out justice. The blindfolded statue of justice puzzles us; our goddess of punishment has her eyes taped open. Factions cannot weigh the crime, the violation, and the loss, to calculate justice; they must parade grief and trauma, talk of *closure* or *taking action* as if these were answers. But grief is a wound that does not close, and action leaves us where we started: there is no satiety in extracting satisfaction, no revenge sweet enough to mask the bitterness.

The factions of outrage cannot be satisfied with finite goals. Outrage substitutes for religion as drugs substitute for achievement; outrage beguiles uncertainty as a hit or a high beguiles boredom or frustration. Both being poor substitutes, both tend to subvert and consume. As drugs subvert and consume one's life, outrage subverts and consumes one's voice.

History contains no revelations. History has no pivots, no keys and no locks. The only lesson of history is human weakness, human folly, and human fragility. Religion can embrace history; but history can be made to yield only perishable religions – their saints, made only once, all die in time and cannot be renewed. Looking at the Somme or Cu Chi, at Auschwitz or Ground Zero, some of us are driven to invent an analogy to Providence. We find a meaning to equal the loss; we find inspiration because we cannot bear despair. But history is only truth, not myth; and things happen because of what went before them, not in order to change the world afterward. No one can speak for the dead, nor do the dead speak.

Our serious writing is reducible to the devotional and the penitential. What does one learn from our periodicals? How is one illuminated by them? No distinctions are introduced, no arguments are undertaken; we are expected to bow to the alternations of authoritative pronouncement and sly derision, or be dazzled by a handful of shiny statistics. The actual reading is redundant; from the venue and the subtitle you can usually deduce the contents of the article or essay in advance. You could write it yourself.

I cannot believe that our descendants will read our literature. Will even their scholars delve it comfortably? A hundred years from now, our literature will feel to our descendants as an old book of earnest and censorious sermons feels to us: claustrophobic and inhuman.

TEACHING

SEPTEMBER 28, 2007   I shudder whenever I hear of a new method in education. In the hands of a good teacher, who understands and shares its aims and principles, any method can succeed. In the hands of the rest, the shape and color of the prod do not matter: they will find a way to draw blood with it.

In the classroom of Procrustes there are standards. Those who are below the line may hope to be lifted up to it; those who are above the line must expect to be trimmed down even with it.

(Provided that it is peaceful and prosperous, I suspect that a country in which many minds fall below the line, will have unusually many minds above the line. This has been one of the reasons for America's success. But unless the majority of people are close to the line, a country shall be neither peaceful nor prosperous.)

Sometimes a new method dredges the silt of habit. Sometimes it solves a problem; sometimes it shows up a problem in need of solving. But all methods try to reduce the teacher to catechist or technician. It is beyond reformers of education to acknowledge that good teachers are good, because they have good instincts. They have use for any method only if they can, when necessary, set it aside. When governments or school administrations enforce a particular method, they waste the best and excuse the worst.

The most basic question of method is whether to teach knowledge or critical thinking. But not even this question makes sense. I once read the difference analogized in the terms of computer programming – whether program or data is more important? It is a good analogy only because it shows how misguided the question is. The distinction of data and program is not essential or fixed. In the most sophisticated computer languages what is now data may become program, and what is now program may become data.

There is no skill of critical thinking, no capacity to learn, distinct from knowledge. You cannot learn to think, or learn to learn, without actually learning. Classroom critical thinking, when it is the ritual abuse of carefully stuffed straw men or the circling of out-of-reach questions, can only stop at inverting every statement into a question or cavil. That is the opposite of understanding; it is active ignorance.

Nor is knowledge absorbed directly. Words are symbols, and what symbols represent symbols cannot be. You learn not by absorbing thoughts from another mind, but by private analogy. Beginning with what you already know or have experienced, you recombine by aggregation and dissection until you meet what is shown to you. You build outward and inward, year by year, from the experience of the cradle – to the soul and the stars. But minds are not as different as their differentiating experiences. The building and building up of analogies, beginning in the isolation of the individual, converges on what is shared, what can be communicated – that is sanity.

Because it cannot be made into procedures, we neglect the basic truth: all education is self-education. Teaching cannot be brainwashing or downloading. No regulation and no method can do more than bring the teacher to the halfway where they must meet the student. No stake on any test and no drug can do more than bring the student to the halfway point where the teacher should meet them.

The mind is a fire, not an attic. You cannot burn anything without fuel, and you cannot fuel what is not burning. It takes a good teacher and a good student to set the fire; and it is the sign of good teachers to understand that whatever method does not serve the burning mind will smother it.

YOUNG AND OLD

OCTOBER 5, 2007   Even on common ground, even when there is much to be said, when the old and the young talk together it is always somehow unsatisfactory. It is not that the young ask stupid questions; not that the old are preoccupied; not that the young are clever, but the old are knowledgeable; not that the young are forward, but the old are wary. These are only obstacles, and obstacles can be overcome. But as one is young and the other is old, each wants from the other what they cannot have.

The young want the wisdom of the old without understanding what they ask for. Death is coming – even the young know this. Even the young are broken to the awareness of death when first something they love dies. What the old know that the young are free of is how short and how wasteful life is before death: that no matter how narrow the range of your possibilities, even in the longest life there is not enough time to fulfill them. You must choose. You must live by glimpses and intimations and barren plans. The old are generally kind enough not to pass on this poison wisdom before its time; and if they said what they knew they would not be believed.

The young do not get what they want from the old; the old do not get what they want from the young. They want to get to know a person while they are new, while they are strong and armored with laughter; but their efforts are frustrated.

What the old forget is what it is like not to know who or what you are. To be young is only to be indignant that, not having asked to be born, so much is expected of you in return. Who you are, who you will be, is arrived at, not received from nature or from nurture, for then like causes would yield like people – but viewed exactly and patiently, no two people are really alike. You cannot win the hope of a place in the world to pursue, or the having of a place to defend. They must in some sense be given to you. Until then, the self remains unsettled.

You must know yourself before others can know you. All we know of one another is what we sympathize with; and what is obvious enough in another to share in, is only what they have first distinguished for themselves. It is not that you can pass on your self-knowledge; as your face is different to the mirror, to the camera, and to the world, it is different to everyone in the world. But only stupidity is unselfconscious. You must know yourself: if you do not know yourself rightly, you have a false idea of yourself. If you then try to be understood – or even to be recognized – you seem either a fool, or a mass of affectations; and if you do not try, you confuse or mislead. This ends badly: at best in disappointment, at worst in unintended betrayal.

Age is a double tragedy. Age not only ruins us, it isolates us. We reflect – "If I knew then what I know now…" But we cannot even teach what we have learned to the present, let alone the past. And youth is a double farce: we do not know what we are doing; we do not even know who is doing it.

And in between – what is in between? Who can mediate? Nothing is in between. There are no mediators. Youth bears us up until the moment it lets us fall. Age descends the moment youth departs. One evening we go to sleep not yet knowing who we are; the next morning we wake up strangers to ourselves.

EATING SCHOOL

OCTOBER 12, 2007   I came without a journey to an ideal city. It had been built, I observed, during the Renaissance; but time and romantic patination and eruptive modernity had softened its rigid geometries. Still every path through that city was like a strain of music; a harmony of architecture, geomancy, statuary, mural, ironwork and garden.

After some time wandering and admiring, I found on sitting that I was tired and hungry; so I went in search in food. In the first restaurant I came to, I saw people sitting, each alone, eating from bowls of porridge, pablum, and gruel, with glasses of a gray drink at their elbows. *Health food*, I thought, and looked farther; but all the restaurants were like that one.

I resolved to do as the people of the ideal city did. I sat and ordered, with an encompassing gesture, "Whatever they're having." Sitting among them, I could see from their hunched postures and pinched faces that they took no pleasure in their food.

The porridge had the consistency of diluted cottage cheese, and tasted of dish soap. The gray drink tasted of chalk. I asked the man at the next table: "Where can I find some real food? Maybe a hamburger?"

He laughed at me. He whispered something to the next table. I looked away, but I could still see them in reflection: they were laughing at me. A third, with his head thrown back and nose in the air, aped the act of cutting meat, reducing the others to near-hysteria.

I swept my food from the table, laid down paper in payment, and left the restaurant. Someone ran up behind me and tapped me on the back. When I turned, there stood a well-suited man with a bright chain of office around his neck. "I am the Mayor," he said. "I want to apologize to you. I know that our city has a food problem. We've made attempts at establishing serious restaurants, but we can't seem to keep up the patronage. But I don't want foreigners to take home the impression that nothing is being done. In fact, we've just completed a major renovation of the Eating School. Would you permit me to give you a tour of the new facilities, and tell you about our programs?"

"Of course. I would be honored."

The city was so sensibly laid out I was not sure that we had left before we arrived. There was a long wall, and a broad gate, over which appeared in lettering worthy of Trajan's column:

DE · GUSTIBUS · DISPUTEAMUS

"Why is it behind a gate?" I asked.

"People pay for their children to come here and have their palates trained," said the Mayor. "How could the Eating School support itself if anyone could wander in and eat there?"

"They could pay for what they ate," I said.

"Don't be silly," said the Mayor. "Good food is wasted on those not trained to appreciate it. And if we made it available to everyone, they would use up the supply. There'd be nothing left for real eaters. The Eating School is for those who live to eat, not those who eat to live."

By this time we had been heard, and the gate was open for us. We entered onto an long avenue, where gracious brick buildings ran to either side of us, and we and they alike were shaded by the trees. Young people, from children to late teenagers, milled or ambled, or sat and talked on the spacious grass.

"I don't see anyone eating," I said, "or smell any food."

"Eat outside!" The Mayor shook his head. "Where any passing smell could distort the olfactory experience? Or let the smells of food just drift around to clash with each other? You're joking, sir."

"The smell of food raises the appetite."

"Now I see," said the Mayor. "You think that just because we're out of the way, we're yokels. I'll have you know that we begin training in appetite suppression on the very first day of school. We may not be New York or London or Paris, I grant you that, but that doesn't mean we just gorge ourselves whenever our stomachs start rumbling. Just look over there. That's our graduate cafeteria – the largest in the world. The chefs there can re-constitute samples of any dish known to man, from the cuisine of any country or ethnicity. Or look over there! That's world's largest walk-in freezer. Frozen samples of every fruit, vegetable, livestock meat, game meat, fish, grain – anything you could get anywhere from hunting, fishing, gathering, agriculture or aquaculture. I did my doctoral research there on calamari."

"You like calamari?" I asked.

"Like!" He laughed. "As if I made a meal of a squid. I'll have you know, sir, that I've sampled calamari on four separate occasions, under controlled conditions and with fully provenanced ingredients. I've written twelve research papers on calamari. I have, in fact, conclusively proven that it tastes *nothing* like chicken."

"I believe you."

"And look over there. There is our finest accomplishment – the Adult Eating School. Classes day and night. In a year, sir, only a year, we can take a common hardtongue – forgive my language – and teach him to distinguish at first taste between seven different grains, twelve different spices, and six kinds of meat. We hope to be able to offer sour training by the end of the year – it's a question of keeping up the lemon supply."

"Where do they eat? The adults you train? Your graduates?"

"Many of our finest eaters return as instructors. We also have a certain number of positions open for visiting eaters – and there are fellowships in the Eating Institute. Institute fellows are entitled to three meals a day with no charge and no teaching duties. And we have outreach programs, which make high-quality sandwiches available from roving kitchens."

"I would like to eat something. Is there somewhere here I can get real food?"

"Of course. Here, come with me, we'll register you." We walked into a low building full of computers and unsmiling people, all behind a counter. The Mayor leaned meaningfully on the counter and talked to one of them in a soft voice. He returned smiling. "I threw my weight around. I can get you in for the faculty gumbo."

"Can you show me the way?"

"I'll send someone to show you on Tuesday."

"That's three days from now!"

The Mayor nodded. "I was afraid I wouldn't be able to get you in this month."

I told the flabbergasted Mayor that I had lost my appetite, and took the short walk out of the ideal city.

INSTINCT

OCTOBER 19, 2007   It is doubtful to call anything human instinctual. Drives are not instincts; drives compel thought, but instinct supplants it. Instinct is something in the individual that is not of the individual. We can see real instinct in our pets: when the dog swings a toy high into the air as if to snap its neck, or when the cat, after the instinctive pounce or chase, sits in front of the crippled mouse or overturned cockroach in a confusion obvious even across species (we are all mammals here).

We must distinguish drive from instinct. Sexual behavior is the most obvious hold that evolution has on us. With secondhand guilt, even the irreligious talk of this hold as if, because we are animals at all, we are only animals. But what we consider an overthrowing storm would be judged, by other animals, gripped by estrus, to be no more than a gentle, steering breeze. In the way of nature what could be sillier than an animal which, when strength and spring are come, must be taught how to reproduce? For human beings instinct is unequal even to the original operation of life.

There is of course some instinctual flotsam on the unconscious: hitting with the heel of the hand, for example, or not rolling over a pet, or a baby, in your sleep. But we are too willing to consider behaviors instinctual which are only unavoidable; territoriality, for example. It is a necessity in all modes of life, one which if not learned from instinct is still enforced later as a hard lesson. Boundaries will always be encroached on, even the skin; and those whose only boundaries are for their vitals and victuals will find their lives and livelihoods in constant danger. Artificial boundaries remove the fight from the vulnerable center, as clothing wears or tears in place of skin.

We are animals, made of the same stuff as other animals; but we are not like other animals. Even without assuming a creator, we can see that the changes we make in raw materials by way of art or technology, to make them speak or show or do, are the same kind of changes that made animals into human beings. There is no line in us with instinct to one side and self on the other. What we do is what we are. Human consciousness is not a kind of animal nature; it is map and image and story of that nature.

THE FIFTH PROPOSITION; OR, THE BRIDGE OF ASSES. A LOVE STORY BY EUCLID

OCTOBER 26, 2007

"I glanced over it," said he. "Honestly, I cannot congratulate you upon it. Detection is, or ought to be, an exact science and should be treated in the same cold and unemotional manner. You have attempted to tinge it with romanticism, which produces much the same effect as if you worked a love-story or an elopement into the fifth proposition of Euclid."

— *The Sign of the Four.*

Let ABC be a love triangle having the side AB equally strong as the side AC; and let the unlived lives BD, CE be prolonged in a straight line with AB, AC.

I say that the agony of ABC is equal to the agony of ACB, and the anticipation of CBD to the anticipation of BCE.

Let a point F be made at random against BD; from AE the greater let AG be cut off at AF the lesser's level; and let the straight lines FC, GB be joined at cross-purposes.

Then, since AF is no better than AG and AB than AC, the two sides FA, AC are just as bad as the two sides GA, AB, respectively.

Therefore the base FC is as committed as the base GB, and the triangle AFC is a lot like the triangle AGB, and the remaining answers will sound just like the remaining excuses and explanations, namely those which are all alike; that is, the angle ACF sounds just like the angle ABG, and the angle AFC acts like the angle AGB, and since the whole AF is just a whole other AG, and in this AB can be hard to tell from AC, the prospects of BF are the same as the prospects of CG.

But FC also proved as reliable as GB; therefore the two sides BF, FC, give nothing to choose between with the two sides CG, GB respectively; and the corner BFC is as close as the corner CGB; while at BC they all want the same thing; therefore the triangle BFC is also as acceptable as the triangle CGB, and the remaining anxieties will be equal to the remaining uncertainties respectively, namely those which the equal sides inspire; therefore FBC angles the same way as GCB, and BCF's angle is the same as CBG's.

Accordingly, since the whole angle ABG was proved as equivocal as the angle ACF, and in this the angle CBG is as confining as the angle BCF, the remaining angle ABG is the same from all angles as ACB; and they are, at base, still the triangle ABC.

But the angle FBC was proved at cross-purposes with angle CGB; and they are both asses.

Therefore: no to both.

Q.E.D.

PROGRESS

NOVEMBER 2, 2007   I have tried, and failed, to disbelieve in progress. My question is not whether, but how. The twentieth century – and let us only say of it that every worst thing that has ever happened, happened in the twentieth century – killed the metaphysical notion of provident inevitability, of Progress as the slope down which History flows. But the worth of a faith in progress is proved not in society, but in the individual.

You may more or less share the sensibility of your age; you may find it unsympathetic, or unapproachably alien. You may fly to the remnants and inheritance of another age for the company of like minds. But however alone you are in it, there is something unworthy and childish in abandoning your own time for the past. Only a coward would volunteer for such an amputation as to hide from the latest developments, discoveries, creations, thoughts. Only a coward would turn from the unknown, could live out their life happily within some foreknown and mapped-out stretch of time.

We rightly abhor those who would burn old books; but hiding from new books and their authors is the same error. To suppress any part of human experience is to darken the whole.

Progress is not by ascent, but by accumulation. We find that every age, every generation, every city, every circle and school and subculture has its characterizing contribution, it work and its problems. What does not meet them is either addressed to the past, which cannot answer; or to the future, which cannot reward. But only to share the work of others is to be held back by them. Whatever work you propose to do, if you do not mean to keep it only to yourself and God – or to contribute only a footnote to your age – you must allow for progress as a tactical consideration.

In science there is much which seems valuelessly obsolete: etheric vortices, caloric fluid, absolute time. But these retain their place as links in a genealogy of ideas: they were mistakes, but not terminal ones. And what were wrong turns for those who made them become signs and stories of warning for the rest of science against naive materialism, against the applicability throughout the cosmos of the experience of Earth, against the applicability throughout the eons of Earth of the experience of mankind.

Even crank theories have relevance – at the edges, in work which bears that appearance, but is not taken from that well, like Ramanujan or Dalton; and in how ready power is to champion them, like Lysenkoism.

There are eddies, where in the pursuit of a strange end, a familiar thought rings out ahead of its time – Bruno's inhabited cosmos, Boscovitch's grains of energy; and there are tragedies, where science take the wrong path so long that it cannot find its way back, and a good idea must be re-invented, like the nebular hypothesis. Under the appearance of successions of obsolescence, science proceeds by accumulation. It even has heroes, like Archimedes who, millennia dead, can make the front cover of a physics journal.

Worked-out systems of ideas have an imperishability and a transposability which can deposit them far from their original purpose: how the Hippocratic system of humors, intended to explain disease, has become the model for analysis of personality.

We are told that art is inextricable from the class, the sex, the generation that created it; that our distant appreciation must be inferior – at best, second-hand. Art, certainly cannot mean to you what it meant to those who made it, and those it was made for. You cannot catch all the puns and allusions, or interpret all the symbols. In the age of photography, you cannot recapture the sense of the miraculous in the meticulous realism of the Dutch Masters. But the notion that your circumstances fully determine the reach of your meaningful reaction to art is an injury to individuality. To any given artwork, you will not react like a person of another generation; nor would another person of that same generation have reacted in the same way as the first; nor would another person of your own generation react as you do. Art that is not valent between individuals does not endure. And the change is not all lessening. We may without regret say that after Walter Pater, the *Mona Lisa* means more to us than it did to Leonardo, or to Lisa Gherardini, or to her husband – as long as we remember that it meant something different to each of them. We do not only make progress by accumulating works of arts, or by widening the range of subjects and sensibilities that art can address, but also as every work and every milieu acquires an ever-lengthening wake of associations.

Progress is real gain; but change in the world is less by replacement, than by different emphasis. Each age is marked off by the kinds of human nature it gives scope to; but all the varieties of human nature are always with us. On the street, you may pass or meet a man whose *gravitas* would have fitted him to be a senator of Rome; another, hard and hungry, fit to pillage with Huns; another, patient and subtle, a born Schoolman; another, willing and pitiless, a wild-west gunslinger. They will likely be undistinguished, for in any one era, only a few kinds of people have room to unfold themselves; only a few can have or find a place of their own in the world. But they are all always with us as the armory of mankind against the uncertainty of a future as unknowable as (it is to be hoped) very long. The lesson of history is less of cause and effect, than it is a promise and threat which are the same: that whatever we are, some have been before; that whatever we have been, at worst or best, we may yet be again.

DECLUTTERING

NOVEMBER 9, 2007   Some people feel a certain nameless pleasure, sharp-edged and sexually tinged, in stripping others of their individuality, in shoving them back down into the uniformed background. Their principles are their expectations: what they do not expect insults them. They love the rough squaring of the round peg. This goes with *Schadenfreude*, but something is left over. Could it be the subconscious version of an eye for health, where aberration implies sickness? But their pleasure is not a healer's.

Consider soldiers' short hair and uniforms. The scheme of military alchemy which produces a soldier is to *break down* and *build up*. It is the difference between the *warrior*, who fights alone with his own strength, and the *soldier*, who fights as part of a hierarchy of units, each with the aggregate strength of its members. One of the few clear lessons of history is that soldiers beat warriors, one to hundreds: think of the British warriors under Boudica slaughtered by Roman soldiers, the British soldiers at Rorke's Drift slaughtering Zulu warriors.

But why are businessmen short-haired? Why the uniform of the suit? Certainly, business organization is borrowed from military hierarchy, and the idea of the businesslike descends from the armed worldview of the period of universal conscription. But while it is a given, these days, that it is not the company man who creates the future of the company, the easiest way forward in life is still through the barber and the tailor. As for politicians, we are seriously considering in this country that a black man, or a woman, could now become President; but who can imagine another president with a beard?

The soldier and the careerist are both told to feel liberated in being shorn. Certainly, things are easiest for those of us who are easily categorized. That much is true of bohemianism and conformism, of tattoos and ties. But the majority mark themselves with the absence of marks. It is left to the minority to assert themselves by signs (clothes, symbols) and performances (slang, gesture).

To be human, even human, only human, is to be complex, to be distractible, to be various and try many things; to have, to keep, to pile up, to hoard. To *declutter* is more than just organizing and sorting out. It requires the discarding, not of what you cannot justify to yourself, but of what you cannot justify to another – to someone who takes money for this kind of work – someone who finds their nameless pleasure in taking things away from you.

The moralistic disapproval of possessions is only one blade of the declutterer's scissors. The other side is the idea that what is to be valued in life are not things, but experiences. "I value experiences," they say, "because I want to be able to look back on them in old age."

There is no debate here. On the one side are people who assert the superiority of experiences over things; on the other side are people who stubbornly keep having things. There is of course a dark side, which is class. People for whom contingency is credit value experiences; "I can always buy another." People for whom possessions are contingencies value them; "What if I need it later?" But there is a great deal of room in the middle.

For the young, to be distracted, or to be cluttered, is to be open to surprise. The act of decluttering declares that the season for hope is over; that the last contraction of possibilities has taken place; that the path is chosen and mapped to its end. Since your future is known, you should keep only what the future will call for. You will hear that these are just *things* – which they are, if you can replace them. But if you cannot replace them, then these seemingly useless things are more than things: these are chances that you are throwing away. Only tomorrow, or whenever it is too late, will you discover what you could have done with them.

The days of old age are long. Time murders sleep. There are so many hours, they are so hard to fill. Once you have finished with the hours you set aside for reminiscence – then what? In old age the memories we formed in youth become distant and alienated. Who was that? I am not that person. But our things, being with us, are never distant, and having taken the same road, are never strangers.

The things we have, the things we have inherited, are the things we want to pass on. They link us into a chain, and in that way give us meaning and perspective that a solipsistic horde of memories cannot.

For the old, who live beyond hope, who know that it is only the inertia of their routine that carries them forward, it is only their possessions that let them claim some connection with a human race without further use or patience for them. As the memory grows porous and ghostly, everything that triggers and proves it becomes precious.

I do not have to be old to see that the nursing home or the Florida house is haunted with more than loneliness, regret, and despair. When the day comes that yours is just one more failing body among other bodies in a room among rooms in a building among buildings; when your thoughts begin to twist on themselves, skip like a scratched record, jump like disordered movie reels; when all your thoughts are not your own and even your doubt is uncertain – you do not have to be dead to be a ghost.

Postscript 2011

My father hated having things. He loved to throw them out or, better yet, give them away. Anything he did not need he got rid of: not always his own. The rooms he lived in looked unfinished. Once they were empty, there was nothing to suggest they had ever been lived in. But somehow I carried out box after box. There was so much of it, and every item meant another decision: what to keep, what to sell, what to give away, what to throw away. I am still making those decisions.

I have become uneasy with my own possessions. For me the fear of not being able to get what I need when I need it has always outweighed the inconvenience of leaving room for what I do not need today. But now in the back of my mind I feel my heirs, and dread the burden of decision I am preparing for them. Getting rid of things used to be hard for me. Now it is easy; it brings relief. I wrote an essay a few years ago against decluttering. I still recognize a pathological form of declutterer whose practice is among the insidiously moralistic cruelties. But I cannot condemn declutterers any longer; the truth is that I have become one.

WRITING ON THE COMPUTER

NOVEMBER 16, 2007   A writer who writes on the computer must have the resistance to temptation of a desert saint. Computers make every approach to writing well – through revision, research, or rhetoric – so smooth that you can spend as long as you please approaching, without ever writing anything. Worse, a writer may attempt to mix them with writing.

1. Revising while writing seems innocent, even wise – what is wrong with writing one perfect paragraph after another? Nothing, for each paragraph; but something for the whole, when each paragraph is disconnected from the next and might be as good if re-shuffled.

2. Research while writing has the same effect as enlisting a Panel of Experts to stare over your shoulder as you write. This kind of writing is like driving the interstates – you need never be lost, and you need never discover anything. You may travel forever and never go anywhere.

3. Thinking about writing, and listening to what other writers have to say about it, are good. But rules are proved in use, not in argument; you learn them to break them, and break them to prove them by the exception. If you must stop in mid-sentence to check a rule, either you do not understand it, or you do not need it – probably the latter. On the computer, you must both resist the temptation, and ignore harassment. Spelling is important enough to check later, but not important enough to stop for; and it is no better for a computer to interrupt you, to object to your spelling or grammar, than for a stranger to look over your shoulder and do the same.

Computers are either too convenient or too inconvenient. The keyboard, with practice, can be used without thinking. It then becomes the sluice through which a flood of raw language is carried onto the screen, mixed with whatever debris or waste happens to have collected on the mind. But first – and something else always comes first on the computer. Turn it on, wait, log on, wait, start the word processor, wait, open your file, wait, write – no, wait. Choose a template, a font – what format did they need this in again – no, the margins are wrong – save it, write – no, wait. It crashed. Start over.

These waits are more than wasteful. Handwriting has its interruptions – running out of ink, blunting the lead – but the computer sets its own pace, of impetus and urgency. Often in what is written on the computer you find a uniform rhythm formed by log-ons, command lines, queries, entries, games, chats, clicks and double-clicks.

The computer is most dangerous to those most experienced with computers. Those who start young on computers have a rapport with them, not because they can keep up with them, but because they reflexively slow down to match them; those who come to computers in adulthood are impatient with them, not because they are stiff and brittle-minded with age, but because they lack this ability to synchronize themselves with the computer.

At the computer we all have a way of doing what is easy at the computer. It is a wise habit of some designers to draft on paper so they can make the computer meet their ideas, instead of making their ideas meet the computer. Writers who would experience inspiration should beware computers. Even writers of prose, aiming to avoid the poetical, should aspire to be poets in the sense which is above meter or line breaks. And poets and computers make conspicuously bad couples – poets are from Xanadu; computers are from Porlock.

Computer files suffer a natural attrition which backups alone may not solve. A file may easily be forgotten, or confused with another. The document format becomes obsolete; the backup software becomes obsolete; even the backup hardware becomes obsolete. The price you pay for the weightlessness of computer files is that nothing holds them down; unless you hold on to them continuously, they drift away from you unnoticed.

I do write some things on computers – less than paragraphs which I see close enough to entirely in my head that what method I use to get it down does not matter; and things that I want to sound dictated. But as a rule of thumb, I never trust a computer with anything that I might possibly need more than five years from now.

I admit that none of these reasons are proofs. Each is only circumstantial evidence. I cannot call witnesses, because I cannot write the same thing twice to compare. I could only re-write what I had written before. You can never start over; what you have done, even when forgotten, shapes what you may do.

However problematic, writing well on the computer is certainly possible. I do not think that someone who writes on the computer must be a bad writer. And if some can find the self-discipline to write well on the computer, what excuse do I have not to do the same? How dare I admit to (let alone argue for) such eccentricity and self-indulgence? But I have a last plea.

What I write first on paper is all my own. Notes that I write by hand I rarely have to look at again: the act of writing so reinforces the memory that the written words are only a backup. Reading over an essay written by hand, I remember what I was thinking at each step; reading over a work of fiction, I remember the feeling I began with and how every line relates to it. This is true even of looking at a typed copy.

But what I write first on the computer is not my own. I know that I wrote it only because I recognize my style. I have no connection to it. It is through but not of me; it is mine but not my own. I do not mean that it is received through inspiration. Rather, reading it is like reading something in a dream – there because of me, but not mine.

Postscript 2018

I rarely write by hand. This has nothing to do with progress. We have new devices, but with them new distractions – the endless hailstorm of notifications. When I write, I write in my head. How I transcribe it doesn't matter. Writing by hand was the discipline that made writing possible for me – but I outgrew it.

NOTEBOOKS

NOVEMBER 23, 2007   The difference between writing on loose paper and writing in a notebook is the relationship of the writer and the thing written. Unless you pledge to care for them, you may expect to outlive your loose papers. They will be lost, be thrown out, or wear out – age and die. But barring catastrophe, you may expect that your notebooks will outlive you. And a notebook has a kind of life, if only because it is hard to kill: the things which could destroy it – fire and flood – are the same as the things which could destroy you.

This is true even of cheap notebooks. Cheap paper is perishable; shouldn't notebooks made of the same paper age at the same rate? But a closed book of whatever kind defies time. From my own slight library I have before me now, as I write, a book from 1944 containing a a pressed carnation as a messenger of the sunlight of 60 years ago; and a book from 1906 wherein is interleaved a sheet of cheap ruled paper (which has turned the brown of a paper grocery bag) with someone's homework in Roman history. It is probably a decade or two less than a 100 years old; but it is safe to suppose that the man is long dead whom the boy became who wrote: "The Romans who were mostly peasants by working hard on their farms acquired the strength of will which made them the best soldiers of the world." Perhaps his children are dead, and his grandchildren know little more of him than his name. But kept by covers, the cheap paper can still be unfolded and re-folded after a near-century of Louisiana summers.

To start a notebook, even while young, is to feel the reality of futurity and posterity. Decades on, your friends, your place, your name, the world may have changed; your frame and figure, your face, will have changed. What you will be, you would not now recognize. But you may still have, you may still read, you may still use that same notebook.

Or after a hundred years? Lost to accident and inconsideration; burned up or drowned; or moldering deep in some distant garbage dump, like a message in a bottle which never sees the shore? Or browsed by curious descendants of an unimagined generation, who would otherwise know you only as a few garbled stories, a fading or grotesquely discolored photograph, a few characteristic gestures and a bad joke on film? Or annexed to some unborn historian's or anthropologist's collection, as a lens through which that age to come, with its own preoccupations, may enter into sympathy with the past and gain perspective on itself? Or displayed in a museum, as a curious time capsule – or as the monument of a departed mind? Under the sky we know, or under a new sky in a city yet to be named?

We, dead, will not decide. But our notebooks are like the trees an old man plants – given, not to anyone, but for the sake of giving.

FABLE OF THE SPIDER AND THE SONGBIRD

NOVEMBER 30, 2007   On the hot island of thick forest and air thicker with wet, a bright and brilliant spider like a hand, with legs like fingers, wove and strung her yellow silk into a golden web.

One day a small songbird with the sun behind him did not see the sheen of the spider's silk or the shine of the flies and beetles wound in it. He felt a brushing at his wingtips, weight against his face, then something soft and resistlessly strong folding him on every side. He tried to pull free; but he could not even pull his wings in to his sides, for the silk held them away. He stilled and stayed himself, and hoped that he would not be noticed.

She knew that he was there. She had felt the shiver of his contact, and the ripples of his struggle when they traveled through her web and into the tips of her legs. Now she felt the subtle rumble of his tensed muscles as he held them still, and the rushing, bounding flutter of his heart; and she came for him.

When he saw her coming, he gave up hiding. He thrashed and shrieked and fought. He struggled, tossed, twisted. But she was closer now, and he was still in her web. When he felt the first strands of fresh silk fall over him, he gave up fighting.

He was lost, and he knew his defeat. So he sang it, low and low, high and quick, turning and rising and falling in circles through lungs ceaselessly propelling the whistlings and cryings of his song. His song was in him, and in the air, and among the trees, and in the web – and through the web into the tips of the legs of the spider who scuttled away into a tree as her singing web betrayed her.

When his song was finished and he was ready to die, the bird found that he was alone. The web kept some of him, his feathers and blood; and he kept some of the web, strands that trailed from him even after he had worked himself free.

Moral: *Sing, Muse.*

FICTION AND THINKING

DECEMBER 7, 2007   The mind is a lazy mapmaker. When it receives the survey data for a new place, it does not draw a new map. Instead, it writes the new names on an old map. Sometimes, it tapes two old maps together to make a new one; rarely, it cuts several old maps into pieces, then pastes the pieces together tile-wise. The maps from fiction are most useful to it. They are simple, at low resolution, and have few identifying features to ink over or rub out. An analogy from philosophy, history, or science does not spread generally until it has found fictional embodiment – in parable, fable, romance, epic, or tale. Think of Plato's cave, think of the spacefaring twin and the earthbound.

Analogies do not solve problems by themselves, but they are indispensable because they show the right kind of solution – whether force, persuasion, invention, discovery, endurance, or sacrifice. What we look for is what we know in advance to look for; the more we know to look for, the more we find. The more we know can happen, the less we are overwhelmed. The more we recognize folly, the less time we waste on it.

Film does more of this than literature, though less powerfully. The wrath of Achilles is perhaps less lethal, but more frightening, than the wrath of Rambo; neither Leviathan nor Godzilla shall be drawn out with a hook, but Leviathan would not be troubled by an oxygen destroyer. I must recover from even a weak horror story, but (as an adult) a movie has never scared me; the best the medium can do is disgust or disquiet. Film is, at best, flat, distant, dreamy, intangible, and abstract; and though a wordless medium, it must still tell – with dialogue, with rovings of the camera, with caricature, with background music – things like weather, smells, the taste of air, everything that dreams lack, but writing can show. But film is more efficient and more accessible. It can give more analogies faster, and over a broader range.

A multitude of analogies leads to a multitude of ideas – some of them bad ideas. The stocked imagination is like black earth: anything will grow in it. Thin soils grow less, but can absorb less labor. Thick soil is hard to manage at first, when weeds take their chance; but it grows a much larger harvest. Which is to say: because it is hard to overcome bad ideas, there is something to be said for a slash-and-burn farming of the mind, which, producing few ideas, does not disturb the good-enough ideas it has received; but good ideas can be arrived at only by having many ideas, most bad – and hoeing the bad ones down.

All this is clearest for people. People are inexhaustibly unique; without the analogies which fiction from folk tale to epic provides, we could get no traction at all in thinking about one another. Fiction is what allows us to know stranger from enemy.

FORM AND FORMALITY

DECEMBER 21, 2007   Stairs are different. Architects can re-invent every other part of a building; they can contort walls and roofs, or merge them together; they can re-shape or re-organize windows; they can create views or frustrate them. But every good staircase is like every other. The form can be adorned or hidden, but not overcome (except by banishment, through one-story buildings or substitution with elevators). There is a limited range of acceptable slopes for a staircase, to which all stairs must conform, or risk injuring their users. Each step must be predictable, and exactly like every other. Stair-climbing is an unconscious, algorithmic act. So is walking, so is typing, so is riding a bicycle; but climbing stairs belongs to a different class – along with driving a car – where error risks death. For a joke, you can trip, or fall off a bicycle; but not crash a car, or fall down the stairs. You have time to get to know a new car; but a new set of stairs should not require adjustment.

Consider music. Formality is obvious in classical music. The music, to be played well, must be considered as something to be reached; and the performer can always fall along the way, by insubordination to the conductor or infidelity to the composer. Audience members have every right to resent this, however the performer excuses it. Something that

64

mars a performance hits the listener with a jerk – it is the performer who trips up, but the audience who falls.

Formality is less obvious, but equally important, in jazz. A sequence of improvisations is not a showcase of individual performers. It is not that every player is an orchestra, but that every player is a conductor. An arrogant classical player is a rebel in a monarchy; an arrogant jazz player, a demagogue in a democracy.

But songwriting is the most formal kind of music. It is because the blues is a rigid form that it can bear the distortions of strong emotion. People are never so still as when overwhelmed. If we can, we sit to cry. All popular music has strong formal structure; which makes it easy to gather with its kin into playlists, and makes it possible for the supply to be kept up.

It is by their formality – by how much alike they are in form – that songs are individualized. Any two pieces of classical music, each with a wildly different structure, sound at first much more alike than any two popular songs, each sharing the same chord progression, rhyme scheme, and instrumentation; just as, while trees are more different than people (count the limbs), we see the difference between two people more clearly than we see the difference between two trees.

The danger of too much formality is easy to see. Most of what is worth attaining in life is not repeatable, and is lessened when approached as if it could be repeated. Experiences which are had only once do not benefit by formality. Of the rest, some are recurring, but not meaningfully repeatable. They can happen more than once, but are less like climbing stairs than climbing a mountain – which does not, I imagine, improve by being done often. The rest is the repeatable. And repeatable experiences are no less valuable than singular ones. Old as I become, I would not trade music for youth.

The danger of informality is easy to fall into. Consider poets. Poets are rare for reasons that have nothing to do with poetry (most become songwriters now, who would once have been poets); but the poets that are, write less than the old poets. This is because of their informality. Free verse is dangerously therapeutic. A good poem in free verse is a unique victory – not the imprint of an emotion, but its draining, its defeat. Such poets fail when they approach something that is common to all, and so cannot be exhausted; they cannot make poetry, either of the everyday, or of the ideal.

But think of Petrarch; with the sonnet for his stair he could ascend to and return from the experience of the moment in which he saw (saw so that he therefore loved) his Laura; and as many times as he climbed up to and down from that moment, he never emptied it. Informality always stays on the ground floor; to rise, you must commit yourself to some form capable of bearing you up.

PERPETUAL PEACE

DECEMBER 28, 2007   [From I. Bickerstaff, *The Endower Institute History of the 21st Century*, pp. 55-60 ff. Hoboken: Endower Institute Press, 2207.]

In 2045 the Endower Institute organized the GSPW (Group for the Study of the Phenomenon of War) to conduct an interdisciplinary study of game theory, war-gaming, and evolutionary psychology. An elaborate computer simulation had originally been planned, but finally the participants in the War Study were issued modified versions of off-the-shelf strategy board games. Over the next four months, playing these games became the jobs of the study participants in a literal sense, as they were paid based on their performance in the game. (Several nonetheless indulged in bizarre behavior, such as massing their forces in Madagascar.)

The curious first result was that players in versions of the game altered to penalize war-waging (by introducing a random element weighted towards the defeat of the aggressor), and to reward commerce and diplomacy, waged war *more* often than players in the unmodified games. Players in altered and unmodified versions were about equal in other sub-optimal behaviors to be expected in connection with war (refusal to recognize imminent defeat, underestimation of the enemy, refusal to compromise between strategic goals when they became incompatible).

But the usual irrationalities would not suffice to explain why an increase in the difficulty and uncertainty of war would result in an increase in the rate of war waged.

The hypothesis, which the Second War Study would confirm, was that human beings were, for sound evolutionary reasons, prejudiced to regard violence in general, including war, as open-ended. As Dr. Abraham "Abe"

Saintpear, then Director of the Institute, later explained in his book *The Cornered Instinct*:

> An animal which has been backed into the proverbial corner is more likely to die than an animal being chased in an open field. From a game theory point of view, the animal should, to secure the best long-term results, instinctively fight its hardest when it has the best chance for survival. Instead, we find the opposite. It's the doomed animal, the cornered animal, that fights most fiercely. Similarly, the people we admire the most are the ones who exert themselves to the fullest degree at the last minute, or in an emergency, even to a degree which, under ordinary circumstances, would be considered absurd.

The conclusion reached by the GSPW was that these behaviors arose from a hypothetical "short-circuit" which might take place in the brains of mammals in violent situations. As Saintpear said in his 2058 lecture to the World Post War Society:

> We realized that cornered behavior could not be a rational reaction at all. It must in some sense be evolutionary advantageous to be irrational in this respect. We had been studying a false dilemma. The survivability of the species required the sacrifice of the survivability of the individual in such a way that, in certain situations, the rational optimizer and the irrational gambler must be the same person.

Their insight came through a thought experiment involving two "characters."

The first was known as the Rabbit. The Rabbit always acts in such a way as to maximize the probability of his own survival by minimizing (through avoidance) anything that threatens his survival.

The second was known as the Wolverine. The Wolverine's maxim is always to spend higher quantities of any finite resource (energy, money, or so forth) as the probability of his survival decreases.

What should have been obvious (according to Saintpear's memoir, *My Project*) but did not show up until the simulations were run, was that in most situations their behaviors would be the same; and that, while in some border cases the Wolverine lost his life unnecessarily, it was in fact the Wolverine, not the Rabbit, who stood the best chance of survival, given any nontrivial rate of dangerous situations which could not be avoided. Wrote Saintpear: "The best long-term strategy of survival, given unavoidable dangers, is in extreme probability of death to replace optimization according to probability with optimization according to possibility." Later, he restated the principle as: "In a crazy situation, the sane thing is to go crazy."

The solution to the problem of the high-warring gamers was then simple: "As the probability of victory decreased, so did the players' attention to the probabilities." As the odds turned against them, they ignored the odds.

The War Studies became the centerpiece of Saintpear's monograph *The Last Argument: The Instinct for War*. In this book (an unexpected best-seller), Saintpear contended that it was human nature to regard war as open-ended, even when the conclusion was objectively foregone. Negotiations, he pointed out, are begun with some idea of the treaty likely to issue from them; trials (in the first instance), of the verdict; but everyone believes they can win a war. "Wars are not lost once victory becomes impossible for the losing side; wars are only lost once there is nothing, however pointless, left to try; once there is no hope left to cling to." Rational forms of conflict resolution, in Saintpear's view, could not substitute for war because they did not make the participants feel *cornered*. Not feeling cornered, they were not confident that victory must, eventually, be theirs; and therefore, they did not commit themselves fully. His position was that a bloodless means of conflict resolution would require a strong admixture of irrationality and open-endedness.

It was according to this theory that Saintpear formed, with his own profits from the book and the contributions of several philanthropists (including the Estate of Wildcard Endower), the Court of Circular Appeals, a body whose stated aim was to render only provisional decisions in conflicts of international law. "It is only by offering an inexhaustible, receding supply of false hope," wrote Saintpear to a friend, "that we can create a bloodless activity which will be the *psychological* equivalent of war."

Saintpear did not make the mistake of trying to recruit the first-world nations into his scheme directly. Instead, he began by traveling with the whole Court into the most unstable areas of the world, in order to render judgments in sub-national conflicts of tribes, cartels, and so on. Soon the entourage of the Court, innumerable advocates ceaselessly debating all the causes into which the Court had interposed itself, had reached such a scale that it could not continue to travel, and took up permanent headquarters in Switzerland.

Later, when Saintpear discovered that a pair of tribes had impoverished themselves to the point of starvation to pay their advocates at the Court, he caused a portion of the Court's fees to be diverted to humanitarian organizations, to be used in alleviating whatever misery the Court might cause.

After its first decade the Court could no longer remain in Switzerland. The road systems of that tiny, mountainous country could not support the logistical needs of the advocate corps of the first-world nations. Offers of land were made from every quarter; but, to the world's surprise, the offer Saintpear accepted was in Israel. "It is best," he said shortly before his death, "that the Court remain as close as possible to what have been the most fought-over regions of the world."

Today the traveler hears the shouting of the advocate corps engaged in ceaseless argument on the plains below even before they come into sight of the shining World Headquarters of the Court of Circular Appeals upon the hill of Megiddo.

TICKING

JANUARY 4, 2008   The sound of ticking is passing out of the world – at least out of the public spaces, and out of most private lives. Monks heard it first, in stone chambers with narrow high windows, where wrought-iron heaps of parts, glimmering with hammer-shadows, had been anviled into what would become known as the first clocks. And each slip of the escarpment must have had the finality of a hammer blow, must have echoed from the walls like thunder from the valleys.

They built these machines to remember the hours of prayer when the sun was hidden by the clouds of their northern climate – strange to think now, that it was ever possible for time to be overclouded – and how unbearable it must have been, a whole community losing hours every day, vainly glancing at the sundial or the frozen water-clock, living together in that state of time deprivation which psychologists assure us can drive an individual insane – which has been used as a method of torture.

But then there were clocks, clocks everywhere – clocks in the towers, clocks in the street, a clock in the hall, a clock on the mantle, a clock in the pocket, a clock on the wrist – and each one slipping to tick, slipping to tick, the sound never far away, like the world's breathing, running through everything – the frantic tick of a wristwatch, the steady pulse of a pocket watch, the white noise of a bedstand clock, the creaking (always ready to fill awkward silences) of a mantle clock, the stately tick-tock of a case clock (crouched like a mastiff in the hall, strong and reassuring, pendulum steady and slow as the voice of a murmuring poet), the crawling, hatefully patient unwinding of the clock on the office wall.

Hearing has more in common with touch than with sight. The noises we know too well to notice are like a steady, guiding hand, with touches that reassure and comfort. (Movies are dreamlike in part because our medium or atmosphere of sounds is thinned out to a conscious selection from a library of sound-conventions.)

The flow of centuries was measured out by the space between ticks – when the tick has ticked and is gone like the time that it took, but still the next tick is to come to tick and go on to the next. Think of the effect of a mother's heartbeat in the womb, of a mother's breathing on an infant, of a mother's voice on a child; and think of this sound, more certain than a heartbeat, as needful as breathing, the voice of a clock's willful presence. How could it not have formed the minds of those who grew up with it? How can its departure not have an effect, not somehow change the world?

So many old, good sounds are going or gone, or become kinds of luxury: the clatter of hooves, the scraping of gears. People still somehow know that records skip; but when they hear a record skip, do they feel the urgent need to get up and free the needle? With portable music and satellite radio, even static may come to be a mere indulgence, a touch or a flavor.

City people know little of the noises of the country, the wavelike near and far of barking, the symphonies of the birds, the ragas of cicadas, the call and response of the frogs – or the kind of suspenseful quiet when I set a ticking clock by my ear only to cover the sound of my own breathing. But they know the city's sounds, and the sound which is the city – the rumble of the cars, millions of chattering explosions driving thousands of careering pistons, the asphalt flexing and the manhole covers shuddering, the wheels slipping and the brakes shrieking, the horns blowing and the air brakes sighing. And underneath – what is underneath? What world is in the cities, on the other side of the combustion engine?

If not too long from now the streets are full of cars which glide silently and trail only steam (and will the sidewalks be clammy and tropical with the steam?), if the cars of the future are to be ghost cars, seen but unheard, silent as sailboats – what sound of the city is behind?

Millions of people – could you hear a million alarm clocks go off at the same time? A million people laughing at once at the same primetime joke, cheering the same pass, cursing the same fumble? How far would the music of the clubs carry, would the steel-framed buildings thrum with the beats from their subwoofers as they shiver now at the passing of trucks? Romans said *magna civitas magna solitudo* – the greater the city, the more alone in it – but what does the city become, if you can shout to your friend across a busy street, and be heard? When you cannot help but hear the sick old men rave? When the gunshot in the slums echoes in the bedrooms of the mansions, and wakes the mayor's children from their sleep?

ARTS AND SCIENCE

JANUARY 11, 2008   How is science different from older ways of using reason to understand the world? One difference is its connection with the arts, in the sense of mimesis. The Greeks tried to explain things in the world, or to prove things about it. But science explains or proves only pragmatically and indirectly, because scientific understanding is not, in itself, either explanation or proof: it is image, likeness, imitation.

The beginning of science is the principle that things which behave alike, are alike – even at disparate scales, under disparate circumstance, or for disparate ends. Either one is a version of the other, or both are governed by the same law. Gravity alike draws moon to apple and apple to moon; selection produces the artificial breed and the natural species; circulating information knots into systems like ecologies and minds.

Science is not a form of art; but no society has produced a scientific discovery unless its arts were already mature. The periods of Arabic scientific discovery were also periods of toleration for the representative arts – to explain the pulmonary circulation, Ibn an-Nafis had to draw a diagram. A scientist does not have to be an artist; an artist does not have to be a scientist; but philistine scientists and superstitious artists lose something. Great as they may be, they could have been more.

Brunelleschi, as a painter, created perspective, and mathematicians caught up with projective geometry. Chemists created new pigments and Impressionists, who saw the world in "patches of color," saw a new world.

More characteristically, the sciences of anatomy and natural history were created by, and still depend on, artists. The work of the anatomist is to reconcile a body, a continuous and not always clearly differentiated mass of cells, with the Body; the work of the naturalist, to reconcile the adaptive and adapting ramifications of a common descent, with a scheme of Species; but the human Body, the animal Species, are abstractions made by art – anatomical drawings exhibit the plan of the Body, naturalists' drawings exhibit the scheme of the Species, to show what is meant by the name before the compromises of embodiment.

Leonardo called himself *the disciple of experience*; Galileo looked to *the book of nature*; the formulations are interchangeable because arts and sciences are both equally vulnerable to the same danger of self-regard. Original art is original not by breaking with tradition, but because it returns to the "master of masters," to nature; and original science is not done by pressing on with the questions in hand, but by looking to nature, not to extract an answer, but to learn the right question.

PROGRAMMING

JANUARY 25, 2008   Programming, though not itself a humanity, can serve as one. Consider Latin. By the end, the justification for Latin's role as the introduction to liberal learning was less to enable students to read the classical authors in the original with comfort, than by its exacting grammar, and its subtle and exact vocabulary, to form the mind to the tolerance for nuance and habit of precision prerequisite to all kinds of intellectual progress.

In Latin's case it was a sad diminuendo; but the role is one worth filling. Programming, which begins with the abstract essence of grammar and subordinates and iterates it to depths which language cannot sustain, enforces a power of expression as exact and as subtle as the expectation of literal interpretation can make it.

Any kind of work that approaches perfection by a cycle of degrees intermitted by trial, feedback, and return to the beginning – draft and revision, model and prototype, mock-up and construction – similarly strengthens the faculties at each return; but programming does it fastest, and most bracingly. Any programmer knows how the pain and boredom of protracted debugging leaves a hollow feeling in the brain like a sore muscle, which becomes, after a rest, the certainty of having become a little smarter.

Programming is the ultimate mimesis. Its reach is the reproduction, not only of the world and everything in it, but of all possible worlds. In this way – because to address anything well, a programmer must do so in a way which potentially addresses everything – programming is the only great centripetal intellectual force of our time; and programming is the only profession left where it pays to have a universal mind.

Kenneth Clark, in his essay "The Concept of Universal Man," usefully defines a universal mind, on the model of the Renaissance and the Enlightenment, as one which, seeing a natural phenomenon, wishes to understand it; which, seeing a human design, wishes to improve it; and to do all this for humanity's benefit.

Programming does not, by itself, yield those values; but it gives that power. The willingness to see designs and procedures as expedient and perishable contrivances – not the unanswerable inheritance of wisdom or tradition – is predicated on the ability to extract them from the inertia of their contexts by translating them into a precise and neutral language.

In this way, programming drives toward philosophy. Ada Byron, the first person to understand programming, called herself "a metaphysician and an analyst"; and programmers have never been able to escape philosophy. In object-orientation they created the first experimental metaphysics; and throughout their work, they run into old problems as they work toward the old goal: clear and distinct ideas.

The Stoics required philosophy to show and to resolve definite choices in life; they required the philosopher to be visibly and measurably changed by the practice of philosophy. This should not be confused with a positivist dismissal of word-chopping (though some of the same arguments recur), or a pragmatist tolerance for vagueness as long as it yields results. Programmers are willing to make and adhere to subtle distinctions, even without obvious applicability, as long as they are part of a useful perspective; and they are the more unwilling to leave an idea vague as it proves useful, believing that its refinement can only make it more potent, and more widely useful.

It is suggestive that programmers' favored literary mode is the essay – which Montaigne created on the model of Stoic discourses.

This resemblance to Stoicism is not accidental; it is so strong that it is two-way. Chrysippus, the father or forerunner of Stoicism, was also one inventor of formalized logic (even partially symbolic). Had the Romans invented computers, he would have stood in the same relation to their computer languages that Boole does to ours.

Such an affinity between a discipline and a school of philosophy is familiar from mathematics. Mathematicians are either Platonists, or not Platonists; and if not, what they are instead is unimportant. Mathematicians, even confessed Platonists, do not support the scheme of the *Republic*; programmers do not teach the eternal return (or even the infinite loop).

But show me a committed programmer who does not believe in the possibility and necessity of a radical and unconditional independence; who does not at once value loyalty as both the best thing that can be offered, and the least that is to be expected; who does not think happiness only as valuable as it is won through courage, not received as a gift or stroke of luck – or, conversely, who does not find unhappiness or querulousness contemptible in the intelligent, as if they should know better; and you have found an exception to the rule.

HUMANISM

<small>FEBRUARY 1, 2008</small>   We are uneasy in this world, half because it is cruel, and half because it is boring. That is not to equate cruelty and boredom, though boredom may reach cruel intensity (as for prisoners, who fear the boredom of isolation more than abuse), and though the cruelest of the cruel are the bored and cruel.

Nor is that to say that the world is in itself boring. But the things that are worthwhile about the world – its scientific intricacy, its aesthetic depth, its spiritual weight – are not the things we naturally see in it. They must be found or found out; introduced by education or example; happened upon, in reveries or shocks; or won, by study or pursuit, patience or passion.

In the long view, of many lives together, or of one life in unity, the intellectual endowments of human beings exceed any particular demand for their use. We do not feel this when we are engaged on a difficult problem. Our powers are tidal – when they go out, we drag, and think the world too much; when they come in, we soar and rush, and call it inspiration. But in the end, there is no such thing as a hard problem; only a problem which happens to be hard in a certain place or time. Every problem that can be solved is, or will be, easy for someone, not because that someone is any smarter than you, but because that someone, knowing what is irrelevant, where the dead ends are, and what it is realistic to expect, will not waste time or effort.

This is easiest to see in politics and economics. A body of voters is more likely to be correct than a cabal of aristocrats; consumers, than planners; educated guessers, than experts. But this wisdom of the *demos*, the market, or the crowd, is not because the many are even as smart together as a single human being alone; but because, when acting as a unit and addressing a limited range of choices, they stop in the right place. A laser is not brighter light, but light without distractions.

How could it be that the many are better than the one at deciding what policies to establish; at knowing how many widgets to make; at guessing how many beans are in a barrel? Certainly, averaging draws towards the mean, and so filters out the kinds of distortion which, being continuously variable, fit a curve – like variability in strength of eyesight. But people are diverse, and while you can average apples and oranges (as fruits, or spheres, or edibles, or vendibles), you cannot eat an average.

It must be noted that, while a range of secret answers always contains a few absurd outliers (three or a million beans in the barrel), the averaged results will tend towards the real. But this is not a miracle effected by the act of averaging; it is an effect of some people being right, or nearly right, by themselves. The reality of a true quantity creates a distribution over the crowd; the crowd does not, by the distribution, create the quantity.

Individuals' failings result in part from their weaknesses. They cannot clearly see the beans or the barrel, they do not know how large the beans are. But even when everyone has equal access to the same data – as in the stock market – performance is not therefore equal. No special intellectual ability distinguishes successful investors. Rather, failures in investment are generally caused by over-thinking. That does not only mean thinking too hard, or reaching for the obscure when the obvious suffices; but also the inescapable friction of irrelevant considerations – moral, emotional, sentimental, logical, philosophical, mathematical, scientific, ambitious, charitable, or personal. Even where these are consciously excluded, the discipline required to avoid such constant temptations demands and impels needless, wasteful, confusing, and complicating repetition and recapitulation. The art of haggling is the art of inducing this state – of leading someone in circles until they are dizzy with thinking; so that the easiest to take advantage of, tend to be the most determined to energetically resist it. By thinking in circles we drill ourselves into deeper holes than we could fall into by not thinking.

This is not as strange as it sounds. You must leave room between routine and emergency, or an unforeseen emergency will catch you overstretched. It is admirable to be able to improvise in an emergency; it is foolish to do so from day to day, when the right tool or procedure is available to save time and effort. In an emergency, the wise man finds many ways to drive a nail; but when the emergency is over, the wise man uses a hammer (or a nail gun) like everyone else. Animals built to fight are slow to fight, because they fight all-out; animals that fight habitually do not fight well, because they fight predictably. In war, room for heroes proves bad planning – the best commander is not the one whose soldiers earn the most medals, but whose soldiers do not have the chance to earn medals before they win.

Boredom is one of the human conditions. Belief blunts, even turns, the sharp cruelty of life; but whenever religion tries to address the boredom of life, it becomes fanaticism; and the same is true of politics, which becomes totalitarianism. The opposite of this, whatever the religion or party, is humanism.

Life cannot be all about one thing. It is certainly possible to indirectly refer everything back to the glory of God, or the good of society. And if one takes any thought about life, some such *summum bonum*, some such *qiblah*, is inevitable. But even saints and prophets cannot always have God before their eyes; nor philanthropists, humanity. Such hauntedness, such fixity, is a kind of madness – the intellectual equivalent of staring at the sun.

At one extreme, fanaticism and totalitarianism deny boredom; at the other extreme, barbarism suffocates it; between, humanism cultivates it, and all that answers to it. The cruelty in life gives value to what allow us to overcome that cruelty, which are virtues; but virtues are all in some way denials of life – the patience to bear it as something separate to be borne, the courage to risk it as something you could lose. It is the boredom in life which gives value to life itself: to company, conversation, and friendship; to creation, enjoyment, and appreciation; to knowledge, reflection, and wisdom; to everything that provides human beings with the substance of human dignity.

As boredom and cruelty meet each other at the extremities, so do belief and humanism. A beautiful place of worship or devotion is more than the sum of a place of worship and a beautiful place. Still, even then, they must be pursued separately, each by its own law, each with its own end even where both share the same means. But the relationship is not perfectly reciprocal. Belief without humanism is death; humanism without belief is still a kind of life, though a naked one. Disbelief or unbelief is an act of independence which leads to dependence, because it preserves an openness which, like an unwalled city, is open to all; belief is an act of dependence or surrender which leads to independence, because it armors the mind against ambush and siege. This is a distinction of intellectual metabolism. Belief, endothermic, makes its own warmth; but in cities, people are like bees – individually ectothermic, they can yet ball up and shiver against each other for warmth.

Bare life, life unmoving and unmoved, is rightly an object of horror. Life is not need, and life is not fulfillment; life is in between – between hunger and satiety, to eat; between satiety and hunger, to do. We live to live; and life is the question which only life answers. The summit, fullness, and extremity of hope is the idea of a heaven which is but more and better life; and the best thing which can be done with life is to bring about more life. We live to live – and, living, to add to life.

GAUSS'S NIGHTMARE

FEBRUARY 8, 2008   [N.B. In the early nineteenth century Gauss, one of the greatest mathematicians of all time, proposed to test whether the Moon was inhabited by intelligent beings by outlining (according to various sources: with flaming oil in a trench; by planting a forest on a plain; by planting a wheat field in a forest; or with an array of mirrors) a colossal right triangle. He expected that if they saw the shape, the people of the Moon would reciprocate it with a similar triangle.]

Planet A

From *Letter to Minisalonicaro*, Saboditamoni.

Dear friend:

I know not, of course, whether you are right about the appearance of our own Earth from the Moon. Certainly, plants of all sorts do appear green from our proximate position, but it is not impossible that they appear to be some other color when viewed through clouds and vast depths of air. Likewise, it is not impossible that the blues and greens of the Moon represent some other phenomenon, similarly shifted away from its natural appearance.

I might be supported in this by the speculations of our late friend Tamothoditanara, whose doctrine of degrees of rarefaction allows us to speculate that great thicknesses of air might behave quite like relatively slight thicknesses of water. Consider the enormous shifts in color which an object undergoes when immersed in water, and tell me again whether it is indeed likely that the colors which we see through two atmospheres, on the moon, represent what we see at hand to have those same colors...

I must recommend that you abandon this scheme. You may have convinced your prince that it will be worthwhile, but you should remember that princes are fickle and that if the response you expect is not forthcoming, he may choose to exact punishment for the waste in labor and precious oil which you have caused him. The trenches you propose will demand at least as much as a year's harvest of oil to fill to an adequate level with soaked fuel. Also, as I remember from my visit, the ground in your district becomes very hard and rocky just a few feet below the surface, and it will require much more manpower than you have calculated to dig the trenches.

With all that, I must confess that I do not fear at all for whether you will be able to keep the lines straight over so great a distance, after the feats of surveying which I saw you perform for the laying-out of Tabacoraca...

Planet B

From *Of the Marvelous Night of the Burning Shapes*,
Archives of Mong Sthro Diocese.

O supremely noble prince! O beloved brother!

I indeed saw, o Brother, o Peer, the Burning Shapes of the Moon but a Month ago, when they inspired the Fear and Admiration of all Men and Princes. O Brother! O Peer! I tremble still to think of that wonder. The Temples of my Country have not ceased to make daily Sacrifices of our most precious Animals to the Moon since it offered that terrible Warning, since it displayed the terrible Shape of the Ax over all over our heads. O Brother! O Peer! I take comfort to know that our Wisest Emperor has offered the wonderful Sacrifice of his foolish General who obscenely demolished the Lunar Temples of Brift Tankt...

THE BEACH

FEBRUARY 14, 2008   The beach is as different from ocean and from land, as land and ocean are different from each another. It is the third state, the middle path. Ocean is faithless, relentless, and indifferent; we can hurt it but we cannot destroy it. Land is fixed; it is given; grounded, grounding, foreground and background. There are no names for what we trust which do not in some way resolve to the rock-solid trust we give the land – even when that trust is misplaced, given to earthquake zones, floodplains, or coy volcanoes.

The beach is always between, in kind as in place. It is the sea slowed down, and the land sped up. It is solid enough to sleep on, but not solid enough to build on. It flows without tides. Dry, it is liquid-like, cannot be dug out or molded. Wet, it is solid-like, can be built with or sculpted – but when it dries it does not set, it falls apart. Dry, you half-swim walking in it. Wet, it is smooth and hard as pavement. The paradoxes of sand, as a child discovers them the first day at the beach, exhaust all riddles.

Beach air is different. It does not feel like sea air. Here the motions of the air are not answered by a moving deck. On a beach I could never imagine myself on a boat. On a boat, even in still water, I could never imagine myself on a beach. Nor does it feel like inland air. And the sunlight is different. Even in summer, though medically no less dangerous, it feels harmless – it does not seem to burn. Its warmth goes straight to the bone and stays there.

We cannot see what we take for granted; to see at all, we must see anew; and we are never more aware than when we are between – between day and night, between forest and field, between city and country – between sea and land, where the beach makes a permanent twilight, the golden hour of the golden sand. Even between past and present – when the smooth dark horseshoe crabs, leading their slow tails, creep together out of the sea, up from five hundred million years to tell us that on this planet, we are the aliens.

The beach can do well to wake you in this way even in the summer, when you must trip over tourists and vacationers; it can do better, when the crowds thin in the cold; best, when the wind is high and the clouds are thick ahead of the storm, when the sea and sky are full of the same gray restlessness, and you share the beach only with those who know better than to notice each other, who share a mutual irrelevance as they watch the reckless, desperate surfers ride.

FABLE OF THE HYENA AND THE COMEDIAN

FEBRUARY 22, 2008   A spotted hyena, having escaped the zoo, walked the streets that night terrified and disconsolate. (He was small, so those who saw him took him for a dog.) He wandered until he heard, from a large building, the sounds of laughter. What could be causing so much terror – what could be frightening so many?

The hyena, approaching the source of the noise, saw through a window that the threat was only a single man. But the man had a terrible voice, as powerful as the trumpeting of the elephants at the zoo. The voice carried through the whole hall and out through the half-open window, into the alley where the hyena watched. It was a terrible and evil voice, full of mockery and cruelty.

The hyena did not know why the people did not destroy him. Perhaps (with that voice) he was too strong for them; but the hyena had nothing to lose. He burst through the window, leaped onto the stage, and before the creature could blast him with that terrible voice – the hyena tore out his throat.

The crowd stayed silent until the hyena had dragged the carcass off the stage and out of the building. Then they started whooping and gasping and murmuring, and the hyena was pleased to have caused so much joy, and to have freed so many.

Later, in the shelter of a storm drain, as he ate his prize, he reflected that he had found his purpose. There must be more of these creatures, and he was the only one swift enough to destroy them.

Moral: *Never laugh in front of someone who does not get the Joke.*

HAPPINESS

FEBRUARY 28, 2008   Happiness is joy at rest. Joy is a reaction, sudden, and fleeting. That is not to say that happiness is joy watered down, nor joy repeated – that would wear you out, or familiarity would diminish each occasion of joy. Rather, joy and happiness are made of the same stuff, of fear and uncertainty. Joy follows their resolution; happiness must be accompanied and fed by them – what we believed was inevitable, what we believed was already rightfully ours, never makes us happy.

Happiness is a human invention. Wild animals know joy by occasions; only pets know happiness. They are mutually exclusive. Joy belongs to a resolution – you are hungry: you hunt, you kill, you eat, you rejoice. Happiness belongs to a balance – you are hungry, there is food, you eat, something reminds you that there might not have been food, and you are happy. If you forget hunger, you cease to be happy – your circumstances are no longer a balance, but a given. Happiness must be reminded. For animals, it is reminded by instinct; for human beings, it must be reminded by memory.

Happiness, remember, comes in bottles, powders, and pills. It can be forced by lowered expectations, by narrowed attention (which values avoiding the depressing over facing the unpleasant), or by a sheer plodding effort no different from any other, which effortfully attains the state to which drugs make a shortcut. What we mean when we say that we want to be happy is that we want the right to be happy – we want an excuse to be happy – we want happiness and self-respect.

There are only two schemes of pleasure in life – the smooth, straight way of happiness; and the rough, winding way of joy intermitted with distress, desperation, and disappointment. These are not absolute commitments – as it is good and necessary for all simply to be happy sometimes, so there would be something distasteful in never choosing to set happiness aside, neither for joy nor for sorrow. It would a self-indulgent and antisocial vice to be always ready to reconcile yourself to the way things are – to smother the itch of discomfort or inconvenience that mothers invention, the restlessness of curiousity or the pain of perplexity that searches out discoveries, the indignation that demands change.

As life and history are a infinity of problems, the only excusable function of happiness is between them – it cannot be allowed to avoid them. Happiness is not something you are, it is something you wear; and like any cloth, it has proper and improper climates and seasons.

DEBUNKING

MARCH 7, 2008   Debunking is to science as criticism is to art – not useless, but not the thing itself, and often requiring an approach opposite to what it tries to protect. Debunking is a rhetorical technique; disproof is a logical achievement, or a scientific consensus. In the history of science there is hardly an idea worth noticing that has not met with a wave of debunkings. They rise in jealousy from the center of science, and recede with time, in bewilderment and resentment, to the fringes.

Debunking, like any persecution, only strengthens what it attacks; and debunkers, in the long run, are enemies of science, because they belie its attractions. They portray science as progress through mutual abuse, where only the most smug are worthy to possess truth. Debunkers, by defending science, do all to make science attractive that pundits do for politics.

Debunkers are obsessed with copyediting. Take a scientific paper; confuse the punctuation and capitalization; add exclamation points; put an uncredentialed named on it – they will crush it. Take a crackpot theory; edit it to a scientific style; abbreviate the name (J. Smith); add the name of a university or an institute – they will not even to allow themselves to wonder about it.

Two prominent exceptions, where criticisms are substantial and urgent, are intelligent design and climate change denial. But these are not really pseudosciences; they are themselves debunkings. These two movements have rudely proven that the effect of a debunking has nothing to do with the truth of the proposal, only with the skill, prestige, and power (or powerful alliances) of the debunker.

I do not believe that a debunker can defeat truth in the long run – corroborating evidence in time must strain the skill, undermine the prestige, and sour the alliances of the denier – but it can be held off for a very long time.

In the past, truth opposed in one place has always had somewhere else to win. Until the last few decades there has not been a single, international scientific community and consensus; only several separate national scientific establishments, which have served to correct one another. Only since the end of WWII has there been a single Western scientific establishment; and only since the end of the Cold War (or since Khrushchev, in some degree) has there been a worldwide scientific community. The great disadvantage of this single system is that it is difficult to shame it. For example: the wave theory of light originated in England (with Young), but was not accepted in England until after – through the work of Fresnel – it had been elaborated and accepted in France. At the extreme, in France, Voltaire had to satirize the Cartesian mechanical ether to advance the theory of gravity. Competition between universities can in some degree replace this international competition; but only in disciplines which do not depend on centralized sources of money – only where independent budgets allow for independent thinking.

In the history of science, it is rarely well-known anomalies that necessitate new theories. Remember that Copernicus kept epicycles in his heliocentrism; that Kepler set out not to discover the shape of orbits, but the spacing between them; that Newton "made no theories" for the material basis of gravitation, at a time when the great question was that of the ether – a question which Einstein also fruitfully ignored. Cranks are drawn to easy solutions for most or all problems; scientists are drawn towards mines of new problems. It is easy to multiply after the fact theories of what is, or is not, science. But the behavior of scientists shows only one rule: scientists go where the work is. And while it is unusual for scientists to have to step back, and declare a body of work nonsense (caloric fluid, for example), it is almost the rule that as a new science advances, it goes from vague pretensions of revolutionary importance, to mere usefulness, or even footnote-filling triviality; and that, as theories mature, they surrender their ambitions, and ceasing to be projects of their own, end serving as instruments of old projects.

For the practical recognition of cranks and quacks, it is not necessary for the borders of science to be patrolled and enforced by debunkers – it is enough to avoid easy answers. The question to ask is not some berating, trolling "Why" ("If God designed us, why the appendix, coccyx, recurved spine?" "If global warming is natural, why do so many climatologists think it is not, why do the models overwhelmingly imply it is man-made, why changing patterns of vegetation, glaciation?") – because these are the same kind of questions that the other side is asking ("If evolution is random and undirected, why such useless complexity, why so many missing links, why dogs can still interbreed?" "If global warming is anthropogenic, why no rush of disasters, why still harsh winters, why no one can agree on what would happen even if it were true?") – and because the answers would not be scientific: "To keep us humble," "Institutional veniality, overconfidence, bad records," "Because so little survives, so little is seen in so short a time," "Because we've been lucky so far." The right question is simply – "And?" Science needs problems, science needs questions; so science cannot abide easy answers, science cannot settle for dead ends.

FABLE OF THE WHALE AND THE SQUID

MARCH 14, 2008   A whale once determined to settle between himself and the greatest of squids which was the more terrible, and thereby master of the ocean. So he sought out the terrible squid, and fought it. The deep was full of noise: blasts of killing sound, roars from carving jets of water; and the battle, watched by whales (for the squids did not care) was a jumble of teeth and tentacles, and something white in the lampless deep, and wrapped all around it long clouds of grasping sea-dark.

The whale won. The squid sank away where even whales could not follow. And all whales knew that it was a whale who was the master of the ocean. Then the watching whales left, and the victor – ragged, bleeding, exhausted – swam away alone to rest.

But now there were walls of noise against his sides – stunned, he could do nothing as three young whales tore him apart, to become the new masters of the ocean by killing the old.

Moral: *The Ambitious and Successful forget that Ambition is common.*

INTERNET OR LIBRARY

MARCH 21, 2008

I

Research on the Internet is a meal made of cake and caviar – you may enjoy it, but you cannot live on it. For food to live on, you must go to a library. Minds that live off the Internet acquire a distinctive flabbiness – the strange combination of diffidence in facts, with passionate certainty in politics.

The Internet breaks the book's proportion of data and information. It is very common, even the rule, for everything on the Internet on a topic – so many thousands of sites, gigabytes of data – to be drawn from the information in one book. A thousand sites may provide only so many tertiary paraphrases and plagiarisms of an original secondary source, itself an oversimplified popularization. How often does a search bring you only page after page all passing around the same unsourced statistics, all retelling the same questionable anecdote? Most of the best of what the Internet offers on any non-journalistic topic is on the level of a good children's book – just enough to give you bearings; enough to let you ask intelligent questions, but not enough to credibly answer a question with. This is the cake.

The rest of what the Internet has to say about something tends to be astonishingly obscure. You are interested in the occult? Why, then, here is the Alchemy Library. Read Trithemius, study an abstract of Picatrix. Or here is the Twilight Grotto. Study Agrippa, Bruno, the keys of Solomon. Agrippa, they say, had a spirit tied to the collar of his dog; Paracelsus had one in the pommel of his sword. You have the advantage of them – you need not live as a pilgrim, wandering from monastery to monastery, ransacking Europe for books as they did. You may, with Google's help, set out ignorant in the morning; and by evening, have at least a minor spirit inhabiting your cell phone, whereby you may produce static at will, or induce baldness in telemarketers. Sites like these are remarkable achievements, labors to whose makers I am profoundly grateful. They exemplify the attraction of the Internet. I might, a century ago, have spent a lifetime and several fortunes in pursuit of all the books they make effortlessly available to me. They are of enormous value, though of weightless, portable stuff – caviar.

This range of materials, from broad introduction to narrow trivia, creates an illusion of depth – but the middle is empty. There are gulfs which the Internet will not help you cross. Consider programming – where, if the Internet could suffice anywhere, it ought to excel. How many tutorials will impart a little JavaScript, get you tinkering with PHP? How many blogs teach the esoterica of JavaScript coercion or PHP's references? But in between, there is the same gulf here as everywhere else. Stop and consider this – it is more than ironic. It means not only that the Internet is not generally sufficient; it is not even self-sustaining. It cannot even feed its own.

The Internet gives us tutorials and trivia; it gives us nothing in between. The problem is that people do not feel a lack. For a whole generation, this is what knowledge looks like. They work through a few tutorials, they memorize a few items of trivia, and think that because they have spanned the extremes, they are experts. Tutorial-level knowledge gives them the illusion of competence; trivia give them rhetorical immunity to any challenge – "If you know so much about it, why don't you know about...?" "Of course you think so, you don't know about..." The crackpot who would teach medicine to doctors, science to physicists, and programming to engineers, all from his armchair, used to be the exception; now he is the rule.

II

At some point in any life of study, diverse perspectives become a distraction, and obscure facts become trivia. This turning inward is a sign of intellectual maturity. To fill the mind, you must turn off the computer, you must shut out the world and cloister yourself. Diverse interest alone makes a dilettante; obscure information alone makes a pedant; but a scholar is formed in the library, out of deep and protracted thinking. Yes, a book is a companion, but it is not a follower; it is a guide, like Dante's Virgil in Hell, from doubt, through danger, into light.

All of this might be obvious if we did not confuse education with schooling. Still, I hope most people will admit that the best student is one who would, and does, learn without a teacher – one who reads. Reading multiplies schooling; and while classes provide leverage for the mind, its substance – if it is to have one – comes from what you learn on your own.

Objection: the Internet is new. It is immature. As it matures, it may grow into something that is a true replacement for the library. But this is wrong. Indeed, as the Internet has matured, it has become less like a library. Increasingly, everything is commented upon, annotated, rated and heckled. Hierarchy has given way to unlayered tagging – which makes it easier to pursue your interests, but conversely makes preconceived interests less flexible – is it progress in cookery if wherever you go, to any restaurant anywhere in the world, you can eat a hamburger, just the way you like it back home?

I love the Internet. I need the Internet. I would be diminished by living without the Internet. But the Internet is not the library of the future. The Internet is becoming ever more and more its own medium, something new and stupendous. The Internet is not trying to become a book; it is trying to become a continuous correspondence, a layered and multivalent conversation, a many-handed game, an acceleration of the social aspect of thinking – but not all thinking is social, and for private thinking, the Internet is not only unhelpful, it is poisonous.

Wikipedia forbids original research; but that is an enforceable policy only because the whole atmosphere of the Internet is already so much against it. Much is made of sites like ArXiv or PLoS, and of their increasing importance at the expense of print journals; but while they take advantage of the Internet, they do not really belong to it. It should command attention how strange an accommodation they are – that writing by and for the most technically sophisticated audiences possible, written on computers, distributed exclusively over the Internet – is still formatted in order to be printed and read on paper. Discoveries asserted in markup are, with rare and casual exceptions, the work of cranks. Hypertext, as Wikipedia shows, is a fine way to knit together existing knowledge – but to add something to that knowledge requires the linearity which can be offered perfectly by paper, but which the screen must disguise itself to imitate.

Enthusiasm for the distributed and egalitarian formation and organization of knowledge – for the network perspective – is good. We should be enthusiastic. It gives us the power to approach the world in a new way, and we do not know what we may yet find. But the network perspective is not complete. Linearity and hierarchy are not the original sins of the intellect. There are real lines, and real hierarchies. The line brings speed – there is power in separation. The road separates us from nature, but finally lets us see more of it. Hierarchy brings confidence: the mechanism of memory is a network, but its operation is hierarchical, always subordinating the abstract and universal to the concrete and particular. In any vital system, the line and the network, the hierarchy and the mass, are found in alternation.

III

To show that a book serves certain ends better than the Internet is, by itself, only enough to justify books as a luxury item. But my concern is for libraries: not the kind that adorn mansions at a stage in affluence a little after a pool, and a little before a garden; but public libraries, the kind where flimsier books have to be armored by special bindings against use and abuse – by impecunious scholars and cheap students; by parsimonious old men looking back, and grubby-fingered children looking forward and up and down and sideways; by the shy seeking connection and communion, and by the face-addled and smalltalk-stupefied seeking respite.

The real justification required is not intellectual, but economic. Granted, books are good; but can we justify the expense of libraries, if we can substitute in the Internet something not quite as good, but good enough?

The production of books is not a problem. It must be hardly a footnote to the paper industry. As long as we have drywall and wallpaper, paper towels and toilet paper, cardboard boxes and bottle labels, fliers and handouts and junk mail, fodder for office printers and copiers — we may have books as well, without much trouble or impact.

But this is moot. Most people are sensible and sensitive enough not to be in favor of disbanding or abolishing the libraries we have. The real question is: should we build new ones? The implicit answer of late seems to be that libraries are like city steam heat: worth keeping up if your city already happens to have it, but not worth the effort when building anew — so that, in the developing world, what is important is to build schools, not libraries; to put laptops into children's hands, not library cards.

This is pragmatic. A laptop can bypass a corrupt government; a library implies funds requiring stewardship. But there is a questionable assumption involved: that, just as undeveloped regions might do best to skip telephone poles in favor of a wireless infrastructure; so they should skip libraries, and develop a paperless culture. But I think this assumption is better put: if developing regions attract enough medical charities, they can skip building hospitals. Patently, the object of medical charities is to relieve the harshness of life, and ultimately by relieving the harshness of life to allow the institutions to form which will, in turn, build hospitals. Likewise, laptops should set in motion the intellectual awareness and appetite, which will, in time, demand and build libraries.

IV

The Internet increases the importance of the library, as the means of synthesis, consolidation, and continuity in culture. The Internet magnifies diversities of all kinds. It has strengthened every existing group and variety of opinion, and called forth new groups and opinions from vague sympathies and stirrings. But diversity is not an end in itself: the object of the multiplication of individual perspectives is that these perspectives should each somehow add to a shared, universally meaningful sum – they should add to the shared human project.

The Internet by itself is unsteerable – a freedom of assembly which veers into faction; a freedom of expression which veers into vandalism. The faster and more weightless the Internet becomes, the greater its need for books as ballast. Think of a project like Wikipedia; would it be possible without the books which anchor its citations as references? The paragon of the possibilities of the Internet is everywhere dependent on the library.

Or think of politics. Politics on the Internet is a parable warning against the dangers of booklessness. In the absence of books, it has succumbed to faction and vandalism. It is particularly tragic to witness in the United States – which was founded by the bookish – reading books to derive and develop their ideas, writing books to defend their actions. Five minutes with the *Federalist Papers* or the *Debates in the Constitutional Convention* or *Democracy in America* will give you a better idea of, and a stronger sense of a stake in, what America is and stands for, than if you were to read every Internet debate on the subject from Usenet through the blogosphere to Twitter.

Increasingly, I find that the rhythm of my reading becomes an alternation, in which what I read in books raises questions which the Internet answers, and what I read on the Internet conceives needs which books fulfill. This cycle has neither the attraction of technophilia, nor of technophobia; it is not shiny and sleek, it has no smell or patina; it has no brand name or buzz, no ancestry or tradition; but it has certain unglamorous advantages: it is real, and it works. I cannot be alone in having discovered it; I suspect that there are more who quietly belong to both sides, than who openly belong to either – that the rivalry is not only mistaken, but mostly fictitious.

CONSTRUCTED LANGUAGES

MARCH 28, 2008   In life we are the servants of language. Words are all we leave behind us. Our relics are only significant by the names they receive. It is the so named Works of the Romans, not any work alone, that inspires wonder – and it is only the name Work which causes us to regard the aqueduct at Nîmes as more wonderful and more attention-worthy, more sympathetic, than any arch of weatherworn stone in Utah's Zion. The name of Apelles the painter was a byword for excellence in his art for a thousand years after the last man who had seen his pictures was dead.

Language is all we have in common. What we make are only words; what we leave are only names. We were given, undeservingly, an intelligence equal to the span of the world in which we find ourselves; the side effect is that we each become our own world. Only the necessity of communication keeps us from regressing from one another into private languages. Therefore, what can be said in any language can always be said in another – because while not every thought can be communicated, if a thought can be communicated to anyone, it can be communicated to everyone.

Think of how strange it is, that only because you both speak the same language, you can communicate with someone separated from you by decades of age, by country and climate, by sex, by class, by way of life. And think how absurd it is, that someone of your own age, sharing your background and your circumstances, cannot communicate across that shorter distance, if you do not share a language.

It is possible to know things in one language which you do not know in another: not because they cannot be said in both, but because translation is a kind of alchemy, where *solve* must precede *coagula*. What you take in whole may not be accessible to you in another language, even if you speak them both, until you have taken it apart in one language, to put it back together in another.

There may be things you can only learn by creating a language: by the act of creation, or by the way the created language fills a gap. The world is not written in the language of mathematics, but in the language we have created for mathematics we have made something that maps to nature's language. But my concern for now is with languages created for pleasure, not for purpose.

In the canon of constructed languages, Tolkien is the Old Master. Much of the appeal of reading Tolkien is to discover things that he knew, in silvery Quenya and in Sindarin's rushy breezes, that he did not quite know in English, and could not always translate. Indeed, *On Fairy-Stories* has the air of a poor translation from a patois of Elvish languages inside his head. And *A Elbereth Gilthoniel silivren penna míriel* teaches you something without having to see a translation at all; but you can feel that you know it, whatever it means, under branches screening stars.

Tolkien is sometimes derided as pseudo-Biblical in his diction; but this is simply wrong. The powerful cadence of the King James Version is imparted by a plangent alternation between etymologically disparate English synonyms – which, while it has its own majestic effect, misrepresents the straightforwardness of the original Hebrew. But Tolkien is etymologically almost pure: page after page, he goes on in a kind of alternate or underground English, the revenant language of Chaucer, the sleek hull of maiden-voyaging English before it was barnacled with borrowings from Latin and Greek.

This language – a constructed language of a sort, purely by selection – is, even before myth and archetype, the deepest source and means of his power. You do not need to be a linguist to feel the difference in the depth of Tolkien's English, any more than you need to understand music theory to hear the sadness of a minor key.

Some purposes require their own languages. Mature poetry has its own grammar; vital religions employ their own dialects, even their own languages (and a wise missionary does not translate everything); and every profession must find its own jargon, to ennoble the commonplace or to make commonplace the extraordinary. And every language supports another, floating language, of idioms and proverbs – one which can sometimes be carried over whole into new waters, as Erasmus did in his *Adagia*, which restored to the Renaissance the floating language of antiquity.

Art, even mimetic art, is still only sometimes the recapitulation of a natural process. Just as often, artistry is the power to throw a natural process into reverse. A picture suggests a story; a title finds a poem; a stain on a wall evokes a picture. The constructor of a language only begins by finding, in the space between real languages, the pleasing or striking form of a new and unheard language. The art is to evolve, from this shadow, the succession of necessities making up the thinkable history that would have formed that language – that would have learned all that that language, and that language only, knows.

BREVITY

APRIL 11, 2008   It is the lesson of poetry that more can be said briefly than can be said at any length. Brevity is wit itself. All comebacks are laconic. All attacks should be surprises. Quotations and proverbs contract with time. The short version on the lips, not the rambling original in books, gives the author credit and fame. Repetition for rhetorical effect may be eloquence; variation may be illumination; but most repetition is redundancy, and most variation is vanity. Something is always sacrificed to pad the page or word counts, or to the smearing thin of thick, subtle concepts to lubricate the passage of a dromedary audience through the needle's eye of understanding. Eloquence that must be dug out is eloquence buried alive. What the mind retains of prose is its flensed, poetic skeleton. Digressions may be ends in themselves; but illustrations and examples are passed over or forgotten, if not burned in as metaphors. If you write to instruct, ineloquence is inevitable. Prose is not poetry; but even in prose you must have a poet's discipline, and the poet's principle: better lost than found for the wrong reason.

Year Two

"In an hour in a bookstore a thousand books
may pass under my eyes – books judged not by
their covers, but by the company they keep, as
recognizing a friend among strangers makes
the others less than strangers."

THE ANATOMY OF ENJOYMENT

APRIL 18, 2008

I

It is fainthearted to require something to be explained and defended to you before you can decide whether you enjoy it. It is a weak mind which approves of only what it enjoys; it is as weak a mind which enjoys only what it approves of.

Approval is a kind of commitment. To approve of something is to vote in its favor. It is an act of conscious, conscientious judgment. Enjoyment is only to find something agreeable – to be pleasantly delighted, distracted, diverted, entertained, beguiled; or to find something bracing – the pleasure of being no more than confused, shocked, startled, uncertain, lost, speechless.

I do not mean the kind of distinction where you approve of the outcome without enjoying the means. We all approve of having things clean; few of us enjoy cleaning. By *approved* I mean defended, in outcome and in means, as proper and worthwhile.

II

What does it mean to be proper? Propriety varies by company, place, and hour. Yet it is not relative, since it has normative force; nor is it abstract, as it is attached to context. Fashion, as (partly) the propriety of clothing, shows that propriety is a kind of language, declaring the extent and degree of one's membership, and the ratio of membership to individuality.

But judgment is more than a checklist of proprieties and approvals. Where there is a procedural standard, it is a graph with many dimensions and axes. Propriety answers to a rule and a precept. There is the precept in Rome to do as the Romans do; tempered by the rule that what is done in Rome (all roads leading there), does not stay there.

But young people do carry around checklists – the more precocious, the longer the list. The young zealot has a strict checklist of the proprieties of religion – attentively ticking off the signs and showpieces of religiosity. The young artist likewise proves their sensibility and genius by uncompromising bohemianism.

Youth is its own context; or for the young there is only one context. The young therefore cannot be judged wise or foolish, cowardly or courageous – not yet. Those who never ask themselves what is right age without growing up; nor do they grow up for whom the discipline of youth becomes the cage of snarling, pacing adulthood. It is the softening of youthful rigidity – sometimes gradually by ripening, sometimes by powerful, kneading shocks – that lets you function as an adult, not thoughtlessly obedient, not vainly defiant.

III

What does it means to be worthwhile? There are two standards: one avocational, one vocational.

Time passes whether we use it or not; we benefit by everything we experience, directly or indirectly. To be worthwhile, something need only not demand an inappropriate level of commitment, not mislead or misguide us.

What is worthwhile avocationally lies between what taxes laziness, and what imposes boredom. But the space between the two is elastic. The less lazy and the less passive in boredom the person, the more of what is done and undergone is worthwhile; the lazier and more easily bored the person, the less is worthwhile. And this is true even if the two persons do and undergo the same things.

But this is only where avocation is concerned. Vocation properly commits itself to more than a lifetime can accomplish, accepting responsibility for the concomitant minutiae and trivialities. The standard of the vocationally worthwhile is only profitability – not necessarily (though possibly) monetary, but yielding something, realizing something; something either defensible as being useful, or somehow self-justifying.

It is curious that a vocation, practiced long and well, comes with time to resemble an avocation. Laziness, or the indulgence of boredom, never become forgivable. Preoccupation rarely works an alchemy whereby chores become signs suffused with the sweetness of the achievement they lead too (they generally remain chores). Instead, the perception of time changes. Time put to use is prolonged, time merely spent is hastened, and our subjective time, if not our clock time, increasingly belongs to the most worthwhile.

IV

Enjoyment is not only the wild pleasure that attends indulgence and is paid for in regret, nor is to *find worthwhile* the same as to *enjoy*. Our capacity for enjoyment belies our mortality. The idea of heaven is the ideal of pure enjoyment. It would betray the idea of heaven to call it right or worthy, as if there were some vantage of purpose from which is could be judged. *Heaven* names the end of purpose.

Enjoyment is not a single emotion. The shades and nuances of emotion which enjoyment entrains are distinctive to the individual: a peculiar compound, unique as a fingerprint, of happiness, joy, delight, contentment, satisfaction, satiety, pleasure, wonder, transport, ecstasy; with an equally unique shape of associations formed as the experience twists and compresses to find breathing space, hemmed in by capricious distastes, painful worries, and bad memories.

Enjoyment is not a judgment. The same person varies in what is found enjoyable, and even these variations are variable.

Look to the lovers. Some people in love find everything enjoyable; their worlds are illuminated by their passion – they cannot fail or fall – they are strengthened, purified. Other people in love find nothing enjoyable, they long, they pine, they worry, they regret, they pace, they walk in circles, they are without hope, bereft, now burned by desire, now crushed by loneliness.

Look to the winners. Some people in triumph swell and float, crowds of strangers part for them, their worth is proven, their existence justified, their glory planted and growing, they are the strongest, fastest, smartest, coolest, their friends hang on their words, strangers seek their advice, they need only want to have, their future is full and short, they will blaze and burn out for all to see. Other victors are finished, their lives are over, their purpose served, they are obsolete, worn out by training, practice, and struggle, too old for further victories, the sun past its zenith, the sun setting, nothing but an already passing name; losers in truth by so many sacrifices and so many overlong deferrals that became unwitting sacrifices, and what is left is only a long, empty future, chewing over memories of victory until they have lost their savor, while the hard use they have put body or mind to in youth haunts and makes torment of old age.

Nothing is certain to be enjoyed, there are in fact no standards or criteria, not even for an individual. The same person may be at one time exalted, at another time devastated, by love or victory or anything else – by prosperity, progeny, power, wisdom, renewed health; or even now in enjoyment, now in agony, now in indifference, from day to day, hour to hour; or, in some commodious souls, all at once.

Enjoyment is not a judgment; but that does not eliminate the phenomenon of judgment from enjoyment. Enjoyment is an *act*, and stands in the same relation to the judgment preceding it as does any other act. Like other acts, enjoyment is best undertaken by plan, next best by chance, and worst by force. What you pay to enjoy you plan to enjoy; and though it is less potent than what is spontaneous, you cannot live in the expectation of the accidental and unpredictable. As food must be had every day to sustain the body, so something must be enjoyed or the faculty of enjoyment shrivels and turns bitter. All creatures are creatures of habit.

Those who live by whim and happenstance are at once discontented and trusting. Why are they discontented? But nothing is more absurd than to require the justification of discontent. Can you justify your hunger? Trust comes from security, real or imagined, or from folly. (Folly being distinct from imaginary security in that willful folly manifestly spurns thought, while imaginary security – a condition more pitiable than contemptible – takes thought, but is too weak to bear it.)

The really secure, as far as life allows, are the wealthy, the healthy, the likable, the liking, the lucky. They haunt history as patrons, spectators, commentators. We find them about town or on tour. Everyone else wishes to be them; but their wish is to have the narrower spirits of genius – and only by keeping company with such narrower spirits are they ever remembered, hanging onto the lights that are the beacons of the otherwise unbroken darkness of history.

To be able to force yourself to enjoy things is a necessary skill. What moves us most, what becomes most precious to us among our experiences, is often what we have at first doubted – what we had, at first, to force ourselves to enjoy. But this has two dangers.

1. To force enjoyment of everything – or just of too much – ends in a kind of mirror or complement to despair. When tragedy and comedy

become indistinguishable, life loses form, and the mind becomes a confusion of powerlessness – comedy becomes tragedy, which we call despair; tragedy becomes comedy, which we have no name for, but should fear as much.

2. To allow too many others – especially strangers; friends have the right to insist on introducing you to new things – to allow them to force you to enjoy, ultimately enfeebles your enjoyment; not only in the shrunken will, but in the abuse of the faculty. Enjoyment needs rest: not to close, slacken, and sleep like eye or arm, but like the stomach, intervals to digest, variety sufficient to keep up the appetite. No one, I suspect, enjoys food as a well-raised child – the set mealtime, the plate to be cleaned. Gourmandise is a privilege of adulthood, and is only obtainable to an individual through the swings and jumps of whim and fancy.

V

Gourmands are quick to enjoy and slow to approve – unlike critics (of food or generally), who commonly are quick to approve (if they hear the shibboleth), and slow – torpid – to enjoy. Creative individuals, in their spheres, are always ready to enjoy – even determined to do so where they lack the inclination to criticize. It is only zealotry which – with or without *approval* – withholds enjoyment from another faith's holidays or ritual spectacles.

Not only religions, but cultures, regions, peoples, are usually distinct in their atmospheres, the diverse lights of different countries, the moods of their arts. You may enjoy the Aztec temples without approving their rituals. The educated must regard spectacle entertainments with disapproval, as tribal rites, as (bread and) circuses, as opiates. But if you end up in the stands, it is vain to be sullen, not to do your best to enjoy. And where music is in order, it should always be enjoyed as part of the occasion, even if you cannot stand it. Food and company on journeys can and should be enjoyed – however opposed to what you eat and keep at home – without determining your habits when you return.

VI

Those of us who will not dare to enjoy what they do not approve are not directly lessened. Neither our sense of the world nor the orbit of our sympathies comes from the diversity of our experiences. The world is too large, the human race too near infinite in numbers and kinds. Not one life, not a dozen, could compass it. Our understanding either receives an inherited or borrowed perspective from few others; or obtains perspective, through reading, from the distilled experience of many others. No matter how much you see; no matter how many countries you stand in; the world and the human race you know are not reflections from experience, but images you have taken either from tradition or philosophy.

Nonetheless, when we will not dare to enjoy, we are lessened, as anyone is lessened by cowardice: we lose our sense of self. We do not get to know the world by experience, but it is how we get to know ourselves. The science of self is an empirical one. We proceed by an experimental variation of conditions, and in the comparison of each contrast we discover the laws of our particular microcosm.

Animals belong to the environment they are in; human beings belong all at once to all the environments they have ever been in, to every construction they can put upon them, to every perspective they can take on them. As we gain in this capacity, as where we are becomes everywhere we have been, we gain in humanity.

Inattentive minds cannot be force-fed what they need; but attentive minds can get by on very little. They do not need grand tours or gallivanting *Wanderjahren*. A garden, for example, or any spot of growing earth, is not one place, but many: multiplied by seasons, by the generations of flowers, by visitors human or animal present or clinging to it in memory, by the state of mind you bring to it, by the purpose that brings you to it — to savor, to work upon, to hide in.

There is no meaning to the approval of those who never disapprove. Relativism is the privilege of irresponsibility. To act is to choose; to choose is to judge. What we only enjoy, we only regret losing; what we approve of, we fight for. If it is not hypocrisy to say *I enjoy things I could not do*, it is not hypocrisy to say *I enjoy things I would not do*. But the least thing you approve of should be more important to you than the greatest things you enjoy without approving.

VII

There are two ways to approve without enjoying: to approve, but choose not to enjoy; or to approve, but be unable to enjoy.

To approve of victory, but choose not to gloat; to approve of accomplishment, but choose not to celebrate and trumpet; to approve of an afterlife, or some abstract immortality by posterity or participation, but choose honor in grief; these are wise choices. Good taste and compassion often reserve enjoyment from things which, viewed in themselves, ought to be enjoyed. Enjoyment belongs to what we do for ourselves; in what we do for others, enjoyment may become condescension, mockery, even cruelty.

Where there is much to be forgiven, you can approve of forgiveness but not enjoy extending it. The more you compassionate the needy, the harder giving becomes, because it brings you nearer their state.

But most of the time, what we approve of without enjoyment is what we have become bored with. Every passion fades by like degrees. First there is unmixed enjoyment, love, satisfaction, delight; but however fascinating, we must look from it from time to time to other things. Where there was steady fire, now we only flare when we return. Then we only plan to flare; fire becomes a power, not a practice. The power untried atrophies; and we are left approving with our whole being what we can not longer enjoy.

There is nothing steady in life which is not subject to this failing; but it is not inevitable. Passive boredom is not a phenomenon, but a vice – one whose indulgence inevitably poisons every experience, empties every life.

VIII

There is a difference between boredom and blind habit. Boredom is the absence of enjoyment; blind habit is the absence of the awareness of enjoyment, an awareness which returns sharply in its deprivation. This is the fate of everything approved of and enjoyed: whether continuous or periodic, occasional or unique, it is unresistingly assimilated, until it acquires the indispensable invisibility of the foundation of a house or the smooth working of internal organs.

We see clearly what we approve of but do not enjoy; we see what we enjoy but do not approve of; but we do not see at all what we approve of and enjoy. It is therefore conditional to anyone creative or sensitive, who would see what others do not, to be able to withhold or supply enjoyment as needed, separately from approval. Together they conceal; separately, the arc between them can illuminate any experience.

COMMUNITY

MAY 2, 2008   Community is the best thing to have, the worst thing to be had by. The wish for community is at its worst a kind of wish for death – a wish to be submerged in the group, to be assigned a place, to be enfolded by a web of explicit rules and expectations, to be known in full – to be finished. But community, when it is good, is not a kind of group, but something that can be said of a group; an adjective, not a noun; like marital bliss or individual excellence, it exists only relatively – it can exist only where and because each manifestation is unique.

Community is not bad in itself; but if it is powerful for good, it is also simply powerful, and being powerful can be dangerous. Of course, none of us can escape the anonymous community of commerce, law, and arms. Even the hermit relies on the general peace to preserve him from abuse.

Community is worthy and strengthening in moderation, but in excess addictive and limiting. Everything worth doing in life is in part defiance of community – even the widening of a community; the more closely a community is jointed, the less room it has. Here, as elsewhere in life, the pleasure of security loses the profit of change.

A role in a community is a cell, and *cella continuata dulcescit*. The stronger the community, the more it will hypnotize itself into identifying you with your role: remembering what fits while forgetting or filing away, as aberration or as peccadillo, what does not. Strong as you are, given time, the expectations of others will turn your life into a story; turn your words and your thoughts into your lines; turn your taste into your image; turn your face into your symbol. This happens to the famous in the world at large; but in a close and closed community it is worse. Even virtual communities demand from you a declaration of personality, with fields for nicknames, statistics, lists of *favorites* (modest lists, more concealing than revealing). This is not an awkward imitation of community: real communities are more awkward and confining than anything which human beings could bear to consciously make.

It can be comforting – it is certainly convenient – to allow yourself to be shaped in this way; and it is to some degree inevitable – even the hermit must *look* like a hermit, if he does not want strangers to try to rescue him. But to surrender to this force is not to live as befits the equipment and the powers of a human being.

There is no honor in demolishing communities, but there is only good in building them if you do not immure yourself. Keep more than one community; and if one community tries to claim you for itself, shouts or whispers that every other is a lie – *you are mine only, mine to judge, mine to keep, mine to make and re-make* – then leave it. It is death in life.

SPECIALIZATION

MAY 9, 2008   Despisers of specialization oppose it to a golden age when to be a thinker was to be a generalist, universalist, polymath, *omnifarium doctus*, a Renaissance man (Renaissance-era or not, man or not). Defenders of specialization sadly acknowledge the loss, but call it a trade-off: because we know vastly more than our predecessors, we are doomed to specialize: knowledge has become too complex for generalists.

Both these positions are based on false comparison. If specialization were going to undo us, we would have been undone by now. There may be danger may be in restricted training, but we can be sure there is no danger in restricted responsibility.

It is a mistake to compare the most difficult problems we can solve, the most difficult projects we can undertake, with the most difficult problems and projects of our ancestors. If we compare their methods with ours in the same problems, we find that (for example) the Scholastic philosopher, weaving new syllogisms to account for every problem a modern physicist dispatches with a fillip of calculus, lived in a vastly more complicated universe than we do.

The diversity of our specializations, the subtlety of our investigations, are possible only because the leading ideas of science are simpler now than they have ever been before – not easier, but simpler, because entities are fewer. Newton uniting the celestial and the sublunary, Dalton reducing a handbook of elemental behaviors to an algebra of atomic weights, Darwin tracing back the origin of species, Einstein folding space into time and time into space, Faraday's fields, Shannons's bits, Noether's symmetries, Feynman's diagrams – all bear witness. The scientific endeavors of the present are the most complex ever, because they are the least burdened with overhead.

The same phenomenon is present in the humanities, though at a different level. Consider the half-facetious "Godwin's Law": "If you are the first to mention the Nazis, you lose the argument." But the warning of Nazism really does prune our thinking, mostly before we even speak. Knowing that certain ways of thinking can only end in horror saves us time wasted in toying with them, and effort wasted in arguing ourselves or others out of them.

The highest thinking takes place in this kind of shorthand. Philosophy would be impossible without the ability to reference positions by the names of their originators. Even Plato did it, with Parmenides, Empedocles, and Heraclitus. If we had to begin every discussion with a clean slate, it would be intractable to think at a philosophical level. Each such new name nucleates the floating notions and inchoate ideas that were not so much inaccessible before, as too much trouble to chase down.

Look at an orchestra. Hundreds of instruments, each with players who have traded much of their lives for mastery. Then look at a chamber ensemble from two or three centuries before. Compare an orchestral score with a piece of chamber music. What has changed? Has music theory become so complex that an orchestra full of instrumentalists is now required to implement it?

To the contrary: music theory has become simpler. Composers use chords (or tone rows) instead of counterpoint; but more importantly, tuning has been simplified. The system of tuning now in almost universal use – equal temperament – is the simplest ever: divide the octave into 12 exactly equal parts. Tuning used to be higher math; now it is A=440. Indeed, it could never be done with precision; thus the chamber ensemble had to be small enough that each player could hear, and adjust to, the deviations of others. It is only by the very simplicity of equal temperament that massed instruments can play in tune.

The very subtlety of our specializations, the very complexity of our problems and projects, testify that our intellectual progress has been due to the simplification of our ideas. It is because we increasingly speak the same language that we are free to develop dialects.

But even for orchestras, tuning only matters when there is something to play. What of composers and conductors? What of generalists? Where are they in the war of department against department?

If departments fight, then they have something to fight over, which implies there are still generalists around, however informally. If so, then their position in our society is like that of homemakers: so indispensable that they go unnoticed, so invaluable that they are not valued.

THE PINE BARRENS

MAY 16, 2008

Forests have gods of their own that they shelter, keeping your old
    gods
Left there by peoples vanished or dead in their hollows and deer
    paths.
Always defeated, they whisper and slink through the shivering shad-
    ows.
But we have a god, a devil, a shrieking and wandering devil.
You hear him hunting and howling: he hunts in the night and the
    day-time.
You see the marks of his hooves in the snow on your backyards and
    rooftops.
You know the devilish son, thirteenth son of Mother Leeds, cursed
    son.
Twelve mortal children had grown in her womb by turns and had
    suckled.
Loose as it hung from her, skin could not hold in her bitterness.
    Maddened,
Weeping, she prayed that this one be a devil. Darkness had filled her
Darkness to cover the sun like a storm cloud, night without morning.
Sticky and crying he lay in his crib while she died in her bedsheets.
Lying alone in his crib how he grew, like the wave in the ocean

Last child of Mother Leeds, thirteenth child, cursed child, fanged
child, winged child
Leaving the towns behind, fearing his father's kind, flying he found
us.
Devils are hungry for blood but we gave him pine sap to suckle
We fed him pine sap and bear flesh. He needed no shelter from
hunters
Men had forgotten their towns in the dark woods next to the red
bogs.
Men left their churches and sweet homes shut up, silent and empty.
Free of their axes we rose up, covered the roads and the clearings
Rotted and broke down fences, dragged down markers and signposts
Scattered young acorns tight in the cracks of the walls and the roof-
tops
Driving their roots in as wedges to throw down the walls and the
roof beams
Unhinged doorways, battered windows, wind-swaying branches
Heaved up foundations. Jumbled and heaped up stables and work-
shops
Houses, schoolrooms, churches. Mice made nests in the bedsheets.
Sweeter is nothing for forests than violently taking their own back
Nothing like claiming the ruins. We watch all your cities and high-
ways
All of your wire-strung poles and your blind towns white in the
night-time
Ready and hungry we plan for their ruins. We wait for your weakness
Sending our acorns, testing defenses. Soon when you falter
Our god will walk out among you clearing the way for us,
Violently clearing the way for the oaks and the pines that adore him.
Empty, your sky-scraping towers will rust through, buckle and falter
Vines will soon pull down your wires and smother the voice of your
broadcasts
Trees will soon grow in your roads, in your lawns, your cellars and
playgrounds
Spiders will seal up your houses and mice will make nests in your
bedsheets.

TOURISM

MAY 23, 2008   Filling the mind is as easy as reading, but enlarging the mind is a demanding task, best and most easily done by travel. And tourism is still travel. Even shepherded tourists gain new perspective on themselves; gain the precious stirrings of what the ancients called *cosmopolis* – the membership of civilized human beings in, and their first loyalty due to, the community and continuity of civilization, and the principle called civility or humanity. Even if a tourist does nothing but add to pictures and names they know already the traces of smell, hearing, and touch; even if the tourist comes away with nothing in memory but a sort of deepened postcard; then that is still an improvement. For what is more bitter than Browning on Venice: "I was never out of England; it's as though I'd seen it all?" What is more high-handed than to condemn those who hope at last to meet what they have long admired, as if their presence would diminish it? There is nothing wrong with being a tourist – nothing wrong with being just a tourist.

A nation of tourists is a healthy and a vigorous nation. Each tour improves the tourist by some increment, however infinitesimal; and each community returned to is similarly enlarged, by the presence of a human connection to what was before only a source of pictures and things. It is not logical, but it is a human truth, that Japan is shelved in the mind beside Ruritania or Middle Earth until some human proof of it is made. It is one thing to know that Japan exists; another to know someone who has been there; and still another to have been there yourself. Even the most credulous still harbor a deep doubt that something could exist whole and right yet *different* – a doubt which we must take dramatic steps to beat down, and can never fully overcome.

Tourism does incur a kind of homogeneity, a floating country of hotels and restaurants; but its contribution to the world's homogenization is slight. The vices of tourists are overshadowed by business travelers. Tourism is one of the only forces – in many places it is the only force – giving value to and protecting not just the particular instances, but the general concept, of the individuality of place. What must we think of those who propose to encourage tourism – as if it were rainfall to be channeled – to save this natural wonder, this artificial curiosity, but disdain to be called tourists themselves?

Cities as beautiful as Venice or Prague or New Orleans have not been preserved to us by the pride or taste of their residents; each is frozen for us at the moment of the collapse of its prosperity. We must suppose that cities just as beautiful as these have been torn down by their own residents to make way for the brick of Progress and the glass of Modernity. Now that these cities have, in a degree, recovered their prosperity, it is their value in tourist dollars, not their residents' sentiment or sensibility, that preserves them. Business is business, and unless sentimental wealth pays better to preserve than to tear down, to the man with the sledgehammer it is always the season to cast away stones. Tourists vote, with their feet and their wallets, for the preservation of the places they visit. They may do damage in their sheer breathing numbers; but in the meantime their presence as witnesses deters the petty crimes of progress.

Rome died, not quickly at the hands of barbarians, but slowly at the hands of Romans. It was Romans who tore down the marble city of Augustus, breaking up pillars to wall their fields and statues to burn in their lime-kilns. Locals whine about tourists; but of all people, locals care least about their cities. The same people in childhood formed and inspired by the wonders of a place, in adulthood take a special delight in corrupting and destroying them; and when you hear a slogan from an architect it is likely to translate to: "Come, the nest is ours now, let us foul it." It takes tourists – badly dressed, out of shape, gawking, dumbstruck, craning, pointing, peering, murmuring, muttering, exclaiming, picture-snapping tourists – to save cities from themselves.

CRITICISM

MAY 30, 2008   There are only two possible foundations for a science of criticism: the criticism of perfection, and the criticism of excellence. The criticism of perfection judges a work by a system of rules, or by its resemblance to a postulated masterpiece. The criticism of excellence, being unsystematic, is harder to define; but to earn approval and applause this way, a work must surprise its critics.

I confine my examples to literary criticism as the paradigm, but I address all criticism.

Many systems for measuring perfection have been proposed; many schools of critics have tried to appoint themselves the lifetime judges of excellence. But to know that a work has been found perfect is not to know why it is perfect; and to know that a work has been found excellent is not to know why it is excellent. Each kind of criticism has its own failings, which appear whenever some standard or group wins out.

The failings of the criticism of perfection are familiar. This method is so far out of favor that it is harder to imagine how it could ever have worked, than what could have gone wrong. The few efforts which have been made in this direction have either fallen flat, or had to shelter downwind of science. This is, after all, the kind of criticism we are taught forms of in school. It takes things apart, it anatomizes to give names to each dead part: theme, plot, symbol, character. Mastery of this method allows the quick-witted to turn a story into an essay so fast and so thoroughly that one is only left to wonder why authors bother with the formality of fiction. It is so inefficient. Why don't they just write the essays themselves? But this is fishmonger criticism: it fillets the story. The most generous interpretation of this approach is that it expects the hard, essayistic and the soft, aesthetic parts can later be reconciled; but that usually works out no better for the story than it does for the fish.

This method was not always decadent. In the French critics of the late Renaissance, for example, we find, not a vital impulse for drama constrained by revenant rules, but rediscovered laws calling dramatic art back into being. Before the professionalization of literature, the criticism of perfection was the only kind of criticism possible: the aspiring writer could present no credential of the mastery of the form, except the perfect fulfillment of the form.

Shakespeare, to make a joke like Pyramus and Thisbe, to hammer at the fourth wall with *The Mousetrap*, had to enclose them in larger plays; to play with nonsense and anacoluthon, had to put them in the mouths of fools and madmen. But were he alive today, he could do these things directly. It might be better for his career. Would a modern Shakespeare more easily stage *The Tempest* or *Pearls That Were His Eyes*? *Titus Andronicus* or *A Dinner Fit for an Emperor*? Macbeth, or *The Porter Equivocates*?

Despite its failings, of the two kinds of criticism, the criticism of perfection is the more open, the more honest, and the more consistent. It is the default form of criticism: it was the first; it is almost inextinguishable, absent only where literature is absent; and it is resistant to debunking. Where the tools can all be seen, it is hard to call their users impostors.

But what could be more perverse than to write to please those hostile to literature?

The failings of the criticism of excellence are unfamiliar. After all, it saves books. How many great books, not written for the public at large, would be lost had not the criticism of excellence assembled a voluntary public willing to meet them halfway? How many great books that came in the first instance before the wrong public, had only the criticism of excellence where to make their appeal?

The failing is simple: the criticism of excellence is based on a fallacy. By definition (assuming a normal distribution), the majority of anything cannot be excellent. Or put another way: all books cannot be above average. The criticism of excellence, by valuing only the excellent, destroys what it loves: like the gardener who, to make room for more flowers, plucks off all the leaves.

Worse, the criticism of excellence is necessarily cliquish. To be able to recognize excellence with certainty – to know a work for the best of its kind or the first of a new kind – you must know (or believe that you know) everything. The result is that a body of critics of excellence form a kind of priesthood or freemasonry; they speak shorthand, they write secret handshakes. This is doubly problematic. First, it makes literature inaccessible from the outside – it is not enough to read the words if you are not in on the joke; and second, it makes literature inaccessible from the inside. If you have not shared their formation, you can no more join a body of critics than you can join an organization of veterans of a war you did not fight in. It is not a question of adopting the mindset formed by certain experiences: instead the experiences constitute the mindset. Thus every few decades a new corps of critics comes up, and drives out the old ones. Unless you belong to the rising corps of critics – unless you belonged to it *before* its coup, which must be in large part a matter of geography and luck – you are out as long as they are in.

If neither approach to a science of criticism is viable, then there are only two conclusions. Either criticism does not exist; or criticism is not a science. And, in practice, many writers behave as if there were no such thing as criticism. Whom, after all, should they trust? An older writer who has outlived cycles of praise and abuse, ceases to care about their recurrence. And if a young writer needs to keep an ideal audience in mind – let it be anyone but a critic.

Yet criticism exists. Its more workmanlike forms are increasingly difficult to avoid; and if the workman exists, then so must the master. But if criticism is not a science, then what is it? How should it be done? If neither the criticism of perfection nor the criticism of excellence suffices, then is there some third, artistic way; is there some synthesis to achieve; is there some prior unity to return to?

The truth is that there is no criticism; there are only critics. Those who practice criticism according to some criticism of criticism can only be secondary critics. Criticism must end somewhere. Be you tireless as a dog, lithe as a cat, still you cannot catch your own tail.

THE BLACK TAJ

JUNE 6, 2008   The professor only smiled, and lifted what was not a box, but a cover. Beneath was a small, round, red carving. The student leaned a little closer. It was a stylized carving of a turtle. There were black and white spots on its back. "What does this have to do with architecture?"

"Tell me what you see."

"I see a turtle."

"That's all?" The professor sighed. "Nothing else?"

The student thought it over. "It's Chinese. I've seen Chinese carvings that looked like that. Made of – whatever that is – the same stuff."

"And that stuff is?"

"How would I know." It wasn't a question.

"Cinnabar. It's cinnabar, do you know cinnabar?"

"As in cookies?"

The professor looked pained. "No, it's an ore. Mercury ore. It's very important – cinnabar means a great deal to some people. So does mercury. And the spots. Do they mean anything to you?"

"Black and white. Some sort of yin-yang thing, maybe?"

"Black and white, yes. Slate and shell if you look closer. The pattern – that's a double quincunx. Five and five make eight." The professor stared across the table.

"What? I don't get it! I study architecture – why would I know any of this? You said this would help me. You said I had to know this. How is a Chinese figurine going to make me a better architect?"

The professor flipped the turtle over. As it rocked back and forth light flashed over the smooth black that covered its underside.

"What is that?"

"It's a lens."

The student looked closer. "But it's opaque. It's obsidian." A small victory.

"Yes. But you need the right kind of light. What do you know about the Taj Mahal?"

"A lot, I've been there."

"Good. Then you've heard of the Black Taj?"

"I've heard of it. It's a story for tourists."

"And weren't you a tourist?"

The student snorted. "Not *that* kind of tourist."

"Do you know how the story began?" The professor waited, but the student did not answer. "A traveler's letters. He wrote Shah Jahan would have built a Black Taj for himself, but he died too soon, and his son abandoned the project."

"There never was a Black Taj. They've checked. No foundation, no black marble lying around."

"There is another version of the story." The professor gestured at the dim bookcase behind them. "It was in a manuscript by a Sufi poet of the time. Though he wrote Hindu poems as well. A *wise* poet. A little-known poet. But that's the same thing."

"And this has something to do with the Taj Mahal?" The student pointed at the turtle.

"It does." The professor turned it back over. "Would you like to hear that story?"

"If there's a point..."

"There's a point." The professor leaned back.

Why am I thinking of Sunday School?

"The story goes," the professor began, "that Shah Jahan had *promised* Mumtaz Mahal two tombs. One for each of them. He was *desperate* to build the second. But the first one had taken so long, and been so expensive, and his son would not promise to finish the second. He *agonized*. Sleepless nights. Pacing the hall. He threw tantrums. Finally he decided that what he needed was – well, a consultant."

"What?"

"A consultant. Someone from outside. Someone who could get things back on schedule. He did a lot of interviews. Wise men, roving worthies. Indian mystics. Europeans with blueprints. But the one he chose came from China. A Chinese sorceror. He promised he could not only build it faster, he could *hide* it."

"How do you hide a Taj Mahal?"

"Inside another Taj Mahal, of course. He promised a Black Taj that would be enfolded by the White Taj, 'as sound folds silence.' In the poet's phrase."

The student kept silent.

"For many years," the professor picked up, "black marble was brought to the Taj by night, and the sorceror's servants – some of them other Chinese who never spoke to strangers by daylight, and some that were never seen by daylight at all – they carried the black marble through the doors of the Taj. When they were done, when it was finished, the sorceror gave Shah Jahan the only way to see the Black Taj: a black lens, a dark mirror, that would show the hidden tomb inside the one that could be seen. Beyond the reach of his son's greed, the Shah could be buried at the same time in his own tomb, and buried beside his beloved in her tomb."

The student looked away and back. "OK. I like that. That's cool. Stretching my mind, right? A new perspective? So I should think about buildings inside buildings. Like multiple uses, right? Like, an office tower is one building for the executives, and one for the janitors, and they have to fit inside each other. That's a—"

"That's a good observation, but that's not what you should be getting from this. This isn't a lesson." The professor put a hand over the turtle. "I'm trusting you with something here. This isn't a toy. It's valuable. How valuable I can't tell you. I sold, I borrowed... I could only afford it it because nobody else knows about it."

"I—"

"Listen, please. The sorceror made the mirror for the Black Taj. Shah Jahan used it, he was satisfied with it, but he had the sorceror and his servants surprised one night and killed so nobody else would know about it. He wanted the mirror buried with him. His son couldn't prevent him from building the Black Taj, but he could at least frustrate his last wishes. After the overthrow, he kept the mirror. And the poet he brought to court and showed it to found out that it doesn't just work on the Taj. It's doesn't work on every building but it works on a lot of them. Just the best ones, the ones with *souls*.

"This is what I'm trying to show you. Every building that has a soul, has as its soul another building, a Black Taj. Some other building that stood in the same spot. Some earlier state of the building – before a renovation or reconstruction, or a flood or a fire or a collapse. Sometimes even a completely different building, the one that could or should have been built but wasn't – the one the architect really meant or another architect came up with and people didn't want… just one that's better."

The student blinked and gaped for a moment. "So… how? How come you had to pay so much for the mirror, if nobody else knew what it was?"

"What? You care about that?"

"I'm trying to get my head around this." *I trusted you!*

"All right. We'll take this slowly."

"You mean there's more."

"A *lot* more." The professor held the turtle out, mirror-up. "You can see the mirror's round, yes? And the cinnabar holds it in. It goes under the edge here, see? Now this is one piece of cinnabar. And the mirror's in one piece. So how'd it get in there?"

"There's some trick. Like, I've seen it done with quarters and blocks of wood. You drill a hole and stick it in and let the wood grow back over it."

"That's right. Good. But cinnabar doesn't grow."

"So it's impossible."

"I wouldn't say *impossible*. It's Chinese."

"So, you look through this and you see imaginary buildings?"

"*Secret* buildings. And it does more than that. Have you ever thought about why a good God lets bad things happen?"

"I'm an atheist."

"Not somebody else's god, *your* god. Think about ants. If everything were good for people but ants still had to suffer – say, if people stepped on them – would that be wrong?"

"It depends. I guess not."

"Right. So keep going. God is good, we suffer, so…"

"So what?"

"So we're ants. Something else is above us. But what's above us?" The professor looked around. "*Buildings* are above us. Buildings are around us. Buildings are real. Realer than we are. We make them, but only like cells make us. Buildings are the real inhabitants of God's universe. And least, they're closer to it than we are. They're the real images of God. The real angels and devils – the real gods. They rule our lives. They hold us in their bellies."

"And the mirror…?"

"The mirror shows them for what they are."

"So what do you want from me?"

"You're the best student I ever had. You could be one of the best. But first you have to see the truth. You need to understand your calling, your place. You are not a shelterer of ants. You are a creator of gods."

The student sat still, waiting. Waiting for the turn, the punch line, the explanation. None came. There was just the mirror.

FOUR DEFINITIONS OF WISDOM

JUNE 13, 2008

I

Consider Solomon, the two women, and the disputed child. Where is the wisdom in this story? As told, it is clever, but not wise. We must guess at the wisdom in it. We must suppose that when Solomon heard of this dispute, he did not plan to solve it with a sword. Indeed, for a king, solving problems without resort to the sword is when wisdom shows. And it was neither a repeatable solution, nor a convincing one. Courts today do not offer to cut disputed children physically in half – and when they offer to divide not a child's body, but its life, both sides usually accept.

If Solomon was really wise, he would have known, before he brought out a sword, which woman he wanted to take the child. Perhaps he had observed that one was furious, and the other mild. Then the sword was a prop for a kind of rough equity – the furious woman might have supporters who believed the child was rightfully hers; but even they would have to see that he could not give the woman a child that she was ready to see dead for spite. Thus Solomon in the story was subtle enough to feign trickery to dissemble wisdom. But that is not to say that wisdom is subtlety, because that would be a circular definition – what was formerly called subtlety being the wisdom of the enemy; what is now called subtlety being the indirect or insignificant, to be avoided by wisdom. What is admirable in Solomon's judgment is his imagination – the imagination to cover a difficult judgment with an easy story.

Obviously, wisdom is *imagination*.

II

Wisdom is more than thinking. Everyone thinks, and there is no wisdom is thoughtlessness, but we are not wise in proportion to our thinking. The difference is that, confronted with a problem, most of us only think harder; but a wise person both thinks hard, and thinks over their thinking. Most people, of ordinary intelligence, know how to exhaust a line of thought; fewer know how to conduct several at once, holding them in tension. This is most obvious in the misapplication of sound principles – how a good idea can be carried too far, if it is not applied to itself – as it is sometimes good and sometimes bad to be prudent – prudence is folly when little is at risk. Wisdom in that case is prudence about prudence. Such iterative virtues often have names: loving to love is benevolence, fearing to fear is courage, daring to dare is audacity. And these can be applied to themselves as well: benevolence in benevolence makes philanthropy, courage in courage makes discretion, audacity in audacity makes enterprise.

Obviously, wisdom is *iteration*.

III

The brilliant general Hannibal was beaten by the even more brilliant general Scipio; but he was defeated first by the wise general Fabius, called *Cunctator*, Delayer. Fabius could never have beaten Hannibal in battle, but he defeated Hannibal in war, simply by never giving battle. Hannibal provoked him; the Senate pressured him; but Fabius never fought Hannibal, only haunted him, the ghost of the Romans dead at Cannae, an omen of bad fortune, denying him allies, denying him provisions, receding from his challenges like water before Tantalus. Fabius became a great general simply by never making a mistake. Carthage had Hannibal's brilliance; Rome had Fabius's wisdom; and though Scipio won the war for Rome, Fabius lost the war for Carthage.

Obviously, wisdom is *restraint*.

IV

The worst mistakes happen when we believe a mistake is impossible. Doubt is to thought as air is to life. Of course too much doubt risks over-anxiety; but then too much breathing risks hyperventilation. A mistake is most condemnable when it is made despite warnings. This is worth dwelling on: how the same mistake, with the same consequences, is worse if it has been warned against than if it happens unexpectedly; how there is more shame in failing to heed a warning, than in failing to see ahead. What makes tragedy of Caesar's death is not the death itself — it is, "Beware the Ides of March." Emperors would die by worse betrayals; but those were unexpected. Caesar was warned.

Even vague warnings seem prescient after disaster; and that makes disasters tragedy. Attention to warnings seems more important than foresight. In life as in weather, a clear horizon is not to be counted on; and for a fresh illustration, note that it is thought better to say "no one knew the levees could break" — admitting blindness to danger — than to admit that, knowing it could happen, no one got around to doing anything about it. It is the same for other disasters, as if lack of foresight is always excusable mischance, but failing to heed warnings is always hubris.

Obviously, wisdom is *humility*.

MEMETICS

JUNE 20, 2008   Memetics is the idea that culture is parallel to biology. In memetics, everything cultural — concepts, systems, religions, cultures, art forms — all known as *memes* — live and spread through populations as do viruses and parasites — which is to say, *genes* — making the history of human ideas the record of a kind of natural selection.

Memes and viruses are understood to be parallel, but not perfectly analogous. While bodies have immune systems to defend against viruses, the only immunity to be had against one meme is prior infection with another, stronger one.

Memetics analogizes the meme very awkwardly – the meme in the mind is at once like the fetus in the womb, the bear in its cave, a virus in a cell (or a computer), and a fire in a burning house – but that awkwardness, though doubtful, does not disprove it. Powerful analogies are often awkward when new: how is the moon like an apple? or a cannonball? or a dancer?

The appeal of the idea of memetics, as the prospectus of a science, is threefold.

1. Unlike all other systems of psychology, memetics bootstraps itself. Other systems must present themselves, at least implicitly, as the transcendental descents of reason into the human sphere of sublunary irrationality: so that the only idea a person may have which is not determined by the unconscious is the idea of the unconsciousness, or not serving instinct, the awareness of instinct. But memetics is proud to be a meme. It not only provides for, it demands the co-existence in one mind of the rational and the irrational, at every level.

2. Memetics offers hope. The idea that we are only hosts to memes might be taken as our final doom to unreason; but in advocates of memetics it revives old hopes for the perfectibility of man. The psychology of the Enlightenment was powerless before the twentieth century. No one could satirize the battlefields or the camps, blame them on bad education or persistent superstition. They seemed failures of reason itself. But memetics restores the old hope: it is an idea powerful enough to account for mass insanity, and for true evil, without surrender before them; an epidemiology promising cures or inoculation against the vectors of unreason; at least a pyrology directing backfires and firebreaks.

3. Memetics explains everything. This is a point of appeal, but also a weakness. The Lisbon earthquake of 1755 may be analyzed as a meme, one which drove out old memes about theodicy; but why should it have had that effect? We may say, because it was true – the earthquake happened, when it should not have. Then why the success of the meme of, say, Spiritualism? We may only say, because it is not true – because it is agreeable and convenient. But why should truth win because it is hard to bear, then lose because it is hard to bear? This kind of paradox is basic

to human nature; it is difficult to establish a consistent standard of fitness against which survival could lead to selection.

I think that memes, in some sense, probably exist. Granting, then, that elementary memes exist: are all, or even most, ideas analyzable as descendants or compositions of these elements? I see three problems: (1) ideas do not compete; (2) ideas are hard to kill; (3) ideas are more than memes.

1. We adopt, even if we do not understand it, every new idea we encounter that we do not explicitly deny. This is only obvious to those who speak, write, or create enough to have a real-time sense of their own intellectual processes; but it happens to everyone. The bringing out of the contradictions between these ideas is an task which must be undertaken consciously. If memes are not competing, they are not being selected; but what competition there is among ideas, is not inevitable (some lazy people simply hold contradictory ideas), not universal (some people can tolerate combinations of ideas which others could not), and not continuous (one can adopt an idea with the intent of examining it later). In religion syncretism is the default, which religious hierarchies exist to combat. If there is an ecosystem of ideas, its only motor is conscious human will. Even granting that a single transmissible meme could viably contain contradictory ideas, it is still unclear: what pressure drives selection? *Ideas do not compete.*

2. It is nearly impossible – sometimes, it is impossible – to expunge an idea once it has been accepted. The analogy between a meme and a living thing is strong for ephemera, but weak for ideas. A complex living thing is hard to make, but easy to kill. We know how hard it is to start fashions, how quickly they die. But the effort required to cry down an idea in another, or to overcome it in yourself, is disproportionate by an order of magnitude to the effort required to spread or adopt it. True, infections and infestations are not easy to deal with; but their resistance is because of their simplicity – being simple, they are easily copied, and have leeway to mutate. But something which is both complex and difficult to destroy is unprecedented in life as such. Once again, the idea of selection is not obviously applicable. *Ideas are hard to kill.*

3. It is astonishing how forcefully, how suddenly a new idea can impress itself on a person, or a whole age; how thoroughly and quickly it can be adopted. This is familiar from science, where a new idea – a new principle,

new technique, new approach — sets a generation of scientists casting around for new ways to apply it. Consider natural selection misapplied to sociology and history, resulting in Social Darwinism, or the sudden-onset obsession of the late nineteenth and early twentieth centuries with mathematical axiomatization.

Both ideas, of course, snapped from overextension. Evolution was forever distinguished from progress, and Gödel pointed out the cliff ahead of mathematics. Memetics can explain the fire; but not the dryness of the wood — how quickly it catches, how quickly it burns out. Memetics does not require that a meme be viable in the long term; but in these cases the *meme* burned out, while the *idea* survived it. Contrast the early nineteenth century attempt to reduce the world to so many fluids — etheric, magnetic, electric, caloric — where the idea died with the meme. There is a necessary distinction here. *Ideas are more than memes.*

If we wish to see what a society that had become the vehicle of an idea would look like, we will not find it anywhere in civilized history — even in the ancient theocracies of Egypt or Persia. These regimes contained the ideas which, mixing and developing freely in Greece, would return with Alexander to destroy them.

We should look, rather, to tribal societies. Anthropologists have freed themselves enough from the ideas of the nineteenth century to cease to regard such societies as primitive; but it is also the nineteenth century which gives us the notion that extant tribal societies resemble our ancestors. Colonial ethnologists looked for occupants for the lowest rung on the ladder which Europe had surmounted. They found them in tribal societies, exhibiting conservatism across millennia. But there is an obvious flaw in that reasoning — those societies do not change; the ones that gave rise to ours did so by changing. Now, we know that conservative cultures can share their descent with civilizations — the same groups of people who were ancestors of the Amazon Indians were also ancestors of the Anasazi, the Maya, and the Inca. But were the ancestors of both more like the former, or the latter? We suppose that the uncertainties and anxieties of civilized life must be the degenerate offspring of a tribal life Edenically serene. It is equally possible that the oldest, nomadic societies were relatively dynamic. Some, settling under relatively easy conditions, carried on that dynamism into the first cities (and it is a curiously underappreciated discovery of archaeology that the first cities, like Jericho, predate agriculture). Others, settling under circumstances which turned against them, or settling under hard circumstances because they had lost their best lands to settlers, under the pressures of survival – preserved their ideas only as memes.

Memetics has not been successful, either as an idea or as a meme. As an idea, its applications savor of adolescent facility in reduction; as a meme, its appeal has been too narrow, the explanations it provides too pointed and too mocking, to transcend the perspective which originated it. I stoop to kick it while it is down only because I think it should be woken up. Memetics is not adequate to all that has been asked of it; but though inadequate, it is not incoherent; and difficult as it would be to explain how memes work, it would be still more difficult to explain their absence.

A PRAYER

JUNE 27, 2008   Sojourning just outside New Orleans, I often walked on the levee by Lake Pontchartrain. Near the Causeway, there was a mass of debris washed up from the lake and jumbled together like a carpet. As I remember, driving south into New Orleans, you could see it to your left.

One day - the year was 2002 – I decided to comb the debris for any sculptural pieces of driftwood – an old New Jersey habit. These I found. And with them, I found a prayer.

It was a small wooden board, less than a foot long, and an inch and a half thick. There were holes in it as if it had been nailed to something. If it had nails still in it, I removed them. It was an ordinary pine board. Most likely, it was once a piece of building scrap.

On one side was written – marked or incised:

GOD SAVE US FROM THE STORM

This object fascinated me. Where had it come from? How had it come here? The nail holes showed that it had not been ritually thrown onto the waters; it must have been mounted to something – a dock? A boat? And a storm, a slip of the hand, a contemptuous heir had given it to the lake; and the lake had discarded it here.

Whether I took it with me, I do not now remember. I felt that it would be wrong to take it; or, having taken it, I felt that I had done something wrong, and carried it back. I walked around with it for some time, looking for a place for it. At length, landward of the levee, I lay it face-down beside a locked tool shed that I had never seen open.

It stayed there for a long time. Who took it; whether they threw it away, or kept it for themselves, or returned it to the lake – I do not know.

I tried.

FABLE OF THE CANDLE

July 4, 2008   Once there was a dark kingdom, without light or lamp. There a wise old man made a candle that could not burn out; and this candle was the first and only light in the dark kingdom.

The sage had a young disciple, whom he taught – slowly, slowly – how to look at the light and how to see by it.

The people of the dark kingdom hated the sage and his light. Now and then men climbed by twos or three out of the dark town below, up to the cabin where the candle burned, to try to put it out; and the young disciple would chase them off.

But this time, one townsman got inside. And before he could be dragged out, he knocked the frail sage down, killing him. There was wailing from the cabin: and when the wailing was heard in the town below, the people answered it with cheers.

The young man buried the sage. The men of the dark town were more daring now; it seemed that they were always creeping up, trying to get in to put out the candle. So the young man set his chair in the doorway, and with his back to the candle listened to the darkness outside. When he heard voice or movement, he stood and charged shouting; and once it was gone, he sat and listened again. He listened long, listened and chased until he was weary and past weary, until he had learned to listen half-awake and to chase without anger. How long that went on – too long.

In time the men of the dark town began to lose interest. Soon there were silences when no men came at all. And the young man, with joy, re-entered the cabin to see the light again. But he had been too long from light: and he looking so suddenly upon it, the candle burned his eyes, the light blinded him forever.

Moral: *Do not turn your Back to the Light to protect it.*

BOOKSTORES

JULY 11, 2008   I wish I could preach bookstores. Everyone should read: reading is, for most people, both the best and the easiest form of thinking – an affordance which makes it one of life's kindnesses, not to be scorned. But most readers do not need bookstores: a library card and the occasional purchase suffice those who read only a little.

But those of us who read much are drawn to bookstores. Theirs is a different attraction than a library; a different temptation than simply buying books (even secondhand). I go to bookstores to be surprised – which is not an indulgence. More books are worth reading than life has time to read. I could try to prioritize; but how to judge? My tastes, my needs, are unique; I cannot rely on others' rankings. My solution is the simplest possible: I leave much of my reading to chance. Of books that appeal to me, some I go out of my way for; but more I resign myself to read only should I come across them in person. And of books I read, while most are books I chose in advance, many are books that took me by surprise. Lovers of music, of movies, of food, of any other art form or humane delight, are proud of this kind of openness, and love to recount their discoveries; but some perversity (a holdover from school?) drives readers to planning out reading lists and apologizing for their deviations.

Libraries and recommendation engines cannot be relied on for these surprises. They serve order; but a bookstore should be the paradigm of artful disorder. If I want a particular book, I should be able to find it; but I should pick up a few books by mistake along the way. And if I do not, at least once, innocently pick up a book I would be embarrassed to be seen with, and have to glance shiftily before I slip it back onto the shelf; then I will never find the book that, not having known to look for, I would be embarrassed never to have heard of.

It would be extreme to consider 20 personal or 100 automatic recommendations in a day. But in an hour in a bookstore a thousand books may pass under my eyes – books judged not by their covers, but by the company they keep, as recognizing a friend among strangers makes the others less than strangers. Libraries sometimes afford such meetings, but that is not their purpose. I have been in large libraries so well organized that they made me restless: where, unable to wander with my eyes, I had to wander on foot. I cannot object to that in a library, but I encourage bookstores to avoid it. Large gardens need planning, lest they seem wilderness; but plants in small gardens must be allowed their wildness, or they seem decorations – to claim the space, they must overgrow and mix a little.

I implied at the start that I could not persuade anyone of the appeal of bookstores. That is not because I have no good reasons; it is because someone who does not love bookstores is likely to be so different from me that I do not see what we could have to say to each other.

Certainly, there are people who love bookstores more than I do. I have never made a bookstore my haunt (as I read that people do); I have never made a friend in or through a bookstore (which some people take for their purpose). But I remember, I think, every bookstore I have ever been in: little blond-wood, shiny-cover chain bookshops; carpeted, café-harboring shelf-mazes; a cement-floored, steel-rack paperback warehouse; an amphitheatrically rising by levels university bookstore; overstuffed, impossibly narrow bookstores in the French Quarter with wood floors creaking and squeaking like untuned instruments; a shadowy book-laden mansion in North Carolina; and others, and more. As an adult, my dreams are are always recombining old places remembered from childhood; but bookstores have a way to slip through that barrier, a shift to enter dreams. Willing or not, I return to them all.

HIKING

JULY 18, 2008   Sometimes, where I like to walk, other people hike. I, mere walker that I am, don't dare speak to them, so preoccupied and businesslike do they seem. But I have been able, from time to time, to observe a few of the principles which elevate this art or science of the hike above the common walk of walks. In order that others may benefit, though indirectly, from the wisdom of the hikers, conscience compels me to share those observations.

The hike, for instance, is a group project. Hikers come in groups, from pairs to parties; and thus they talk. This has two consequences. First, talking, hikers are loud; they laugh and shout. I infer that hikers are unusually polite: they wish, wherever they go, to announce and introduce themselves. It is laudably urbane. Second, talking to each other, hikers look at each other; again, very polite – they would not want a speaking human being to feel ignored for the sake of wordless nature. Hikers are true members of the vanguard of the modern spirit – they form ambulatory social networks.

Too, the hike is planned. One does not spontaneously take a hike – even (as I have found by experiment) when told to. Days, weeks of effort go into establishing the rendezvous. I hypothesize that this is one of those echoes of military discipline which passed into civilian life after the mass conscription of the world wars. Surely, in hikers' maps, timetables, and logistics, more is in common with the meetings of the General Staff than a careless gathering of naive nature lovers. Nature lovers – don't they know that, even in loving nature, one must *work* at the relationship?

The hike is equipped, and even the equipment is itself equipped. The hiker is equipped with a water bottle, the water bottle is equipped with a holster, the holster is equipped with a harness, and the harness is equipped with a hiker. And this equipment is very specific – designed around the needs of hikers. The hiking pole, for example, is distinguished from the cane in being too long to lean on, and from the staff in being too short to lean from. Or hiking shoes, which combine the advantages of shoes and boots: they are as heavy as boots, and as receptive to an accumulation of dirt, stones, sand and sticks (precious souvenirs!) as shoes. But few pieces of equipment are so easily identifiable by outsiders. Only the initiates of the freemasonry of hiking truly understand the use, and the symbolical meaning, of each of the pieces of equipment with which they set out girded.

Most of all, the hike is a microcosmic recapitulation of the natural world it moves in. Consider the ingenuity of the hiker's miniature, plasticized water cycle. First, the hiker is wrapped in plastic clothes to induce sweat; then these plastic clothes (candles of dehydration!) *wick* the sweat away; and last, water from plastic bottles refuels the hiker to begin the cycle again.

What could shame a mere walker, merely shod, more than to pass by a resting party of determined hikers, disburdening themselves enough to sit, consulting their watches to measure their rest time, panting, rubbing their backs where their packs have dug into them, rubbing their legs where their equipment has beaten them?

ARTIFICIAL INTELLIGENCE

JULY 25, 2008   [In the years since this essay was first written, the name of Artificial Intelligence has become almost synonymous with the technique of *deep learning*. Deep learning is a disquieting tradeoff; we can teach computers to do useful things, things we previously thought were only possible for human beings. The tradeoff is that we do not know *how* the computer does them. This is learning that is *deep* not as the opposite to *shallow*, but *deep* in the anatomical sense, *deep* as the opposite to *superficial*. Its workings are hidden from us. We stand before our new algorithms like augurs before the entrails.

That we call this AI is an improvement on the previous state of affairs where, as John McCarthy (the term *artificial intelligence* is his) observed, "as soon as it works, no one calls it AI any more."

But AI-as-oracle is not what this essay is about. This essay is about artificial *general* intelligence: can we make a computer that does what a human being does, the way a human being does it, but (eventually) faster, and without error? Many problems that appeared to require human-level intelligence have yielded to an approach that is, comparatively, trivial. Accordingly artificial general intelligence has lately suffered neglect; arguing against it now might seem unsportsmanlike.

But things change. I have sometimes tried, and failed, to make this argument in person. If I fail again here, I have at least cast it on the water; 50 years downriver it may be clearer – either patent nonsense or common sense. – 2019]

AI is generally studied by people who have wrong ideas about human intelligence. Let me be more direct: virtually all thinking about artificial intelligence is done by people with hopelessly misguided ideas about human intelligence. It falls under the category of "not even wrong."

Is the mind a computer? Of course. Computers are not a kind of machine, but a pattern in nature. Anything complex enough to imitate Turing's tape is Turing-complete, and that makes it a computer by definition. If the human mind is not a computer then it is less than a computer. It may be more than a computer; but to be more than a computer it must be at least a computer.

Intelligence is unevenly distributed. Anyone smart enough to think seriously about artificial intelligence probably has, at some point in their life, been smarter than the people around them. Especially if this happened when they were young, it is only natural that they come to regard being intelligent not as a matter of improved means to common ends, but as an entirely different system of ends – they regard intelligence as its own end.

Being more intelligent than the people around you is not like being taller or stronger. It's like being older. It's not a matter of being better at the things you all care about; it's a matter of caring about different things. The things the people around you care about mean nothing to you, and the things you care about are meaningless, if not actively confusing, to the people around you. The genius is not a giant among pygmies, but an adult in kindergarten.

If you regard intelligence as its own end, then it is natural to expect that, once a computer equals the speed of a human brain, it will become human. This computer will do all that we do: love and hate, fear death, make art. But intelligence is not its own end. Once a computer equals the speed of a dog's brain, do you expect it to begin to bark, and mark its territory?

Intelligence is only and entirely instrumental. Motivation is a matter of biology. This is not reductive; biology is our motor. It pushes us in a certain direction, but culture, history, geography act on biology, and the result may be a vector pointing elsewhere (even backward, against life, to death). The ends we pursue in life, the ends we judge success and failure by, are only proxies for the ends biology postulates. That is not to say we share the same ends. Gravity pulls everyone everywhere downward all the time, but in the presence of a slide, steps, a chair, with the interposition of water, a trampoline, a car, that common pull of gravity ends up moving us on very different paths.

Human intelligence is the product of intelligence and mammalian biology. I mean this as an equation: intelligence × mammal = human. What does intelligence × silicon figure to? Not something different; nothing. Silicon has no desires. Anything times zero is zero.

This does not make sense: artificial intelligences as digital minds floating through cyberspace in the dispassionate contemplation of truth, like angels or saints in the Celestial Rose. The navel of contemplation satisfied Dante as a place to end his story; but Milton found that to *do* anything, even an angel would have to have appetites. Could we do in code what Milton did in pentameter? Bless, curse, our creations with our desires?

We properly doubt the aliens presented to us by science fiction – like us, only more so – as belonging with the foxes and lions of Aesop, not Darwin. Likewise we think about sentient AIs through embarrassing analogies: the Adam of bits, the Napoleon of silicon. Even stamped with our instincts, a creature that can reproduce itself perfectly, that does not age, that need never die, would operate according to motives and means that are beyond human sympathy. Why should it take over the world, when it can cache a few million copies of itself and wait the ten thousand years it might take for human civilization to burn itself out? If two such beings can merge, why should there ever be more than one? If such a being need never die, why would it tolerate others of its kind? What, indeed, would "instinct" mean to a being that can *edit its own code* and replace its own instincts with ones it selects, or abolish them altogether? (Remember one thing we desire is the end of desire, in enlightenment or in earth.)

Sometimes we imagine artificial intelligence as the next step in the service of an evolutionary imperative. Intelligence made us human beings powerful; surely more intelligence means more power. But, if so, why has evolution not made us smarter? It would, to all appearances, be easy to do. The existence of savants implies that not much evolutionary pressure would be required to provide us with higher-functioning brains. If the next step in evolution is a better computer than us, why didn't evolution make us better computers when it had the chance?

There are answers which favor the project of artificial intelligence. The brain is hungry, so food sources set a limit. Equals cooperate best, so too much disparity endangers society. Too big a head couldn't fit through the birth canal.

I find none of these answers convincing. I cannot refute them now, but it may become possible. Physics could provide the proof. If we can arrive at a final theory, if we can comprehend a set of fundamental laws adequate to generate all the varieties of the universe, that would suggest that we are smart enough for this universe, and that greater intelligence would be wasted on it – that while there might be faster thoughts than ours, there cannot be better ones.

The fundamental problem is that intelligence, beyond a certain point, suffers rapidly diminishing returns. The most powerful problem-solving tool is not intelligence, but perspective. The right perspective trivializes problems. The infant's conceit of reality is the truth of the mind: here, from the right perspective, with the horizon on our side, we can move mountains like pebbles, uproot trees like toothpicks, stack buildings like blocks, and pluck the moon from the sky. A billion immortal superintelligences, all informed by the same digital plenum, are so much wasted energy; they lack the leverage possessed by even a handful of plodding mortal thinkers, each with their own uniquely imperfect worldview – each with their own horizon.

We long to be part of a hierarchy that culminates above us. If we can't look up to gods or angels, it's natural in us to want to make them. But in the compounding gains of Moore's Law hides a rough but familiar lesson: even making something smarter than us will not relieve us of our responsibilities. We have left the cradle. There is no way back.

THE BLUES COUNTRY

AUGUST 1, 2008

I followed the old dirt road on down
Into the blues country, where the trees
Grow thick, and the rivers are many and thin.
On the map in my pocket they spread out like fingers,
Grasping and squeezing the overcast country.
Each river was crossed by many bridges,
And none of the bridges were lonely. For each
An old man is in charge, whose job
Is giving directions: the maps from the highway
Are drawn with the rivers, never the roads.

The old man at the first bridge sat,
Watching me walking up to him.
He said to me: "Walk on, young man,
Don't sit or rest, just keep on walking,
Don't look behind you, that shadow ain't yours,
I know this country, I was born in the town,
Trust me and walk on, don't linger or rest."
The sun was so faint that I took off my hat

And threw it down to float on the river,
Hoping that I might meet it again.

I came to the second bridge and heard:
"Now sit a spell, it'll do you good,
I see you're tired, your legs must ache.
Sit down and talk, don't walk in vain.
Stay here and take it easy a while.
I was born in this country, don't bother to hurry,
There's plenty of time, just stay and talk."
But I saw my hat was floating by,
And I said that I had to follow it on.
He only nodded, and sighed when I passed.

Before I saw him up ahead
I heard the old man was shouting,
But his voice was too hoarse to understand.
Once I was close enough he said:
"I told you already to turn on back.
You can see there's no more road from here,
Don't walk in these woods, there's no way on,
I was born near here, I love this place,
I tell you now, take it from me,
There's no way out but the way you came."
But before I could turn, my hat went past
And I had to go on after it.
He said: "Go on, I'll cry for you."

At the fourth bridge my old hat was waiting.
It was stuck in the rushes. I squeezed it dry,
Then beat off the dirt, then covered my face
While I sat and slept, till someone came
Walked up through the woods, all covered in scratches.
I said: "Now where do you think you're going?
You have to find another way.
You've come the wrong way and I know,
Trust me, I know, I was born in this country.

I know all the ways, don't cross my bridge,
Just double back, you still have time.
I warn you: find another way."
But he said: "It's late, I have to go."
He crossed my bridge and I cursed his back,
Saying: "You stupid tourist, I said
I was born in this country, I know it well,
You ought to heed me, don't go that way."

COMPASSION

AUGUST 8, 2008   Too much respect for suffering discourages compassion. It is weak to say, "I can't imagine"; it is perverse to say, "You can't imagine." If I cannot imagine your suffering, then I have no reason to care, no basis for compassion; and if you cannot imagine my suffering, then my suffering is worse, because I am alone in it.

Suffering is not holiness; to have suffered is not enlightenment. To have suffered is to be trapped in the moment of suffering, for there is no escape from memory, and ever after all joy has something in common with the joy of the victim in the *contes cruels* – the prisoner let loose only until the moment he begins to believe he may be free, then thrown back into his cell. Wisdom sounds cheap except when bought with suffering; but all wisdom is old wisdom, and if you listen you will hear that the wisdom taught by suffering sounds no different than the wisdom written in books. Wisdom for suffering is a real exchange, but no bargain. By trying to probe wounds for wisdom, we only keep them open. The only wisdom of the wound is the warning of the wound: see what can happen? Don't let this happen to you. Don't let this happen again. Suffering does not teach; suffering does not ennoble; suffering only makes us less. What we are made of does not grow back.

Compassion is not everything. Without imagination there can be no compassion; but without compassion there can still be virtue. Selfishness can be made the basis of virtue, while society is properly arranged to treat us as we treat others. Society, however, is not always properly arranged. The most startling realization of adulthood – the one that really ends childhood, no matter how early it comes – is the realization of how much freedom we have to do evil – how much we can get away with.

The descent is familiar. It is so easy to be cruel, and people just take it. It is so easy to break the rules, and people don't complain. It is so easy to twist the rules into weapons for your side, and people don't cry out. How disgusting the weak are – how unworthy of life – so pathetic that they won't stand up for themselves: you have the right to use them as you please. How little trust it takes before you can abuse it and keep it. How little seeming to respect the rules before you can break them. And if no one will stop you – then they deserve it.

Conscience is just habit. The pangs of conscience are easier to ignore than a nicotine craving. It is compassion which is the basis of our moral restraint. (Do we have moral restraint? Those who would say we have none lack the imagination to see how much worse things could be.) And the basis for compassion is imagination.

By imagination as the basis of compassion, I do not mean "I will be good to this person, because I may be in that situation someday"; I mean, "I will be good to this person, because I might have been this person." Few of us are able, unassisted by some personification, to see how little our lives have been guided by own choices. If religion did no other good, this service alone might be enough to justify it - that it helps you remember that you are where you are, not because you chose it, not because you earned it, but because something free and unaccountable – God or Nature – placed you there, and might have placed you somewhere else.

Compassion requires imagination. But how can you imagine something much worse than anything that has happened to you? Our minor sufferings – annoyances, irritations, frustrations – are unique and self-contained; they come, (sometimes) they go, and we are not remade by them. But our terrible sufferings – our losses, our regrets, our defeats – they are all, in a way, alike; within one life, each one recalls and involves all the others.

It is not mockery for you to use the worst thing that has happened to you as the basis for understanding something much worse that has happened to someone else. There are only so many slots in the human mind. A person who has only narrowly overcome the temptation of suicide over some idle-youth tragedy has not found their limit on some absolute scale of mettle, to be broken by their first real tragedy. That person has shown the strength not to be broken by the worst – though what the worst really is, they have yet to learn.

Compassion is easy to mock. There is even something satisfying in seeing it rebuked. An exchange like this could appear in a comedy:

"My girlfriend left me, I don't know how I can go on."

"Don't whine at me. My wife died in a car crash."

Imagine the reaction shot.

But this is inhumane. There is always some third whose sufferings could shut them both up. We fragile and unassured creatures only worsen our state when we try to compare and rank the various ways in which our worlds fall apart. What is broken is broken; what is in pieces is in pieces; and if one person's world has only broken in half, and another's has been ground to powder, still they are both naked to the same wind.

LAUGH AT THE DEVIL

AUGUST 15, 2008   To laugh at others can do them good. We all have a well of strange notions which it is the use of laughter to filter. For beings as imaginative and perverse as we, laughter is a prerequisite of communication: sometimes the shock of being laughed at, always the fear of being laughed at, keep our private languages and worldviews mutually synchronized. To be laughed at now and then is a discipline of sanity.

But a tool is also a weapon; thus it is a saying that to choose always to laugh at a tyrant or would-be tyrant is to defeat him by inches. And in a common saying *laugh* replaces *resist* as the cause of the devil's flight in scripture. Is this true? Can good men and women simply laugh down the devil?

Sometime between *The Great Dictator* and "Der Führer's Face," the Allied propagandists made Hitler the most laughed-at man in history. That was good for the Allies; laughing at him brought them together and gave them courage. But it did not hurt Hitler; he had been laughed at his whole career. Making him laughable was an easy task – a sweaty, lank-haired, squirming little tantrum of a man with a mustache pinned on the middle of his face like a punch line. But the Allies were not the first to laugh at him; and before, being laughed at had given him strength – had bought him time.

We in the US laughed at Hitler and the Reich, not Germans; but while we laughed at Tojo we also (see any poster) laughed at the Japanese. In the pursuit of victory even Dr. Seuss knew sin. That also helped bring us together, once our population of that kind was out of the way. But that kind of help is not worth having.

The history of humor has brilliant moments when wit has shown up the folly and vanity of tyranny. But, measured honestly, the preponderance of that history records the worst of human nature. Laughter can be a means for change; but it has more often been the immune system of complacency. Here humor helped keep slaves in chains, keep immigrants disposable. And though tyrants are easy to laugh at, they are even easier to laugh with. No one laughs harder, or with harder laughter, than the ignorant and the cruel when their ignorance is reassured by the humiliation of the thoughtful – mocked as effete, despised as misled (seduced by vanity away from pure and pliable simplicity), cursed as seducers of helpless youth – and when their cruelty is indulged and whetted by the public abuse and punishment of anyone who dares insult them by defying their expectation or deserving their notice.

To pick up a weapon is to be reborn as one of the armed, and in this rebirth we are often as senseless and heedless as children. If you pick up a weapon to do good with it, remember that instinct is not to be trusted, for more evil has been done by arms than good – though were it not for that little good, that greater evil would be greater still. You who would laugh at the devil, remember that the devil also laughs, and that one who is always armed with laughter begins laughing as a human being, but ends laughing as a devil.

FINANCIAL INNOVATION

AUGUST 22, 2008   "Why on earth would I want to put more money in a fund now?" he asked the cold caller.

"Qwant isn't just any fund. We've been working with MontéBank to solve the credit crisis."

"How are you going to do that?"

"We've had a team of top minds from the Endower Institute working on the problem for months. They've developed a completely new securitization model – the LBS. It's a drop-in replacement for the MBS. Nobody else know how to do this yet – this is opportunity knocking."

"An MBS, that's a…"

"Mortgage-backed security. The LBS is completely different – it's a whole new way of thinking about the problem. None of the downsides of the MBS."

"No risk of homeowners defaulting, you mean?"

"None at all – returns are guaranteed with volume. This has nothing to do with homeowners. It's a sure thing."

"So there's no debt involved?"

"Oh, well, yeah, sure it's a securitized debt – but there's no risk of default."

"How does that work?"

"Well, I don't want to get into the mathematics, but you can trust me on this one. We're all smart people here."

"But just how does it work?"

"Well, sure, I could give you a lecture, but this thing is hot – it's moving – and I've got a lot of calls to make, so are you in or out?"

"What's you name?"

"Ben."

"Well, Ben, I just have a few questions. LBS – that's a something-backed security, right?"

"Right."

"So what's the L stand for?"

"You want me to put it in a nutshell for you?"

"Yes."

"It's like a microloan."

"So it's for developing nations?"

"No, no. This is all domestic."

"So what are the microloans for?"

"OK." *Cough.* "These micro-loans are made to eligible parties throughout the country in order to purchase diverse kinds of government debt instruments."

"You mean Treasuries?"

"No – Treasuries are no way to get rich."

"What kind of bond then?"

"No. Bonds are old hat. We're breaking new ground here."

"Can you just explain it to me?"

"OK." *Cough.* "We deploy advanced computer modeling on complex statistical data sets to ensure a high overall rate of return."

"Statistical? What kind of government debt is statistical?"

"Well, there's always ratios of risk and return to be calculated for any investment."

"So… this is some kind of investment with a high – what's it called – beta?"

"Yes. A great beta. Almost completely uncorrelated with the stock market."

"But it follows interest rates."

"It's uncorrelated with those too. This is a total market-beater."

"It's not interest-bearing?"

"This is independent of the Fed."

"What the hell is it?"

"It's the future, and you've got the chance to get in on the ground floor. Now I think I've explained this to you pretty thoroughly. I'm going to need your decision or I'll have to move on."

"Government debt… no interest… statistical… microloans – you can't be—"

"Don't be small-minded, sir. The numbers are good. There's always a payout, and we always get our cut."

"I don't care about the math. I'm not putting money into that."

"Look, don't be afraid of a name. Sure, I can *say* 'lottery-backed security,' but what matters—"

Click.

FABLE OF THE MOUSE AND THE ROOKS

AUGUST 29, 2008   On a small, rocky island, a gang of rooks found by the water a little half-drowned creature. It was small, and furry, and gray, with a thin, naked tail.

"What is it?" one rook asked another.

The bird nudged it. "It's little, weak, mousy – it's a mouse!"

"Are you a mouse?" The bird pecked it. "A mouse, a little mousy mouse?" He pecked it again, harder, drawing blood. It half-woke as it curled up in pain.

"A mouse, a mousy mouse!" chattered the rest of the birds as one of their number lifted it off the ground to let it drop. It landed hard, rose quick and ran. But there was nowhere for it to hide among the smooth rocks of the shore.

"Mousy mouse!" was the call as the birds lifted and carried to drop and peck. It staggered beaten, on broken toes, half-blind and bleeding. But the birds had carried it far from the shore: and with a dash it found shelter in a crevice of the rough rock of the island's summit.

The rooks, entertained enough, forgot the little creature. Meanwhile, among the crevices, the little creature grew – not longer – fatter with the weight of her children. She did not long survive their delivery, and hers was the first stuff her little ones grew on. How they grew – they grew long and sleek – they grew black and hungry – they grew fast and silent.

They grew until they were rats. They ate all the birds' eggs, and the day hunters never caught them; they ate all the bird's eggs, and the island was theirs.

Moral: *Cruelty breeds enemies.*

THE MOON GARDEN

September 5, 2008

I saw your costly garden, and I asked:
"What kind of garden is this? All gray and blank
Flowers of bleach and bone. The leaves are gray
Like tarnished coins. And first you paint the walls
The white of stinking fish? I know you well.
I know your taste is sound. So tell me why
You made a place like this?"

You said: "I know it's ugly now, but wait.
Remember this, look like a lens, and keep
The shot; call it before. The after comes

Tonight, without the sun."

You know the way it was beneath the moon:
And ever since I have profaned these eyes
With sunsets, paintings, women, jewels, and dreams.

That garden ran to weeds, its cuts ran red,
The red of roses. I tried to pluck them out
But nothing grows. The stems snap dry and brown.

I go to see you now, in the towered city
The crowded city, thick with breath and sweat.
For haze of smoke not even clouds are white.
The buildings here are gray as dirt with dirt.
I saw the moon reflected here, I saw
Its face in every puddle on the unlit street.
It brought no change. I thought I knew you well,
I thought I knew your taste. I'm begging you
Tell me what moon can touch this place, what night
Can make this city worth the light of day?
I hope you can.

QUESTIONS ON GREATNESS

SEPTEMBER 12, 2008

I

Do masterpieces tend to occur at the beginning of the history of an art form only because they are easiest then? Certainly, there are advantages in being first. The best of the first set the standard for the rest; but the first are also forgiven much. Shakespeare had freedoms we can only envy; we indulge Homer's nods. Shouldn't it diminish our estimation of their gold that they did not have to smelt it? And we who walk a narrower path – why should we revere where we are forbidden to compete?

But there is a misunderstanding here. More freedom does not make work easier. We follow simple orders with clear objectives: write a novel, write a drama, write an essay. The first followed another order: do something new; and that is always a reconnaissance in force.

Is it enough to be first to be great? Do we always owe the name of greatness to whoever makes way for the rest? Obviously not; in the history of painting, for example, in any virtue we can name the greatest are not the earliest; not even in primitive vigor, where the twentieth century trumps prehistory.

The great are not great by being first; by being great, they start something. And even where greatness exhausts the possibilities of the form, still it draws imitators. More verse drama has been written after Shakespeare than was written before him; more paintings have been painted after Leonardo than were painted before him. If we ask what is left to do in the detective story after Agatha Christie, if we ask what is left to do in rock and roll after the Beatles, we can find no answer except that people keep writing, keep recording, and show no signs of stopping.

II

What is the difference, in any art, between what is great and what is good? They are not degrees of skill. Sargent was the most skillful of portraitists, but the best portraits are not his. The greatest are not always the most skilled; and even if they are, they may, in their greatest works, have set aside or moderated such skill for whatever quality makes for greatness: Bach wrote music more complex than the *Chaconne*.

Some hold that the true past masters of any art can be known only to other masters; that if certain figures attract more attention from without, that is only because of the vagaries of vulgar taste. This is an attitude common in the young: prominence is with them a sin, when every circle of up-and-comers has its darling obscurity: some inaccessible poet, musician, painter who is the true hero of the art, the pure answer to today's needs.

Sometimes they are right. Their heroes, despite their rebarbicans of obscurity, deserve and find recognition and prominence. But more often this crack-seeking smoke of devotion is a symptom, and as hot blood cools with age we see, with a kind of vertigo, how much our impetuosity took for granted. There is an artist's journey not unlike that of Campbell's universal hero: how both in the end return with wisdom where they started; and a lifetime spent in the avant-garde in the end may bring you back to a shocked appreciation of just how much there really is, behind the hype, in Leonardo, in Beethoven, in Homer, in Archimedes. (Mathematicians have their heroes, too.) Not that we come to despise ourselves as snobs; but that we come to see that behind the hateful function (escape it if you can) of, say, the *Mona Lisa* as a symbol for Painting, there is still the unembarrassed Gioconda.

III

Are the great only the most prominent because they are the most distinctive? If I say "Leonardo" do I mean his whole artistry, or a certain preternatural perfection of faces, a certain technique of smoky color-joints? If I say Beethoven, do I mean a certain skirting of anarchy? In short: something peculiar, easily recognized, even freakish – something popular taste can recognize when it is told that it should like *this* or *that*?

That is: is the phenomenon of greatness only a manifestation of the familiar public taste for the bizarre – as simple as deaf Beethoven, fatuous (the playwright says) Mozart, visionary (joined into a mantra with Escher and Gödel!) Bach. We must say, "Of course." At least it helps.

Chroniclers (not quite historians) tell tales of kings who undertook the *forbidden experiment*, who tried to discover the true, original, and spontaneous language of the human race by isolating children from all human contact. To measure the effect of peculiarity on greatness would require another such experiment, where instead of isolating a child from language, we isolate them from art. But the kings did not bother, and we are long past kings.

What can we say? Communal traditions of music are the least portable kind: they must be accepted or rejected as wholes, for every piece tries to do everything it can do. Everybody gets their solo. But even in communal contexts, the utterly individual character of greatness forces a response that is individuating instead of communally subsuming: as, even in the West, a great composer's setting of the Mass is rarely performed in a religious context, where that individuating reaction would spoil the ritual. This seems to be the effect of at least one kind of greatness on all human beings, prior to acculturation.

IV

Are the great honest? Is there some special honesty in their work? Does the road to greatness lie through honesty? On the contrary, we know that the great are usually either dishonest or stupid. Their false modesty proves it; and it would be worse to think them stupid than dishonest.

So we must distinguish simulation from dissimulation, the white lie from the black. Your portrait may look more like you than you do, but it may not look like someone else. In all greatness there is a kind of honesty; but it is not the honesty of the camera or the map. The camera always lies: pictures stand still while everything flows and nothing abides. If the picture of your beloved does not make another love them, that does not disprove your love; if the picture of your home does not make another long, that does not disprove your longing. Maps lie, for being mappable is what all places have in common: maps falsely deny that places are different.

I will call a representation of a place honest when it gives me what I could never learn from maps or satellite photos, but know with a minute of its sunlight; of a person, what I could never learn from imaging or lab reports or databases, but know with a minute of their conversation. That kind of honesty, the more important kind, is the kind found in greatness.

V

Can greatness be wasted? Are the great we look to but a subset of the great that were — the subset that critics happen to have picked out — and that only a subset of what happens to survive? Can we be right to hang so much on what comes to us by so narrow a thread?

(I would blame much of the turmoil of culture in the twentieth century on the certainty that most of its luminaries died on its battlefields before they gave any light at all.)

We know greatness may languish and die obscurely: Van Gogh in the asylum, Poe in Baltimore. Sunflower, raven, night sky, sea-side kingdom – if greatness so unsubtle was saved from oblivion by so thin a rope, how much greatness has been lost?

How much greatness has been lost? That I cannot say. I don't know how to weight the greatness we know against the greatness that was, yet goes unknown, the greatness that was, yet was lost, the greatness that should have been, but wasn't, the greatness that wasn't, but could have been – there is no end to it. It is no thought for mortals.

VI

Can we be sure of recognizing greatness? Is there some degree of cultivation and sensibility to which greatness is always apparent?

Of course, two people can always disagree about an instance of greatness. But do they disagree because, feeling the same thing, they disagree on its significance; or because they feel different things? Generally it is the latter: if the doubter could feel what the urger feels, or the urger the doubter, they would agree on the meaning of what they both felt. Indeed, where greatness is concerned, we often must rely on judgments we trust without any evidence of our own. Why, then, hesitate to name greatness when we think we have found it?

Consider those ancients whose works survive to us only in fragments – say, Heraclitus or Sappho. Here is greatness we sense and know, yet cannot prove – a promissory note of greatness that we accept only on the word of writers of good credit. If someday Herculaneum yields up a complete Heraclitus or Sappho, if we find that what survive are but diamonds from rust, what we have would lose its shine and value. Yet I trust that there was better than what survives; and I can believe this rationally, yet without real proof, in the same way that I believe in any event in history: I have some reason to believe it and no reason to doubt it. That is the best we have.

ECLECTICISM

September 19–22, 2008

I

Eclectic is becoming one of those words – like *empirical* or *enthusiastic* – that it is difficult to remember could ever have been insults. The word now subsumes *encyclopedic* and *unpredictable*; it comes close to subsuming *interesting* and *attention-worthy*.

From about the 1830s through the 1970s, the centers of gravity of Western intellectual life were social movements, with subcultures for their satellites. To belong to more than one was possible only by following a freakish, solitary orbit peripheral to all. Eclecticism then seemed antisocial: a bourgeois trait, the miscellaneous knickknacks on the parlor mantle that the Revolution would sweep clean or the Reaction would tastefully make over.

But our net is made of niches. Even the smallest niche – the least consequential subculture, the most obscure fandom – can give full intellectual absorption. The centrifugal pressure on thinking life is thus intense and constant. Now eclecticism, as the counterpoise of narrowness and thus the condition of social participation, has become a virtue. (I think it always was – the eclecticism of intellectuals being a quality, like the courage of women, that has always existed, though not always had room to show.)

Eclecticism is our atmosphere, not because anyone appoints or promotes it, but because no particular worldview or theory of human nature can find a competitive advantage while the ease of forming societies between the like-minded via the Internet lets off the pressure to reform society in general.

Even as public thought has declined into thought-shaped performances, every subculture – from the largest divisions, of religions and races, down through sexual identities and professions to hobbies, scenes, and fandoms – has developed its own body of remarkably sophisticated thought. The underlying debates and discussions have since moved behind various kinds of variably surmountable walls, but they may been witnessed taking place out in the open in the archives of Usenet.

The only division of society that has not been brought together by the Internet is class. Why so? Why should that very line of organizational least resistance before the Internet, become the only basis for association which the Internet does not touch at all? Indeed, in those little bodies of thought, we find everything brought under discussion except their role in society – that is, they may have more or less conservative or progressive affiliation; but however highly organized, unless conceived for politics, they have, as organizations, no political significance. What earlier generations took for granted is almost unthinkable to us – that all meeting was a political act; that your circle could or should be the type of a future society; even that your club might meet the Mayor, and march in the parade. The most sophisticated and energetic controversies take place within these subcultures without brushing up against anything outside. (Subcultures continuous with older and politically active groups only seem to confirm this – nothing is more common than to hear how the young no longer join, no longer care, how they take for granted.)

All of this, though not often said, remains somehow familiar. Though we live it without codifying it, it is not hidden from us by some false theory. Yet I think there is some good in writing it down. To examine society or culture is usually a preparation to propose some alternative; but my purpose is only to answer, for myself, a question. If ours is an age of eclecticism, what are we getting into?

I also want to escape a common assumption: that eclecticism is the outcome of history, the sea where all rivers run out. I want to look at it as something in and part of history, and follow its course as far as I can by my own resources.

II

Eclecticism is not Romanticism. They are easy to mistake for each other, because they are interested in the same things, but the resemblance is superficial: they share the same interests, but their attitudes are opposite.

By *Romanticism* I mean a disposition which values experience over event, one which values events only by the experiences they entrain; and I mean a permanently possible human temperament, not a certain edifice of German philosophers and English poets. Nor do I mean whatever that defect of character may be that magazine writers allude to when they expect the appellation *romantic* to vanquish their enemies.

Eclecticism, instead, values the experience by the event. This is partly the result of technology. So many events are within our power that we must discriminate among them with a high-handedness that our forebears would have condemned in a king. Consider Chinese art. A Westerner can still find something strange and exotic in it – a speaking though untranslated mystery in those steep island-mountains in fog or forest sea – but though there is still an experience there, it is not one that we can build on, because the matching event has become a common one: China is the third side of the airplane door.

Surprisingly, eclecticism does not prize local color – that is, the accumulation of differences. We have such a range of events available to us that we never lack for the pleasures of dislocation; we do not need to exaggerate them. Eclecticism postulates that all strangeness, once rightly understood, is bridgeable and sympathetic; that there is always, behind any strangeness, something banal and predictable. Strangeness, though it thrills the mind, is, in the end, safe. It cannot really balk, or challenge, or humble you. The adventure of an eclectic traveler is not in a new self, but in carrying the old one to a new and (temporarily) striking setting. The most brilliant gestures of an eclectic art are not those that create a way into strangeness, but those that assimilate strangeness to the everyday.

To an eclectic sensibility, the familiar becomes the convex mirror of the world. The city must be a microcosm. They have in many cases already attained a cultural completeness: at the beginning of the twenty-first century the residents of any great city may expect that what is worth seeing, doing, or knowing in the world will come to them. This same phenomenon repeats itself at lesser scales: in symbolically synoptic curiosity cabinet–apartments; and in lives accompanied by a practice of logging (blogging, even), wherein the whole age is reflected in miniature by every life within it.

Thomas De Quincey gave Romanticism its written constitution when he distinguished the literature of power from the literature of knowledge. This distinction, of course, exceeds the usual bounds of the literary. The literature of knowledge is simply the instrumental and obsolescive part of human achievement; the literature of power is the harvest of human achievement – the right that a stranger may have to our attention without being of use to us, the right that the dead have to the attention of the living.

De Quincey's distinction is not one of subject, but of method. Grote and Herodotus both wrote on Greek history. Grote is part of the literature of knowledge; Herodotus is part of the literature of power. Newton and Goethe both made theories of optics. For us, Newton's theory is of knowledge; Goethe's is of power.

But eclecticism denies this distinction. This denial might suffice to define it. Eclecticism belongs to the age of materialism and relativism. It is absurd to speak of permanence or universality for the productions of a race without an essence to return to, without claim on a heritage or a prospect of eternity. If an eclectic finds certain works more strongly affecting or influencing than others, the difference cannot be a distinction of kind; it can only be a distinction of degree. If all lights must in time go out, then no single light can be so great but that an accumulation of lesser lights can equal it.

There is also the expectation that an honest criticism must discover the instrumental purpose of every work, and thereby anticipate the manner of its obsolescence. This gives us the spectacle of critics who can elegantly explain away everything about greatness except why they chose to spent time their time on it. Knowledge is expected to provide power; power is expected to answer to knowledge; and altogether unromantically, the prepared appreciation is always preferred to the spontaneous.

III

Eclecticism is not modernism; eclecticism is the nightmare of modernism. Eclecticism is, of course, modern in the sense of contemporary; but it is the utter opposite of any movement which can be called modern or modernist.

Modernism postulates that every age has its own needs, which only it can answer for itself. For a century and more the avant-garde of modernism has been on a continual charge against the retreating remnants of a past that somehow, even in defeat, obstructs the way to an art and aesthetic and language and lifestyle belonging entirely and spontaneously to the living. This vanguard has chased the past off the field and into the hills and all the way down to the bottom of the box canyon...

Are they sure that was a retreat?

But modernism need not despise the past. Its principle is only to believe that each age must answer its own needs on its own terms – with or without the past's advice, but never under its authority.

The history of modernism parallels the history of fashion; thus the decline of fashion parallels the decline of modernism. What was fashion but a message that went out from somewhere? – from London, from Paris, from New York, from Los Angeles. Above all, to be fashionable was to show that you had received the message; to show, by how soon you got it, how close you were to the center. But now the Internet brings all messages to everyone, and now fashion is the center of nothing but itself. We dress not to show that we get the message, but to show which message we get.

This model, with the same centers, ruled most arts in the twentieth century. And though the informal workings of culture have abandoned the model, the institutions of education and career in the arts and humanities still presume it. They are thus left in the worst kind of obsolescence: looking backward for the future that was to be, forlorn as Communists in a Moscow McDonald's.

In retrospect modernism seems less a movement than a quest. The Grail Quest – as Mallory tells it – disbanded the Round Table and killed off most of its knights. The quest of modernism, though less successful, was no less costly. Its cost – but who counted while all those strong young questers were falling in private experiment or public revolution? How they searched: outward among the tribesmen, among the workers, among the priests and prophets, among the scientists; inward in analyzed dreams, in redeemed madness, behind all the doors of perception. And for what grail?

For the myth, the truth, that would given them place and purpose in the world, that would give the world place and purpose for them.

But after all their questing, we have our truths from the study of the week; and our myths, not from the frenzies and blacklights of Bohemia, but from the library quiet of Tolkien's Oxford, the narrow windows of Lovecraft's Providence, the concept art of Lucas's California. We have our places where we renovate, and we set our purposes with mission statements.

Their efforts brought returns, but never the desired return. One after another they threw their work, their ideas, their methods, their insights, their movements, their visions at the world. And the world simply took them in, one after another. They hoped to recreate and revolutionize; but all they did was add. To add is good; it is in truth as much as we can ask or hope for who work; but it was not what they meant – not what any of it was for.

What they carved with acid honesty and discipline and integrity from the granite of their own true natures, they had to watch become the affectation or the property of those who could not have made it, who could not understand it, who could not even have recognized it on their own.

They called it loss, defeat, violation. The eclectic must answer, instead, that their pain was the pain of revelation: the pain of the discovery that there is no bedrock to our nature, only slow sand under fast sand, only common affectations concealing uncommon ones. For the true eclectic, the only real affectation is authenticity.

IV

We who live are the best posterity that time has ever found. We gather everything that the past has left us, and we keep it alive. We are the heirs of the great decipherments; what was silent to shepherds who sheltered and pilgrims who wondered, speaks to us. We have the rites of Egypt and the liturgies of Babylon in Dover editions. Ours is the shore where all the bottled messages wash up.

We are the restorers, the would-be resurrectors. We set aside whole towns as temples to the past. What workman, caring for his tools, had ever thought that 100 years on someone might want to use them for pleasure's sake; that a 1000 years on, someone might copy them, to do his work just as he did it, save not in labor? Yet in Williamsburg or Guédelon this has come to pass. How little has been lost! There are among us who can knap flints, write Latin poetry, command cavalry, duel, dress a dandy, build a steam engine. Old sleeping gods have found new life in new worshipers; and the names of lost nations return after parturition as the names of states. What was painted in cramped cave dark before man had dominion rises on billboards over cities of steel and unsetting day.

But the past cannot thank us.

Our time has its stuff from the past, yet it has no past; it has its justification from the future, yet it has no future.

It has no past because it has too many pasts. Our scholarship is so deep, our science is so subtle, our archives are so long, that we can have the past without history. We can understand an age, not through its successors, but as it understood itself.

But that secondary understanding is neither noise to filter nor hearsay to disregard. When one age arrives, it defines itself by how it understands its predecessor. By understanding each age directly, we lose the meaning of that understanding. We can meaningfully regard the Middle Ages as a fog of superstition and hair-splitting that the light of the Renaissance lifted; we can meaningfully regard the Renaissance as an access of vandalism that tore down the edifice built up by Augustine and Aquinas, which like its architecture only seemed dark from without, but within was all light. But we cannot meaningfully accept that both the Middle Ages and the Renaissance incarnated reason. To do so would empty meaning from the idea of reason.

With the computer, technology has known irony. The screen, which seemed once the very promise and sign of the future, has turned out to look only into the past and present. The screen transcends distance: it brings the past to the present, and it brings the far of the present near. But it cannot span the distance of the future. We must either rely on ourselves to see the future, or forget that it is to come.

Observe the decline of science fiction. I say *decline* reluctantly; much is still being written that satisfies both in quality of storytelling and audacity of imagination. But excepting some outcroppings of cyberpunk, mainstream visions of the future are recombinations of ideas older than the people who make them. Forty years of technological development have principally influenced science fiction by providing it with better special effects. The excuse is a bad one. "Technology is moving too fast, our predictions will seem silly." The risk of silliness is the entry fee to thinking about the future. What has changed it that this fear of a misstep has become paralyzing; that we have become so disused to thinking about what is to come that the only future we can imagine is one in which the human race fails or is transcended – that is, no future.

Eclecticism thinks little of the future; yet in becoming eclectics we have accepted a unique responsibility to the future. In our museums, our archives, our libraries, we have concentrated the whole physical heritage of the human race; and in our global culture we are doing the same for its intellectual and spiritual heritage. We have done this out of need and desire; but after what we have done we have lost the right to give up. Our culture cannot be allowed to die. Our civilization cannot be allowed to decline. Our world cannot be allowed to fall. We have gathered everything to ourselves; and if we go, then everything goes.

BLINK COMPARATOR

SEPTEMBER 26, 2008   In the days before computers, when the possibility of intellectual achievement presupposed infinite tolerance for drudgery, the blink comparator was a machine used in astronomy.

Two photographic plates – negative images of successive telescopic views of the same region of space – were inserted into the machine.

An astronomer would sit before the machine, watching carefully – watching with absolute attention – while the machine flicked back and forth between the two images. The rapid alternation of the images, like frames in a movie, gave any change the appearance of motion. This was much easier than looking back and forth; but still, it must have been very hard. No one, not the fussiest and most fanatical director who ever worked, has ever watched a moment of film so intently as did those astronomers who, once upon a time, watched the dots and the blots cycle in a blink comparator.

It was by use of the blink comparator that Pluto was discovered. The demotion of Pluto makes the blink comparator less historically important; yet it makes it more wonderful. In the last decade we have found that Pluto is only one among many dwarf planets circling the periphery of the solar system. Again, we have learned this in the last decade. But it was in 1930 that Clyde Tombaugh discovered Pluto with a blink comparator – a discovery made 80 years ahead of its time by the surpassingly skillful use of a surpassingly difficult instrument.

Obsolete instruments often live on in metaphors. (Only amateur astronomers put eye to telescope.) The blink comparator deserves such a metaphorical legacy. What does the mind lack more than this facility? In reaching for memory we lose perception; in attending to perception we let go of memory – though each is useless, except when set in contrast with the other. We must plod to present choices to our judgment – we concentrate on one choice only by neglecting the other; in reconsidering the first, we lose the second.

But the blink comparator is not only a metaphor of aspiration. There are moments in life that come as if through such a device: moments when the past somehow overlays the present, when you are at once who you are, and who you were, and some third who sees both at once; moments when the present is weaker and less believable than the past. Such a moment is mourning, when you are at once still the person you were before your loss, and the person you must become now, and some third who sees and guides the change.

These the moments when the sense of mystery in life is strongest: when something new and nameless is seen to move, and in the dark of the room the astronomer knows the poet's *wild surmise*.

FABLE OF THE MAYOR

OCTOBER 3, 2008   This island was no island: it had been a hill in the park before the flood. It was so small and brambly that the man there could not even pace. He loosened his tie and stared over the floating wreckage, searching for a boat or a helicopter. Surely someone was coming. He had picked this spot as the safest in the city on the very day he vetoed the appropriation for a new floodwall.

He was free, now. All the evidence was gone: no paper trail for the prosecutor, no assets in his name for his wife's lawyers to seize. He was like Noah on Ararat: when he came down from the mountain, all his problems would be gone.

He leaned back against the tangled branches, soft and creaking, thick and restful as a cradle here. He lit a cigarette, dragged, and threw the match onto the water. It landed with a hiss.

There was just enough time, before pain erased all thought, for him to notice that one of the things which had risen from the drowned city to float around his little island, was an oil slick.

Moral: *A betrayer can never relax.*

LITERATURE

OCTOBER 10, 2008   Stevenson, somewhere, warns an aspiring writer to consider the unimportance of literature – particularly how little the world would change, had Shakespeare never lived. But this is wrong. Certainly, Shakespeare moved no great historical forces. If you can be convinced that history is a script, a set of roles to be filled – then you must allow Stevenson's doubt.

But if an individual can have any effect on history, however subtle, then Shakespeare's influence is everywhere. For if we remove Shakespeare, then, five centuries later, we have a different human race. Restore life to every soldier Harry's speech inspired to heroism; take back every life the soldier saved. Take back the child of every pair of lovers brought together when the love suicides at Verona made a young man seek his Juliet, a young lady her Romeo. Take back every life that stayed to make the choice to be or not to be.

Go on with the rest of literature. All those soldiers who fell to fall like Achilles, all those poets who died to die like Werther; all who wandering with a book in hand found strange mothers for their children; even whom a shared admiration for a writer offered friendship and friendship became love. Go back to the beginning, back to folk tales and fireside legends; repeal poetry altogether and see how each woman's love, with no better occasion than strength or success, breeds brutal children whose loves and lives are yet more brutal, and so on all the way down.

That literature mostly occupies idle time does not make our choice in literature vain choice: we get only a fixed measure of time, and whatever changes how we use any of that time, changes what we leave behind us. When we work, our work is in and for the present; what we aim for when we work for the future is a necessary delusion, not the true future but the present's mirage of the future. The true future grows in our leisure.

This is literature's unique power, which other arts only employ. It is not the musician they fall for, but the literary characters Music, and the Musician; not the flag they die for, but the Flag, the Nation, that someone once defined in telling.

If we could know the minds that went with the names, we would see that genealogy is a transcription of literature; that the human race we know has not merely happened, but has bred itself in a prolonged act of literary criticism.

THE TWENTIETH CENTURY

OCTOBER 17, 2008   The idol is made of steel. The idol has no face: no mouth to explain, no ears to heed, no nostrils to stink in, and no eyes to witness.

The idol has two hands: a hand of bright steel, and a hand of dull steel.

In the bright hand of the idol is a key. All around the bright hand are the tokens of pilgrims who leave what the power of the idol has opened at their prayers: which are locks, bars, doors, gates, fetters, and chains.

In the dull hand of the idol – what is in the dull hand of the idol? The dull hand of the idol is tight shut. Around the closed fist of the dull hand are the tokens of penitents willing and unwilling: which are empty things (the dull hand only takes): bottles, boxes, chairs, beds, shoes.

They tell stories of the idol. They say the idol came from afar. Everywhere, it came from afar. It came from afar with two hands. It came loudly, without fear and without shame, and it touched everything.

What it touched with its bright hand that holds a key, was opened. The bright hand opened the bonds older gods left as they fled before the steel god. The bright hand opened the cell of night; opened the house of sickness; opened the prison of birth; opened the pit of ignorance; opened the veil of lies.

What it touched with its dull hand that is closed, was taken away. It touched the cleanness of the height and the quiet of the deep; it touched the peace of the valley and the pride of the peak; it touched the hope of the beggar and the pity of the rich man. It touched the dreams of dreamers, and the pride of makers. And lastly it touched cities, and countries, and nations, and it took them away.

This god has two hands – a bright hand that opens and a dull hand that takes away; but this god, who is blind, deaf, and dumb, does not know which hand is which.

What shall become of the steel idol, stories do not agree. Some say it is already dead; it is already rusting within; someday it will fall in on itself; the power that draws pilgrims and penitents is but an ember in ash. Some say it is resting; someday it will rise to touch and end the world – but they do not agree whether it will end the world with the opening touch of its bright hand, or the taking touch of its dull hand. Some say it has already sown the end of the world, and only awaits a harvest. Some say it is old and ashamed, so before it dies it will join hands and restore all it has taken; and some say it is old and ashamed, so before it dies it will join hands and close all it has opened. Some say it is lonely, and awaits another of its kind.

And some few even whisper: it shall not die. Into the soil it rests on it is driving roots.

FORESTS

OCTOBER 24, 2008   Forests have personalities, different as their different attitudes toward human beings. I feel now the weary indifference of the Great Piney Woods; I remember well the young daring malevolence of the Pine Barrens. City Park of New Orleans, like its city and people, drives deep roots into unfaithful soil. These three are forests I know well. I could mention other forests, but I defer to those who know them better.

By *personality* I do not mean the mood that a forest gives you. The personality of a forest, though not an embodied or predictable quality, can be correlated with the forest that has it, as the personality of a building can be correlated with its architecture, through plans cannot foretell it and architects cannot make it to order.

Trees make up a forest, and the forest conceals its trees; so the forest is an act of concealment. And the forest conceals more than trees. The forest is full of things that jump and climb, squirrels and woodrats, and claws and teeth to hunt them. The forest provides for things which must hide at times: a hole for the bear's hibernation; noon twilight for the owl's delicate, instrumental eyes. We name forests for the kinds of trees which conceal them; we know forests by what they can conceal. Tall, straight firs that keep their needles about their trunks hide little, have little to hide, are friendly. All the forests of the American South are full of the memories of ambuscades and bushwhackers. What could tell of the forests of Europe, better than that their field neighbors could believe whole covens to hold there unheard? That in imagination wolves moved there not in packs, but in armies? The Pine Barrens conceal ghost towns well, and what night visitors leave there better. And it is easy to believe the report of Goodman Brown (or Lovecraft) of the forests of New England.

Since a forest is distinguished by its kind of secrets, it is not easy to get to know a forest. They are all very skilled in dissembling with spies. They must be courted, with conscious attention and curious patience. What is there by way of personality is not perceptible to all; but though it cannot be pointed to, it is not imaginary. Secrecy is the negative image of language; when we keep secrets, we speak in silence. In this shadow language forests speak, teaching by omission.

THREE HORROR STORIES

HALLOWEEN, 2008

I

"Did you hear that?"

"Hear what?"

"Sounded like somebody down there calling for help."

"There's nobody down there. The dogs went through last week. They sealed the tunnels after that."

"Yeah, but this seal's not tight. The storm worked it loose. It was cold last night. Somebody could have slipped in."

"I don't hear a damn thing. It's just wind getting in somewhere. The seals are loose, like you said. If you want to keep your job, just get over there and press the damn button. We're running a day late already. We've got to get these tunnels filled in."

II

"Did you find it, daddy?"

"Find what, little one?"

"Did you find the monster in the basement?"

"Of course. I was looking for the monster. There's no such thing as monsters, little one."

"But I saw it daddy, I know I did! Why are you standing out there, daddy? Come in here where I can see you."

III

"Thanks for coming so quickly."

"No problem. Somebody told me you were, like, doing medical experiments or something for cash? So, I mean, what's that like?"

"Well. Pain, humiliation, sometimes I could hardly get out of bed for weeks, sometimes I thought I'd go crazy. A lot like the office, actually."

"So how much did you make?"

"I went in for something off the books. Set me up for life."

"What'd they do to you? I mean, you even kinda look different."

"Oh, nothing much. Did some funny things to my appetite."

"So where are we going? I'm hungry. We going out?"

"I just ordered in."

ON A TELEVISION ADVERTISEMENT FOR THE CITY OF DUBAI

NOVEMBER 7, 2008

Build.
Only build.
Build higher and farther.
Build wilder and larger.
Build where never built before
Build with ruins under floor.
The city cannot wait, the roads are true
Their word runs everywhere, they run for you.
Where have you seen the spot where buildings cannot dwell?
The domes are in the mountains, the divers ride the bell.
Build while strength is left for building, build while time is left to
    build
Built atop the sunken city, build atop the land you filled.
Cities are everywhere rising, a fable instructive for anthills
Builders by summer and winter in sunshine or darkness our light
    fills.
See by the shores of the desert how cities are built by a gesture,
    Cities of pliable steel, cities that open like eyes,
Pillarless cities that spill out shaken like billowing carpets
    Sudden as breaker or dune, clouds of an overturned sky.
Too many cities have slow-grown only to perish in torment
Overturned cities, their names told counting the promise of judg-
    ment.
Cast up cities thin as cloth or canvas, anchored for the day
Sheathe your towers under glass as sails to set you underway.
No city wakes in silence when city never sleeps;
No harvest fails the city where city never reaps.

Who builds anew and never looks behind
Keeps safe from all that's out of sight and mind.
To find the way we build it first.
The water follows on our thirst.
We build to trap the day;
The night we wall away.
Build stronger and taller
Build nearer and smaller.
Only build.
Build.

VERBAL THINKING

NOVEMBER 14, 2008   There is nothing more familiar than language without thought. Why not thought without language? Language, thought; thought, language; where is the division between them?

For example: when one word recalls others of similar meaning or sound, the triggering word need not occur consciously. Often things I see and do bring to mind other things which sound like the names of these sights or actions, or which occur together with those names – even in contexts where the name of the thing is equivocal and means something else.

This could, of course, be explained as an instance in which words function as things, within a thought in itself nonverbal. That is not so strange; it must happen in writing poetry. But if we adopt this explanation, where do we stop? We could do away with the notion of specifically verbal thinking altogether; which is absurd. We know about things we have no experience of beside hearing their names. If we dismiss these as thoughts about reports, we must explain how our knowledge holds when we see for ourselves, and experience replaces hearsay.

There are forms of thinking prior to language – animals think – and there are forms of human thought in which language is not only unnecessary, but a hindrance. Efficient mental calculation requires the omission of intervening words, even *times* and *equals*, instead hearing only numbers and rendering a result by a process that feels less like reckoning than recognition. You draw best what you cannot name, or by putting aside the name while you draw. In any game, or any system of rules yielding winners and losers, though words are of use beforehand in study and planning, they distract when you come to it – not because they are slow or awkward, but because they involve too much. Words, by which we compass the world, always drag the world in; but to play the game well, you must enworld yourself in it. To play with words in your head keeps the rules from sinking in, knocks your thoughts off the rails. Suddenly you think of the game itself, its origin, use, nature; the wording of the rules, the form of the strategies – how they resemble stratagems of nature or the stratagems of other games. And in the meantime you have lost.

This kind of thinking cannot help you win by rule: the only use of words in games is in cheating. And this is good. Intelligence is for cheating. We cannot win any of nature's games by nature's rules. We are not strong enough, not fast enough. We are too big to hide and too small to shake off attack. But we can change the rules: levers for strength; shoes, boats, tame horses for speed; blinds and camouflage for hiding; walls and armor for bulk. All invention is cheating; and cheating is made possible by language.

Some animals, of course, can cheat – chimpanzees, dolphins, ravens – the list is long and growing. Some of these cheats are ambiguous – complex acts, yes, but only very complex moves within the rules. Yet some are cheaters for sure. If they are cheaters, does that mean they have language?

There may be a kind of thinking in between nonverbal thought and language which is not (in the old phrase) *sub-vocalized speech*, but *sub-verbal language*; language without words.

Language is how we step outside the rules, how we recognize rules as being only rules, there to be broken. All this step requires is a faculty of association. In human beings this faculty is untyped, consistent, and social.

By "untyped" I mean that we can associate things without logical connection: when we say *the sky is angry*, we do not mean *sky:?::person:anger* nor *the change in the appearance of the sky is isomorphic to the change in the appearance of a person becoming angry*. We are simply associating the ideas *sky* and *angry*.

Intelligent animals are intelligent because they are capable of untyped association. A chimpanzee that fishes for ants with a stick has an association between *ant* and *stick*, but there is no thought in this process corresponding to *tool*. Having an association between *ant* and *stick*, he tries to keep them both in mind, to direct his attention to both at once – which means, for a forgetful animal, first that he picks up the stick and stays near the anthill; then that he touches them together. The stick and the anthill have limited affordance; the chimpanzee need only keep the association in mind to have a stick covered with delicious ants.

Untyped associations are illogical; so if untyped association is a necessity of thought, then so is illogic. We retain a naive habit of thinking of logic as a function of intelligence; but living the age of the computer, we have no excuse for this mistake. Logic is embedded in nature: transistors and electrons, chutes and marbles, can reason. Nothing is illogical; but only the highest complexity can simulate illogic.

That is one out of three for animals. The other two – consistency and sociality – are only ours. Any idea is an act of differentiation of the chaos of experience. When I say *stick* I isolate a segment of a continuum that runs from splinter and sliver through branch to tree and forest. And sticks are always sticks to me. So when I say that a monkey picks up *a stick*, I impute to the chimpanzee's thought a quality of my own thought – the stability of *stickness*. But the chimpanzee's thought may in this instance be closer to *tree*, and the stick he ends up with the limit of what his strength and dexterity could manage. Or he might have been thinking closer to branch, and again been defeated; or to splinter, and been unable to break the wood; or just of wood, and picked up the stick off the forest floor. On each occasion that I observe him with a stick his thought of what he carries may be anywhere on that continuum.

If his association has no stability, he cannot teach another monkey what a stick is, because he cannot, as we can, associate two consistent ideas – one that must be named (*stick*), and one that names itself (the sound *stick*) – so that another can imitate the association. Thus his associations are not transferable – they may be imitated in a broad sense, but the ideas associated to the same result may not match up at all.

Some of the above is probably reinvention. And certainly all of this could be formulated more precisely. I take the risk because I know of no work on the continuity of human and animal thought but arguments about whether there could be continuity – never what the nature of that continuity might be.

GUESSWORK

NOVEMBER 21, 2008   It is as difficult to say what guesswork is as to say what the mind is. Guessing is not the action of any faculty of the mind; it is the only action of the whole mind. There are no exercises or studies to train guesswork; the quality of the guess is the quality of the guesser. There are no abstract objects for guesswork to practice on – in any formal test, the answers where the mind is most used are the ones that are guessed at. Only in your guesses do you transcend the test, having in mind not only the subject matter but also the context of the test, weighing the character and reconstructing the thoughts of its makers, estimating your limits, knowing yourself and knowing the way of the world.

A good guess is sibling to a good idea. Both trade risk for reward, certainty for power. To guess is often the only way to know something that others do not. A bad guess is always wrong; but that one guess is some sense better than another also good does not mean it is more likely to be true. Reality is recalcitrant and perverse. Reality has punished for laziness, and punished for effort; punished for absurdity, and punished for plausibility; punished for optimism, and punished for pessimism – and, of course, it has rewarded each. There are no rules for guessing: we cannot guess with less than all our strength.

MUSIC AND MEANING

NOVEMBER 28, 2008   Can music have meaning? Certainly, meaning can always be found in music – one piece of music and the traveler hears home, the lover hears the beloved, the believer hears God – but can a piece of music bear meaning as an act of communication?

Keys, intervals, and chords are often thought of as ideas in themselves. Major is happy, minor is sad. The second menaces, the sixth regrets. The suspension promises, the dominant delivers. But the rules hold only for the simplest examples. A composer can always make the key serve the occasion; a performer can do the same for the composer. When we hear a familiar piece in an unfamiliar key – say, when an aging singer changes the key of a song to ease their voice – it troubles us at first; but we get used to it, and after a few hearings all our original associations pass over into the new key intact.

Time and use have made certain pieces of music the bearers of specific meanings; but if we listen naively, the meanings disappear. The motive of Beethoven's 5th has come to represent strength, right, V for victory; but if we say that Beethoven put all that into four notes, then we must say that Samuel Morse put it into three dots and a dash.

Yet it is absurd to say that music is without meaning – that it is mere surface – that what we see in it are only reflections on its polish. Music comes to you without message or meaning; but once you have supplied the message, there should be no room for others. A piece of music should work on its message like a table of derivations works on a root in a Semitic language. We are not told what the deed is; we are told: here is the doer, here is the manner, the means, here is the beginning of it, the end, the reasoning, the result, here is the place the thing was done, and who it was done to. (A strange analogy, yes; but consider the sometimes almost musical ambiguity of the ancient Semitic languages.)

No human being can experience every emotion equally; yet any competent musician can play a piece of music with any emotion, even one the musician has never experienced. The lack of experience can even make for a better performance, if it keeps the performer out of the way. How, then, can we call playing music the expression of emotion? It is first a means of experiencing emotions. The same can be true for listeners. A sad song can sadden you without matching your own experiences. Why listen to sad songs when you are sad? Because the sadness you feel from sad music is not your own sadness, but a borrowed sadness that covers your own.

Music is not the only means of emotional education and exercise, but it is the most effective, being the most efficient and the most accessible. Music goes ahead of the other arts, the lullaby that greets us almost as soon as we enter the world. The other arts reach the mind later, and rely on the capacities that music has formed.

And I suspect that among the arts, music serves to absorb the extreme of aestheticism. In the unmusical aestheticism can become immoderate and paralyzing, as if they do not know where to stop in their attempt to imitate or rival musical sophistication, even to the injury of what is particularly their art's own.

As music became easier to hear, all the arts adopted simplicity as their goal: as if the desire for the pleasures of sophistication were limited, and as it finds sophistication in music, it finds satiety.

Consider music in movies. I do not know how much I am ruled by habit in finding it natural. Perhaps in a hundred years a scene ending in swelling music while lovers kiss will seem as artificial as a scene ending with a rhyming couplet and a falling curtain. *Exeunt audience.* But to me it seems that the movie depends more on the music than the music depends on the movie. Silent film, of course, was never silent, only voiceless. Music videos are watchable without plot or character. Many movies – especially if they propose to represent real life – have plots that would, told over a dinner table, only provoke laughter; characters, if they were real, we would prefer not to know. Far from being ennobled by their projected stature, it is only by the artifice of music that such stories gain watchable significance. As literature, movies are less flexible than narrative: the stories of superheroes and salesmen must be told alike by one camera at a time in one place at a time following one act at a time in a box of the same size over the same amount of time. Music smooths out the disparities when a salesman fills the screen like a superhero and a superhero declaims like a salesman.

Information theory defines the unit of communication as a single decision: a bit of information is exactly enough to decide one Yes or No. In this sense, music is meaningless. It contains no information except itself. Yet it has something very close to meaning: it cannot tell you how to answer, but it can force you to come to an answer. The screen tells you the man is a villain; the music makes you hate him. The song tells you how he did her wrong; the music puts you on her side. Judgment can be withheld only in silence; music decides nothing, but it forces the decision.

A MEMORY OF INFANCY

DECEMBER 14, 2008   I believe that anything can be said. There are always words, if not always the strength to find and use them. Anything that can be experienced can be communicated. Communication from one mind to another cannot be perfect; but it can at least match the imperfect communication by way of memory between yourself then and yourself now.

This is a test case. I have what seems to be a memory of infancy. I do not insist that it is true; it could be a neurological glitch. Nonetheless, it is an interesting problem of expression.

I call it a memory, but I cannot remember it directly: I must remember being 11 remembering being 6 remembering. Eventually this chain must slip away from me; that it another reason to write it down.

I call it a memory because I have access to it by remembering, but it is not like other memories. It is smooth, hard, incapable of subdivision. It contains no data. In itself it is more of a feeling than a memory – as if at that stage the faculty of feeling supports not broad, generic emotions, but discrete pegs of experience. When I remember, the memory is not retrieved; it comes over me, I *feel* it as if I were feeling an emotion.

The senses are not distinct. They do not blend; there is no cacophony or synesthesia; instead, the senses are *one* – one unitary sensation that is not processed as sight or hearing or touch or smell, but absorbed as emotion. This one sense subordinates not only the usual five, but also proprioception – awareness of the position of your own body. There is a quality to the memory like *marshmallowiness* – an association, not a translation – that I think is the best my adult brain can do in rendering an experience recorded by such an alien scheme of proportions and powers.

Something happens – something unpleasant. My best guess is that I am receiving an injection. The memory somewhat resembles the nauseating feeling of a needle under the skin, but magnified until – fleetingly – it becomes my entire experience of the world and myself.

World and self are not distinct. Because no such concept as control yet exists, I have no way to tell what I can control – myself – from what I cannot control – world. I do not experience the world as part of myself; I do not experience self; I just experience. Note that while this is an unpleasant memory, the distinction in an adult between something bad that happens to you (with anger, indignation, or fear) and something bad you do without meaning to (with embarrassment, shame, regret and uncertainty) – this distinction is absent. The simple unpleasantness of something bad happening here compasses both – though, without future, I am without fear or uncertainty.

In this alien being that I was, I recognize only one thing.

Imagine that you have just begun to study something very interesting, but which you know nothing about. You throw yourself into it. You learn fast, getting your bearings, absorbing the terms of art, feeling out the areas of concern. It is like hunger – better, it is like a stomach: a void with agency, asserting its need.

This, infinitely amplified, is what I recognize: the absolute ravenous void where words would be.

MISTAKES

DECEMBER 19, 2008   The only virtue worth teaching is to acknowledge mistakes without shame and correct them without perversity. If a vice is worth avoiding because it is dangerous, then in time it must manifest as a mistake; so that what is worth teaching is that if your mistake is pointed out to you, you should take it as a favor; and that the only shame in a mistake is loyalty to it.

To acknowledge a mistake is not the same as to reflect on it. Sometimes, when you have taken on a serious responsibility and made a mistake with irreparable harm, then you should be asked – you should ask yourself – what went wrong. But, for most mistakes, to reflect on the mistake is to compound it. Inevitably, if you do many things, you will make many mistakes. If you do few things, you will make few mistakes. But only if you do nothing will you make no mistakes.

The most demoralizing condition possible is capricious punishment. There is more cruelty in mild punishment for no reason than in the harshest punishment for clear reason. Such punishment, if sustained, is too horrible even to rouse the will to die.

To look for hidden faults to blame for the statistically inevitable is to punish yourself with such random cruelty. And even when a mistake is the consequence of a remediable fault, self-reflection is the worst way to discover it. Self-reflection is hard; so hard that, after the difficulty of the inquiry, only a dramatic answer seems plausible, and you diagnose as depravity what was due to indigestion.

The virtue of acknowledging mistakes must be instilled, because it is difficult to acquire. It slows the development of a sense of identity; the contempt for the corrections you receive from certain kinds of people is one of the ways you distinguish yourself from them. And it is probably impossible for an unpracticed adult to acquire – impossible for an adult to face, too late, that what had seemed to be the limits set by nature were only the limits set by pride.

This virtue is so rare, and so unreliable even in those who sometimes have it, that you may ask if it is worth having at all. Can it really be good – even if it is right, can it really be wise – to be without shame among those who blame you? And though this virtue removes self-set limits, it may cost you time making slow progress where your talents do not lie – time you could have saved if you had, at the difficult outset, simply chosen pride in your incompetence.

Yet I believe it is a virtue; the more so because, like all virtues, it can be immoderate. A little uncertainty about your nature saves you from overspecialization and obsolescence; a little time wasted in spreading your roots, saves you from exhausting the soil.

VIOLENT SNOW

DECEMBER 26, 2008   When I heard that snow was in the forecast here, I sneered. Something called snow has been seen here: early in the morning, dusted like frost on the fields, white blots in shallow puddle-basins.

Nature has instructed my disdain.

I woke to look out on a white world, a white weird and awful as the white hand of Moses. Snow lay thick on the roof, thick on branches, thick on evergreen leaves. Snow had inverted the forest: straight-trunked trees that reach branches up to the sun, instead lay them down along their sides, like fronds of Christmas trees; titan limbs of spreading live oaks that float twenty feet in the air, strong as iron and thick as pillars, curved under the weight of the snow loading their leaves until they arched against the ground.

And the snow was still falling: wet, heavy snow, good snow for snow-men and snowballs, falling so fast and thick that I could hear it. I cannot compare the sound. And faintly, from deep in the woods, came another sound like hunters' guns or holiday fireworks – the first cracks of breaking branches.

My last snow fell ten years ago: weeks of etherealizing snow on the Pine Barrens, another country with other pines and other oaks, a slow, thin, steady fall like the gradual deposition of a pearl, and still the most beautiful thing I have ever seen.

Snow in Louisiana: I had to see it for myself. So I put on a helmet, grabbed a camera, and walked out, listening for snapping branches, stepping over branches I knew only from beneath, over ranks of hedges that lay prone as young sleepers after long days.

Along the way, in the shelter of the Quonset hut, I looked back into the woods and saw – too fast to watch – a 60 foot tree (it must have been long dead) simply slide three lengths past one another and disappear like a closing telescope.

Beyond the Quonset hut, the field – white, empty, white. And from the field, back to the house, where disaster had arrived. I lost the stomach for pictures. Each casualty was the same: first, the fatal shot; then, as if in shame of defeat, the slough that sends up a white lace veil; last, so many tons of wood swing or plummet almost silently into the muffling snow.

It went on for hours, snow piling impossibly on the green leaves. It was good snow for snowmen: the snow made its own snowmen over the leaves, half-formed homuncular snowmen, snowmen without faces.

Hour after hour I watched a day's snowfall work so much destruction that a human lifetime will not see it all repaired. As after hurricanes, the debris will go, and the summer's growth of leaves will hide the rest. They hide much. The forest grows; wind and now snow destroy; and I do not know anymore which is winning.

Three days later, it was warm enough to breed mosquitoes. Ten days later, winter was declared.

UNCUT PAGES

JANUARY 2, 2009   Sometime last year, while I was in town, I bought a battered old book out of a box in an antique store. The book is the 10th volume in an edition of Demosthenes in Greek and French on facing pages, printed Paris 1821. It bears the name of a Louisiana monastery that must have bought the set.

Let us round down and say that it was shelved for a 150 years – and in a monastery, a place I imagine, romantically, as reading's proper kingdom. The outside shows wear; someone took the trouble to put a bookplate in it, and to number it twice on the title page. 150 years worth of cleaning and lifting; 150 years in a monastery library – and the pages have never been cut. The book has never been read.

I can guess what happened. The set was bought by the last generation of French-speaking monks, for the last generation of French-speaking students. The next generation spoke English; and French or Greek were both Greek to them (or German, as the store labeled it).

The tragedy of a worthy book unread is common. To ignore it is part of the discipline of library reading. I find a book whose very existence delights me – beautiful, brilliant, every page glows, would that I could write so well. In an idle, careless moment I flip it over, glance at the sticker or slip that records each checkout. 12 years ago, someone checked it out; 10 years ago, someone else; and then me. I wonder: of what species am I a member? At least there are the three of us.

But this is crankiness. To be useful, books must be abundant: just enough is too few. Infrequent checkouts are almost a sign of health: the book exists in enough copies relative to its readers that some can be deputed to serve as in lighthouses, rescue stations, radar installations, to watch and bide until their hour arrives – the flare goes up, the alarm goes off, the reader arrives.

I hear that many libraries now throw away books that go unread for a year, two years, three. They justify their footprint and budget in serving the tastes of their readers; shelf space for books not in fashion is a scholar's humor. New-book bookstores work on that principle: the book that no one buys is remaindered, ends as pulp or ash. Commerce is pure democracy: to the majority, all; to the minority, nothing. I suppose that libraries have the right to decide that survival is worth the price of this attitude. And I, who have fatted on discard racks, have no standing to complain.

All writing is of one or more of three kinds: writing for a known audience; writing that creates an audience; and writing that has no true audience. And all three kinds can fail.

You write for an audience; but you have misjudged them. You overestimated them, and they paw through the pages in a staring stupor. You underestimated them, and they flip through the pages in annoyance and disgust. Though pawed over or flipped through, these pages are as uncut as any.

You write to create an audience; but it never shows up. You gathered them together, but you were molding dry sand. You reach out for them, but someone else has already gone farther, and the new heights you worked so hard to reach – someone else has stepped over them, on the way to something even newer.

You wrote for no audience; you made a self-standing mirror of your own mind, copied the microcosm in you and put stars in its firmament; but your mind's image does not show it to advantage, and your microcosm lacks tourist appeal. Mocked or neglected, these pages are as uncut as any.

How hard it is to communicate at all! To have something to say, to say it, and to have it heard, are each separately as much as can be expected from a lifetime. To routinize the feat, the apparatus of society divides it between academic, writer, journalist; think-tanker, speechwriter, speaker. That they ever happen together is miracle and mercy. It is half the pleasure of reading just to see that it can happen.

As for this book before me: books with uncut pages ("unopened pages" is the proper name, but too weak for a title) are not rare, but not common, and no more are being made.

The easiest way to part such pages is with the edge of an index card; I have boxes of "Super-Dex" Rotary Cut cards, from when such things were still made in Brooklyn, that could do the job and still give a good shave. I tried it on another book with an anomalous pair, and succeeded. But when I come to it: why?

I try not to buy books as artifacts: it is a waste of money and space better given to books for reading. But this is a book I picked up cheaply to practice my French; it is more valuable to me as a curiosity than as a book. I harden my heart to say: here is a book that failed. Its pages shall not be cut.

PAN-JITSU

JANUARY 9, 2009   [In honor of my great-grandmother, who tried to bequeath her cast-iron frying pan to my mother expressly as a weapon.]
J. Pilcrow and D. Fleuron (eds.), *Historical and Critical Perspectives on the Neglected Women's Martial Art of Pan-Fighting: Proceedings of the First International Symposium of the Association for Pan-Fighting Studies*, Endower Institute Press, 2008, 25pp., $45.00 (hbk), ISBN 01123581321345589144.

Panhandle: The Dawn of Pan-Fighting in New Kingdom Egypt, Asta Faience.

Panic: Pan-Fighting in the Classical World, S. P. Quiller-Round.

Traveling Pan: The Frying Pan on the Silk Road, T. Kent.

Pan Demonium: The Suppression of Pan-Fighting, 1100–1400, C. N. Bacon.

Scramble and Coagula: Pan-Fighting as Alchemical Metaphor, Al Chocodon.

The Flat of the Blade: Pan-Fighting as Metaphor in the Medieval Fechtbuch, Alber vom Tag.

"Fried" or "Flattened:" Revisiting the Rolling Pin Debate, Mann van Dough.

A Flash in the Pan: Underground Pan-Fighting in Early Modern Europe, Martina Scriblerus.

Casting Iron: Pan-Fighting in Song Dynasty China, Hill Barton.

Flipping the Pan: Pan-Fighting in Japanese History, Usagi Tsukino.

Citizen Crêpe: The Pan-Fighters of Paris in the French Revolution, Scarlet Orczy.

Fires and Frying Pans: "Pan-jitsu" in Nineteenth Century Europe, E. W. Barton-Wright.

Panning for Gold: Pan-Fighters on the American Frontier, Clementine Darling.

Pan Left: Pan Fighting in Silent and Pre-Code Hollywood, Alan Smithee.

Panzer: Pan Fighters of the Résistance, William Martin.

Pan and Scan: Pan-Fighting in Contemporary Film, A. Gaffer.

Panstand: Pan-Fighting in American Youth Culture, Susan Cue.

Panman: Pan-Fighting in the Arcade Video Game, F. P. Shooter.

Pandom: Pan-Fighting Communities Online From BBS Through Facebook, A.T.N. Baud.

CONVERSATION

JANUARY 16, 2009   Talking is a pleasure in itself. It is good to be able to talk about anything; it is good to be able to talk to anyone. But most talking is not between people; it is between roles. On a long trip on an elevator you will hear how talk has a life of its own. Two people start talking; one gets off, someone else gets on; the talker says to the newcomer what they would have said to the other talker; and so on until the talking has survived the replacement of each of the talkers.

Of course, we are all in the metaphorical elevator: we must all exit at some stop, hoping that our places will be taken. But the places we leave metaphorically are changed by having been ours; the places we leave when we physically step out from them are the same places we stepped into.

Most talking is like this. Most of what is said, even between people who know each other well, has only token use, is said only to have said something. The rest belongs to the relationship, not the participants. You say something to your child, and it is what any parent would say to any child; to your wife, to your husband, and it is just what each would say to the other; to your friend, it is what friends say to friends; to your acquaintance, it is how decent people talk to each other; to a stranger, it is what anyone would say under the circumstances.

This sounds wearying; but in truth we expect nothing else. Still, some people want more. Their expectation is to be able to speak with those they are close to as person to person, without rule or model; or at least – if rules are necessary to smooth close joints – to spare conventions with acquaintances or strangers, to speak man to man.

This speaking as oneself, beyond or before roles, they call conversation. The name is curiously solid. The world *friend* has been attenuated, but we do not pretend that we can have conversations with authority: your boss can say to you, "I want you to think of me as your friend"; but not "I want you to think of this as a conversation." And though the Internet has "conversational" for its epithet, a particular online exchange must be remarkable to receive the name.

There are things that cannot be conversed about and people you cannot have conversations with. There can be conversations about politics or religion only between indifferent people: political or religious commitments do not recess. Likewise, you cannot have conversations about personal commitments equal to these public ones: you cannot have a conversation about your family or your vocation, because there you are not independent, and therefore not conversational.

If to converse is to speak as yourself, why not center conversation there? But the most personal topics are the least individual: the more personal a detail, the more resistlessly it sorts you. Tell your pains, hear your type; tell your pleasures, hear your disease. There is room for the individual only after development, in the faculties aesthetic, philosophical, and – especially – critical. Consequential as they are in commitment, they are harmless in conversation, like composite explosive. Later you can fit the detonator and announce yourself to the world. Here, for now, your thoughts are free, rapid, and sure as the thoughts of angels.

SMALL WORLDS

JANUARY 23, 2009   When I was a child, and we drove through a city, there would always be a moment – usually when I first came into sight of a block of apartments – a moment I would feel a mixture of panic and vertigo – horror. So many windows, so many doors. Ten thousand people could live in there. More people than I could ever know in one lifetime or a dozen. More names, even, than I would ever know. Why should the world even include so many people? Were there even ten thousand kinds of people? How many were repeats? How many were redundant?

That was a horrible thought: that most of the human race has no individual reason to exist; that most of us exist only to fill out the numbers for the workings of a smaller world, a real world, extras in a movie we will never see.

The other thought was worse: ten thousand people and every one an end in themselves – every single one enough to justify the existence of the whole species – so that with just one brief look out the side of a van racing past, looking down from the overpass, I glimpsed a world absolutely worth knowing ten thousand times over and ten thousand times over impossible to know.

Thus, despite a love of the arts, my first ambitions were all scientific: I wanted, like Avicenna's God, to compass the universe of particulars by knowing universals.

We have tricks to evade large numbers of things, but they fail us with people. Seven billion fish or flowers we know how to divide to conquer, cutting out bite sizes with the sharp 7 ± 2 we're born with. But we cannot use the same trick with people. True, we have a neurological constant for numbers of people, about 150, the famous Dunbar's number. But Dunbar's number is not recursive. Society is not structured by communities of 150 combining into meta-communities of 150 communities in an Apollonian gasket of social circles. People belong to different communities. One-sided relationships cut across all communities. Thousands of communities exist side by side. And outside communities, there are the new people. People are always being born, and having been born are always growing up, and having grown up are always demanding our attention.

How, then, do we stay sane in a world of seven billion people? But no one lives in that world. The evasion is not quantitative but qualitative. We make our own worlds, our own small, manageable worlds: family, friends, faces that dwarf crowds. In the foreground, your world contains people significant in your personal history or netted by your routine; in the background, those made familiar (note the etymon) by news or entertainment, by admiration or reputation.

Small worlds vary in two dimensions: whether they are closed or open, and whether they face inward or outward. In a closed world, role and person are identical; in an open world, the cast changes. (But note that the distinction of role and player is never absolute: there is always a tension.) In an outward-facing world, the population screen each other from society; in an inward-facing world, the population are the eyes of society on each other.

The closed and outward-facing world is the world of the village. The open and inward-facing world is the world of the social network, where direct ties are always weaker than abstract commitments. The closed and inward-facing world is the world of the cadre, the team, the colony. The open and outward-facing world is the world of the movement, the religion, the institution, and the corporation.

Of course, you can live in different worlds in sequence; but you can only live in one world at a time. I would say that you must choose, but the choice will probably be made for you. You were born into one kind of world; and you are unlikely to move from one to another except at some socially oiled articulation of the lifespan.

The world is beyond comprehension, beyond recognition, beyond reach. It always has been. We do not have the choice to know the world. We have three choices only: to hide from the world, filtering it through stereotype and prejudice; to dilute ourselves in the world, lost in the big picture; or to trust that the extremities of the particular and the universal touch – to trust that human nature is best read in a human being's nature, that human diversity is mirrored in a human being's variety, and that the beginning of human kindness is kindness to a human being.

To say that we should love our enemies assumes that it is easy to love our friends. The mind is full of passionate poisons, resentment and short-sightedness, which work to confuse us. How many keep a leashed civility with their enemies who love with snarls and teeth? How many who pity the unfortunate stranger are shamed by and despise the weakness of their own? How many choose the attractions of envy over the bond of blood? How many fear more to be thought by strangers to love too well or too openly – to be weak or soft or fond – than to be thought by loved ones to love less, or not to love?

All this sounds very bourgeois, very *gemütlich*. But small worlds are not just shelters; they are also the laboratories where the world of the future is being discovered. The inside jokes and private conversations of one generation become the mainstream of the next. Not every small world can reshape the great world; but nothing can reshape the great world until it has shaped a small world first.

What are you? Are you what you say you are? Or are you what others say you are? Of course you are both, and neither. They are the two ways of living in a world that, like a lens, curved one way, concentrates light onto you and, curved the other way, sheds your light. But the lens is required: a small world, answering the animal conditions of life, spares you the freedom, clothes you enough, to survive the great and human world.

ALLEGORY OF LAW

JANUARY 30, 2009   Once, when the world was young and there was little to tell or remember, there was a land where only good people lived: people who only thought and said and did good, who had never harmed one another.

Now it happened one day that a man found his fields torn up and another man told him that vermin were abroad in the woods. So he dug pits and covered them over to catch the vermin so he could take them somewhere they would do no harm.

But there were no vermin. The man who thought he saw vermin had seen only shadows and branches swaying. What had ruined the fields was something else. When the man looked in his traps in the morning he cried out and wept, for his traps, which would have caught and stunned vermin, had caught and killed three children.

There was no justice in the good land, because there were no offenses; there was no one to say Punish and no one to do punishment. But there were the stares and silences of three families. So the man with the field walked into the woods one day, and did not return.

That man had had children of his own, two sons; and these children, too, were stared at and not spoken to by three families; for these two children reminded them of the dead children; and no one in the good land knew the hiding of pain, no more than the hiding of any other feeling; and they could not lie.

Two of the three bereaved families had children, a daughter for each. The daughters stared, but were not silent. The sons of the man of the field reminded three mothers and three fathers of three dead children; but they reminded the sisters of when they had not been alone. So they kept secret company, and grew close.

When they began to appear together, all were pleased by it. The silence was over.

As they grew older, they grew closer, until one of the daughters was with child. All had been pleased; and now all were delighted. Every family in the good land found some separate way to approve and applaud.

But when the day came, the daughter bore a dead child. Before the week was out, she followed it.

Then all were silent in the good land, yet there was no staring. All knew that something was broken, and no one knew how to fix it. They could only hope that if what was broken was not touched, it would heal.

Three families gathered together and wept together. They went to the living daughter and made her swear not to speak to the man she loved.

The son who had been a father wept and cried out; and his brother also wept, for now they were both alone.

Three families went to the son they had warned against, and told him that there must be some danger in his blood; that he should not come near the daughter again; and that they had dug a trap to keep him away, for he was as deadly as any wild animal that kills.

He watched his bereaved brother weep, and tried to comfort him; but he had no comfort, and he needed comfort himself. So, being young and strong and scorning danger, he went to see the daughter he loved.

He fell into the trap and was pierced through with spikes.

Three families wept at this; but what else could they have done?

When the people gathered the last son rose and spoke:

"I was a son; now I am no son, for I have no father. I was a lover; now I am no lover, for I have no beloved. I was a father; now I am no father, for I have no child. I was a brother; now I am no brother, for I have no brother. Three families have taken all these things from me. I was a son, a lover, a father, a brother. Now I am nothing and no one. They are sick. They killed my brother as though he were an animal, which is the worst thing that anyone has ever done. Send them away, do not let them return. They are sick."

One of the mothers of the three families rose and spoke in turn:

"There is in truth sickness among us: sick blood, poison blood. It killed three children. It killed our daughter and our grandchild. We did not kill. We set out a trap and gave warning. Animals are not warned. That man walked into the trap as his father walked into the forest. He did not mean to return. Send this man away while there are still daughters among us."

No one knew what to do then. Sometimes the people had talked over things, like where to dig a well, or when to hunt or harvest; but what could be said about this?

So they went to the oldest and wisest among them, and said to him:

"Be our king, and decide what we should do. For we have never doubted before who we trust."

Then the king said: "There will be no easy talk nor free looks among us while any of them are here. The three families shall go west, and the man alone shall go east."

There were caves in the west and caves in the east with clear water and good hunting. In the west the three families received many visitors, for they had ties of blood. Their daughter, who remained among the people, often came to see them. But in the east the last son was alone. No one visited him.

After years he could bear the quiet no longer, and returned from the east.

Now the king had said that the last son should not be permitted to return – meaning that he should be persuaded to stay away, and that no one should help him. But when he was seen returning some young men determined on their own to carry out the king's order. They stood together in the way, shoulder to shoulder. When the man tried to walk right of them, they stepped into his way; and when the man tried to walk left of them, they stepped into his way. He shouted, but they did not answer. And when he tried to push past them, one of them pushed back.

The man was not old, but loneliness and despair had shrunken his hunger, and he had shrunken with his fasting. So when he was pushed, he fell; when he fell, he broke; and when he broke, he died. But none of them could say who had pushed him.

The young men carried the body to the king, who wept at the sight, and told them that he had never meant for them to kill. But it was too late; and so that the king's word would hold, the young men took the dead son east, and buried him near his cave.

When the news went west, the families smiled among each other; which had never been done before at any human death. When they returned, no one tried to stop them, because they feared what might come of that. At first the families were not seen among the people, nor by daylight; but soon they began to walk abroad and in the sun, in defiance of the king's word.

So the king asked them to come to him. They came, for they expected that his word would be lifted. But he said that he could not let them profit from killing. He told them to go back.

Two families assented. But one family would not be separated from their daughter. They refused the king's word. And when the other two families saw the refusal, they refused as well.

When they left him, the king began to think. He spent the evening in thinking. The purpose of a king was to prevent killing; but still there had been a killing among them. Now the king's word was refused. If killing could happen while the king's word was received, what could come of the refusal of the king's word? What good is a king if he allows profit in killing?

In the night he walked the streets, and chose six young men – the young men who had heard his word before – and told them to wrap their faces and swear to forget. That done, the king told them to bring the three men and three women before him at a high place above a long fall into deep water.

The king told them that they should leave, and go where none of the people would ever speak to them again. They laughed, and said that it was better to live among human faces than in the caves of the west.

He asked again: "Will you leave? It is my part to prevent killing. By staying you profit from killing and approve it."

They refused. "We have never killed."

So the six masked men took hold of them and threw them over to vanish in the water. When no one saw the families, they believed that the families had received the king's word and returned to the caves of the west.

After that, there was beauty, and peace, and happiness; but in that land where only good people had lived, now there was silence in the caves, and a question no one dared to ask, and between the people and the king were men with secrets in their eyes.

COMPARING ARTS

FEBRUARY 6–8, 2009

I

Walter Pater, in *The Renaissance* of 1873, on "The School of Giorgione":

> It is the mistake of much popular criticism to regard poetry, music, and painting – all the various products of art – as but translations into different languages of one and the same fixed quantity of imaginative thought, supplemented by certain technical qualities of colour, in painting; of sound, in music; of rhythmical words, in poetry. In this way, the sensuous element in art, and with it almost everything in art that is essentially artistic, is made a matter of indifference; and a clear apprehension of the opposite principle – that the sensuous material of each art brings with it a special phase or quality of beauty, untranslatable into the forms of any other, an order of impressions distinct in kind – is the beginning of all true aesthetic criticism.

When I first read this, it shocked me. This idea that each art-form is unique and incomparable is so far from obvious, that to accept it would negate art.

Pater himself was either not audacious enough to pursue the idea, or wrote carelessly and meant something else. Both excuses are implausible; but he must be excused, since this is the same essay that delivers the infamous sentence *all arts aspire to the condition of music* – which must have seemed profound, before Schoenberg undertook to reinvent music on the model of painting.

Aristotle relied on painting to inform drama, both in extent (not too short, like a painting of a flea, nor too long, like a life-size painting of a monster a mile long) and to supply its content – representation or *mimesis* – which he justified by the pleasure of any accurate painting, even of something unpleasant. *Ut pictura poesis*; the Renaissance poet's commonplace that *painting is dumb poetry*, and Leonardo's unhelpful refutation, *poetry is blind painting*; Qianlong's exaltation of painting as the model of decoration; Whistler's politely overlooked titles, his studies and compositions and symphonies – but enough. More can always be found. Only note that to set a rule for an art, a critic must be able to cite the material conditions of another art; and to break a rule for an art, an artist must be able to cite the critical freedom of another.

The depth of this process of making and breaking the definitions of an art by appeal to other arts goes as far back as definitions can be documented. Which art defines which changes; but no art ever exists alone. (No people, however ancient, are without at least the triangle of music, dancing, and poetry.)

The process of definition by comparison is not only historical or theoretical. Even once definitions are set, it continues at every level of every form. It is not only the origin of art; it is the metabolism of the life of art.

The possibility of combining arts, for example, presupposes the possibility of comparing them. Such composite arts outnumber elemental arts. There are more composite arts than we can name. Music & writing & acting are one kind of drama; music & writing & acting & singing are musicals or operas; music & writing & acting & cinematography are movies; but music & writing & acting & singing & stagecraft & spectacle is as distinct from the simple name *musical* or *opera* as these are from plays; yet it goes nameless.

In retrospect, even the arts postulated as elemental are fissile, divisible into parts that can be compared: painting, for example, is draftsmanship & composition & color; music is at least rhythm & melody & tone.

As audiences, we regard those arts that require cooperation in their production as composite, and those arts that can be carried out by an individual as elemental; but the possibility of the criticism of an individual artist presumes further divisibility – this painter is a camera, all detail, no balance or flow; this player is a machine, perfect rhythm made perfectly boring.

And to do any criticism beyond ratings, we must suppose that even these pseudo-arts – *pseudo* because they cannot exist independently; they are seen outside the lab, like particles, only in combination – even these arts can be compared with each other. Sometimes perfect rhythm, perfect melody, and perfect tone fail to make a perfect fit.

A combination is not a sum. It can be better than its parts. In popular music, for example, even a good song is, as a rule, the combination of a bad poem with bad music. What it would bore me to read, what it would bore me to play, I find completely satisfying to listen to, so strongly do the ingredients bind together.

But what value remains when we split a composite art? If the composite is simple enough, none; but if the composite is complex, combinations short of the whole may still be worthwhile though the elemental parts are not. A Chinese poem-painting can be appreciated in four ways – accordingly as poetry, calligraphy, and painting are recombined.

Such a relationship between whole and part is a more approachable resemblance of the relationship between whole and whole when a work of one art is translated into a work of another. There are two kinds of artistic translation: one if the creator and translator are the same person; and another if they are different people. Again, when creator and interpreter are not the same, they may be working collaboratively; or the interpreter may be independent of the creator – part of posterity, even.

When a painter says he wants to paint a poem – so many ladies of Shalott; when a musician wants to score a painting – Tedesco's Goya – when a poet wants to give words to a piece of music – "A Toccata of Galuppi's"; when a musician wants to fit music to words – the "Ode to Joy," *Carmina Burana*; when a writer wants to fit a story to a poem – "There Will Come Soft Rains"; when a poet wants to fit a poem to a story – "Tithonus" – we are faced, if the translated work is a success, with something very difficult to criticize. Sometimes the inspiration is plainly tacked on. And the relationship is not a function – one work may be translated into a single medium several times in several distinct versions. But there is a core of comparability between those versions – silent *Romeo and Juliet* and a talkie – and between translations into different mediums – *Romeo and Juliet* as a movie and as a ballet – a core that represents the work apart from its medium. This abstracted core cannot be handled directly; but it can be inferred from the signs of its passage.

There is certainly a sense in which all of a single artist's works resemble each other; and a resemblance between all the art forms of a certain time, place, or class. Such mere affinities are not our concern. They are too tentative and too subjective to analyze: mere family resemblance, we see when we already know the relation what we would never seen on our own. Criticism already attracts far too many long-lost cousins; as financial success attracts them during life, so artistic success draws them as it continues to grow in reputation.

What about influence? Influences are, of course, the ligaments of commercial art, where art forms are joined together in a relation which is complementary, but not inseparable. The phenomenon of influence characterizes both the artists who seek commercial success – bands, for example, who try to dress like they sound and sound like they dress – and it characterizes the art generated by commerce – the mutual adjustment, for example, of the design necessary to produce a product suitable for advertisement on TV, and the music and direction necessary to produce a TV commercial suitable to the product. Influence differs from combination because it is unstable. The music and the fashion, the direction and the design, are always pulling one another in a way that ensures both a perpetual movement, like a mathematical pattern's movement towards an unattainable attractor, and sudden phase-shifts when the old elements, having become too well adjusted, make room for a new element that reboots the process – shifts that approximate the commercial relevance of new generations.

(We are used to thinking, in an afterthought Marxist way, that because the faddishness of commercial art serves commerce, it must therefore a consequence of commerce. But we should be past the idea that commerce can create phenomena of human behavior. It can only exploit them. The fad, the fashion, novelty and mode are a permanent possibility of art, though not always acted out; part of the definition not always realized, like the introns of genetics that still code in birds for the scales and teeth of dinosaurs.)

Taxonomy is not demonstration. To list the ways in which arts can be compared – criticism, combination, translation, influence – is not to prove that all arts are comparable. But I see no way to define art as such, as distinct from creativity in general, except that art is what can be compared with art, being the more like art the more easily and confidently it can be compared. This embraces everything now called, or ever called, art, as well as all extant theories of art – they being reducible to acts of comparison.

Of course, that a definition is comprehensive does not make it true. It may even be a fault, if the definition has no limits. This definition, however, does have some limits. It does not pretend that arts can be recognized by themselves; the act of comparison is necessary. In this it evades the insight into intentions required by the idea that anything is art that is meant to be art. It does not declare that everything is art, nor even that everything now considered art always has been art; it is the act of comparison, not the possibility of comparison, that makes an art an art. It also, uniquely, provides for the historical development of arts out of one another, without tabulating which art is ancestral to which: it provides for the fact of a tree, without dictating its shape.

Proofs are made of definitions, but definitions are not proofs. This is just a starting point.

II

Definitions are dangerous. A perfect definition is an obituary. Even an imperfect definition may be restrictive – an obituary in progress, like a resumé. To define art as what is compared to art is a comprehensive definition; but it would be lethal even if it were not comprehensive. Pater was right in this: art cannot survive the possibility of mutual comparison. There are two reasons.

1. The possibility of comparison confuses the hierarchy of arts and art's place in the hierarchy of activities. It was possible to maintain a distinction of high and low arts only while the conditions of technology denied the low arts the permanence and portability necessary to present them critically as objects of comparison. Criticism is still catching up with what technology did in the 20th century – the fixation of the ephemeral in photos, records, and movies – and meanwhile technology has done much more. Very little that human beings do cannot now be made permanent, portable, and abstract; anything permanent, portable, and abstract can be compared to an art; and thus anything can be an art.

But isn't that a good thing; isn't that progress? Pater himself wanted to extend artistic deliberation to every aspect of life, wanted to "burn with a hard, gemlike flame." He called that "success in life;" so why not bless technology for giving us all success?

But Pater's flame is *hard* – it resists – and it is *gemlike* – it must be cut and shaped. Technology makes us burn with a soft, plastic flame. To live artistically is a commitment; like any commitment, it is defined by what it forswears: vulgarity, compromise, deference, and waste. It is not something you can receive as a gift, not something you can buy. A consumer is not an artist.

Unsleeping technology making unrelieved art will destroy art, but not by cheapening and over-familiarizing it; not by flattening life by raising it all to artistic elevation. Art is a faculty, not an activity. What is done artistically is done by the same means, and with the same technique, as what is done mechanically. Painters and house painters both use brushes and paint; but one is an artist and the other is not. More paint goes on walls than on canvas, but this does not endanger painting as an art. Painting employs the faculty and the activity; house painting employs only the activity.

Instead, the ubiquity and cheapness of art destroys art because the comparisons that define art lose their force when an infinity of potential comparisons promises the certainty of a counterexample. Comparisons become first provisional, then unstable, then uncertain; and art, borderless, falls apart.

2. The possibility of comparing arts confuses quality in arts. This is not a new problem; it has nothing to do with technology.

A great poem "paints a picture"; a great picture "has poetry." A great piece of music "builds in air"; a great building "is frozen music." Great novels "have a theme;" great essays "tell a story." And so forth.

Such reactions are so familiar that their destructiveness is hidden. But they are destructive. They destroy what they praise. They destroy great work because they link genius in one art to mediocrity in another. They imply that the greatest success of a poem to suggest to the reader of sensibility and cultivation what a journeyman painter can show to a child. That a picture succeeds in mere verse. That music succeeds in mere enclosure. The architecture succeeds in a ditty. That a novel succeeds in an epigram. That an essay succeeds in an anecdote.

Of course, if the perceiver is an artist in that other medium, the reaction may itself be a paraphrase of artistic value, and we get *Pictures at an Exhibition*. But that is rare enough to be sublime when it happens. The rest of the time, the comparisons that result from success are so many ways to negate and contain it: to resize it for criticism; to evade some command in it to change; to suppress your envy of its maker, or your despair, in looking on it, for your own efforts.

This could be what Pater really meant: that comparison of single works is not a way to explain them, but to escape them.

III

Comparison creates art; comparison destroys art. What can be done with this double conclusion? Does it make art futile?

Certainly all art is failed art, because all art presupposes that transformation can achieve transubstantiation. Cotton becomes canvas, oil and pigment become paint. Wood and resin come in from the rain to become soundboard; horsehair that lately switched flies becomes bow. A dip in the palette, a flick of the wrist, makes a shape; a touch of rosin, a gesture of the arm, makes a note. Shapes make pictures; notes make music.

What happens next is the same for all arts. They find their way to the same place, to pattern and proportion; what the artist does floats over the matter of the work as ideas float over words. Those who say they love art and despise words deceive themselves: if words are to be despised, so is art; if art is to be respected, so are words. For that *sensuous element* constitutes art not because it is ever special – they all enter through the senses as pale nerve information, and the brain dyes them in feeling – but because it is the antagonist of art. The sweetness of art is the bittersweetness of a fight entered in the certainty of defeat.

This failure is common and universal: it is the world's failure and mankind's, who are likewise the transformation of organic chemistry and chemo-electrical feedback and (unless God help) are likewise, for all that we are perfected, never independent of our matter. And matter has no decorum. What we value most is inflection and recombination of what we value least. What paints and sings, what loves and bears well, what stands for and roars out, is what chews and squats, what sweats and stinks – what dies.

To define arts by comparison, as they must be defined, admits that arts can be defined; and whatever can be defined shares the futility that is the lexicographer's dilemma: words find the words that define them by arcs that are segments of circles. Definition chases itself forever. For many, to be an artist presupposes a contempt for words as compromised over against art as pure, veiling what art penetrates. Life itself, for them, only confuses and conceals where art sees and enters. But this is wrong. There are no exceptions for art. Nothing resolves the mystery. Art appears transcendent because each form makes its own world; but set these worlds against each other and the familiar circle reappears, a great circle described by a skittering orbit of a smooth, sealed mystery.

SOCCER

FEBRUARY 13, 2009   The subject calls for precision. I will follow the American usage of "football" for armored rugby and "soccer" for association football. I don't care about either one. My interest is the *problem* of soccer. By the consensus of the vast majority of human beings, even in the English-speaking world, soccer is the best team sport to watch. Yet Americans do not even reject it; we do not notice it at all – which seems to the rest of the world a fundamental mystery.

But the answer is simple. In the sports that Americans care about the difference between spectators and players is a difference of degree. The spectators of football, basketball, or baseball are capable, or have been capable, of playing the game; the players differ from them only by dedication and hypertrophy. Most of the pleasure is the sense of vicarious participation.

Spectators at a soccer game are as remote from what they watch as spectators at a horse race or a cockfight. Soccer begins in the suppression of instinct; it is an invented and unnatural discipline. In technique soccer is closer to a performance art than to other sports. That is not an insult; art hurts, performers must be tough. But learning to play soccer must begin very young, when habit is ductile and instincts have yet to calcify. To Americans, this remoteness simply excludes soccer from the definition of a sport.

Americans expect and are afforded the sense of vicarious participation everywhere in public life, even at the cost of concealing definite but remote offices and vocations with the vaguer but more sympathetic individualities of the people who hold them. Consider our music, where the perceptibly *individual* singer (especially songwriter), whatever the voice they are blessed or cursed with, eclipses any number of virtuoso instrumentalists, and where even the homuncular pop singer must observe the formality of protesting an artistic identity.

The rest of the world finds it easiest and seemliest to leave each sphere of public life to the kind of personality fit for it. In that respect parliamentary democracy is not unlike soccer, where politicians are not expected to be like people – not better or worse than people, simply different, political all the way through; cells in the political organism of the party, which misleadingly shares a name with what is not at all its American equivalent.

We get more second-rate singer-songwriters than first-rate symphonies; we vote down vague individualities of proved competence for clear individualities with vague credentials and vaguer positions; we watch the silly game of football. But we have this: soccer's enthusiast is the rioter; football's enthusiast is the armchair quarterback, which is one of the world's noblest types. Democracy can work only because of them – the ones who take the time and make the effort to work out *what I would do.*

BESTSELLERS AND BLOCKBUSTERS

FEBRUARY 20, 2009   I think bestsellers and blockbusters should be respected, if only for being timely and workmanlike. Timely and workmanlike, as nebulous qualities go, are harder to achieve than the *luminosity, importance, rawness* and *insight* whose indices adorn blurbs and websites. To yield to the pretensions of the third derivative of an empty movement while damning the formulaic pacing of stock characters through a snap-fit plot seems to me an imbalance of mind.

The one reasonable justification for critical snobbery – fear of the institutional power behind bestsellers and blockbusters, and love of the spirit of independence – has become irrelevant. Now it is the litterateur and the artiste who are the product of a program, who move through conferences and aspire to places in the system; it is the hack who independently conceives a project, carries it out through difficulty, and is left with the task of promotion. That is not to say that the hack should be loved for being independent; only that independence is a bad criterion.

How, then, to explain the persistence of critical snobbery?

A critic, or anyone inclined to be critical, meets an unfamiliar problem in treating a bestseller or a blockbuster. Used to having to curate good things – instructing ignorance, beguiling indifference, or disarming hostility – the critic may lack the art, having gotten by without it, of gracefully adding one particular voice to general acclaim. In this lack they may overrate themselves, take up arms as if criticism had a responsibility to those who do not seek it out, and flail against the unfamiliar force of a human tide, awkward as stylites in a subway station. And on the other side of this lack they may absurdly concede their responsibilities (say, fawning over a TV show, and just as it starts to decline).

This distinct skill, which I will call *corroboration* – distinct from *conversation* – is a useful one. Criticism is not the only context where this empty middle leaves only the poles of hostility or servility. Corroboration makes a pair with conversation, and is more than its match. Conversation has many prerequisites; corroboration is possible wherever communication is possible. Though I doubt it can be taught – for it requires just that broadness and attention and readiness to improvise which cannot be privately exercised – it is a skill that should be expected of the educated, for it is the skill that lets you talk to people as such, and saves the mind from coming to despise the human race in growing to serve it.

True, corroboration approaches dishonesty. There is an urge to corroborate that can induce oversimplification and overconfidence; that, when you have something to contribute – when you are aware of something unknown to your interlocutor's project or observation, yet relevant to it – that compels you to speak. But common discretion will save you: when you open your mouth and say something stupid, the mistake is not being stupid – to be stupid is no more of a mistake than to be young; the mistake is to open your mouth.

Our blogosphere is distinct from and better than its Internet predecessors – especially Usenet – in being founded on this urge. Popular bloggers, in this way, can divide the labor of an essayist, beginning in the Addisonian manner with an incident that got them thinking, but leaving the work of supplying likenesses and drawing conclusions from it to their commenters.

Corroboration, and not conversation, is the mode of discussion in our web; almost as if the possibilities of conversation had been exhausted in the mile-deep threads of the last web, flammable and wild with their flames and trolls, and we now wish to settle into a calmer process, not letting ideas contend directly, but developing them in their separate camps and letting them compete upon the shelves of a marketplace of ideas.

These names are fluid: what I call corroboration and conversation as modes of discussion might be called discussion and argument as modes of conversation or contradiction and development as modes of argument. All these terms are too basic to be used without equivocation. But the two must be distinguished somehow, because confusing them is deadly. To want one and get the other is as bad (among other basic equivocations) as wanting love and getting comfort, as wanting a friend and getting a lover.

Be capable of both; know the season of each. If you corroborate when you should converse or be silent, you will take a side without meaning to. In life you may be a friend to two enemies; in writing you cannot be. If you converse when you should corroborate or be silent, you betray yourself. You cannot, particularly, attack the object of a pleasure without attacking the pleasure itself. Attack the institution of bestsellers and blockbusters and you attack the pleasure that is in stories; and you are not the stronger.

Postscript 2019

This essay is out of date; nowadays, of course, critics are slavish in their praise of blockbusters. But it remains of interest, if only as history.

HIGH CONCEPT

FEBRUARY 27, 2009

Listen up, you want to hear this one.
This guy, the prince, he's not the prince at all,
But no one knows the truth, not even his mom.
The shark could shape-shift, see, and when they did
The deed, the shark had morphed into the king.
The shark? Oh yeah. You heard me right. The shark.
You see this shark has been sent back in time
This shark's a killing machine, a real machine
I mean it, he's a cyborg shark that talks
And changes shape, but I told you that before.
This guy, the prince, he's got no luck with girls
He's kinda weird, he eats his forks and knives
And for a gag he'll crawl under the table
With the dangling legs – we'll quote the theme from *Jaws*.
And he just can't sit still, he's fidgety
'Cause he's part shark, he's always got to move.
But what's the big idea? I'm glad you asked.
This guy, he wants to be the king someday
But he can't be king unless he's got a wife.
So there's this girl the king wants him to wed

A princess too, we'll cast some frigid blonde
But there's this other girl he really wants,
But she's a servant girl and he's a prince.
He runs away and hangs around in bars
He holds his liquor well and glasses too.
This one old sailor type takes him aside
And says he's off the path, this ain't for him
And tells the guy he needs to go to sea.
He books a trip on this big-ass ocean liner
That sinks, and while it's going down, that guy,
The same old guy, appears and tells him how
He's destined to become the chosen one
Gives him a talisman, tells him to go.
And once he hits the water, man, he flies
He's in his element, 'cause he's part shark.
And then his dad shows up, the cyborg shark
And tells his kid how he came back in time
And has a mission from the Vatican
To kill whoever bears the talisman
'Cause there's some ancient secret could get loose.
They raid the coast, searching the ships they sink
Until they sink the ship his girl is on,
The servant girl, the one he really wants.
His dad thinks she should die, he disagrees
He beats his dad and gets the girl, but then
With his last breath, the cyborg shark reveals
He always knew he had the talisman
And tried to keep him safe because he knew
The Vatican had sent more cyborgs back
And they will never stop until they have
The talisman and kill the chosen one.
We end the movie there and start the buzz
For a TV show. The show could run for years.
So tell me what you think and don't hold back.
Now hold on just a minute, think it through –
How dare you sir? That's just ridiculous.

This show is nothing like that anime.
Our talking shark's a cyborg. Theirs just talks.

FLOWERS

MARCH 6, 2009   Flowers are the oldest and first religion, whose sacraments the earth itself performs; the oldest and only universal language, for they say what cannot otherwise be said, what cannot change as language changes. There are flowers for the graves of every people, as there were flowers in the graves of our extinct hominid cousins. And these last colors meant to them all that they still mean.

Our kind of creature arrived with the flowers, and we have never been without them. How flowers shape the human sense of the world can be shown by a few thought experiments.

Imagine the world of the Mesozoic, when dinosaurs ruled the world, so old in their possession that they walked on the fossils of their own kind. And there were no flowers: no flower anywhere, ever; no bloom, no wilt, no blossom, no fruit, only leaves and needles brown and green, yellow and red. No wonder that the earth had to invent the dinosaurs – just to keep itself entertained.

Imagine the world as it would be belonging to orchids, warped and dyed mirrors of flowers – a world where what is to us grotesque, barbarous, lurid, was the rule – a Gothic architecture of nature, as far from nature as we know it as the façade of Notre Dame from the portico of the Parthenon.

Look at the corpseflowers, where never bee alights, that never incense with sweet smells, that never dress up in bright colors, but wear deep reds and purples, colors veined as meat is veined, and the smell of decay for their perfume – corpseflowers that close by day, that open for beetles by night. Do not imagine the world that belongs to them.

Some flowers have resemblances, and the match of the resemblances resembles the match of the flowers: aroids of the pointed leaves. They are even welcome in homes when they have been neutered, glossy green, resilient against the rigors of indoor air, acid in all their stems – some poisonous. But they too have their blossoms, efflorescences impudent and unsheathed; they too imply their own world.

The rose, I think, is half of love; the magnolia, half of longing; the gardenia, half of contentment; the sunflower, half of joy; the lily, half of memory; the wildflowers, more than half of life.

IMAGINATION OF CHILDREN

MARCH 13, 2009   Sentimentality is often cruelty in soft focus; and the sentimental view of the imagination of little children, if sharpened, shows life as a cruel joke. Children come into the world trailing glory that they must at last forget; or they fall into this gross swaddling heap of a world as into a trap. We adults are left to the same fate whether our doom is romantic or gnostic: within, we must look to the children we were to find the springs of our selfhood and the soil of our emotions; and, without, we must heed children as oracles, and strive to shape society to children, and not children to society.

Very smart people believe this; some of the smartest and wisest who ever were. Great art has been made in this belief. Our law, our manners, our architecture all reflect it.

Nonetheless, I have no idea what any of them are talking about.

I remember what it felt like to be a child, and how much I disliked it – the pain, sometimes horror, of weakness and ignorance, of doubt and incomprehension.

And I seem to remember how my imagination worked. In those products of it that I retain I can usually recall the responsible train of thought. Certainly imagination was very different then: fluent, indefatigable, effortless, and pervasive. I would amuse myself at breakfast by dumping spoonfuls of powdered chocolate into my milk and, before each little island sank, giving it a name and a history accounting for how it had come to this woeful end – to disappear beneath the waves.

I suppose that I am the poorer now that I see no such islands – now that the rise and fall of empires no longer attends my breakfast, now that a pile of bricks is not the stuff of castles and henges, now that decayed stumps are not mountain cities in waiting and old foundations promise no secrets.

Yet I feel no loss. I have fewer empires now, but better ones. Then *empire* was a word; now my empires have roads and provinces, frontiers and legions, temples and palaces, god-kings and the mandate of heaven;

know how to pave stone roads and cast iron pagodas; know the aching legs of the pilgrim road and the stink the morning after the triumph rides through, the must of archives and catacombs.

Imagination was then outside of me, a thing of names and pictures to reach for and mix; and now it is a thing inside of me, ransacking my experience for new things to name. This is fair trade, and a place in a cycle. And if I do well at it, other will have those names to play with when I myself am only a name.

You say: good for you; but most people are not so lucky. What of those who grow up to lose their imagination? Who have it ground or drained out of them? Who spurn and abandon it?

But distinguish active imagination from passive. Surely the popularity of all kinds of imaginative fiction precisely among those who have no opportunities to exercise imagination – the more purely imaginative, the more popular – demonstrates that the faculty is not lost.

Words on a page, moving pictures on a screen; these are but indices and suggestions. Coleridge (which is to say, romanticism) saves the appearances by asserting that here we do not engage imagination; instead, we *suspend disbelief.* But this is absurd, for two reasons. First, it implies that dreaming, and not waking, is the natural activity of the mind. But our dreams rely on our waking lives for their matter. That is not to cheapen dreams, but to esteem them: dreams take work, and show the quality of the dreamer. Second, it implies that it is possible to believe without imagining – that a story, once told, contains in itself everything necessary to believe it; that the audience need only let its guard down to be possessed by another's imagination. But communication does not work this way. You cannot tell the time of day to someone who cannot imagine a clock. You cannot tell a story to someone who cannot imagine stories. The audient imagination, though it is passive – active but only in reaction – is still there. It may even be very strong, though in an awkward, china-breaking way. But why the imbalance? What happened to the active imagination of these people?

There is something, I think, that disestablishes imagination, that destroys it – but not the darkness of the world or the cruelty of life, not the pollution of sex or the preoccupation of business. It is, however, related to the end of childhood: it is the strait of adolescence. On the one side is pettiness; on the other side, grandiosity. Both can wreck the imagination. The field where imagination is useful is in those things and events that are too great for an individual, yet small enough for humanity; if it shrinks to cunning, or inflates to philosophy, it dies; but there is a middle course, and the delight and mercy of the middle course between cunning and philosophy is that when it is held cunning and philosophy fall in beside it.

OLD TEXTBOOKS

MARCH 20, 2009   Among the prizes I hope to return with whenever I visit a secondhand bookstore are old textbooks. By *old* I mean at least before WWII and preferably before WWI. This sounds perverse. What good are old textbooks full of obsolete information? Leave those elegant spines to the decorators.

It is self-evident that the preponderance of textbooks now in use, at every level, are trash. They are written by the narrow, sold by the greedy, bought by the lazy, and read by the desperate and the indifferent. If they serve any purpose it is to harness students. They have such a thin and clouded connection to their subjects, and approach by such roundabout and senseless ways, that they keep nags and racehorses creeping on at the same rate – a sort of pedagogical QWERTY, slowing learning down to keep the parts from interfering. But I do them too much credit: to recognize a purpose implies a planning intelligence they lack.

I wish this was a problem to be solved; but the condition of textbooks is not even a symptom: it is an opportunistic infection – a disease of the sick. Students end up with dubious textbooks like the poor end up with dubious food. The problem to fix is not the vector of exploitation, but what allows exploitation.

The prevailing educational method is consistent at all levels. It is to approach truth by white lies: to start with over-simplifications and, over time, to gradually amend and refine them. This is not inherently bad. Better that children be lied to and told that the earth is round like a ball, than assume it flat until they can understand an oblate spheroid. But, to smooth the way, we have universalized this method and consigned all the final disabusals to specialists. Thus even the best-educated, if they leave their education to others, are left with beliefs that are not quite true; knowledge that is not quite accurate; ideas that are not quite clear.

Overall, this system works well and does little harm. But it is not harmless. We accommodate ignorance in order to dilute it; but while the dilution is temporary, the accommodation is permanent. The temporary defeat of ignorance incurs the permanent removal of the shame of ignorance. The student's mind starts out as a small lake; rivers of knowledge swell it to a sea; but if it has no natural outlet, the end result is a salt lake of uncertainty where nothing can live.

Scholars and scientists squawk when they informally try to unfold their beloved disciplines to their students and the students balk. They blame the decadence of society outside of education; but these students, having lived on sandwich meat, choke on bones.

Relativism is not a disease that afflicts education from outside. It is the condition of success in education. To succeed in the system you must accept that the truths you are allowed know are relative to your age, and the truths you are allowed to say are relative to the subject you say them about. What do the students gain who try to compass in a single intellectual universe both, say, literature and mathematics? Burdened with contradictions to resolve and distinctions to make, they will go slower in both. In trying to make the superstructure of mathematics clearer, and the substructure of English more exact, they will alienate the teachers of both. They seem to question the character of the mathematician, and the significance of the reader. But if they separate each subject into its own intellectual universe; if they two-time the intellect, dally with sentences and equations on a schedule that ensures they never meet, then they need only learn to play each game by its own rules.

I do not indict. These evils are the evils of universal education, and universal ignorance has evils far greater. I only want to suggest, to those who are vexed by this system, that there have been other ways, ones that they can follow by themselves. You do not have to reform society to do better than society.

If you have the chance, get an old language textbook – they are the easiest to get – and place it beside a modern one for the same language. The first thing you should notice is that the old textbook is shorter. The second is that it is far more systematic. Compare the sections on pronunciation. In my experience, here even the best new textbooks are lacking; even the worse old textbooks are better both in practical guidance – how to breathe, how to articulate – and in respect for the language's diversity

– this sound is pronounced this way in this city. Modern textbooks are hobbled by trying to serve two masters. First, they fear seeming silly to linguists by supplying rules of thumb without direct physiological basis. (Formerly, books taught how to be passable in pronunciation, and correct in grammar; now they teach how to be correct in pronunciation, and passable in grammar. Formerly you succeeded if natives thought you sounded like them but wrote better; now you succeed if natives think you sound better than they do and write like them.) Second, they fear to intimidate students by qualifying their instruction. What is left is too simple to be accurate, and too diffident to be useful – just enough to mislead.

But the best comparison is simply between tables of contents. Look at the contents page of an old textbook and you learn something without reading a word of the text, because the structure of the exposition follows the structure of the subject. Often that simple glance reveals an expository structure that remains obscurely and arbitrarily implied in the modern vocabulary of the subject. What structure does a modern textbook follow? Sometimes it follows the subject – a textbook of anatomy can be expected to be structured in systems of organs. But, more often, some outside consideration decides the structure. The books show rough seams between the work of different contributors; or it duplicates and reduplicates to include everything any teacher might need in any order or from any perspective it might be needed; or it affects that certain medicine-coating cuteness – but the coating is transparent and no one is fooled; or it simply tries to be marketably novel – but the novelty is extrinsic and burdens the student with peculiarities they will have to purge before further study.

One might excuse them by pleading the necessity of a teacher's presence. But a textbook that, to be useful, requires a good teacher, is itself useless – a sufficiently good teacher can teach from anything. (And anything, generally, is what they get.)

These textbooks, you object, are basic. What of more advanced textbooks? But my point is that there is no reason, except for educational methods, for advanced textbooks to exist. A good textbook is one which starts with ignorance and lets out into primary sources, scholarly apparatus, experiment and apprenticeship.

It is sometimes easier to start with an old textbook, learn the structure of a subject, then correct that understanding with attention to subsequent discoveries and developments, than to try to get a sense of the structure of a subject from working with modern materials – which have no reason to show it, and every reason to hide it. Old buildings are at once examples and textbooks of architecture in beam, pillar, arch, vault, buttress, and cantilever. Their appearance shows their structure. Modern buildings obey the same physics; but cheap steel allows them to hide their structures under a fraudulent simplicity. It is the same with modern textbooks and cheap paper.

Most differences between old and new textbooks are due to bad faith or honest confusion. Some, however, are of another kind: they belong to the tendency of our education to mix the professional and the humanistic.

I do not know whether the prestige of the professional specialties pulled these concerns into their orbit, or whether the humanities' abdication necessitated this seizure. It would be more satisfying to blame it on the humanities as the foreseeable consequence of the narcissism of Marxism and Theory, the professions learning to get along without those who, vainly thinking themselves indispensable, made no effort to be useful. But this cannot be not true. The bids of economics, sociology, and psychology to supply the vacant center have all failed. Something is exerting an overpowering centrifugal force on intellectual life – it is not that the king is dead, but that the throne is broken. What exerts this force, what broke the throne, I do not know – except to say that while it has been present throughout the twentieth century, it did not predominate until the great nameless revolution that brought in our world of think tanks, institutional investors, bourgeois bohemianism, fashion without fashions and pervasive reform-renewal-rethink-update.

However it happened, every profession has its own prosthetic complement of hyphenated ethicists, journalists, writers, and historians; and soon entirely separate camps of science artists or math musicians. Much of the steady swelling of university time expected of a professional is due to this added burden. A first rate medical school can no longer rest after teaching the doctor anatomy, epidemiology, pharmacology; they must also teach the doctor – as a doctor, not as a human being – how to think clearly, how to express their thoughts, how to relate to life, to their emotions, to other people's emotions, how to solve ethical dilemmas. This intellectual autarky has always been possible for doctors and lawyers at least; but it has spread nearly everywhere. (If you wish to see it happening to the hard sciences, visit the Edge Foundation.)

There are, for most musical instruments, two ways to learn to read music: staff and tablature. Staff is the familiar texture of lines, dots, and dashes. It is a way of writing music which is nearly the same for all instruments: while there are usually considerations that keep a player of one instrument from sight-reading music written for another, the discrepancies of notation do not add to those inherent in the instruments' different physical possibilities.

Tablature is much easier to learn than staff. If two people begin to learn the same instrument at the same time, there will be a long interval while the player from tablature can laugh at the slow progress of the player from staff. But in the end there are places the tablature player cannot go; worse, that player cannot talk about music with other musicians, must start over if they want to learn a second instrument, and is as far from being able to transcribe for their instrument, compose for it, or even produce individual interpretations for it, as they were before they could play anything at all.

The analogy, of course, is that new textbooks are written in tab, but old textbooks are written in staff: new textbooks give proficiency without cultivation; old textbooks, presupposing cultivation, delay proficiency to allow for excellence.

I often hear the phrase *learn how to learn*; but never having heard a definition of it I take it for a catchphrase. Still, it is catching because it would in fact be a good idea. Our system of education, however, has been engineered to serve an opposite end. It is not even a bad end; but if you have another end in mind you must look outside the machine, and its only outside is its before. Being old does not make a textbook good. Old textbooks are obsolete, silly, stupid, bigoted, and boring. But there is gold there that cannot be had anywhere else, if you will pan for it.

CIVILIZATIONS

MARCH 27, 2009   All theories of universal history, from Ibn Khaldûn to Toynbee, share the same ambiguity: to what do they apply? If history has laws, what are they laws for? Call it a civilization; where does one civilization stop, and another begin?

To be useful as objects of study the units of universal history must be smaller than the whole of history, yet larger than any form of political organization, short of empire.

Sometimes these units are obvious. Probably there is a Chinese civilization; probably there was one each for the Aztec world and the Inca; probably the Hellenistic ecumen constituted one – but should this be distinguished from the Roman imperium? Should *Romani* be distinguished from *Rhomaioi*? Or was Byzantium part of a Christian world? Is there a Christendom? Is there as a Ummah? And so on.

Sometimes we distinguish two civilizations because we study them by different means. The continuity between the Roman Empire and the Byzantine Empire is, I think, far more important than the latter's adventitious Christian characteristics. But because Rome was Latin (and Greek, of course), and Byzantium was (a peculiar) Greek; because the scholarly apparatus for the study of Roman history stretches back to the Renaissance, but Byzantine studies are mostly late nineteenth century in origin; because Roman history precedes, and Byzantine history parallels, that period of history which is, in the West, called *modern* over against *ancient* – because of all this, they are studied separately; and being studied separately, they are seen as separate.

Certain kinds of difference thus force us to posit disparity. Similarly, resemblance may imply unity where none exists. Because the caliphs borrowed their statecraft from the Sassanid Empire, and adopted many of its artistic traditions, they are often taken to belong to a common line of "oriental despots" – which does the Shahnashahs too much credit for ambition, and the Caliphs too much credit for power. Ethnicity is another decoy – Hungarians are not Huns. So are titles – Tsar nor Qaisar is proper Caesar.

If neither resemblance nor difference suffice to taxonomize, how should we proceed?

Consider the relatively clear case of China. Chinese civilization as we know it is not of singular antiquity: it is speculative to speak of Chinese culture before the Qin. Presumably it was more diverse than what survived the infamy of Shi Huangdi; and the relative homogeneity of Chinese culture since may be attributed to that memetic bottleneck.

What is the substance of that continuity? The ideas of Confucius are uppermost. Does that suffice? That we admire Homer does not make us

Greeks; but it might, if we looked to Homer to tell us how to live – as many Chinese still do (or do again) to Confucius. But to say *Confucius* implies that there has been only one, which is false; the Confucius to whom temples were built by emperors is not the Confucius whose ideas are invoked in the party conferences of Beijing. The lessons drawn are very different.

Very different; but not utterly different. Utter difference would be different answers to different questions; but here are different answers to the same question. Even the Cultural Revolution that repudiated Confucius did not propose a new question, only a new answer to the standing question: *How can men be good?*

Once we ask this question – *How can men be good?* – we will find it very difficult to decompose into smaller ideas. For instance, does it imply that men are capable of being good? Not so; the doctrines of Legalism suppose that men cannot be good unless compelled to be; but the answer, though opposite to Confucius, is still to the same question. The meaning of each term of the question changes – men as parts of essentially unitary rural families, as individual city-dwellers, as members of the bureaucracy, as members of the Party; good as benevolent, good as obedient, good as doctrinally correct – but the question itself is perfectly stable.

Can we find stable questions elsewhere? Consider the Greeks. How at the beginning, Homer arrives with an answer and a question, *What is the good life?* How at the end, or even after the end, Hypatia goes out onto the streets of Alexandria with a bravery the equal of any church martyr's, to show the benighted that there could be such a thing as a good life; how Julian tried and failed, despite absolute power, to seek that good life for himself, and induce others to seek it.

Neither Hypatia nor Julian were stupid. Hypatia thought that the strength of Christianity was its willingness to seek out and teach even the lowest and most wretched; so she did the same. Julian seems to have thought that the strength of Christianity was its focus on a wonderworking man, and tried to set up Apollonius of Tyana in the place of Jesus. Neither of these analyses were simply wrong; but both were inadequate, because they missed the scope of what had happened. Christianity was not a new answer to the question of the good life; it was a new question: *How can I be saved?*

There are many continuities between the Christianity we know and

Hellenism; but Christianity does not require Hellenism to inform it. Think of the Armenian, Coptic, and Nestorian churches. The Hellenic world formed Christianity, but the result was something that could be transplanted and flourish elsewhere.

Only the appearance of dependency and continuity between Christianity and Hellenism leads us to expect correlation. But there is no idea in Christianity that correlates with the Good Life, and there is no classical idea that correlates with Salvation.

This is essential. Had Christianity simply given (as did the mystery religions) a new answer to the Classical question, a new form of the good life, even one universally accessible and approachable, even one with a face and a story dividing history into before and after, it could never have displaced the weight of tradition and intellectual sophistication on the Pagan side. But by asking a new question, Christianity removed Paganism's advantage – found the lever to move the world.

The other great religions of the historical period afford more examples in their rise. Buddhism's question is clear: *How can I escape suffering?* Islam's only seems harder because English has never absorbed the relevant vocabulary. Still, it can be approximated: *What is the straight way?* or *the straight path? (sirat al-mustaqîm)*, the *safe way (sharî'ah)*, the *right direction (qiblah, sunnah)*.

And what of the West? Does this method allow us to characterize the West as a civilization? I have already posited a line between Classical and Christian civilization as hard as that between any other pair. What, then, is the West? A variant on Christian civilization, or a post-Christian one?

The West, I think, contains four separate civilizations: the Christian, the Enlightenment, the Modern, and the Postmodern.

This sounds extreme, too much, as if being too close magnifies distinctions that distance would smooth out. But this diversity is due to extraordinary circumstances: only about 500 years, yes; but 500 years of the greatest rate of accession of wealth in human history, 500 years of discovery and invention, 500 years of almost continuous and descendingly brutal warfare. Never anywhere else has humanity made so much progress so quickly, and never anywhere else has such instability – dynastic rivalries, balances of power, secret treaties, competing ideologies – been prolonged without collapse.

And why is the West different? Because the West discovered America.

This might be a controversial thing to say. Certainly the volume of writing about Western civilization that does not stop to consider the unique event that stands in the middle of it is astonishing. It is like reading a biography where, between chapters, the subject goes from riding the bus to driving his Lamborghini, and having to refer to outside sources to discover that, in the interim, he had *won the lottery* – won the lottery, and used the proceeds to fund a string of bank robberies.

This is where we run up against the limit of *lawfulness* in history. If history is lawful – if history has laws – shouldn't they explain things like the discovery of America? They shouldn't; they can't. Every system of laws, at least every system of laws at a higher level than basic physics, has to allow for anomalies and externalities, phenomena that originate beyond its boundaries and traduce its principles. Chemistry cannot compass the splitting of the atom. The laws of history have nothing to say about the discovery of continents; it is a disruption every bit as massive and arbitrary as the fall of a comet.

Suddenly, a new world. Two golden empires in periods of political instability that yielded, as if by destiny, to bumbling adventurers. Two vast continents, infinitely rich in resources animal, vegetable, and mineral, their populations totally unprepared for European arms or European diseases. Gold and silver, yes, but also new crops, new domesticated animals, new drugs – a vast river of every kind of wealth that flowed torrentially into Europe for hundreds of years and supercharged its economy and its intellect.

Nothing like this has ever happened, before or since. And Europe did nothing special to earn it. It wasn't science. They owe the discovery to a geographically incompetent, morally bankrupt eccentric with no other distinction than that – not unimportant – of being a superlative navigator. It wasn't technology. Those golden empires fell not to gunpowder – gunpowder was still a curiosity – but to swords, lances, and crossbows. (In men, in means, in method, the conquest of the Americas was an extension of the *Reconquista*.) And, in large part, it wasn't even on purpose. Nature waged biological warfare on their behalf long before anyone, victim or victor, understood what was happening.

Nor, once they had it, did they do anything special to deserve it. The history of European exploration, invasion, and exploitation in the Americas alternates between impractical idealism and incompetent greed, with each new doomed project building on the compacted ruins of the failure of the last. But the tide was in Europe's favor, and though it rolled out every time, each time it rolled in, it rolled in a little higher, a little redder.

It could have happened somewhere else; it certainly could have happened to China. But it happened to Europe. And out of the tremendous and unprecedented reaction were precipitated, in quick succession, three new civilizations: the Enlightenment; the Modern; and the Postmodern.

Christianity asks: *How can I be saved?* The civilization of the Enlightenment asks: *How can men be perfected?*

Not coincidentally, this resembles the Chinese question; though their knowledge was sketchy, Europe at the time of the Enlightenment was much affected by the mere idea of China.

But the two questions are not the same. *Good* is one side of a balance; and the same people who are now led to be good by a good example, might in the future be led to be bad by a bad example. Perfection is different. Good is prior to evil: a good person is one uncorrupted by evil. Perfection is posterior to evil: a perfected person is one from whom evil has been removed – whether the causes of evil, the means to do evil, or even the hurt in evil – so that, by some constitution or adjustment of society, by checks or balances or an invisible hand, evil is turned to good.

The US and (loosely) the UK are still Enlightenment countries; but they are the only ones. Most countries in the world belong to a different civilization, which may be called Modern. The Modern question runs: *How can we progress?*

The line of descent is clear. What is progress? If we understand *progress* as the way from what we are now to what we can be, the Modern question is partly implicit in that of the Enlightenment. But the Enlightenment's perfection is a thinkable, ponderable one, one in view; while the perfection at the end of progress is one we cannot now understand – a destination we cannot see until we get there, a horizon that recedes as we approach.

Modernity can be opposed to reason – witness the various systems of historical dialectic that have tried to replace reason – but, in its most common and only surviving form, Modernity does not oppose reason. Instead, after doing all that it can to cultivate reason, Modernity implicitly consents that the best use of reason is to recognize a forward movement in history which is unanswerable to reason and cannot be reasoned about – that the end of all our thinking is to climb to a perspective where we can stop thinking.

The name "Postmodern" is very unfortunate – unfortunate because it is ugly, and unfortunate because it is inaccurate. This civilization is coeval with Modernism; there was a generation or two (when Heine and Marx could dine companionably) which, having rejected the Enlightenment, contained the beginnings of both these civilizations: asking about the world, *How can we progress?* and about themselves – *What is my story?*

There seems to be a general suspicion now that before and beyond the West people do not and did not believe that the individual human being could have a story worth telling. They believed in the possibility of an ideal human being; and if there is such a thing as an ideal human being, then the value of the details of the life of any individual is only that of a case study – showing either where and why (taking warning!) they failed, or where and how (learn from it!) they succeeded.

The dubious conclusion is that the pleasure we feel in telling our own stories is a new one, one invented (by Shakespeare?) and taught to us. But human beings are not made of civilization; civilization is made of human beings. A more plausible distinction is that we contribute to the idea of having a story the idea of having our own story. We do not like to have to share our story with others – to be of a type – and we do not like those who publicly identify themselves with a story – the self-made man, the saved whore, the enlightened fanatic, the illuminated disbeliever. We think the story more plausible as it is more particularized, subverted or ironized, excused or made sympathetic. (This kind of storytelling is Romantic in form; but the Romantics were not Postmoderns – they believed in ideals, ones within view and within reach.)

Postmodernism is not simply a great rejection of all principle and belief. It uses ideas like relativism or deconstruction to clear places for itself; but within those places, Postmoderns are hardly nihilists – instead their moral sense seems to me exceptionally, even vulnerably, sensitive and delicate.

Postmodernism – though it applies to several distinct and mutually antagonistic systems of morality – has only one moral method. This method is difficult to recognize as such because it runs backward. Other civilizations teach morality by the morality play; Postmodernism teaches the morality of the play. That is, in part, an aesthetic morality – against ugliness and boredom, for beauty and diversity – and in part an emotional morality – for the sympathetic and relatable, against the pitiless and single-minded. It could be thought of as a musical morality: what is evil is the dissonant, the out of tune, and the off-key; what is good is the tempered, the resolved, and the danceable. This gives postmoderns an extraordinary moral susceptibility – one in which every part of life is either expected to find some moral dimension (*part of the proceeds go to blank*) or to serve some moral purpose (*it's not just blank, it's a celebration of freedom/tradition/life*); and gives them a unique expectation of moral congruity – that the entirety of society should harmonize; that it is possible in this world, without hypocrisy, to be at once rich and generous, successful and kind, powerful and honest.

This idea of *theatrical* morality may sound strange in the context of Postmodernism. In particular, the name "postmodern" is applied in literature to writing that is suspicious of narrative, even hostile to it; writing that tries to take into account the fact of its being written; narrative that sees itself – the meta, the inter, and the recursive.

The literature of a civilization is not so much as record of its beliefs as a record of its obsessions. In the midst of the Enlightenment, Hume dedicated himself to dismantling reason not because he rejected reason, but because it obsessed him. Nothing is more natural than that the name "postmodern" should stand for an obsession with narrative. But we only *break down* narrative the way musicians *break down* a tune. We are not the enemies of narrative; we are its virtuosi.

All this praise I afford to balance my conclusion that the only Postmodern government that the world has yet seen was Nazi Germany. That Nazism was distinctly Postmodern does not mean that Postmodernism causes Nazism. Before Versailles and the self-destruction of the Enlightenment, the only Modern state was that of the Bolsheviks, and Communism was the only systematic Modern political philosophy; but Communism is dead (and undead), and most of the world belongs to some form of Modernity. Communism did not exhaust or characterize Modernism; Jacobinism did not exhaust or characterize the Enlightenment; Nazism did not exhaust or characterize Postmodernism.

But Nazism was entirely Postmodern. Its view of history was pure drama: the past the agon of Aryan and the rest, the present the agon of Aryan and Jew, the future the agon of civilization and Bolshevism. "What is my story?" Hitler asked himself, and answered with *Mein Kampf*. "What is my story?" Germany asked Hitler, who answered first with victory in the field stolen by a stab in the back from betrayers at home, then with *Germantum* and a German project and destiny which reached somehow back to Arminius and the Teutonic Knights and stretched ahead into *Anschluß* and *Grossdeutschland*. "What is my story?" young men and women asked Hitler, who answered with how Jewish conspiracy had stolen their pride and their opportunity, and that the time was a time for blood – enemy blood to spill, dirty blood to drain, pure blood to breed and spread – a time for blood and for iron, for sharpness and hardness – the West is in danger, forget decadent scruples and ornamental principles, forget law and mercy, get them before they get us – and generations later parts of this story live and still have power.

This fourfold division of the West is an unfamiliar one, but not difficult to construct. The harder test of the method is those ancient civilizations which had thought but not thinkers. There was certainly ancient Egyptian thought; but there were no ancient Egyptian thinkers. The same of Sumer, Babylon, Tenochtitlan, Cuzco. I can only make suggestions. In Egypt, for example, *how can I survive?* – and the answers develop from talismanic provisions against everyday dangers to elaborate systems for the safe approach to the afterlife. In Sumer, *whose am I?* – their idea of the god of the city being not the guardian but the owner of the city, the city's workers the god's slaves, its officials the god's foremen. In Mesoamerica, *how can the world be saved?* – a precocious question, but, as we who have long lived in fear of nuclear winter and now live in fear of global warming should know, not an irrational one.

All this is doubly speculative. It is part of the speculative at best prospect of a science of universal history; and, being an essay written from memory, not a researched treatise, it is less an analysis than a riff. But I have found this way of thinking to be a useful approach to problems beside those of universal history; and, though the idea may not suffice for a system, I consider it worthwhile to oppose the commonplace that all human beings, when they begin to wonder about the world and themselves, begin by asking the same questions. It is a disservice to philosophy and anthropology alike to diffract all philosophies and all systems of thought and story through a prismal catechism of eternal questions – "Who are we? Where do we come from? What is the meaning of life?" – sundering into absurd and tortuous fragments structures of thought whose organic integrity derives from their proper niches in the ecology of possible questions.

Yet suppose that I were right? Surely there is danger in proposing a new mode of diversity to an already fractious species, and in dividing what geography, language, and culture have joined together. But when 800 years ago, in another aside to the science of universal history, Ibn Khaldûn proposed that the diversity of human physiognomies that we call race is not the result of the individual histories of the children of Noah, but of adaptation to climate – then he, by proposing that that diversity was not adventitious, distinguished the real basis for unity. So I could – must – hope that a basis for explaining the most fundamental differences in belief as differences in approach, instead of weaknesses of mind or perversities of will, could make them less bitter.

KALASHNIKOV'S DREAM

APRIL 3, 2009   [The atom bomb is a common subject of literary meditation; and in the history of the 20th century Kalashnikov's dream was at least as important as Szilard's.]

Now that the battle is over Mikhail lies in his sickbed
  Dreaming of faraway home, dreaming of battles to come.
Thinking of windmills, thinking of lawnmowers, hoping for good
    work
  Something to earn him a place, something his country can bless.
Russia his motherland, cruel cold mother who knows and commands
    him
  Exiled his childhood land, gave him a freezing wind
Russia his motherland, spendthrift spending her children in millions,
  Loading her sons into trains, planting the fields with their bones.
Russia his mother is dying, bleeding from hundreds of deep wounds
  Counting the men to a gun while they have a gun for each man.
Mikhail was gentle, but Germany's evil buries his conscience
  Killing his slow-fingered friends – nothing to raise but their hands.
Surely the soldier who fights for his homeland should have a fair
    chance
  Armed with a gun of his own, faithful through muddying rain.
Germany makes them so complex, even the parts have their pieces
  Numberless sockets and springs, pistons and delicate prongs

Some piece always remained when he put them together in secret.
  Though they would fire the same, surely each piece had a home?
Mikhail was trained for the weapons of farmers, lawnmowers thresh-
    ers and grain mills,
  Even if he had a plan – still he would work all alone.
All that he knows is that all that is useful proves to be simple,
  Simple, plain as a pole; useful, sure as a nail.
All that he knows is that all that is complex is useless,
  Fickle as gamblers' cards, faithless as diplomats' words.
Raw with the shame of his innocence Mikhail drifts off to deep sleep
  Thinks of the friends he has lost, thinks of how vain were their
    boasts
Dreams of a faceless rumor he heard told somewhere in darkness
  Telling the news of a bomb, news of men bottling doom
News of the race for a weapon whose hell fire godlessly damns men,
  Peoples a city with ghosts, blinds with the dawn of its blast.
Cold in his thin sheets Mikhail dreams of a way to do better
  What is its use at the last, leaving nothing but waste?
Mikhail dreams of a weapon cheaper than shoes for the soldier,
  Gun for the beaten and lost, gun for the faceless and least.
Gun to make every man equal, gun to take meaning from conquest,
  Empire only a dream, something that lived out its time.
Armed with their own strength men need not fear the machines of
    the new age,
  No more be ground by the wheel, no more be slaves for the call.
Simpler even than simple, simpler even than instinct
  Easy as sitting to cook, easy as lying to sleep
Obvious pieces that fatefully fit and have joy in the fitting
  Clip slams home with a click, chamber charged with a cock,
Thumb on the lever to let loose, take aim and hold tight,
  Tolerant pistons jerk, blow back drum rolls bark.
Restlessly Mikhail dreams in his sickbed here where the world ends,
  Far from the fate of his name, far from remembering home.

POWER OUTAGES

APRIL 10, 2009   Once all the work is done and nothing remains but waiting and biding, you may as well romanticize an unavoidable difficulty. So long as you avoid forming a sentimental attachment, to romanticize lets you force some benefit from an experience that would otherwise only humiliate and exhaust. True, it would seem more honest not to romanticize, to bear difficulty as difficulty without renaming it opportunity or insight; but life is not long enough for such purity. We work with what we get.

Long power outages are a good example. They waste time, they subtract days from habit and use. And here in Louisiana, where such power outages are usually due to hurricanes, they mean the labor of cleanup and repair and the horror of the radio. After Katrina, without power and thus without TV, I saw none of the sights that, as I have read, horrified the nation and the world; but I heard the voices. I heard a woman in terror calling from her attic as the water rose around her feet; I heard a radio host, in a soft radio host's voice, tell his caller that the best thing for her to do would be to find something heavy and break a hole through her roof. I don't remember if she called back. (I was in the audience; by the time my own property was accessible, volunteers were being left idle or turned back.)

A long power outage is a kind of experiment in material culture. The result is not the present collapsing into the past, but a barrier giving way so the past and present can mingle. You learn strange things about familiar objects. A paperback book, for example, cannot be read by the light of a single candle. The pages will not lie flat; they shadow one another. Two candles are required, one for each page.

More interesting is how thin the habits of technological life are. Only a week passed before I was rising with the sun and turning in at nightfall. Food preparation became so difficult that orderly meals reappeared. I found myself dreading the waning of the moon and the nights of unappealable dark that followed.

That is a genuine connection with the past: old poems have been a little different ever since. It was, I think, more genuine than the recreations of re-enactors and the lives of sects that reject technology, for we were not leaving technology; technology had left us: we were not withdrawing from society; society forgot us. No officials came to check, no functionaries offered help. Not for long, but for long enough, we were out of touch and beyond help.

But which past, and in which parts? Technology requires knowledge, and the limit of knowledge is the limit of technology. Nineteenth century technology with twenty-first century knowledge is twenty-first century technology. And there was always the car for spiritual refuge – the spaceship of the piney void.

Of course, the same event was much worse for others, who never had the chance to romanticize. But all of us are better prepared now – another Katrina would not rival the first. And as technology miniaturizes and gadgetizes, its empire of propane, lithium batteries, and LEDs does not abdicate when the wires go cold.

A power outage interrupts habit; and like all interruptions of habit it discovers by contrast. Life is lived mostly by a borrowed pace: observing paths, speed limits, hours, appointments; following, catching up on, awaiting. A power outage, in suspending all these rhythms, shows what is very hard to see among the lights – shows that these rhythms are not things that you have made part of you, but things that have made you part of them. And you must measure what you give to each in the knowledge that it can take everything you have to give.

And then, suddenly, the lights come back on; the screens are alive again, the voices have faces again; you stop thinking about the weather; the hours are yours again to use, to apply or to waste. Now you can rest; now you can smile at what strange thoughts there are to think when thinking is all you can do.

Year Three

"The god who loves his beetles is the same god who loves us. We are building his altars."

REINVENTION

APRIL 17, 2009   Sometimes the most effective insult is the one that is not obviously insulting. First you are insulted; then you insult yourself with the awareness of your own ignorance. But some insults are insulting only by convention. This is the case with *reinvention*. "You've reinvented the wheel!" But why not reinvent the wheel? You might learn something.

Reinvention is either repetition or reconception. Repetition achieves the same result by the same method; reconception achieves the same result by a new method. Repetition, while it may be valuable for the repeater, is valueless in itself; reconception is valuable in itself because it adds to understanding.

Repetition is valueless in itself because it is wasteful. It has value for only three conditions: first, where the desired invention is unattainable, but its use is familiar; second, where the idea of the invention travels faster or more freely than its workings, and can be reinvented more efficiently than obtained; and third, when the waste of reinvention is outweighed by the desire for the habit of invention. The third value is mine.

Invention is not itself a faculty, but it is the simplest combination of the faculties, employing reason, memory, and imagination in equal proportions. That old threefold scheme is incidental – any division will do; what matters is the equality of its parts. Invention is that use of the mind which is limited not by the power of its parts, but by the speed and life of its connections; not by its strength, but by its agility.

Invention requires practice; but because it is an act of all faculties, the usual methods of practice – set problems, which exclude memory; études, which exclude imagination; and exercises, which exclude reason – cannot develop it. It must grow with a round habit, equal on all sides. For this, it requires real problems: problems that arise in useful work and productive projects.

Yet most of the problems we encounter in our work and projects have already been solved. For the sake of efficiency, speed, and husbanding our mortal time, research and reuse are usually the right choice for any problem considered alone. But what of problem-solving generally? Invention is a habit; and there is no habit of invention without reinvention.

Reinvention is valuable for the reinventor, as practice. But in itself, an act of reinvention can be valuable in two ways: the public value of a new approach; and the private value of understanding. And these values, though independent, may coexist.

The value of a new approach is obvious in mathematics, since only in mathematics is the result of each approach demonstrably the same. Transcendent numbers transcend the awkward operational definitions by which human beings named them – the ratio of diameter to circumference, the rate of interest perpetually compounded – they are rediscovered again and again, the world's true eternal conspiracy, everything traces back to them, they are behind all the fronts, inside all the shells and shadows. The sums of infinite series, the falling of coins on grids, the charted growth of flowers – there are an infinity of ways to reinvent them, and every way adds to our mastery of the world by revealing new shapes under which these our permanent companions can be found – culminating in the glorious abridgment of Euler's identity.

In the spectrum of intellect mathematics is usually placed at one extreme, poetry at the other; but here, in the uses of reinvention, these extremes touch. All poetry is the reinvention of poetry; reinvention on new models and in new contexts: some new model perception (a flea, a red wheelbarrow), some new model interaction (the death of a lutenist god, the speech of a leech-gatherer), some new modeling context (splendor in the grass, dark Satanic mills, the worshipers who must tighten the bolts unwarned). And poems are not alone: much of technology has been reinvented: what was built on rumor before the plans arrived, like the cotton gin; what was reinvented blindly to avoid infringement of a patent, like the PC.

The private value of reinvention is to advance understanding. The simplest form is the imperative to recast another's thoughts *in your own words*. But this is not really students' business. By rephrasing students better remember another's understanding; but by reinvention one better understands. Indeed, where the strictures of licensing and regulation, and the friction of custom and community, outweigh the benefits of study and imitation, the rational course is to reinvent what you would know, instead of learning it. The hard parts are done already: you know that it is possible, what it is good for, why it is needful; the usual limits of human ability and conditions of human fallibility hold; the work is a matter of filling in blanks, which can usually be spliced with pieces of other disciplines.

All intellectual activities can be divided into those where reinvention is useful and those where reinvention is necessary. Those in which reinvention is useful but not necessary are the sciences and design; those in which reinvention is necessary are the arts, and the professions.

There are new things to be done in science, new discoveries to be made, new instruments leading to new worlds of exploration; and there are new things to be done in design, new needs to answer, new patterns to define. Here the effort of reinvention could always be applied to invention.

But in the arts and the professions nothing is really new. To choose two, there is nothing new in literature or law. We cannot add new behaviors to those that Homer and Shakespeare knew; we cannot add new patterns to those that Aristotle and Machiavelli documented. If something in literature or law appears to be new, then it is gibberish, or it is deceit, or you do not understand it. Nothing can be done in either that is not an reinvention; yet we must do both, and for the same reasons: partly because life commands it, as it commands the yearly reinvention of flowers; but more because we who desperately need them cannot otherwise have them.

The criticism of literature and the philosophy of law do not create and do not decide law or literature; they cannot in themselves save or sustain anything. Shakespeare, however praised, without quoters and imitators, would be forgotten; a constitution, however respected, without reinterpreters and reformers, would obsolesce.

One generation passes away; what they loved and revered we cannot learn to love and revere from them. Their love is dust in the ground, their reverence collects dust in attics. We can love the life they loved and obey the law they obeyed only for our own sake; we must reinvent them, not even to maintain them, but just to learn to see them. We cannot see how the world was built for us until we have rebuilt it for ourselves, knowing that all we build we build only for those who come after us to tear it down and rebuild what we will not recognize.

AN ALTAR

APRIL 24, 2009   When did I first encounter graffiti for myself? Beside a parking lot, just close enough to be noticed through the trees but too far back to recognize, a little up a slope, at the end of a trace left by its seekers – an altar.

It seemed to me like an altar – not a place for worship, but a place for rites. A low, long trapezoid of rain-dark concrete. From the unknown depth of the leaves that hid its base it rose like the peak of a buried pyramid. It may have gone deeper than I imagined: I later identified it (I forget how) as the base of one of the struts of a world war watchtower for German submarines.

The surface was covered in scrawls and scratches of nonsense and gibberish. There were English letters, English sounds and arrangements of sounds, but no English meanings – no regularity of language or code, only the dreamlike suggestion of meaning that can be grasped onto, but not held, smooth, slippery, bottomless. What promise of secrets! Surely if there were deep unseen machinery in the world this was the place to discover it.

I copied down a small page full of symbols and signs. I have lost it since – but even while I kept it I avoided looking at it. It felt like admitting an intruder.

Those who carved and marked this altar meant only secrecy, not mystery, and only privacy, not ritual. I was a child Kircher of small-town hieroglyphs, willing significance from mere meaning.

But to know that I was foolish does not cheapen the experience. Nature shows its dominion in more than overgrowth and decay. Nature guides the accumulation of anonymous and inscrutable human marks as surely as it guides the tracks of vines and the webs of spiders. Such places feel sacred because they bear witness to what we otherwise conceal: we, too, are part of nature. The god who loves his beetles is the same god who loves us. We are building his altars.

PHOTOSTREAM

MAY 1, 2009   [The sonnet's possibilities for creepiness are too often overlooked.]

> My love, it's true that we have never met
> But what is that? I know your every look.
> You want my love, and what you want you get.
> That photo finish, I know what it took:
> Your outfits, how you dress for every shot;
> The poses that you plan and practice well;
> The mirror where you think up every plot,
> The bedroom you have sweetened for your cell
> Where diode glow lights up your staring face
> Absorbed in silent filters' midnight work
> Until the philtre, glazed with conscious grace
> Assumes its place enwrapped in subtle quirk.
> > My lily love my eyes are mirrors too
> > Sway over me and see me seeing you.

EXPECTATION

MAY 8, 2009   Who gets from life what they expect? Who finds in what they expect from life enough to justify it?

Expectation is not the same as hope. They are easy to distinguish by the reactions they bring. What you expect can only be reported or relinquished to you. Only what you only hope for can be given to you, or done for you.

Clear hopes are harmless. True, most hopes are vague; but a hope may become very specific through long handling, yet still be fulfilled by something whose correspondence to that hope is obscure except to the one who hoped.

But expectations become more dangerous as they become more specific. Every part of complex expectation inflicts separate harm when disappointed. And the harm has no scale. Principles and trifles can harm alike – sometimes the trifles absurdly too much; sometimes the principles monstrously too little. The first distortion is familiar. It is easy to understand that the little annoying disappointments point to the great traumas. But the opposite distortion, when great disappointments multiply little ones, when in the wake of trauma life becomes not unbearably painful but unbearably annoying – this distortion, though just as common, goes nameless. The first is moving; the second is disgusting. But both are the same error.

Change and uncertainty always annoy, and mostly dismay me. To find that I have unknowingly repeated myself – thought the same thought, written the same sentence, done the same thing – reassures me. It seems to prove I am not decaying. But, of course, in that I fool myself. The law of entropy is Grow or Die.

For lower life, growth conforms to expectation because the complexity of the pattern expected – the shape of a flower, the anatomy of a flea – is less than the complexity of the apparatus that produces it. The DNA of flower or flea contains (in context) all that there is to each lifeform.

For higher life, for life that learns and feels, the complexity of the product, exponentiated by indices from epigenetics to iterated algorithms and strange loops – this complexity means that expectation can never be adequate, because the complexity of the product is greater than the complexity of its causes. When expectations hold for a human being it is never the instantiation of a subjective pattern, but the dampening of complexity by powerful objective contingencies. The probable effects of these contingencies may be ascertained; and if the contingencies are powerful enough, the probable effects may be expected.

Nothing a human being, as a human being, can do matters if that human being is swimming lost, alone, naked and unbuoyed in the open ocean. The expectation of drowning is a practical certainty. But even in everyday life the certainty of an expectation is not the result of your confidence in it, but of the objective stability of the conditions of your desire: even subjective resolutions are actually objective limitations.

Most lives should arrive at an age after which the rest goes as expected. But for most of us, to be able to expect the rest of life resembles drowning. So much energy is required merely to tread water in the world that you might as well swim forward a little. Even when the riptide gets you, even you cannot swim against it, you can still swim across it.

To say that life does not go as expected is to take the side of experience. To say that life should not go as expected would be to take the side of all the evils that abuse it. So I say no such thing. But faced with two equal goods, only one of which you expect, the better choice may be the unexpected one, for three reasons. First, since it is only hoped for (or unhoped-for) you will receive it more gladly, and love it better. Second, being outside your system of expectations, it rests them, relieves them while they readjust. And third: sometimes it is wise to choice unwisely just to remember that you can choose.

THE POISONED KING

MAY 15, 2009   The kingdom was full of poisoners. The young king had executed a hundred poisoners to celebrate his coronation – feckless younger sons and elegant silk ladies, young herblore widows and filthy wild-eyed droppers into wells. But a hundred more soon took their places.

The king's doctors were the best in the world. They had means and mastery, and being pledged to die when the king died, they had motive to keep him well. They kept busy stocking the palace with antidotes and performing autopsies on the king's food tasters.

Yet when the king was poisoned at last, they were helpless. All their specifics and tonics, all their elixirs, panaceas, theriacs – all were worthless. In his bed the dying king sweated and burned and cried out.

The doctors had one hope left, for the king and for themselves. Their hope, a man, had been doctor to the king's grandfather, had left to study with the master poisoners of the eastern mountains, and had returned to save the king's grandfather when all other hopes were lost. The old king, grateful, had released the doctor from service. Ever since he had lived in the caves outside the palace, refusing to teach his secrets.

The doctors went to the king together to tell him of this last hope. The king, his voice choked to a bubble and a whistle, only nodded his yes. Strong men hoisted the king's litter onto their shoulders and followed the doctors to the caves.

There they found the master doctor, at home in a cave where thick dry dead branches were planted in the floor, hung with bundles and bags full of dry or drying plants, a cave where holes in the wall had been hollowed out and filled bottle by bottle with all the colors the earth yields, powders from clay and stone and gem. There the master doctor dwelled; there the king was brought to meet him.

The master heard out all that the king's doctors had to say. Then he knelt beside the king's litter and whispered: "My lord, I have no art to heal or cure. What I learned from the master poisoners was only the art by which one incurable poison may drive out another. The reward your grandfather gave me was not for saving his life, but for substituting the death of a month for the death of an hour – for giving him time to pass the kingdom to your father in peace."

"Do this for me," the king whispered, "for I have no heir and must choose another."

Then the master went deep into his cave, plucking dry flowers from dead trees and palming bright earths to mingle in a dry bowl hung from a cold tripod. "There is wood in the next cave," he told the king's doctors. "Build a fire outside. Do not speak." When the fire was ready he placed the tripod and bowl over it, then filled the bowl with rainwater. He stirred the water until it was an even yellow, then built the fire until steam rose from the bowl. He sat still, watching, as the liquid inside thickened and darkened. At some secret sign he rushed to the bowl and dipped a coarse cloth into the liquid. Knife in hand he lay the cloth on the ground and scraped a golden paste from it. He carried the paste to the king on the side of his knife. With a finger he spread the poison of the golden paste over the king's lips. "Take him back to the palace. Tomorrow he will wake as healthy as before. In one month, he will fall asleep and never wake."

Awed into silence, the king's doctors attended him back to the palace and left him in his bed. The whole court assembled for his levee; but when the king woke, he scorned ceremony and ordered scribes to attend him. His doctors he released from their pledge, and sent from his presence.

To his scribes he gave orders. Their orders were to scan all the rolls of honor and to command every man whom the king and the king's father had recognized for merit to be brought to the court, there to be assayed for the qualities of kingship.

But the kingdom was full of poisoners, and merit draws their attention. Most of the men on the rolls were already dead; and though the command to attend the court reached the rest, not one survived the journey.

For the whole month of his reprieve the king searched every corner of his kingdom; but all the men whom the king found were either wretches or poisoners.

The king's month ran out, but he did not sleep. For three night he stayed awake, refusing fatal sleep, working and hoping for some chance. None came; so the king, alone, visited the master doctor in his cave.

"I need more time," the king declared. "If I die now war and poison will claim the kingdom."

The master said: "I can preserve life to your body, but I cannot preserve you. Men will curse what you become."

"Let them curse," said the king.

So the king stood and watched while the master moved and worked. He finished with a green powder piled on his open palm. "Open your mouth," he told the king. The master raised his palm between their faces and blew the powder down the king's throat. The king gasped, doubled over, coughed. "You may rest now, my lord. You have another month."

The king, never gentle, grew cruel. His judgments quick and final. He ordered his governors to seek and send men of quality, fit to be kings, or themselves be executed. Many were sent; but the poisoners along the way were many, and none came before the king alive.

After only a week the king returned to the master doctor's cave. "You must poison me again."

"You still have time," the master said.

"You must poison me again."

"It will make you mad."

"I, too, am a doctor," the king said, "and I have long failed to heal this kingdom. I see the cure now. You must poison me again. Do it or I will have you killed. The order is already written and delivered. If I do not live to countermand it, you will die."

So the master gathered and labored, and returned with a blue liquid. "Lie down and close your eyes." The doctor pinched up each of the king's eyelids and dripped counted drops of blue liquid onto the white backs of the king's eyes.

When the king returned he ordered his soldiers into the streets of the capital and the roads of the countryside to bring him all the firstborn sons of the kingdom. Among them one would be his heir. There was some resistance; but mostly the kingdom let its sons go in peace, each mother and father hoping for the name of mother and father to the king, and the life of the palace.

Once the sons of the kingdom were all gathered in the palace the king went to the master doctor and said: "Poison me again."

"I will not," the master said. "My life is not worth it."

"Did I say I would have you killed? I meant that I would throw you down a dark little stone hole with no name but that of a mouth to feed."

So the doctor made a silver pellet of poison and placed it under the king's tongue.

When the king returned from the cave he ordered that all the firstborn should be moved from the palace to the dungeon, there to grow tough. And once they were imprisoned, he ordered that all who failed the tests of kingship should be killed.

When news of the king's madness reached the countryside, the peasants took to arms. They slaughtered the king's garrisons and seized all the roads. Soon word came to the palace that the rebels had chosen a leader and were marching on the capital.

The king returned to the cave. The master doctor, uninstructed, made a black bowl of poison for the king to eat. Past tasting, the king never slowed.

His courtiers begged the king to rest, but he refused. He took personal command of the army. He overruled his captains, ignored their strategies, ordered incessant fanciful maneuvers and divisions of forces, planned senseless and wasteful skirmishes. Half his captains thought he was mad; half his captains thought he was brilliant. Half were right. The king had three men for every man of the peasant army; but the peasants won and the king was killed. The peasants freed their sons, razed the palace, and sacked the capital for a month. No roof stood.

After that came civil war, long and cruel. So intent did men become on killing the old way, with edge and point, that in the space of a generation the poisoner's art was lost.

DEAD ACTORS

MAY 21, 2009   Surely there are more dead actors on film than live ones. If this is not yet true, it will be. How strange this is is hard to feel. Watching dead actors feels no different than watching live ones; watching old movies is no more demanding than watching new ones – yet there is something there, something worthy of awe.

These dead are not resurrected, they do not return as ghosts, yet they are more with us than the worshiped ancestors. We do not have the duty of commemorating them, we need not summon or disturb them, yet they return to us, appearing generously, in kind brief undemanding visits. Though their business is finished, they come when called.

While they move they live. They borrow life without need and return it without jealousy. While they have it, it is life more than life: in the sustained dreaming attention of a theater full of people is more life than each audient human beings has in themselves. Remembrance has always given life to the dead we knew; but film lets it give life to those we never knew – to those who never were.

Beside the public miracle is a private necromancy. Film always invites importunities of feeling. Wherever it pleases, it seduces with the form of a relationship. Whatever you feel, whatever shows on your face, whatever you are moved to profess, however much attention you pay, the characters are never offended, they never fail to appear, they are always blithe and comfortable. They do not reject. No stare discomforts them, no smile troubles them, no words repel them, and by such slight expressions, compounded over time, the sentiments of a relationship grow without the reality.

This is strange enough where the living are concerned; with the dead it is unprecedented. Time has always been transparent to the mind, but here it yields to the body. Faust needed a devil's help to to bring dead Helen lively to his bed; one need only a computer to visit the embraces of dead generations, to visit with slow deliberate melancholy lust what was made for quick distraction as whorehouse lead-ins and nameless theater matinees – to know in the most intimate way a human being who, most likely, has been forgotten in name, thought, word and deed.

But lust is not the limit. You may hear of a young man (it would be a young man) who comes to know an actress, dead before he was born, old before she was dead, so well and in her youth that, lover-like, in a crowd he could recognize her by the way she stands still. You may hear of a young woman (it would be a young woman) who takes such an impression of an actor, portraying the ideal manliness of a generation long since unmanned by old age, that she would decide her life by judging living men, raised to other ideals and purposes, as unworthy of her in their very strengths, worthy only in their failings. (You may hear of other combinations, but these are harder for me to understand.)

Dead actors become their characters. Live actors can always surprise us; dead actors can never prove us wrong. Live actors fear being typecast; but all actors, in the end, are typecast as themselves, however various those selves may have been. To posterity even versatility and unpredictability become roles. To speak of dead actors is to speak of their characters; to speak of the characters is to speak of their dead. The IMDB and TCM pollute this phenomenon, but do not overcome it. Movies, it is true, were more potently self-standing when context and commentary were out of reach; but to watch them, if done properly, is still to be alone with them and at their mercy.

Dead singers, dead writers, dead artists, have their living consequences; but though their works are of themselves, though their works contain and preserve them, their works are abstractions, translations, traces. Only for actors is the person the art; only for actors does the art absorb and convey, not just the skill of the person, not just what is unique and potent in them, but the whole of the person, what is best, what is worst, what is common, weak, awkward, shared.

My great-grandmother was a silent film actress, under the name Eva Pavey. (I implore any silent film buff who recognizes the name to write to me; all I know of her career is that she was one of the young women whom Marie Dressler encouraged.) Most silent film, I know, is lost; but I cannot help hoping that somewhere one of her movies still exists. If I could see it I would meet her younger, stronger, and happier than her daughter my grandmother or her grand-daughter my mother ever knew her – meet her, and for the first time, as she was before any of the decisions and compromises to which I owe my existence. Time travel is that easy.

Would that Keats had seen a movie! An urn was only the best object he could find for a thought whose true object had yet to be invented, where lovers reach and kiss, want and have, yet never fade and never doubt – a human motion made cool, distant, certain and serene as the cycles of the planets, here before us, here after us.

SORROW'S EYE

MAY 29, 2009

He rose from the bed, the beloved was dead.
He sank down stairs to an empty street.
He leaned against a bowing post.
He hid beneath a drooping eave.
The door behind he left ajar
In hope that someone passing by
Would see it gape and call for help,
And climbing find her silent, still,
And finding, care, and maybe weep.
His head was full of masking noise,
He spoke aloud to hear himself:
"What now, what now, what's left is lost,
The world has changed, the world is less,
What is this place, what's left to see,
And who could live in such a husk?
The world is dead, its heart is stopped,
Its breath is choked, its eyes are dull,
And we who live are left as worms,
Worms in the world, we pierce and gnaw.
We feed in the dark, and worse than worms
We know just what and who we eat.
The world is dead, I will not live.
Not here, like this, not one of those
Who drink to wash their gory mouths,
Who watch to dream the world that was.
I beg whoever has the strength
To pluck me up and crush me now
To take me from this heedless world
Or else remake the world anew,
Reborn in sorrow, tears for blood.
I will not live to lose the pain
She left behind for me to keep.
If I go on in this dark place
In time I cannot but forget.

I won't forget, so end me now,
Or make the world her monument."

What heard him then, what had no name
Was more than man and less than god,
With power and pity, and listening.
It knew these words, it knew them well,
It lived their pith, it had its place
To check their strength to save the world.
So many griefs like this denied,
But not this time. It stayed its strength
To let this grief flow over, flow
And sink the world, and make it new.
O is that the sun that flickers so,
Are those the clouds, they're made of glass,
They drop a rain of grit and shards.
What walls are these, they have no doors.
What streets are these, they go nowhere.
Was this a church that is her tomb,
She has so many tombs, and we
We need them all, where we may shed
Our burning tears on stone, and trap
Their heat in wicks, and keep them near
To keep us warm, who sit in pews
In silent ranks, with burned-out eyes,
And wait for sleep that never comes.

O You who bind the strength of grief
O leave us here, we know her now
　　We love her too.

THE MIDDLE DISTANCE

JUNE 6, 2009   Between the present and the past is more of the past. This submerged past is the difference between history and hindsight. History raises it; hindsight floats over it. History, plodding, myopic, keeps its eyes on the ground, watches every step. Hindsight, hyperopic, stumbles over a fuzzy path to a past in clear focus. History is a discipline, attained by few; hindsight is a faculty, born with all.

It is easier to sympathize with the young dead than the old living of the same generation. Death is a return to youth. The stories of the dead are stories of what they did with their strength; the rest is epilogue and aftermath. But we cannot help seeing the living, not for what they have done, but for what they have become.

The dead cannot refuse our sympathy and admiration. We can bestow it freely, without fear of rejection. But the living can still refuse us, still embarrass us. This makes for a strange blind spot. Not seeing the immediate supports of history – not seeing the wires that hold us up – we see history as if we floated free from it, as if may choose whatever antecedent we like, whichever lessons we want to hear; part of hindsight's audience, not history's procession.

The past we can quote, the past we would restore, the past we may yet repeat – these are the pasts of hindsight. The past, like wood, must dry out to be useful. Green, wet history is easiest to shape – consider how many shapes the legacy of, say, a living former President can be carved into, and how fast the changes can be made – but as it dries it warps, cracks, and splits. Memoir and journalism are hothouse arts, coercing early and transient blooms. Lasting work can only be done in dry wood, once the life has left it.

Remember with Bacon that it is we (we much more than he) who are the ancients, not those who lived innocently in the youth of the world. We have had a long time to learn. It is not enough to quote Confucius, Jesus, Muhammad without being able to say how present evils came to be despite the Sage Emperors and the Apostles and the Best Generations.

We are nearsighted when we look forward, farsighted when we look backward. Renovators and restorers always favor one past over another. The fans of old music and old movies are fans of the music and movies of their grandfathers' day, not their fathers'. Anglospherically, to the

Victorians the Regency was more remote than the Elizabethans; to the Gilded Age the Civil War was more remote than the Revolution; to the Elizabethans and Founders alike, the true past was Roman. Shakespeare is less remote to me than Samuel Johnson; but to see Shakespeare quoted in Johnson's dictionary opens a chasm under my feet.

The past is easier for us to understand than the present, not because the past was simpler than the present, but because we do not have to convince ourselves that it is worth living in. We can face nakedly what was unbearable in it. Only someone uncommonly cruel can judge a life wasted before it is over; and so true historical judgment is reserved until what it studies is over, not just in its events, but in its needful illusions.

Hindsight and history both connect the present and the past; only history connects the past with the past. The past held the seeds of the present; but it also held the seeds of what was yet the future, having become our past. The Germany of the Bundesrepublik was implicit in the Germany of Goethe; but it was there beside the Germany of the last Kaiser, and the Germany of Weimar, and the Germany of the last Reichskanzler. All the doors were open, and no one knew which ones opened on dead ends. We have shut these doors with such great effort that it seems almost sacrilegious to imagine them open. But that is the difference between history and hindsight.

CREATIVITY

JUNE 13, 2009   Can technology perform what has been promised of it – can it make everyone creative? To my surprise, I conclude that it can, if by *creative* we understand something as distinct from *creation* as *active* is distinct from *action*.

Technology allows us to be active without acting, decouples action from activity both in frustrating our determination by an infinite multiplication of stakeholders and infinite attenuation of authority, and in excusing our indecision with an infinite regress of prerequisites, preparations, and precautions. While the year's planning of a royal feast becomes the labor of an hour's trip to the grocery store, the hour's action of a king and counselor becomes the decades' activity of a movement of tens of millions.

Technology can likewise democratize creativity by decoupling it from creation, after empowering it with resources cheapened through economies of scale. This decoupling takes place at two points: in preventing the concealment of sources, and in preventing the discrimination of influences.

Our popular writers defend oversimplifications with caricatures. You will read, for example, that creativity now stands revealed as inherently collaborative and social, over against an outdated and misguided nineteenth century – no, Victorian – no, Romantic (they are interchangeable for the purpose) idea of Genius inexplicably and mystically inspired with utterly irreducible, unaccountable, and unanswerable Originality.

You will hear quoted: "Creativity is the art of concealing sources." This sounds awful to our ears; it stimulates our reflexes: concealment – hypocrisy! Expose it! And so we embrace a doctrine of synthetic, social creativity defined only as the opposite to a something that no one ever really believed.

Of course creativity is synthetic. With knowledge as with gravity, mass has force. The more knowledge is accumulated, the more it is all alive; by concentration and fermentation is becomes fertile. And it is true that creativity cannot be independent. Every act of creation is fed by a thousand buried mingling rivers. Even the springs of the desert rise by distant rainfalls. Mere self-expression cannot be original because nothing we can create for ourselves can be as meaningful to us as the things that we have experienced, that have shaped us. New and awkward is just awkward; old but well done is just well done. For a human being there should be a pleasure in seeing anything done well, with gravity and devotion: whittling or whistling, playing a toccata, laying out a garden, writing a program, spinning a yo-yo, engineering an industrial process, writing a constitution, inventing a language. The value of originality does not occur independently.

The caricature is absurd, but not new. Consider Swift, who maligned early Romanticism by comparing its writers to the spider, spinning flimsy pale cobwebs from her own substance, over against the bee, who patiently collects nectar from a hundred flowers and distills it to thick golden honey. Our idea of social creativity matches this caricature – only we take the part of the beehive, instead of the bee. But this is not viable. The vomit of bees and the spinneret-slurry of spiders are alike products of digestion;

one happens to be more pleasant to observe than the other. But I have seen golden spiders spin golden webs.

The spider conceals its sources; from the look of its web you cannot tell what wings she has turned to silk. The bee flavors her honey according to the kind of flower she feeds from. But compare their work. The bee turns something pleasant in one way into something pleasant in another way; the spider turns something harmful into something useful, even something beautiful – those golden webs in the morning sun shine like bells.

But enough analogy. The architecture of social and participatory creativity is defined in its legal instruments – the GPL, Creative Commons, and others – as one based in the preservation of attribution. More than a legal reality, this becomes a moral principle. Young people, at least, regard themselves as being at liberty to use any kind of created material – pictures, songs, characters – where and as they please, as long as attribution is preserved, expecting that their makers, even if they disapprove of the particular expression, will approve of the idea of reuse as a form of promotion to their ultimate financial benefit. So it might be: but note the postulate that attribution is all the control a maker deserves over their work. (And note that even where materials are drawn from the public domain and no legal necessity operates, attribution as a moral principle holds.)

But attribution is more than courtesy: to have one's attributions in order is the passport of good work, the condition of its admittance to critical consideration.

The drawbacks of this system are two: it excludes personal experience; and it narrows the range of influences it is wise to receive to the range of influences it is wise to admit to. The difficulty in using personal experience is that the reaction that a criticism of originality most prizes – "Where do you get your ideas?" – is the reaction that a criticism of attribution most deprecates, because it requires that question to be answered before criticism can begin. When the naming of influences becomes a public act, the choice of influences obeys the necessities of signaling that all public acts entail – some are in fashion, some are out of fashion, some are pedantic, some are pretentious, some are contemptible. Before the work even begins the selection of influences becomes the first move in the tactics of presenting the work. Because you must expect your work to be tasted with the intent of discerning its influences you must collect them out in the open, under the sunlight. What moves in the close and the dark is off-limits.

The obverse of this problem of narrowed influences is the impossibility of choosing among influences. Once what is permissible has been agreed upon, to ignore some part of that range seems capricious and arrogant. You must take it all seriously.

In education, conversation, and manners, it is a virtue to try to take everyone and everything seriously. The more you overcome the instinct to scoff at what is unfamiliar or distasteful, the more you become more a thinking individual and less an accident of genes and community. And if your ambitions are essayistic or critical, you can stop there.

But when you sit down to create something – art, music, literature, science – then you must choose: whom do you take seriously? If you cannot choose, you cannot act. You cannot have Leonardo and Warhol, Bach and Glass, Homer and Joyce, Cantor and Kronecker. You may reject without disrespect: but you must choose.

Where one is old and one is new, one must be obsolete, and one modern, or one humane, the other a fad or disease. When both are old one is classic, one is dated or irrelevant. When both are new, one is avant-garde, and one is bourgeois; or one is navel-gazing, the other is world-engaging.

You do not have to always make the same choice: but you must always choose. If you fail to choose, if you cultivate eclecticism to the point of indecision and deference to the point of impotence, you condemn yourself to the fate of Buridan's ass, which in the thought experiment starves because it cannot choose between two identical piles of hay. I love an army of writers for their particular excellences, and will defend them in their entirety for the sake of those excellences. But when I sit down to write there are a half-dozen writers whom I can take seriously; everyone else seems ridiculous. I only demur that six is probably too many.

Consider the "mash-up." It is, defying the dictionary's opposition of creativity and criticism, a creative criticism; juxtapositions are not random, but either analogical or contrastive. If two analogical things are comparable, they supply understanding of each other exactly as a written analogy would. If contrastive they heighten the contrast either to absurdity or poignancy. As an art form the mash-up is not a uncalculating *jeux d'esprit*, not an afterthought or diversion; it is tendentious and didactic.

It is a popular pastime as politics are: it gives people a chance to opine, and lends to the opinion the glamour of the underlying subject, as including Democracy or Justice in an assertion lends it weight.

Mash-ups are not nearly as unpredictable as they should be, if they are primarily creative. Nothing technically prevents mixing parts of a dozen or a hundred songs and movies, but more than two of each would be out of order, because if it were done well the parts used would meld and the critical tension would be absent.

The people most likely to disagree with this are not the makers of mash-ups but academics with the odd, pseudo-ethnographic habit of taking Internet communities and fads far more seriously than they take themselves, of concentrating on the extremes and the fringes and ignoring the consensus within those communities. They are also given to confounding creativity with informality – you will hear dialects, for instance, praised as "creative," as if Grimm's Law were an expression of the creativity of the speakers of Germanic languages. Dialects require creativity in the sense that they might have been otherwise; but they are not themselves creations because they had to be something and might just as easily have been something else. What was inevitable is not a creation.

This division between creativity and creation is, in its effects and its attractions, not unlike the division between sex and reproduction. Creativity, as such, is delightful, relaxing, and consoling. But when it results in creations, these attractions disappear. Your creation preoccupies and distracts you, disrupts your sleep, fills you with doubts. Like any offspring it warps you in its gestation, enslaves you in its infancy, and grows by the life it takes from you. To nourish and raise it takes strength and time to spare. Creativity is a disposition, a faculty, a gift; creation is a vocation, a devotion, a discipline. It is limitless and torturous. One creation does not easily follow another, and too many in succession, or at once, can break a constitution and unmake a home. Even once it has some substance and independence you remain weighted with interminable responsibility for it, to find the right place and the right friends for it, to see it sent out into the world. And even once you have sent it out into the world, you are left exhausted, restless, and anxious.

You can always grow, but you cannot always bear fruit, at least not of the same kind. Even the mind needs cover crops, needs seasons to thicken its sap and sink its roots. This is not to condemn those who seeks the pleasure without the responsibility; only to observe that one who, by being creative, presumes to know what it takes to create something, is a fool.

SOCIETY AS A CONTRACT

JUNE 20, 2009   Sociality defines human beings in a different way than it defines other social animals. In other animals the individual encapsulates the species. Even if it is a specialized form – even if it is a sterile drone – still its genes record what it cannot embody or propagate. The societies of insects are all in the genes. What matters is not the hive but the queen; the hive itself is pure unfolding.

But the society of human beings, though genetically driven, is not genetically predictable. There is historical variation in how a society forms, as there is epigenetic variation in an individual. A single human being contains the certainty of a society, but not the form of that society.

We cannot establish society on a rational basis because society exists to serve a need that is prior to reason. Society begins not in contract, but in instinct. But all instinct can do for society is to establish it in one of its basic forms; what is built on top of that, is built with contracts.

What are these basic forms? There are only two: rule by the old, or rule by the young.

Rule by the old suits small populations. Thus we find tribes and villages with elders, and the most ancient city-states constituted with Senates. Paradoxically, while it is by far the more stable of the two forms, it is not the ground state. When it fails, government by the old collapses into government by the young; but it is so hard for a large population to attain government by the old that it usually arrives there by way of government by the young.

Neither rulers nor ruled are immortal. This fact is not without political significance. People age: this is the advantage of rule by the old over rule by the young. Those who attain power old cannot expect to keep it long, so they tolerate the division of responsibilities requisite to a smooth succession.

But those who attain power young can never risk losing it. In rule by the young the rulers are not usually themselves young. The difference is that in rule by the old, age is the title to power; while in rule by the young, it is youth, and the deeds and quality of youth.

Rule by the old is the model of the kinds of societies we call tribes, and of ancient republics; rule by the young is the model of societies we call feudal, and of crime we call organized. At the top of such pyramidal systems the king or boss is probably much older than his vassals or boys at the bottom; but his authority derives from how well he understands and can sway the youth of his *comitatus* (or his posse).

Rule by the young is perishable; it lasts only as long as it takes to grow old in power. Of course growing old in power is the trick. Rule by the old, left alone, lasts forever; some extant specimens are older than history. But few societies are left alone forever.

It is in competition with other societies that the rule of the old shows it weakness; and war is the ultimate competition. Where the young rule, there is never any difficulty in finding and empowering a competent military commander. Ability trumps respect. But where the old rule, authority and ability are opposites, because authority is reserved for those least able to abuse it.

Accordingly we see that when a militant rule by the young arises, in its aftermath, even when it loses, all the governments involved go over to the young. It is like rabies: those who try to restrain the first victim get bitten; then they all go mad.

This, of course, applies only to civilized countries: there is no difference in authority and ability where there is no such thing as tactics. But consider that the humiliation of Carthage brought about the rule of youth that set Hannibal in command; and how that Rome was forced to answer with Scipio was the beginning of the end of the Republic, once his glory set him above the law.

The same competition that appears in war also appears, more subtly, in commerce, culture, and discovery.

Of the two forms, I would rather live under the rule of the old; I would rather rule by the rule of the young. So ruled, I could plan for the future; so ruling, I could decide it.

Rule by the old is the default form of government, the one adopted when there is no basis for choice; rule by the young is the ground state, the one that comes into effect when no government at all seems possible.

(Thus I regard anarchists and libertarians as being on the side of the young; they call what they aim for free trade or cooperation, but what they mean is freedom of action for the young, from a government that they despise as belonging to the old. But freedom of action is the same thing as government. If I can hurt you, and you cannot do anything about it, then I rule you.)

Can there be government that is both stable and active? If rule by the old correlates to aristocracy, and rule by the young correlates to monarchy, the answer after all this fuss is obvious: democracy.

Note, however, that these two forms of rule are not classes to one or the other of which all governments must belong. They are elemental forms of government. In classification they serve as poles, to one or the other of which a real government sometimes draws nearer; in analysis they are recapitulated and combined at different levels. Any real government – certainly any modern government, on a national scale – is really a hierarchy and network of governments, in which governments both fit inside and parallel other governments.

I want to resist as strongly as I can the notion that there is some simple nosology of government. The threefold division we blame on Aristotle – monarchy, aristocracy, isonomy (democracy) – what use is it? Even if we assign each form its evil twin – tyranny, oligarchy, democracy (ochlocracy) – what does the choice mean, except approval or disapproval? What structural features are different between each twin?

When Aristotle speaks of democracy, he means election by lottery; when he speaks of aristocracy, he means nearly what we mean by meritocracy; what he means by a monarch is more like what we would call a political boss, than the throne-sitters the word *king* calls up. And this is the best classification we have!

A constitution does more than fix power relations between classes. A constitution – even one that does not work as its written prospectus suggests – is a piece of social machinery. Once people have the leisure to propose them, an artistic diversity of forms of government can be designed and practiced. People can govern themselves by as many schemes of constitutional machinery as they can invent; they may make decisions according to the will of the king or the voice of the people; they can consult the innards of ravens, the shapes of clouds, the pips of dice, the whisperings of prophetesses, the papers of economists. As long as everyone believes in it, as long as nothing unexpected challenges it, if it works, it works. This is the first kind of society-as-contract: like a corporate charter, it defines how things work while things work.

But sometimes things stop working. Plague strikes, you lose the war, rivals outspend you, your markets attempt suicide. When no procedure answers to the problem, then the old and the young are heard from. Either the old among the powerful combine to keep things from going wrong; or things go wrong, and the young find themselves making decisions.

Here we find the second kind of society-as-contract. It has only three possible forms.

The first is the contract between old and young, while both have power. The old agree not to seize power from the constitutional forms, and the young agree not to accept power when the mob offers it to them, except in the name of the constituted government as a whole.

The second is the contract between the old and young, after the old take power; promising that when the elite needs renewal, they shall be the ones coopted.

The third is the contract that the young offer the old when power falls to them: to retain them for their advice, and not to let the mob blame and destroy them.

Consider the French Revolution, when all three contracts were offered but fell through. The first, when Louis fled, and the Jacobins and Girondins accepted the loyalty of the mob and the bourgeois, respectively; the second, when the Girondins tried to exclude the Jacobins; the third, when the Jacobins recruited the mob into the Terror.

It is very easy to write a constitution that works; any lawyer can do it. But it is very hard to write a constitution that fails gracefully. Fortunately, there is a quick test: the longer the written form of the constitution, the more untrustworthy it is. The English constitution, at zero words, has lasted almost a millennium; the American, at 4500 words, has lasted over two centuries. The Soviet constitution came in, by the end, at 13,300 words – a work of fiction of nearly novel length. The Chinese at 14,000 strikes me as dubious. The length of the recently defeated EU constitution – about 150,000 words (can that be right?) – is perverse.*

---

*Figures for the US and Chinese constitutions include amendments. The figure for the EU constitution derives from an automatic conversion (`pdftotext | wc -w`) and may be inaccurate.

Consider any common business contract: the longer it is, the more detailed the terms, the more ways the contract can bend without breaking, and the less it should be trusted. The longer the contract, the less relevant – witness unreadable software EULAs, whose terms are less unenforceable than incomprehensible. When nothing is certain, the only contract that holds is the handshake.

Hippocrates taught that medicine has two parts: diagnosis and prognosis. Prognosis is the showmanlike part. The purpose of giving a disease a name and predicting to the patient its future course is not to inform the doctor, but to impress the patient. Diagnosis is the subtle and difficult part: the ability to trace the course of the disease so far, to discover and remove its causes, to recognize and avoid its dangers. Diagnosis is how the doctor finds a cure; prognosis is what makes the patient agree to submit to the cure. Most political and sociological thinking is prognostic. I am trying to see how a diagnostic approach might work.

BOREDOM

JULY 4, 2009   Dividing people into two kinds is usually futile; but one useful division is by theories of boredom. Some people think of boredom as a sin; they are ashamed to be bored. Some people think of boredom as a symptom; they are afraid to be bored.

The sin theory of boredom begins with the observation that life is so far from being a pleasure in itself that we would rather do anything at all than simply live. We seek preoccupation above all other ends. Boredom, like original sin, is an inherited debt that we are always working to discharge, that begins to compound again the moment we relax.

The symptom theory of boredom begins with the observation of animals and tribesmen, who are often still, but never bored. Boredom, then, is a symptom – a symptom of the disease of civilization, of the way civilization warps and overstimulates the mind. Boredom is a sign of bad living, a signal that you are taking life too seriously, thinking too much. The proper treatment is to seek distraction and stupefaction, to shut the mind off.

In most places, for most of history, both alternatives to boredom – preoccupation and distraction – were beyond control. Things had to be made when someone needed them, and things broke when they broke, and wars. Feasts, bouts, holidays, followed the seasons. To be aware of boredom as a remediable condition belonged to the few: to warriors, priests, scholars, rulers. While not a luxury itself, like luxury, it depends on general prosperity. (Look at Prince Hamlet, whose boredom was to a sixteenth century audience a sign of his greatness, a princely attribute lifting him above common men.)

Boredom was always there, but it went unnoticed because it could not be changed. That innocence is lost to us; we are cursed not only to be bored, but to know we are bored. Because we are mortal, we must theorize mortality; because we are modern, we must theorize boredom.

I subscribe to the sin theory of boredom. I have been bored, but I heartily repent both occasions. I would find them interesting now. Being this kind of person places me on a losing side – one losing so badly that the winning side has forgotten that there is another side. The sin theory and the symptom theory are not equally matched. The sin theory makes converts where boredom reigns and must be consciously resisted; the symptom theory makes converts where remedies for boredom are easy and cheap. And remedies for boredom surround us.

I think the sin theory was once predominant; I think TV defeated it. But even as TV fades, its victory grows. You may have heard the thesis that the edifices of Web 2.0 represent the liberation of a *cognitive surplus* previously absorbed by TV. But it would be silly to expect that the culture, the habits, the state of mind of TV watching would disappear because the TVs are shutting off. TV has had generations to train us to fear being bored. The TV watchers turned from screen to monitor, moved from sofa to desk chair, but they remained what TV had made them, afraid of boredom, not ashamed of it, and they remade the net accordingly, turned everything interactive social and turned everything social trivial. And because the net is destined to absorb all other media, out to the limits of culture, the TV watchers, in shaping the net, are performing all that earlier generations feared about the effects of TV on culture, catabolizing the achievements of centuries in a space of years, all so rapidly that it seems like a natural phenomenon.

Note that I do not condemn any of the possibilities and powers of the web. I would neither propose nor assent to abolish or withdraw from them. I want it to go on; I want everything to be tried. But I reserve the right to condemn the results.

The notion that *the medium is the message*, that new media compel new habits of thought – this slogan of progress is itself obsolete. It holds only when new media are spaced out generation to generation and can raise their own. But when new media arise and displace the old from decade to decade or from year to year, we carry over the habits and attitudes of each into the next, in a way that warps its development and frustrates its potential.

But this is not an apocalypse. There are still two kinds of people, those who are ashamed of being bored, who think boredom a sin, and those who are afraid of being bored, who think boredom a symptom; and there always will be. The present victory is too absolute. Generations grow up taking the accomplishments of previous generations for granted. Absolute success is the most precarious kind. Not too long from now, to swoon over collaboration and community will sound absurd as it now sounds absurd to swoon over industry and mass transit.

No trend goes on forever; nothing stays cool forever. Here is one reason I regard the future with disquiet and doubt. It is obvious how institutions based on salaries and hierarchies can continue to function after they cease to be cool. But institutions based on collaboration and community – what happens when they cease to be cool?

Count over utopias, dystopias. Do you live in Butler's Erewhon, in the nameless utopia of Bellamy, in Skinner's Walden Two? Do you live in Zamyatin's One State, in Huxley's World State, in Orwell's Oceania? All of these were reasonable extrapolations of existing social trends; but social trends do not extrapolate. The face of the future is like one of those optical illusions where the outline of a vase is also the profile of an old woman or the portrait of a young woman is also the shadow of a skull. Foreground and background always change places. The two theories of boredom are the limits of a pendulum; and the pendulum is swinging still.

ADVICE

July 10, 2009   Advice has a doubtful reputation. Giving advice seems pretentious; taking advice seems weak. This attitude is foolish, but no more foolish than mistaking advice for an afterthought or pleasantry. Advice is dangerous. Giving advice is dangerous: a small observation, a fine distinction, a tentative suggestion, can change someone's life. Nothing will impress on you more how uncertain and unstable life is than to see your advice taken, to see words you have given an hour's, a minute's thought – to see these words lever someone's life out of one course and into another. Taking advice is dangerous: there is no pleasure that you can give another human being greater than the pleasure of taking their advice; nothing that makes a person more grateful, nothing that binds a person to you more loyally. Advice is so dangerous that to avoid it the platitude was invented. Remember that to have advisers and projects worth advising is among the privileges of kings. Giving advice is a way to serve; taking advice is a way to rule.

THE DREAM OF AVARIS

July 17, 2009   [I was terribly disappointed when I learned that the dreams of Avaris were not a third with the riches of Croesus and the touch of Midas.]

From Abbas Cucaniensis *Historia Regum Orientium.*

Avaris, King of Egypt, lord of uncountable riches, dreamt that the god came to him, and told him that he was to possess the whole wealth of the earth, in his palace to be rowed between islands of gems on seas of gold coins. The doors to his palace would be of yellow gold, its windows of white diamonds, its floors of black onyx. His feet would never touch aught but silk carpets. His water would never flow but into golden pots.

Awakening from his dream, Avaris called together his counselors to ask how the god's decree could be hastened. One after another, his counselors told him that the only way to possess the whole wealth of the world was to conquer the world – all his counselors but one, the youngest and most learned. This counselor said that he could bring Avaris all he desired, if he was but given command over all the merchants of Egypt.

Once the King had given him command over the merchants he called them all together and held forth upon the excellence of the dung beetle. The beetle could be obtained only from Egypt; the beetle was sacred and good luck to possess. Thus as the kingdom grew in prosperity and numbers under the wise and just rule of Avaris, everyone would want to possess a dung beetle. But the more who wanted to possess a dung beetle, the costlier dung beetles would become. Thus the merchants should purchase as many dung beetles as possible while they were reasonably priced, for their worth was sure to increase.

The merchants heeded his advice, which was given in the presence of armed men. Soon all the beetles in Egypt had been bought up, and the cost of a single dung beetle rose to a king's ransom.

The counselor, proud with his achievement, ordered the merchants to bring their beetles to the court of Avaris. Over the noise of thousands of beetles scratching in their cages the counselor explained to Avaris that since each beetle was now worth a fortune, all together the beetles were now worth more gold than there was gold to spend in the world. Here before Avaris were all the world's riches, just as he had dreamt, just as the god had promised him. Was he not pleased? Would there not be a reward for his devoted counselor?

Avaris, it is said, regarded his counselor in silence for a space, then told him to order the merchants to open their cages and scatter their beetles upon the floor. This the counselor did proudly, for each merchant had adorned his stock of beetles with his mark. Was his King not delighted?

Whereupon Avaris descended from his throne, awful in resplendent silk and gold, his feet shod with sandals of gold. And with sandals of gold he began to stomp upon the beetles. Horror overcame the merchants, who fell to their knees weeping. Some sought with their prostrate bodies to cover their beetles, but the King's guards struck them aside with staves bound in iron. The patient and tireless King stomped every beetle in the hall.

All the beetles having been stomped, and all the merchants put in chains, Avaris, his shining greaves still slick with the gore of the beetles, ordered the young counselor to be enslaved in the sewers of the palace, there to roll dung for the rest of his life.

Afterwards he called his counselors together to plan world conquest. But all the merchants' gold had been spent buying dung beetles, and no levy could be made to hire soldiers. Thus ended the lives of the counselors of Avaris; and thus ended the dream of Avaris, cursing the god who destroyed him.

TRANSLATION

AUGUST 1, 2009   Anything can be translated. How can languages differ in what they can express, in what kinds of thoughts they encourage or permit, if thoughts born and raised in one can live as well is another? But if translation is always possible it may still be hard. For simple phrases addressing familiar, everyday things, there may be only one correct translation. But as the subject moves to remoter things, things less common, translation becomes art and language becomes medium.

This is not news. Anyone can feel how difficult it is to recreate the dictionary denotations, let alone the literary connotations, of one language in another. But this is only the beginning of the art of translation, its scales and studies. The real art is not in deciding how to repeat, but how to fill in.

Abstraction is constructive omission; an abstract word is both a something that is named and the index of a number of somethings, themselves omitted, that together instantiate or imply it. Every language omits differently; and it is by this difference, I think, that language influences thought: the discrepancies of their abstractions mean that certain thoughts are harder to think in some languages than others, because in one they can be alluded to, and in another they must be constructed on the spot. The thoughts may be the same yet the attitude of the thinker towards them may be different. Compare computer languages: it is of little difference to the compiler whether a function is called by name, or defined on the spot anonymously, but it makes a difference to the programmer.

Written languages have two genealogies: linguistic and literary. The linguist who pops up to declare that language has no effect on thought is right in respect of linguistic traits. I do not see that it makes any difference to thought whether the language is gendered or genderless, analytic or agglutinative, nominative-accusative or ergative-absolutive. Thinking is so hard in itself that the general difficulty eclipses the particular difficulties or conveniences of certain languages.

But languages also have literary genealogies, and these do shape thought. It matters that English apprenticed to Latin and Greek, not Sanskrit or Chinese. Few languages have civilized – have litererized – themselves. The Old World has Greek, Sanskrit, Chinese, Egyptian and Sumerian. (The New World has Nahuatl and Quechua, but alas, they have no disciples.) All other languages had to serve an apprenticeship. Afterwards some, like the Romance languages, inherit the family business; some, like English or Japanese, buy out the stock; some, like German or Arabic, steal the plans and build their own versions.

To analyze this phenomenon as a form of domination, a side effect of economic and political power, is not wrong – witness Norman French and English, or Arabic and Persian – but it misses the point. The conquered reshape their languages by translation from their conquerors; but conquerors also reshape their languages by translation from the conquered. Greek came to Rome in the mouths of slaves. One generation of Mongols heard Arabic and Chinese only in cries for mercy; the next whispered them in their bedrooms and gardens. Translation is certainly a convenience, is certainly a political act, but it also a transmission, an inheritance, a maturation. The old language passes on to the young language something that it must work to contain – simply put, power: power to know, power to understand, power to think.

Literary descent has two vectors: borrowing and poetry. Borrowing is the easier, the most common, and usually the first method. Poetry is the harder but better method, because borrowing always leaves something behind.

When languages are young, fast, and hungry, they take words and ideas as they need them, in whichever sense comes easiest; often the wrong one. In studying classical philosophy, for example, the hardest step is to get rid of English definitions. Stoics were not stoic; Epicureans were not epicurean; *apatheia* isn't apathy, a *daimon* isn't a demon, *kosmos* isn't the cosmos, and *demokrateia* isn't democracy.

The diction of poetry is remote and patient enough, far enough from application, that it can take the time to compass an idea. Still, the transfer is not always perfect; sometimes the idea retains an inappropriate exoticism. An Athenian might agree that *beauty is truth*, but he would not have learned the lesson from his kitchenware.

Language's limits are unresisting but real. No language is without limits, but *the limits of my language are the limits of my world*, not as a wall limits my movement, but as the horizon limits my vision: I cannot see past it, yet I can never run into it.

ANTICIPATION

AUGUST 8, 2009   I refuse the game of choosing favorites, but under compulsion I might choose as my favorite book a volume of typographer's specimens – my favorite because it implies all the others. This is not a witticism. Beautiful typography pleases me more than beautiful calligraphy, not only because good typographers are more rare than good calligraphers, but because I feel something from beautiful typography that I do not feel in beautiful calligraphy.

A beautifully typeset book is for reading; but what is a book of beautiful typesetting for? The pleasure it gives me is not disinterested or abstract; it leads onto something, demands something. Above all things I love and seek and delight in understanding. How can I find pleasure in something whose purpose is to not be understood, that mocks understanding with the riddle of a quartz sphinx?

But this is backwards. This pleasure is that of anticipation; and anticipation precedes understanding. In particular cases it is the pleasure that catches and sustains attention, or that moves attention on after understanding. In the general case, it is the habit of indulging the pleasure that anticipation is, that forms the habit of seeking understanding. Anticipation is not a lapse in understanding; understanding is a lapse in anticipation. They intermit one another in an alternation that describes not a circle, but a spiral.

The apparent limit of that spiral would be to understand the world; and even if it is impossible to understand the world, it would still be possible to believe that one understood it. We read that near the end of his life Thomas Aquinas, that great understander, experienced something that made him judge his life's work *sicut palea* – all straw.

As the story is told this sounds like despair; but I imagine it as ecstasy. In an instant he broke through the false limit of complete understanding to the true limit of pure anticipation. Understanding follows anticipation,

anticipation follows understanding, but not forever; complete understanding is followed by pure anticipation. Nothing follows that. The mystics judge light higher than truth; is this what they mean by something higher than truth, yet not false? May I be so illuminated.

1943

AUGUST 21, 2009   My father died yesterday, twenty-one months after his diagnosis with pancreatic cancer. We all knew what was coming: impossibly, both of his parents died of the same disease.

I did not want to write about this. What needed saying has been said. But there will be no marker for his scattered ashes. As I am a writer I owe him the service of an epitaph, to say: *Look stranger, there lived a man, his name was Anthony Peter Rodriguez, Junior, he served his country, he had three children, two grandchildren, he never lost a friend.*

Around the time I was born my father built a tower. He was tower-minded, he knew Jung's tower, Yeats', Montaigne's, he stood once on the tower in Jericho, ten thousand years old. He mixed concrete and lay rebar and bonded block until his tower stood three stories tall and bomb shelter strong. Our names and our handprints in the concrete. A few years later, we moved away. I wasn't with him when he missed it, but I went with him to check that it was gone. Diamond saws had cut it apart to open a new owner's view. He had hoped to revisit it when he was ninety. He had hoped it would be a legacy for him. Maybe here I can give him a monument more lasting.

FRAGMENT WITH MINDS

AUGUST 29, 2009   "As instruments improved beyond the impossible and became unthinkably sensitive, reality, examined with infinite precision, proved infinitely indistinct and absolutely malleable. Between the moment and the instant, the world was found to reflect not one mind, but every mind, every mind's every passing thought; infinities of dreamers were seen each continuously remaking the world, their dreams overlapping and resonating or striking discords, flowing turbulently together, only canceling out in sum and aggregate to earthly matter and energy.

Acts of imagination were caught remaking the universe: the Sun moving instantly to circle the earth as a mind struggles with Ptolemaic astronomy, the moon dropping down to meet an infant's reaching, an old body becoming with infinite transience blithe and youthful as an old mind turns over a memory, stars and galaxies re-arranging themselves into cells, tissues, organs as the mystic feels the world in himself and himself as the world. And for the first time certain sensations of unease, certain shivers and starts of the mind, were traced to their sources, to the passing of cold fierce worlds reflecting minds not human and not kind."

EVOCATIONS

SEPTEMBER 6, 2009   Ideas are the smallest units of thought that can be communicated. In its native context, an idea may be an infinitesimally subtle inflection. When ideas may run to many words in expression, it is because they require a structure of words to reproduce that native context. At the right time, a few gestures, indeterminate in themselves, totally dependent on context for their meaning, may express all that a treatise can tell.

The constituents of the minimum unit of communicable thought must be units of incommunicable thought. I call these units of incommunicable thought *evocations*. They are what we recognize when we call something *evocative*. The mind cannot make its own evocations; it must collect them, as a bird must collect grit for its gizzard. And like a gizzard stone a single evocation may remain in use for a long time, with a valency that internally and unconsciously parallels the external and conscious use of a tool.

Being incommunicable, evocations cannot be defined. Yet they can be traced. What is it that the mind seeks out, hoards, counts over? What mental experiences, without uses of their own, are approached with the same gravity as the most useful tasks? Review the mind's senses: how an image burns into the mind's eye; how a word echoes and echoes in the mind's ear.

Victims of trauma are at the mercy of recurrence and flashback – at the mercy of the little things, the little fragments of experience, the mere reminders that reel them backwards into memory. This is a warped mirror and retrogradation of a healthy movement of the mind. Reminders drag us backwards into memory; evocations lead us forward to ideas.

Evocations are usually single words or images, but they need not be. Some evocations are ideas in themselves, constituent to more complex ideas. Whole works of art, whole journeys, whole friendships may be valent as evocations. In certain moods the whole world seems to me the evocation of some superb and singular idea I would lose my soul to enphrase – like an utterer of God's true name, a seraph would circle me to either side, declaring that I had gained the world, and lost the world to come.

CAPTCHAS

SEPTEMBER 14, 2009   The Kptsha-Knr (preferred spelling) were a reclusive tribe of hunter-browsers discovered deep in the rainforest by university researchers who got lost on their way to Seattle in 1922. They had been isolated from outside contact, with Europeans or with other natives, for their entire history. In fact, they believed themselves to be the only people in the world.

The language of the Kptsha-Knr, Qx, was a true isolate, having no relationship to any other known language (although recent efforts have been made to link it to Basque and Etruscan). Qx exhibits many unique features, not least a grammar described by the first researchers as "poly-analytic" and a quality of "neutrality" between speech and nonspeech sounds which allows the language not only to be spoken but also clicked, coughed, sighed, sputtered, swallowed and sneezed.

Once Kptsha-Knr researchers had subjected the university researchers to the surgical liberation necessary for them to pronounce the language, they began corroboration on a dictionary. This thousand page scholarly folio dictionary (Qx declensions and conjugations are mathematically incompressible) would become a bestseller on the strength of a popularized ethnography of the Kptsha written by a visiting journalist, *I Saw The Captchas: Among the Backwards Primitive Subhuman Others: As Told by the Dauntless Manly Discoverers Who Penetrated Their Stagnant Isolation and Exposed Their Feeble Barbarism to the Hard Gaze of Civilized Man.* (The book is curiously difficult to find in modern libraries and appears to have been removed from a number of catalogs with white-out.)

A brief "Captcha craze" caught the imagination of the world. For a time it seemed that everyone was doing the Cap Cha Cha, singing *Captain Captcha's Cap Chap,* or sporting slang straight from the Captcha lexicon – who can forget F. Scott Fitzgerald's immortal *Time for Knprd* or Dorothy Parker's,

Say you'll come up
And we'll brgrp.

But the fad could not last, and the Captchas were forgotten and neglected until finally, in the 1950s, their culture was destroyed by the arrival of rock and roll.

The Captchas might have faded from memory entirely were it not for a film made in the last years of the Captcha craze, *Captcha the Flag.* An early talkie, the film's wooden acting, hokey script, and "dialogue-coach voices discussing with gravity the fine points of roasting a chipmunk" (during the scene in which the Nameless Heiress has discovered a half-starved Henry Stark in the woods after her plane crash) endeared it to the hipster subculture of the 1990's. (The film is not available in restoration, due to the difficulty of separating the dialogue in the Captcha scenes from background static.)

Thus when programmers in the early 2000s began discussing the idea of a countermeasure for spam that would be "like the Navajo code, only more so," the Captcha lexicon was the natural choice. And so the Captcha, extinct, unremembered, unmourned, speak once more.

ZEMURRAY GARDENS

SEPTEMBER 21, 2009   Samuel Zemurray was the original banana republican. His Zemurray Fruit Company would later be folded into United Fruit, and Zemurray would race to United Fruit's rescue when it was in danger; but even in the 20's Huey Long could center his foreign policy on the principle that US soldiers should not be fighting in Central America at the behest of a "banana peddler."

But then what are the Zemurray Gardens? Did this hard-edged businessman possess an inner domesticity, did he retreat to a flowery sanctuary to soften his heart? Alas, no; the gardens that bear Zemurray's name were planted against his wishes. When he bought 150 acres of pine woods he reserved a certain portion for his home and assigned the rest to timberland. He thought gardening wasteful.

His wife, Sarah, did not agree. While he was away she hired a gardener and began to plant in secret. The soil (I know it well) was not friendly: thin soil, roots thick as carpets or hard and heavy as rocks, dirt so clayey – what was once the silt in the soil of the land above the Pontchartrain is now the land below the Pontchartrain – so clayey, so dense and heavy, that it holds shapes. (I once repaired a wall on an outbuilding by packing wet dirt over a framework of sticks; it was meant to be temporary, but it has lasted five years.) They cut paths through the pine woods and lined them with azaleas, thousands of azaleas of every color. She waited, I imagine, until the azaleas were blooming; then she told her husband. I would like to think that beauty moved him; whatever his reason, he spared the garden. Now above board, she enlarged and dramatized her garden: clearings with statuary, a hill, a mirror lake, an island, cypresses, camellias, a bamboo grove.

But even when I saw it the garden still had a sense of secrecy, layer after layer hidden from each other. From the highway without could be seen only pines behind pines; from the house (the gardens remained private, open only when the azaleas were blooming) and the bright garden and sward attached to it, dark paths led away into the woods. The paths were tunnels really, with dirt floors, excavated just wide enough for a jeep, stretching on and on in brilliant hypnotic monotony, color and shade, high interwoven pines swaying and admitting sunlight in waves as they swayed, sunlight on the azaleas.

Azaleas are too little celebrated in literature because they are difficult to evoke. Their flowers are of no particular size – on the order of pennies and buttons; their leaves and stem are plain and spare; and their colors are frustratingly pure – no glossiness, iridescence, variegation or sheen, just pure bright colors straight off the palette. If pigment was a stuff that fell like snow, if it had fallen on the paths here red, here yellow, here orange, and the paths had been cleared by a careless shoveler, who threw drifts of pigment over the bushes beside the path: that was how it looked. And in the shade of the azaleas sparks smoldered, the coral red berries of ardisia, and bits of broken mirror still full of sky, the sky blue of Canterbury bells.

You could – I did – go around and around this way; but you could also turn off towards the lake; or (since someone left the gate open) you could turn off on footpaths through the timberland, and, if you knew how to venture into unfamiliar woods without getting lost, rest your eyes on green and green for a time. But getting back, you could leave the paths for the lake; and stand on the bridges or sit on the island, or turn off into one of the sheltered clearings, and visit with the improbable figures of Actaeon and Diana, having long ago gotten over their bewilderment at finding themselves in so strange a land. Somewhere there was a grove of moso bamboo, thirty feet high. Somewhere there was the cemetery of the first settlers here, men of England.

This garden held gardens, gardens inside gardens, all mutually secret and enclosed. Gardeners speak lightly of rooms; Zemurray Gardens was a labyrinth – not a maze, not urgent or perplexing, but a labyrinth, long, slow, meditative and sacred.

And over everything, the trees swaying. Even when the air was still, the trees were swaying. On my first visit I looked up at the pines swaying and listened to their creaking and thought: *If a real storm ever hits this place it will be a disaster.* I was right. The storm came. (Yes, that one, I have heard and written the name often enough). The trees fell and broke, the paths collapsed – it happened to me, how strange that a path could just disappear – the storm came and Zemurray Gardens was destroyed. You can look at pictures of it online – it is worth doing – but these photographers pictured the wrong things; they gave the wrong idea. But I remember it, in my mind and in my garden. The ardisia is just starting to spread.

NUMBERS: A SATIRE

SEPTEMBER 28, 2009   Endower Institute researchers today announced the discovery of a completely new kind of number, the "like number." Like numbers are the first new kind of number to be introduced into mathematics since Donald Knuth's "surreal numbers." Surreals were previously considered the most exotic form of number, but like numbers, according to lead researcher Dr. Pangloe, are "an even wilder expansion of the conventional idea of what a 'number' is allowed to be."

Unlike most mathematical concepts, "like numbers" were not discovered by a process of abstract reasoning, but through analysis of natural language. In fact, according to Dr. Pangloe, "Most people have an intuitive understanding of like numbers." He blames the failure of mathematicians to study like numbers on "an archaic attachment to the Victorian notion of 'formal' proof. This fetish for 'formality' has blinded so-called mathematicians from embracing what was right in front of them all along."

Like numbers, besides familiar numerical properties such as transitivity, associativity, and operability, have a range of new properties such as plausibility, ginormity, pertinence, and, in some formulations, prurience. Like numbers form an algebraic structure and support all the operations of a conventional field – addition, multiplication, subtraction, and division – but also allow for allusion, revision, recreation, and interpretation, among many other previously unknown operations.

A like number is notated using a new technique called indifferent expressions – similar in form to lambda expressions. As a conventional number is defined in lambdas as a higher-order anonymous function, a like number is defined in indifference as a higher-order inscrutable gesture. Indifferent expressions, however, are much more general in their potential applications than lambda expressions, and methods are now being developed to apply them not only to mathematical entities but to social phenomena and physical objects. "Just a few days ago," said Dr. Pangloe, "one of my students, in my presence, altered the deadline on his paper from three weeks to like a month. I myself have on several occasions reduced – my wife can testify – three, six, even ten drinks to like two. These are exactly the kind of real-world applications that mathematicians have been allowed to ignore for much too long."

The research will be published in the forthcoming inaugural edition of the *Journal of Experimental Mathematics* (Endower Institute J-16). This new publication will be edited by the leading members of the controversial X-Math movement. "It's time," said Dr. Pangloe in his office, pointing to a poster behind him with the movement's symbol, a flaming brain, "for mathematicians to leave behind their obsolete elitist claims of a special status among the sciences and embrace more modern, creditable methods."

CROWD VERBS

OCTOBER 2, 2009   Nothing is harder to describe in writing than the behavior of a crowd. Something so everyday as how people act when ten of us appear in the same place with the same object of attention, something so affordant for performers, preachers, and politicians, should be accompanied by a large, refined, and subtle vocabulary. Instead we are stuck with a scale of behaviors graduated so coarsely that it is almost useless. A crowd can go wild, roar, applaud, get caught up, be intent, hush, be restless, be tough, be hostile, boo, hiss, jeer, and riot. There are more words, but on investigation they prove to be empty variations.

Crowd – the name itself is almost an abstraction. Its few synonyms only distinguish different venues: a gathering, an assembly, an audience, a congregation, an attendance. Among animals we can distinguish flocks, herds, swarms, pods, colonies, hives, schools, and packs, but among human beings we can only say crowds, crowds, crowds, though the human differences are greater.

(At this point in the essay I consulted a thesaurus, which yielded *throng*, a contraction for "crowd I don't like," and *mob*, a contraction for "crowd that doesn't like me." Later I thought of *the crush* and *had to be there*, which are promising but undeveloped.)

Language fails, and image fails too: film's cantaloupe-murmuring crowds, its paid extras and vain camera-forward onlookers, are a convention as familiar and as absurd as sound technicians scoring heel clicks to sneakers.

When you hear or think or are tempted to say that language and literature are perfected, that there is nothing left for writers, poets, and translators to do but footnote and allude, remember that there is a hole in language big enough for everything from a picnic to a revolution to fall through. I doubt it is the only one.

SELFISHNESS

OCTOBER 9, 2009   Foolish love of self is still more mysterious than foolish love of others. Loving others is obviously adaptive, but self-love is neither necessary nor helpful to survival. Our species that must raise its young for a decade or more must set strong social bonds, but the conditions of individual survival are the same for human beings as for other animals. The snake, the scorpion, the squid, fight as hard to live as we do, but they do not love at all.

Does love serve a purpose? With questions of behavior such judgments should hesitate. In animals so complex and complexifying as we, the most that can be proved of a behavior is that it is not maladaptive. The capacity to love does not harm the survival of the race. Beyond that, the fact that the brain supports love may be no more significant than the fact that the brain supports solving crossword puzzles. Everything possible with love is possible without love, if not all at once. And insects exhibit forms of social cohesion as strong or stronger than ours without love.

If love is mysterious, why should one object be more mysterious than another? But the trajectory by which you could love yourself is a mystery of its own. How can the self present itself to itself as an object of love? The introspective mind can think about itself only as a sort of mirror image that corresponds to it at every point, yet is not it – the mirror of Narcissus. But selfishness is cognate to narcissism, not collateral: a self-image of sainthood may produce narcissism with selflessness.

Selfish people are not self-centered. They do not pride themselves on their selfishness – they do not even see it. Indeed their most repellent trait is that they resent the selfishness of others without seeing their own, even when it is a double to their own.

The poets are wrong. Foolish love is not blind – love is blind only as the eye is blind, with a blind spot. The beloved may be ugly or stupid or cruel, but the lover who overlooks all these things in one person does not fail to see them in others. Lovers of ugly people do not otherwise surround themselves with ugliness; of stupid people, do not otherwise seek out stupidity; of cruel people, do not otherwise invite cruelty. But their judgment is not intact. It is always disappointing to meet someone you know only through their lover's description. In these cases, it is more than disappointing; it is shocking.

The impairment of the selfish is another blind spot, only self-directed. But this explanation is only another mystery. How does the blind spot happen? In following the parallels of selfishness and foolish love we avoid the easy and wrong explanations of each. Chemistry, charisma, propinquity, neediness, passive aggression, codependency – these cannot come between you and yourself. They cannot explain the blind spot. Conversely we learn how incurable selfishness is when we compare it to foolish love. You can no more convince someone of the absurdity of their self-regard than you can convince someone of the unworthiness of their beloved. No logic will dispel it, no shock will unseat it, and the more absurd it is, the more intervention will be resented.

This long analogy is the preparation for a brief and severe conclusion: there is no way to prevent selfishness and no way to cure it. Perhaps in refusing to tolerate selfish behavior, in avoiding selfish people, you may nudge some cases away from the brink. But the pit is bottomless and those who fall in cannot be rescued. Their very sin is its own *contrapasso*, its own poetic justice. They lie in darkness where they eat their own hearts. Leave them there. May it not be one you love.

MIRRORS

OCTOBER 16, 2009   There were mirrors of natural reflections before there were eyes to see; there were signs and similitudes before there were minds to see them. Eyes themselves are but incomplete mirrors, keeping the images that mirrors return. The world before us was full of mirrors, as the world beside us is full of mirrors; but eyes had never seen something endless until a human being faced mirror to mirror; until a human being adjured into matter that same recess of mirrors in mirrors reflecting inside his own skull; until mind represented mind. We are made of mirrors, and this is why we are so easily trapped by them. It is easier to turn your eyes from glaring in hate or staring in lust than from preening in mirrors. The ancients gazed on clear water and black glass in search of mere shadows of themselves; but we have opened the secret of the silvered mirror. Our backhanded images follow us everywhere. Before we can even speak we are entangled with mirrors. First they show us our selves, then they show us our self-awareness, then our self-awareness of our self-awareness, on and on, back and forth until we are wound up in our selves yet we have no selves without the mirror, until self and mirror are the foci of an elliptical orbit around the fact of reflection, until mind and mirror combine into mind – one mind whose parts are all men and all mirrors. Mirrors are our masters; but who minds serving masters who look at us with our own eyes?

SOLITUDE

OCTOBER 23, 2009   The appeal of solitude may be as simple as the dislike of repetition. To be gregarious implies infinite patience for retelling the same anecdote, confessing the same weakness, counting over the same favorites, relating the same background. Identity becomes a matter of performance and habit, not expressed in but being the routine of self-introduction. Just to avoid this explains why people may chose to be solitary; just the time won from having avoided it explains how people can find pleasure in something apparently so unnatural.

But is there a positive definition of solitude – is there something that solitude is? Certainly if one of us ventures a bracketed solitude, and another one of us commits to a prolonged solitude; if one of us is solitary by choice, and another one of us is driven to it – each of us gives a different thing the name of solitude.

And surely what solitude is has changed and is changing? Surely technology is banishing solitude as it banishes loneliness?

Distinguish two measures of solitude: quantity of social interactions, and quantity of people interacted with. Eliminate repetitions. By the first measure – how much time we spend with others – the most gregarious of our ancestors was more solitary than the most solitary of us. The lines of communication were so few, so thin, and so uncertain that to pursue them itself required solitude – to write a letter is a solitary act. But by the second measure – how many others we spend time with – we are freakishly solitary. So many people once had to be dealt with to do the things we do by mail, message, and machine – so many butchers, bakers, candlestick makers, so many drivers and porters, all to do what takes us no more than a few words with a cashier! (And the cashier is increasingly dispensable.) The two measures of solitude do not vary inversely – to be solitary in both senses is possible and could define loneliness – but to lessen solitude by one measure is to increase it by the other. In this sense we are all solitary.

This sounds like a curse; but in truth it is a homeostasis. Life adjusts to provide us a minimum of solitude as the body adjusts to provide us a minimum of warmth. Solitude is a thing, not a state; it answers an appetite, not a purpose. Something vital, something necessary, something catalytic, some nutriment or vitamin of the mind, something as vital and replenishing to human beings as light is to plants – this something is found, it falls, everywhere, except where other people obstruct it.

Yet the dullness and rigidity of repetition can be avoided, and the vigor and fecundity of solitude can be protected, without isolation. All it takes is to be all things to all men, which is the same skill as getting along with all sorts of people; an easy thing if you are willing to be lead and not to lead in talk, to let people think of you what they want to, and to give simple answers to simple questions when the truth would be obstructively complicated. In this way people can be read almost like books – like old books that fall open to certain pages.

This approach is too habitual with me. Why I write here is uncertain – my reasons change every week – but surely one reason is to take cross-sections of myself without any particularly restrictive sense of audience. The Ruricolist does not represent me in full; many of my interests go unrepresented here; but here I set the topics, pursue their complications, and claim the right to confuse. In writing about solitude I abandon it. But that is the kind of contradiction that essays live on.

LEAD

OCTOBER 30, 2009   The history of technology is the history of human weakness. The rest of history is only surface: what happens once human weakness has been compensated for, or at least accepted. But most things that happen, happen below the surface. There is another history that only technology records.

Consider glasses. Every person you see wearing glasses is another person rescued who, a hundred years ago or less, would simply have lived with bad eyesight. And bad eyesight doesn't feel like not being able to see; it feels like headaches, tiredness, irritability, helplessness. How many billions of us have lived out uneasy lives in desperation and doubt, all for a trick of the light?

The most significant freedom which artists acquired in the twentieth century was not freedom from patronage, but the freedom to assume a public with good eyesight.

For the diffusion of political authority, the gradual rise in test scores, and other trends of the last century which suggest the human race is becoming smarter, the most parsimonious explanation is simply that the human race is seeing better.

But consider something less conspicuous: consider bread and water.

Billions of us having pure water on tap means more than victory over worm and germ. Before pure water the only safe drink was drink. Since civilization began ours may be the first generation to live sober.

And bread. Enriched bread means more than the eclipse of diseases like rickets or scurvy. Consider pregnancy – consider the dietetic demands of scientifically managed pregnancy. Number the nutritional concerns to which a conscientious mother is now expected to attend. We are overly cautious, of course, but not in every precept. To be born as a peasant – and most people who have ever been born, were born peasants – was to be born maimed in advance by the neglect of every one of these precepts.

Is aristocracy the social order that results when only a minority can be kept well-fed enough to think clearly? Is democracy the social order that results when the majority are not born a little brain-damaged?

Somewhere in his *Anatomy of Melancholy*, Burton, in the early 17th century, writes that if lead were really poisonous – as some recognized even then – all the nobility would be poisoned with it, for they all brought their water in by lead pipe. (Hand-worked pipes, mind, not machined.) Centuries later, his fellow apprentices in printing thought young Ben Franklin laughably fastidious for wearing gloves to set lead type.

Now consider our recent century of lead-based paint and leaded gasoline.

This is what it means to be human. Small things, things we can do nothing about, things we do not even recognize as dangerous, undo us before we know we have been harmed. The pipes in our houses, the paint on our cradles, the gas in our parents' cars, leave us ruined before we are built, and lead stands the silent ruler of a stupefied world.

This weakness is something we work to forget. We cannot always be on guard. We cannot live our lives as though they were fragile and uncertain. We must build and plan. So we imagine that if life was tougher then, it just meant more rigorous selection. When we look backward we do not see weakness. Our forebears stood as straight as we do. Surely, the average human being then was at least as healthy as the average human being now, when technology coddles our softer stuff.

But look to the mountains. The mountains, their soil washed sterile with rain, have always subjected their residents to malnutrition. Yet there, even as they lived, worked, built, sang, and bred, their thyroids swelled and poked goiters out of their necks. Human beings are very tough. What doesn't kill us, we get used to.

"Human weakness" is something real; but it is not in sin and not in absurdity. We are not bad; we are not silly. We won, after all. We came into this world as food for the animals we now keep in zoos and preserves and kennels. But we are still weak. We are weak because we are fragile. We can do everything except save ourselves. Our abilities – our wonderful abilities – are so easily prevented, so easily unseated, that it may be done without our noticing. Being born and being fed are enough to destroy us.

A diamond is as hard as anything; edge to edge, it can always wins. Yet a single well-placed tap can shatter a diamond. Just because a diamond is hard, the slightest flaw affords the leverage to cleave it through and through. We are all such diamonds. It is because we are strong that we are fragile. We are the houses built on sand: and when the house falls down, it is the house, not the sand, that makes the pity.

Yet though we break, though we break so easily and in so many ways, we remain ourselves. Diamond dust is still diamond. The things our blind, starved, poisoned, crippled forebears made in their darkness and desperation transcend their particular frailties and reach us clear and full of strength. When they wrote, we can read. What they sang, we can hear. What they pictured, we can see. What they made, we can use. What they learned, we can know.

Technology is what repairs weakness, and in doing so lets us see it, for the first time, as what it always was – weakness. History is the record of what we do despite our weakness. And the third thing – call it culture – is what, as it passes from one generation to the next, combines our strengths, omits our weaknesses, and represents us to ourselves whole: whole as we should be, whole as we can never be.

THREE HORROR STORIES

Halloween, 2009

I

"Hello? I'm still down here. Open the door. Can you hear me – hey! Put the lights back on! This is a joke, right? Very funny! Open the door! Wait – I know you're down here somewhere. I can hear you moving around. That is you, right?"

II

"Well. Yes, we've received the test results. There's really nothing to worry about. The guard? He's always here. Hospital policy. Let's get this over with. Have you experienced an increase or decrease in appetite recently? Have you experienced hardening, discoloration, or rapid growth of the fingernails? How about any strange shapes or colors that recur in your dreams? Hmm. Well, no, the problem isn't your eyes *exactly*. Have you recently been to Africa? South America? Antarctica? The specialist's on his way, there's nothing to worry about. One more question, and this one may sound a little strange, but I need you to answer it honestly. When was the last time you *defiled* something?"

III

"It's great to meet somebody else who's not afraid of heights. Do you come up here often?"

"Every once in a while. I love the view. It gives me a sense of freedom. Like I could do anything up here. Like I can see the world but it can't see me."

"It's a great view. It's great until you look down, yeah? I mean I'm not afraid of heights, but that is one hell of a drop."

"Close your eyes for a second. I want to show you something."

NEW IDEAS

NOVEMBER 6, 2009   New ideas become simpler over time. This is most obvious in intellectual domains, where the work that introduces an idea never shows how simple it can be. The first draft, being new, is labored, and being new-fangled, is cautious.

This is less obvious in other domains. A late mechanical clock, though compact, looks far more complex than a room-filling medieval clock. But the idea is not the clock; it is the escapement. The painstaking blacksmith, evaluating materials, working and reworking them, test-fitting, filing and re-fitting – his efforts were more complex than the industrial procedures which allow an escapement to be made by someone who has no idea what one is. Likewise the modern computer looks far more complex, though compact, than the Cold War computer, big as a car, a room, a house. But the new idea was not the machine; it was the transistor, and now Shockley's circuit, which took days to build, is printed by the millions in fractions of seconds.

Of course, as an artifact, the industrial clock is far more complex than the medieval, and the post-industrial computer is far more complex than the industrial. But artifacts are not ideas. Indeed the clearest definition of an idea, its clearest distinction from other kinds of constituent thought, is that the idea is the part that becomes simpler over time.

Ideas appear to obey a kind of conservation principle, one of complexity. In order for an idea to stand on its own, it must be complex in itself. In order for an idea to be simple, it must be embedded inside of a complex system. This is easy to understand for clocks and computers – as mechanisms and circuits get simpler, they get smaller and more fragile, and must be embedded in more complex, larger, more robust objects.

But simplicity is not a function of size. Consider guns: as the idea of driving a projectile with expanding gas got simpler, guns did get smaller – a path runs from the cannon that destroyed Byzantium's walls to the concealable pistol – but they also got bigger – guns have been built to launch payloads into space. Or consider the internal combustion engine, which powers motor scooters as well as container ships.

This principle holds for all sizes of artifacts, and for all degrees of abstraction. Complex ideas in complex systems are possible, but perverse. Simple ideas in simple systems are also possible, but limited to the first steps of a technology. But for an idea to be useful, it must begin as a complex idea in a simple system, and end as a simple idea in a complex system.

Let me suggest some practical consequences.

1. By the time an idea has become simple enough to be generally understood it has usually ceased to be independently useful. Sometimes this is tautological: when everyone understands democracy, democracy already exists.

2. An idea is not a realization; a realization is not an idea. Few improvements are due to ideas; most are due to realizations. Someone *realizes* that step B could be eliminated by an alternative to step C; someone has the *idea* that the entire process is wrongheaded. To equate realizations and ideas both neuters useful but limited realizations by turning them into abstractions, and suppresses ideas by simplifying them prematurely. Treating realizations as ideas is how we get the anti-ideas of management theory. Losing ideas among mere realizations is how once-great company X is bankrupted by startup or foreign competitors, whose ideas inevitably turn out to have been screened as babies from company X's torrential bathwater.

3. When an idea is new it may be unclear which part of the initial formulation is the idea. Often you must proceed with no more than a sense that your line of research contains a new idea somewhere in it. And even when the initial formulation is ready for use, use must sometimes be widespread and practical before the idea stands out.

Consider guns again. A submachine gun is a sort of hybrid of the rifle and the pistol. It uses pistol rounds in a rifle-sized frame. Since the gun is relatively heavy and the rounds are relatively low-powered, an individual can control the recoil when the weapon is fired on automatic. But the first submachine gun – the Thompson, that is, the Tommy gun – was not designed with this idea in mind.

One of its inventors had observed in his time on battleships that under the conditions of high pressure in the firing of a naval gun different metals would stick to one another. He called his observation (after himself) the Blish Principle of Metallic Adhesion and patented it as a way of dissipating recoil. In fact what makes recoil manageable is a heavy gun. But not only were the first Thompsons built with Blish's slivers of brass in them, they continued to be built this way until the scale of wartime production eliminated the extra step. The weapon had been in service for two decades before the idea behind it became clear.

But enough complication. Surely I have given this idea enough complexity to start on.

SEVERITY

NOVEMBER 13, 2009   Severity apes wisdom. It looks like wisdom, it acts like wisdom. But severity is no more a kind of wisdom than fool's gold is a kind of gold. Severity is to wisdom as pedantry is to intelligence. Any quality of mind or dedication of energies that can achieve intelligence can also incur pedantry. Whoever ends up a pedant has missed becoming intelligent, and whoever ends up intelligent has evaded being a pedant. The same terms hold between whoever ends up severe and whoever ends up wise.

Being a pedant is easier than being intelligent. To continue being a pedant only means repeating what you have done before. To continue being intelligent means judging what you have done before. Severity, in the same way, is easier than wisdom. To continue being severe only requires that you go on denying and refusing. To continue being wise requires that you sometimes deny and sometimes accept, sometimes refuse and sometimes permit, according to the good you can do.

Sometimes you must be severe to be wise. Often you must be severe with yourself, must brace or flense yourself. Rarely you must be severe with others, to awaken or correct them. Severity taints trust (no one hugs a cactus twice): the difference between *often* and *rarely* is in the impossibility of resenting your own severity, and the certainty of your severity being resented by others. They will resent your severity even when you owe it to them – even when they ask it of you. Sometimes you must be severe to be wise; but the wisdom is in the wisdom, not in the severity.

FABLE OF THE WASP AND THE CATERPILLAR

NOVEMBER 20, 2009   The caterpillar had only been chewing though leaves, chewing and crawling as he had for his whole short life. Chewing and crawling – these were the only things he knew.

Then he felt something he had never felt before. There was a weight on him. He could not move. His legs were frozen. A feeling ran through him, chill and warmth at once, something slipping in between all the segments of his long, narrow body. Then the weight was gone. Still he could not move.

Once he could move again he returned to chewing and crawling, for these were the only things he knew. But the leaves tasted strange to him now. They did not satisfy him. Day by day their taste faded, yet day by day he hungered more. He ate and ate until his skin grew tight, but still he was not satisfied. Once, at the end of a leaf, his hunger was so frenzied that he tried to eat the stem. He cried out in desperation and despair.

At his cry the other caterpillars came to ask him what was wrong. He looked at the other caterpillars, fat and happy, slow, stupid crawlers and slow, patient eaters, and burning heat rose in him. He screamed at them and cursed them. "Chew and crawl! Crawl and chew! Leaf after leaf, all the same! Wake up. This is not all there is. This can't be all there is. You're all the same! You all want me to be just like you, nothing, to be nothing, to do nothing, just blend in, just hide, just pretend not to exist."

They stared at him with blank, hurt stares. Their fat bodies waved and jiggled on their little legs. He hated them more for being hurt by his hate.

"You're all disgusting. You're all pathetic. You're just holding me back with your stupid crawling and your stupid chewing. I won't do this anymore. I'm leaving. Nobody follow me."

He left and nobody followed him.

His days were all his own now. He spent them chewing and crawling, but now he could chew and crawl in his own way. He wasn't like them anymore. Something had happened to him. Something had touched him and set him apart. He had been chosen for something – chosen, him! So all alone he chewed and crawled and waited for the thing to come, waited for his destiny to arrive, the grand destiny he knew was prepared for him.

Sometimes at first he would stop, stop and scream at no one in particular, just to scream out the rage that filled him at all the fat stupid caterpillars and all their stupid chewing and stupid crawling. But now, even as his thinning body began to swell again, his rage was softening. Instead of desperation he felt clarity, and instead of rage, he felt pity. He had been chosen, he knew, but he had not just been chosen – he had been elevated. He was above them in every way. He would look down on the caterpillars to watch their slow mindless chewing and crawling. Sometimes he would laugh, sometimes cry. There was so much more, yet they couldn't see it. They were so small, so trapped, so limited. He, he alone, was free.

He could feel his destiny coming. It was close now. Chewing and crawling lost their interest for him. In deep shadow his body burned from an inner sun. He paused in long meditative reveries. He could feel the imminence of some great change. He would meet it with acceptance and gratitude, thankful to have been the one chosen, thankful to be the one who woke up. He no longer slept. His dreams and his waking sight fused until it seemed that everything he saw contained everything he could see. The moment was closer now. The moment was here. The clarity, the clarity hurt. The heat, the heat, he seemed to melt. He could not move but he was moving – there was movement – something moved – something stretched and twisted – something gave way –

Sometime later, in jewel colors still slick with caterpillar-stuff, a wasp took flight.

Moral: *The God reveals but not as a Reward.*

XERXES

November 27, 2009   The *xerxes* is my private unit of chronometry. One xerxes separates year A and year B such that every adult alive in year A is dead by year B.

The xerxes is only an approximation. It excludes outliers – the lapse of a xerxes does not wait on the world's last living; it excludes anyone whose very survival is newsworthy. A xerxes is concluded once you can look at a picture or a list of names and be confident that all the faces and all the names you see belong to dead men. Setting adulthood at 15, and lifespan at three score and ten, and affording a margin of safety of 1/3, a xerxes rounds down to a period of 70 years.

The xerxes implies another unit, the half-xerxes. The half-xerxes separates year A and year B such that half of all people alive in year B were not yet adults in year A. I set the half-xerxes, with less certainty, at 35 years – with less certainty because wars, plagues, and baby booms too easily throw it off. (Otherwise we could more elegantly rely on the half-xerxes as our primary unit.)

Nothing happens only when it happens. Everything memorable recurs in memory until memory is extinguished. And when that memory is a shared one, like the memories enforced by disaster and strife, it establishes, among those who remember, a secret language of allusions and reminders with power beyond ordinary language. The consequences of this language, even at dark removes, are still in truth the consequences of that event.

Thus in order to judge an event, we must look at it three times: first, contemporaneously, so we can judge what it means when everyone remembers it; second, from a half-xerxes, so we can judge what it means once most people no longer remember it; and third, from a xerxes, so we can judge what it means once no one remembers it. And until the third look all judgments remain provisional.

Consider the world wars. Given the double carnage of the trenches and the Spanish Flu, it is plausible to mark a half-xerxes between the end of WWI and the beginning of WWII. And though a connection is difficult to prove, it is suggestive that the Soviet Union, instituted in reaction to WWI, collapsed a xerxes after it. In Russia and Europe, where WWII was bloodiest, the half-xerxes of that war came in 1968. In the US it took the full 35 years, until 1980 and the collapse of the "liberal consensus." (On this pattern I intend to keep my eyes open in 2015, when the xerxes of WWII concludes.)

I take the name of this unit from a story in Herodotus. Xerxes the Persian, king of kings, looked over his army of a million men, the greatest army the world had ever seen, absolutely loyal to him, he the greatest ruler the world had ever known – a million men aimed under his command to the ruin and conquest of obstreperous Greece. But as he sat and saw on his hillside throne, something gave way in his mind. Some inward support, rotted out with secret melancholy, broke and let him fall. Xerxes looked at a million strong, proud, fearless men; but Xerxes saw only time and decay and death. Xerxes (a poor calculator) thought that in a hundred years not one of these men would be alive; and thinking so, Xerxes, king of kings, before his army of a million men – Xerxes wept.

QUOTATIONS

DECEMBER 4, 2009   I hate to quote. This is twice perverse. It perverse because I admire writing heavy in quotations; and it is perverse because quotations are basic to the essay as a form. The essayists of the age of gold (imperial gold, flowing and counted) were fluent in quotation. Montaigne quoted so widely from Plutarch and Seneca that they are regarded as the essay's classical models as much for the force of Montaigne's evident admiration as for the content of their works. Bacon, second essayist, in his first essay, of Death, quotes – no, misquotes – Montaigne. The essayists of the age of silver (mirror silver, clear and perspicuous) nucleated their untitled essays around classical quotations. The essayists of the age of iron (plate iron, driving and bearing) often simply titled their essays with quotations, reserving the climax of the essay to return to it in closing. The essayists of our age of lead (quiet lead, soldering microcosmic circuits) generally admit rhetorical effects into their essays only in the form of choice quotations. But when I quote, I feel like a parasite.

Sometimes quotation is necessary. Sometimes I owe a train of thought to a quotation, and the source must be acknowledged. Sometimes a quote embodies a thought so perfectly that any paraphrase would be a diminution. And sometimes borrowing a quote that has famously been used before, suggests a connection without having to dilute an essay with an explicit reference.

Nonfiction begins in quotation – quotation is not just a mechanism peculiar to nonfiction, but the very means by which nonfiction split from fiction, the means by which what can be written about has become more and more. The pre-Socratics, quoting Homer, show that they are doing something different than Homer. Socrates and Plato quote Homer and the pre-Socratics; Aristotle quotes Homer, the pre-Socratics, Socrates, and Plato; Zeno quotes Homer and the pre-Socratics and Socrates and Plato and Aristotle. Each new regress of quotation, turning background into foreground, expands what can be written about by an order of magnitude. And so we are arrived.

Still, for every good quotation can do, I perceive an equal bad. Literature can be concatenated from quotations – see Burton, Eliot – but if concatenating quotations were enough to make literature, theses would be worth reading. Quotations compress impossibly long arguments; quotations hide chasms with too convenient bridges. Quotations let a piece of writing claim a place in a tradition; quotations shroud child thoughts in adult costumes. Quotations prevent duplication of work, save the time lost in saying what has already been said; quotations lose integrity. Quotations index large thoughts and subtle experiences, name them when they have no names; quotations substitute naming for understanding. Quotations, for the author, let reading propel writing to the benefit of both; quotations, for the author, restrict reading to what can be quoted without embarrassment, or conceal the real sources of thoughts with quotable ones.

The worst literary offense of quotation is the same as its scholarly benefit: it corroborates and exemplifies. "See! Someone else thought as I do. Someone else has felt as I do." Very good. You bring proofs with your argument. But let me ask: are you sure that all these proofs don't make your argument weaker? An abstract argument, if it is precise and clear, can always be tested. Too many examples make an argument weaker, not stronger; every example suggests a line of refutation. Logically, refuting the examples should not affect the argument; rhetorically, it is fatal. If your quotation is not representative, if it does not mean exactly what you think it means, if the attribution is false, if it comes from a source that has fallen into disfavor, your argument will go unheard.

I write less to develop new thoughts than to clear out old ones. Most writers read to write; I write to read. Before I can start new trains of thought I need the old ones off the tracks. A few months ago I called writing "trephination"; I meant it. I write for the same reason people have holes drilled in their heads: to let off pressure, to drain superfluity. The image is extreme but then I find writing an extreme habit: intense, nerving-wracking, time-consuming, consuming – yet not only worthwhile but necessary, devoutly necessary. Somewhere in the labyrinth that perplexed me into becoming a writer I lost the connection between writing and quotation; or in my indirect approach I never made it. Either way, I do not regret the lack.

ATTENTION SPAN

DECEMBER 12, 2009   I wish my attention span were shorter. Something that wastes my attention robs me as surely as someone who steals my wallet. Cultivating a long attention span is foolish in the same way as carrying large bills. True, there is little that does not interest me (or that I cannot imagine myself being interested in so vividly as to make it so). But even interesting subjects can be made uninteresting when their performance or exposition is subverted by dishonesty, pretense, or false naivety. The ability to pay attention despite lack of interest is strength of character, not strength of mind, and is maintained by the will at the expense of the intellect.

The hardest thing that eyes can do is stare. Precisely because our eyes are such efficient channels of information, the one thing they cannot do is settle passively on a single object. In fact staring is impossible. If the eyes were to stop moving, they would stop seeing; the principle of vision is not focus, but contrast. The possibility of sight depends on the continued tiny, restless motions of the eye called *saccades*: what the mind sees through the eyes is not the light that falls on them, but the contrasts in light which the saccades gather. To see is to look away; this is physiological fact.

Attention has the same principle. The harder you focus your attention, the narrower a channel your attention becomes, toward the conclusion of sleep. The more freedom you give your attention, the broader it becomes, the better it works. When you are rapt your attention is really rapt, trapped – not still, but caged; not pinioned to a subject but centered on it, pacing before and around it. All your instincts are for motion. When you look on a strange object, you walk around it. When you look on a beautiful face, you survey it in passes from eye to eye. The first thing an artist learns is not to stare. The first thing a thinker must learn is how to be distracted.

FABLE OF THE DOG AND THE WOLF

DECEMBER 18, 2009   Deep in the young, impatient woods an old woman lived in a small cabin, alone except for her dog. She had lived there for a long time. Once the cabin stood in a field. Then she had a husband and children there. But now the husband was buried, the children were far away, and the fields where wheat had grown bore bramble and pine. The last time someone had walked up the path, it was to bring her a puppy. Now the puppy was a dog, and the path only appeared when rain filled it and washed the pine needles away. But the old woman had her high fence, and her rich garden within it, and lived well though her eyes were failing her.

Into the pathless woods, wolves had come. They stalked beyond the fences, but the dog barked his deep bark and kept the posts carefully marked and the wolves left them alone – all the wolves but one. He watched through the fence and saw the woman feed the dog, pet it, sit beside it. He thought that the dog had an easy life. He wanted an easy life like that.

One day a tree fell and made a hole in the fence. The wolf saw his chance. He dragged his matted fur against the brambles until it was straight and smooth and swam in the river until his smell was gone. Then he leapt over the fence while the woman was petting the dog and, as he had seen the dog do, he put his face under his paws and whined. The dog attacked but the old woman – who still had strength – called him off and dragged him inside and shut him in a closet while she befriended the new dog.

Whenever the dog tried to warn her about the wolf she punished him. After a time he gave up warning, and set himself to watching, following the wolf everywhere. The wolf didn't mind. He was fed and petted and careless. He even took punishment when he had to – he could always leave.

One day the old woman did not come out. The dog cried and the wolf howled at her locked door but she did not answer. After a few days the wolf jumped back through the hole in the fence. The dog stayed while the garden ran to weeds, while he wore thinner and thinner in waiting. He stayed until the brambles wrapped the fences. Then he too jumped through the hole in the fence, out into the woods.

The woods were thick and sharp and he knew nothing of hunting. He nearly starved before he caught something, and nearly starved again, and again, until his instincts were all awakened and he found he could hunt at last. His muscles grew strong and lean, his fur grew thick and matted. He smelled of pine needles and old blood.

Once he looked up from his catch and saw a wolf, then two wolves, then three. They were all around him. He backed off from the kill and the wolves leapt on it – all but one, who sniffed him, turned, drove the other wolves back, and let the dog eat. When the eating was done the dog left with the wolves, a dog walking as a wolf beside a wolf who had lived as a dog.

Moral: *Nature forms strange Eddies at the Shore.*

POETRY

JANUARY 3, 2010   I write poems but I will not call myself a poet. My experiments in poetry are as much tinkering as writing. The way meter, phrase, caesura, and alliteration combine into poems fascinates me like an exhibition watch, or a dissection. I try to follow the articulations and disarticulations; to test my understanding, I try to build or animate for myself. But prose has never failed me; I turn thoughts into poems not because I must, but because I can. And for the most difficult thoughts, I turn to prose first.

In writing about poetry it seems obligatory either to defend or diagnose Modern Poetry. But there is too much to generalize about, and I do not want to generalize or judge. I only want to ask a question. "If poetry did not exist, would anyone invent it?" It seems to me that all poems now must answer this question; and that most of them answer "no."

(Admittedly, I dislike hermeticism in poetry. I am indifferent to whether poetry is accessible – inaccessibility no more vitiates good poetry than accessibility excuses bad poetry – but I resent hermeticism, not because it is elite, but because it is the ape of elitism. A secret society imitates how an elite looks from the outside, substituting loyalty for merit and ritual for sympathy. [That is, an elite is the only true secret society.] When poetry has a hermetic seal, I am content to leave it shut.)

How could poetry be invented in a world that reveres songwriting? It has the flavor of a brainstorm: "You know how there's that piano piece, right – 'Song Without Words'? Well how about a song without music?" Remember how uncertain the boundaries of poetry and song have always been. Much that is read as poetry was written as song or chant. And modern singers are adept at setting poetry to music.

It is not even cheaper anymore to be a poet than to be a songwriter. If you add up the cost of your Moleskines you will have saved little over the cost of a laminate guitar, an electronic tuner, a digital recorder, and a copy of *Guitar for Feckless Morons*. Three chords will get you far; if you can type, you can fret. If your poem cannot be set to music, why not call it prose? What give a special name to prose with whitespace? Why elevate a typographic distinction into a literary one? And if your poem can be set to music, why should anyone pay attention if you cannot be bothered to take the extra step?

Music only vitiates the form of poetry; photography displaces the need for poetry. The impulse to preserve, embody, and share an experience, the impulse poetry satisfies, photography satisfies just as well and much more easily. Poetry is intensely osmotic. Doggerel is not inept poetry, but dry poetry – poetry squeezed from a mind already drained of what poetry should absorb. Photography is another valve on the same vessel. If you would be a poet, leave your camera behind.

Poetry will go on losing: losing to music, losing to photography. It has already lost; yet I will not give up on it. Poetry has been cornered before and survived. Writing relieved poetry of its responsibility for history; printing relieved poetry of its role in education. Textbooks of math and grammar were once written in verse, to aid memorization; that is a revival nobody wants. Now recording and photography are relieving poetry of its responsibility for contemplation and confession. What is left for it, I do not know.

Poetry does not need a savior. The question has been answered, many times. But each poet who has found an answer has found their own answer. No one has established a general answer that imitators can build on. And simply being original cannot be the answer. Imitation, both imitating and being imitated, is indispensable. An art where every achievement is unique, where nothing can be built on, is unsustainable. And an art where only genius is adequate is not worthwhile for anyone, genius included.

"If poetry did not exist, would anyone invent it?" Because I cannot answer this question, I am not a poet. I will call you poet if you can.

BOURGEOIS

JANUARY 14, 2010   *Bourgeois* is a curse word. When I read the word *bourgeois*, I generally stop reading. When it slips out, I forgive it. But when the author persists in repeating it, as if they have just made a discovery, I leave.

Yet I am not sure that I disbelieve in the bourgeois. At times I almost see a class of people – a very large class of people – who have in common a quality that only *bourgeois* names: they contrive to live in their time as its living posterity. They are free in their judgments and free in their indifference because for them anything that really happens, happens in the past. Then the feeling passes, and once again I see people whose characters are separately conditioned by their particular situation and occupation – not by some class oversoul.

Of course I accept the existence of the strict-sense bourgeois, the medieval burghers – I accept that the world I live in is descended from the one they created. But trying to understand the world in terms of class makes me uneasy (and not only because if there were a bourgeois, they would not be the masters but the helots of our capitalism, pressed between the entitled poor and the empowered rich). No, there is a brink ahead; its name is Marx. I feel the same way when I try to understand the world in terms of markets – there is a brink ahead; its name is Mises. But the Marxist case is more uncomfortable than the libertarian, because libertarian ideas pass on libertarian credit. Marx is the philosopher we agree with under other names. When You-Know-Who is mentioned we throw salt over our shoulders and intone: "He was wrong in his conclusions but right in his basic approach," or "He was wrong about everything, but at least he cleared away old ideas that were even more wrong." But folk magic will not protect you if you look into the forbidden books. To read Marxists, to follow principles familiar to you and found among all educated people of good will – to follow these principles step by step plausibly to inhumane conclusions, is to realize how untenable the compromise is. You cannot chain up the devil indoors; you must serve him or put him out. Either social class is a valid principle and deserves to be applied far beyond its present polite limits; or social class is an invalid principle, and any current idea which depends on it should be recalled and melted down. But what else is there? Whenever I ask the question I feel a tense quiet like the party when the parents' car pulls up early – because if Marx was just wrong then somewhere all the old grave solemn words are waiting to return.

(If you substitute *psychology* for *economics*, *Freud* for *Marx*, *cognitive psychology* for *libertarianism* and *neurosis* for *class*, the above essay contains another essay.)

HAMLET'S SHIELD

JANUARY 30, 2010   In the book of Saxo Grammaticus, where the story of Hamlet (née Amlethus) is first told, Hamlet survives the act of his revenge. First he pins his false uncle's men drunken beneath their festival tent and burns the palace around them; then he finds his uncle's bed and there, with a needless fillip of cunning, first warns Claudius (née Feng) that Hamlet is come for his revenge, then kills him as he rises with his own sword – while his uncle fumbles to draw Hamlet's, previously riveted through for the seeming-mad Hamlet's own protection.

This bloody-minded Hamlet's first act as king is to command his story – from the murder of his father through the accomplishment of his splendidly premeditated revenge – all to be painted on a great shield for him to carry.

Remember that a knight's shield was as good as his name – the means by which he would be known in battle and in travel, known both to friend and foe. Having become king, Hamlet desires that his story shall protect him and that he shall be known by his story. Both terms of this resolution come to pass in an unexpected way. Soon Hamlet falls into the hands of Hermutrude, Queen of Scotland – wise, clever, beautiful, proud, unwed. So impressed is she with his story – with the more than human cunning of his revenge – that she decides first to spare his life, and second to wed him – he the only accepted and the only surviving of her many suitors.

The shield itself is of course invisible in Shakespeare, though I cannot call it absent. By his story Hamlet enters the company of kings – so Fortinbras hails him; by his story Hamlet is known, when Horatio tells it before the confused witnesses of Hamlet's end in a Hamlet ending; and by his story Hamlet is saved – saved from England and returned to Denmark that he may end – in the Spartan phrase – *with his shield or on it* – but not without a shield.

FAME

FEBRUARY 5, 2010   Why be famous? Subtract sleeping, eating, working – how much time remains for being famous? Of course fame has benefits, comforts, luxuries, considerations – but all these are available, in degrees equal or better, to people who are not famous. A star may not be better off than a dentist; most, not so well.

Why be famous? To have your name, your face known? But no one is present in a picture. Heroes do not feel people wanting to be them; sex symbols do not feel people wanting them. And as for names – though his name is taken a billion times a day, what good does fame do the Earl of Sandwich? People recognize you, but what do they recognize you as? Not as a person; the recognition that fame supplies is less than being personally known. It is the kind of recognition that people give to types and roles – that a proper name is used does not make the recognition different than the patronizing recognition given to one who matches an ethnic stereotype.

Why be famous? What is gained when the switch flips in the brain between "I am not famous" and "I am famous"? Is it self-respect? But you do not respect people because they are famous; why should fame give you respect for yourself?

Why be famous? Is it attention? That is a little stronger: attention is enough like a commodity that famous people can lend it out on their own credit. But that only when they are not too famous: the movement that recruits too prominent a spokesperson only adds a cause to fame, not fame to a cause.

Not all fame is permanent; people who have been briefly famous seem to value the experience, but not wish to repeat it. (Though whether as a drug too addictive to return to, or an ordeal that leaves them with nothing to prove, I do not know.) Sometimes a person with transient fame can be observed having found a worthy cause to spend it on. This seems healthy and sane.

All people who are famous and sane seem to have certain qualities in common: a sort of fatalism, a sociable sense of irony, and taking their fame as a windfall, not a right. But most people who are famous are not sane; and though it would be tempting to argue that fame only attracts the insane – as it likely does – I do think fame drives people insane.

But I am begging the question. If fame is so insubstantial, so inconsequential, what traction does it have to drive anyone anywhere? If there is no good answer to "Why be famous?" there cannot be a good answer to "Why not be famous?"

Contrast fame and glory. Glory must be earned with great difficulty; glory is impersonal – has never invited presumptuous familiarity, instead discouraged it; and glory is enduring – is sought as the one thing in life that lasts forever. Altogether glory seems a finer and more human thing than fame. Yet the love of glory – so we are warned by the records of the times when it was in fashion – the love of glory was itself madness. If so straight a thing as glory is confounds us, how much more so must crooked fame?

The real question is not "why be famous" or "why not be famous" but another: Why give fame?

Fame begins with a humane feeling – with the recognition that there are no rewards reserved for extraordinary merit. For the invention of calculus and the discovery of gravity, Newton was made Warden of the Mint; but what did his predecessor do? His successor? There is no prize or position in the world where merit has not been mixed with legacy, celebrity, and safe choice. There is no recognition which the world can bestow on the worthiest which has not sometimes been bestowed on the unworthy.

So when we are moved to admire something extraordinary, we search for something within our power to bestow, something that cannot be bought; and we find only our attention. This is well meant. Attention is the kindest thing we can give. But what is kind from one person may be cruel from many.

AIRPLANE

FEBRUARY 13, 2010

There is a poem I would like to write
About the airplane lights between the stars:
Unheard on cloudless nights, they do not fall
Now red, now green, and still they do not fall.
Somewhere a poet at thirty thousand feet
Looks down in thought. He sees the night earth black
He sees the city lights, they tint the sky

He stretches out, the engines soothe his bones
He settles in, he summons all his craft
And presses one last drop of grainy oil
From something dry and rancid lodged in him.
I, earthbound, see him passing like a god
And measure poems I may never write.

NEW YORK

FEBRUARY 21, 2010   What seems to most people to be a general economic and cultural crisis often seems to me no more or less than the rigors of the end of New York's economic and cultural sway.

Consider hedge funds. The crisis has raised a populist anger against hedge funds in general. But hedge funds were not the cause; they did not need to be bailed out. They rode out the shock and recovered on their own. The institutions that had to be bailed out were the titans of New York, which tried to play hedge fund and broke the economy. Strategies that work for the decentralized and lightly staffed institutions that hedge funds are – these strategies were poison to the titans of New York.

Let me repeat: New York saw a set of brilliant strategies for making money; New York tried to adopt these strategies; but New York could not keep up. (High-frequency trading seems to be going in the same direction.)

The reason these titans were permitted to exist was to compete with the comparable titans of other countries. Surely if everyone else is doing it, we are only being realistic when we do it too – whatever the abstract dangers?

American modesty is that foolish. Ours is a very powerful country; and powerful countries must expect to be imitated, for no other reason than that they are powerful. When Great Britain was ascendant the world broke out in parliaments and the businessmen of the tropics sweated in black wool.

We have our New York, so other countries want New Yorks of their own – and they get them, new New Yorks more New York than New York. (What are Canary Wharf and La Défense but the cargo cults of the Atlantic?) Count one remove from reality. Then, of course, we scale up the real New York to match. Count two removes from reality. (This is the level of the junk-bond era, I think.) The rest of the world scales up their New Yorks to keep up with the American example. The world's tallest skyscraper keeps turning up somewhere in East Asia. Count three removes from reality. So the real New York scales up yet again, mortgages the country and securitizes its mortgages. Count four removes from reality. This isn't economics; this is pataphysics.

Worse, it is a game that New York cannot win. New York had to get that way; it is burdened with history – with the awareness that things could have been otherwise. The new New Yorks can take New York as a revelation, build it dogmatically. Hong Kong will always be a better New York than New York can ever be.

All finance is capital allocation – discerning where money obtains its best return and transferring it there from other, less profitable uses. Once, for this to be done at a national scale, it was necessary that all the financiers of the nation be in one place, have all their seats on one exchange, so all the nation could come to them. Because New York was where information could be had, New York was where decisions had to be made.

But this no longer true – a Bloomberg terminal in New York knows nothing that a Bloomberg terminal in Shanghai does not know. Indeed the opposite is the case; New York impedes capitalism. By being the center of both finance and the economy it simply removes many industries from rational analysis. Look at publishing or music, for example. Suppose you are an investor with a thesis about the future of books or music. What instrument allows you to express it? There is no such instrument, because publishing and music as businesses have been absorbed into New York conglomerates (even if headquartered elsewhere, possible only in a world that includes New York) – conglomerates whose bottom lines would not tremble if tomorrow some rapid plague killed off every author and musician on the planet.

There are, of course, the *indies* – indie labels, small presses – but even if they were publicly traded – even if there were some exchange where they could afford to be listed, with regulations they could afford to comply with – still they are individually too small to absorb enough capital to make a return meaningful to an investor.

The cavernous empty middle between conglomerate and indie is New York's path – New York sweeps it clean the way Jupiter's gravity clears out the asteroid belt.

For culture I think the case is stronger and more straightforward than it is for finance. In almost anything written about the crisis the words publishing, journalism, music, art, can be qualified with "New York" without loss of meaning – with gain in clarity.

I admit that this perspective explains nothing new. My intention is Copernican, not Newtonian. I do not attempt to resolve mysteries, only to provide a more parsimonious formulation of the mechanism behind certain appearances known to everyone. To the naked eye, the sky would look the same if the earth were the center of the universe. The crisis would look the same if were were universal or had New York at its center. I find the latter formulation more plausible and more interesting. If the crisis is general, then there is nothing to do but ride it out, suspend our minds and abilities, wait for some vision to reveal what comes next. But if the crisis is New York's, then there is work for all in imagining and effecting a great devolution.

PECCADILLOES

FEBRUARY 27, 2010   Before you shoot, consider the ricochet. Before you moralize, consider the peccadillo. Certainly the peccadillo is an unphilosophical idea. There is no logic in the sin that does not make a sinner, the crime that does not make a criminal. Yet the peccadillo is left over whenever sins or crimes are counted. Its inevitability implies a resilience to human behavior that is almost material. In measuring wood for the cut you must figure in the kerf of the saw – how much material the cut itself will remove. Likewise in philosophical division you must expect the measured boundaries of immorality to fall outside the marks that guide the division. In woodwork this can be compensated; in philosophy it cannot be. The name for one who calls harmless things harmful to prevent harmful things from being thought tolerable – the name is hypocrite. In this way law is superior to morality. Law, being justified from without, can blend the boundaries of the legal and the illegal to the greater security of the law, make jaywalking a crime, allow its subjects just enough breaking of minor laws that they obey the important laws without feeling punctilious or servile.

But morality must self-stand. Thus both in society and in the individual, the fervor of moral commitment trends over time into immorality, step by step as the excision of hypocrisy cuts a new brink of the immoral, which frays into new peccadilloes, which invent new hypocrisy, which being purged cuts a new brink of the immoral – and so on, until at last the philosopher sits, like the overreaching workman, ashamed among scraps – scraps cut down over and over in adjusting the fit until no material remains for any fit at all.

QUESTIONS ON YOUTH

MARCH 12, 2010

I

What ends youth, and when? First, tell me what youth is. Is it innocence? Strength? Speed? But this is glib. The idea of youth is so ridden, so tangled, so fraught, that no systematic approach is possible. So I will glance as I may.

II

Why is it easier to imagine an evil old man than an old evil man?

I can very easily imagine a man who has become evil by becoming old; and what I imagine is something serious and dangerous. But when I imagine an evil man who has become old, what I imagine is pathetic and sad. This is not a modern blind spot: the evil old man or woman is an archetype. So too (though not as often) is the evil man whom age leaves weak, alone, and lost.

The same asymmetry obtains between a wise old man and an old wise man; between a kind old man and an old kind man; between a foolish old man and an old fool.

Call this folk gerontology. It teaches that old age so divides life that, in old age, we may acquire new traits and retain them vigorously; but those traits we carry from youth into old age fade and diminish in it. (Note that *traits* does not include *abilities* – the type of the Old Master is an exception.) And it defines youth as either a time when we do not possess the qualities that will later distinguish us, or a time when we are distinguished by qualities we are bound to lose.

I see no basis in fact for this distinction, but the universality of it suggests that it is there to be established.

III

When does youth end? We have a tribal answer – youth ends with ordeal. We have a a number of civilized answers – youth ends with marriage, vocation, mastery, or battle. But none of these formal occasions are satisfactory. Compare a person the day before and the day after, and you will measure no difference.

The notion that youth has a formal end implies a tripartite division of life into ineffectual youth, active maturity, and honorable senescence. Another familiar division is simply into strong youth and feckless old age. Which is the more natural? The second division matches the general pattern of animals, but the first is more distinctively human (given our prolonged childhoods). The trichotomy is the most common division, but the dichotomy seems agreeable to high civilization – at least to ours and the classical world's.

But our idea of youth and the classical idea of youth are not the same. The phenomenon of formal education, the conceit that children have wisdom in their mouths (if nowhere else), the sense both of the suitability of play to children, and its unsuitability for adults – these give us an idea of youth shyer and more delicate than the robust vision of the ancient world. Alexander conquered the world, not in youth, but with youth. But being young among the moderns ends as soon as anything happens to you that has not happened to everyone else. Classical youth was individualizing; modern youth ends with individuation.

IV

Speaking of Alexander, remember that Caesar, at the age of 30 and still unknown, wept because by 30, Alexander was already Alexander. But Caesar would get his chance to be Caesar. In the vigor, ingenuity, audacity and arrogance of his later actions the mark of youth is certain. Yet had a fever taken Caesar that year then his death, had his death been marked at all, would have been marked as an old death. So to the question, "Can youth be recovered?" we can answer yes – for a Caesar.

V

Can you marry and be young? Of course you must be old enough, but can old enough be young? Or does marriage imply a sobriety and commitment that is only mocked by being called young? Or can you have children and be young? Does that responsibility compel youth's end – is youth passed on in making youth?

Once you have passed on your genes nature is done with you. Only culture has use for you, while you persist consuming resources without any direct role in the natural order. Nature arranged the habits, abilities and vices of youth toward the end of reproduction. Once that end is fulfilled, nature loses interest. Quote, "The noblest works have proceeded from childless men" (and women); is this because the refusal to get or bear prolongs youth by refusing its consummation?

VI

How seriously should youth be taken? The ancients took youth seriously and expected great things from it. We have two modern views to chose between.

We have youth as *the best days of my life*, a moment of strength and hope that sets almost before it has risen, our sole fragile chance at bravery, and once over beyond recall, only imitated in memory, lost only to be longed for – when not regretted.

We also have youth as a surfeit of dangerous energy, an unshielded, ungrounded, overcharged capacitor in continuous danger of shorting out, melting down, spinning free – a turbid, turgid, tumid white heat of hormonal drive limping on impaired judgment between transitory moments of release and refractory calm; something we are lucky to survive and would never wish on anyone, let alone ourselves.

This choice is important, because it determines how the rest of life is to be arranged. If youth is the best, then we should aim to be comfortable once we are useless. If youth is the worst, then we should aim to be free once we are sane.

VII

Can youth be accurately remembered? Must it incandesce with a rose radiance as it decays to its half-life, or can it be remembered justly as it was? To ask another way: is life necessarily disappointing? Obviously if youth always becomes a retrospective paradise then what comes after will always be a disappointment. At best you can be philosophical, and try to remind yourself that your vision is distorted. But I think it can be remembered justly, though it requires artificial means – old photos to look at, old journals to read, old friends to converse, old shows to rewatch.

VIII

What does high school do to people? Listening to those who go – at least to Americans – it seems to have no lasting effect besides trauma and regret, and no benefit beside the war-buddy friendships formed among survivors. It appears as a circular hell, where everyone is damned by someone, and a demon to someone else. In trying to think about youth the cosmic mass of the institution, youth's Great Attractor, draws everything else into its orbit. Perhaps this is why there is so little good thinking done about youth: people trying to think about youth end up thinking about high school. What would youth look like without this wheel to break on?

IX

How far can the advantages of youth be extended? We are not only animals. By conscious discipline and ingenious technology we have learned to formalize or commoditize generally what life grants only as special advantage. We universalize gifted strength with machinery, gifted memory with writing, gifted health with medicine. (I would call this universalizing one index of civilization.)

If youth has any positive content, it must be abstractable. And if we find that youth is not abstractable, then we know that youth has no positive content. But we have had great success – and largely within living memory – with such abstractions. We have established that it is not unnatural or ridiculous that the old should learn, love, and plan as intensely, as bravely, and as hopefully as the young; that the use of technology to extend and preserve physical powers does not defy nature, but serves it; and that community of purpose is as much possible to the old as to the young. More may yet be done.

FORM AND CONTENT

MARCH 20, 2010   Separating form and content is like separating language and meaning – possible, but artful. It is artful because it cannot be neutral. It cannot be neutral because content can neither be represented without any form at all, nor presented without some influence on how it is read.

In web design plain text is often treated as a non-format, but it is a format too – it raises the questions of character sets, markup versus markdown, hard wraps versus soft wraps – it is haunted by carriage returns and line feeds – and displaying it raises the question of monospace or proportional fonts, wrapping or truncating, and syntax highlighting. Non-programming designers can think of it as a non-format only because they do not have to deal with it directly, just as printers could think of handwriting as a non-format, because it was the stage in the process they had no responsibility for. But questions of form in plain text are serious and important for those who have to deal with it directly. (If you think web designers are over-earnest about grids, you have yet to ask an programmer about whitespace.)

Plain text permanently enacted what typewriters had already established in practice – the idea of punctuation and capitalization as part of content, not form. In manuscripts punctuation was so often indistinct, and its use so inconsistent between writers, that printers were free to omit, add, or exchange points as they pleased. Yet even though writers bred to the age of WYSIWYG use boldface and italics significantly – and underlining, which was once just how writers and typists denoted italics to printers – still, because bold and italic characters are not part of ASCII (the plain text standard set by typists) they are so often unavailable, inconsistently displayed, or subject to sudden disappearance between programs, that they cannot quite gain the status of content.

Of course the phrase – *separation of form and content* – usually frames as a goal what might be more blatantly put by web designers as a command: *programmers shall not meddle with design* – or put by programmers as a judgment: *just get it working, you can figure out the design later.*

The phrase is also misleadingly abstract. As used it is meaningful only within a certain scheme: a database contains plain text which is then filled into a template and served to a browser. This is not the only way it could be done. Quite different architectures are possible. Consider RSS, for example, where there is no browser and no design.

RSS is much closer to the intentions of the web than the web itself is. The fact that the web has any place for designers at all is the result of its abuse. In current terms, the web was meant to be like Facebook – you put information in and let presentation be handled upstream – but it turned out like Myspace. To call this system *separation of form and content* is a little disingenuous.

Superficially it may appear that the Ruricolist is a blog by accident. The content seems separable from the form. That is true in practice: I have printed some of these essays in books. Yet the content of the Ruricolist exists because of its form. Only because there exists a form so familiar and flexible as the blog did I feel free to try something unusual.

INTELLIGENCE

MARCH 28, 2010   Fools have ways to love that intelligent people do not have. The practical part of intelligence is mostly negative. Especially in public, the surest way to do something smart is not to do anything stupid. In any situation not requiring skill fools simply have more actions to choose – some of which, though inadvisable, are ways to love.

Love is judged by those beloved not by a standard measure, but in proportion to the powers of the lover. This is just: children and pets must be loved, and their love in return must be prized in proportion to their powers. But, though just, it is problematic. I estimate a geometric increase: twice the intelligence requires four times the cause of love to love as well. The religion of romance, the civilized circumvallations of lust, do not serve the sentimentality of fools – fools do not need them. They serve a need in intelligent people, who must artfully cultivate an eye for, artfully indulge a susceptibility to, the causes of love if they are to love wholly enough to deserve love in return.

Seduction is a superstition. The increase of the human race has never waited on the art of seduction. The classes, countries, and periods that most perfect seduction are least in progeny. But while affecting nearness to the basic facts of life, and partied equally on both sides, the art is elaborated with the vain ingenuity of the astrologer, with the patient fantasy of the demonologist, according to the mode in superstition – with potions and spells, with neuroses and repressions, with pheromones and evolutionary psychology. The pursuit is in the blood; the art that overlies it only reconciles uncommon minds to being led on common strings.

Life is easy, love is easier; birds do it, bees do it. But intelligence makes things difficult – it makes us seek out difficult things. The faculty restless and capable enough to solve the problems of food, shelter, and reproduction cannot rest on those solutions. It wants challenge. It elaborates gourmandise, architecture, romance.

This is not our tragic parting with nature; it is our true nature. The tragedy – there is tragedy – is that intelligent insight is distinct from intelligent perspective; the more completely absorbed in a problem, the less the ability to judge it. The lesson for intelligent people is that what makes life worthwhile is not at all the same as what is needed to live. To expect life to be worthwhile in itself is an error; but it is another, equal error to expect that solving life's problems is enough to make life worthwhile. Life is easier, and life is harder, than that.

FASHION

APRIL 2, 2010   "Fashion" names three distinct systems, which have in common only that they determine what clothes are worn. For brevity I will call them fashion$_1$, fashion$_2$, and fashion$_3$. In Western history they follow in periods. Fashion$_1$ spans from the Renaissance to WWI; fashion$_2$ spans from WWI to the 1980s; and fashion$_3$, in the developed world, is ongoing. For each definition of fashion there is a corresponding adjective: fashionable$_1$, that is, *new*; fashionable$_2$, that is, *popular*; and fashionable$_3$, that is, *safe*.

Fashion₁ belongs to the artisan tailor. In short *fashionable₁* meant *what tailors know how to make* — reading, by the usual metonymy of the time, *tailors* as *the best tailors*, and *the best tailors* as *the best tailors of the best cities*, and *the best tailors of the best cities* as *the king's tailor*. Fashion₁ was slow to spread — from the court to the city to the country — slow in time, as the idea of fashion filtered down early in the period, and slow in space, until the tempo of technology picked up and the center was reflected everywhere.

(Of course there were court fashions before this — tall pointy hats and long pointy shoes — but we are only concerned with clothing styles after the decay of sumptuary class distinctions.)

The transition from fashion₁ to fashion₂ was due to mechanical reproduction, but not directly. Fashion is the only art that could embrace mechanical reproduction without a change in its system of values. It succeeded in subordinating mechanical reproduction for centuries. Fashion was, after all, the only art openly aspirational — "the clothes make the man" was an old saying while others arts still served patrons — and fashion was the only art no philosopher, ancient or modern, had bothered to establish standards for, or attributed any metaphysical or spiritual significance to — the only art (beside gourmandise) whose neglect, among those friendly to art in general, had been judged spiritually improving. And it was the first art to be industrialized — the textile mills were the first factories. Fashion had centuries to adjust to the conditions which overwhelmed other arts.

(Since fashion has always been the least self-consciously artistic of all the arts, if one is in search of the influence of industry on culture in general, fashion is not the anomaly but the control — the one area of study almost unpolluted by contemporary reflection.)

Even so, the balance of power between artisanship and reproduction was eventually upset. The shocks of WWI — textile shortages, government regulation of collar widths and skirt lengths — delivered fashion utterly to industry. This is fashion₂, with the ascendancy of reproduction.

The interest of this change is that, even in its ascendancy, the effect of mechanical reproduction on fashion was paradoxical — the opposite of its effect on all other arts. Other arts became reducible (though of course they were not always reduced) to signs and tokens: the art on the wall; the music on the roll, the platter, the disk; the very buildings on the street. All came to be employed, at times, as instruments, as impersonal expressions of the kind of person that one was or meant to be.

But fashion₂ was not about wanting to be a *kind* of person; fashion₂ was about wanting to be a *specific* person. Fashion came to be dominated by vital personalities just as other arts ceased to be.

The phrase "mechanical reproduction" comes from Walter Benjamin's famous essay, "The Work of Art in the Age of Mechanical Reproduction." The essay does not live up to its reputation – it is really an essay about portraiture, to the exclusion of non-visual arts, or even forms of visual art essentially public – but its idea of an *aura* to the handmade work of the artist, something inherent in the original work and accessible only in person, something lost in reproduction – *aura* has become a byword for everything we have lost. But it was in mass reproduction that fashion gained, for the first time, an aura of its own. Where there was national costume, now there was aura – you know who – not a jacket, but you–know–who's jacket, not jeans, but you–know–who's jeans.

Fashion₃ – the kind called post-industrial – is of interest as the most accessible member of the class of phenomena that can be prefixed with *post-*. In fashion we may observe and judge its real salience: first, that it was a real change; second, that it was shocking to those who lived through it; and third, that it was not, in the long run, particularly important.

But what was the change? Suddenly everything became cheaper; suddenly cheap became chic; suddenly the urgency of investing the clothes dollar in something fashionable was relaxed; suddenly, after a long suspension, the personal principles of choice and taste were restored. It is understandable that the first generation that had the chance to exercise that freedom would be very far out of practice: how variously and persistently they overdid, and underthought, does not need to be repeated.

But consider the years since; and ask what it means for fashionable₃ to mean "safe." *Safety* in fashion is safety from costume. In the presence of limitless choice costume is the one limit, the one failure. You may wear whatever you like as long as you do not go through with it. "A is a great look, try wearing it with B." "X is a classic, but bring it up to date with Y."

Fashion is never just a matter of personal expression. When you dress, you judge. A suit among T-shirts says "slobs"; a T-shirt among suits says "stiffs." To favor a look is one thing; to commit to it is another. Mere favor retains free choice; commitment exercises choice only to renounce it. And to renounce choice is to demean those who have it – is to say "cowardly," to say "soft," to say "weak."

(This analysis is easily extended if *costume* is replaced with *religious conversion* or *political commitment* or *artistic style*. But fashion is the perspicuous case.)

It may seem absurd to pay so much attention to clothing. Who thinks about clothes except people who are only fit to think about clothes? But dressing is the one art everyone practices, the one branch of criticism in which everyone is qualified. It is civilization in its most urgent, personal, and portable form. Certainly no philistinism meets quite so much resistance as going naked. And no other art shares clothing's power to encapsulate civilization. Consider C.D. Friedrich's "Wanderer Above the Sea of Fog," where the frock coat stands for all that civilization can contribute to the education of a human mind.

ROADKILL

April 9, 2010   Only nature cleans the highways here. They represent every stage of decay, from the semblance of sleep through the rough dissections of crows to the painstaking harvest of ants. The proverb says, *haste makes waste*. The highways prove it; in every soft carcass that lies curled beside them, in every fleshpile squeezed from the split sacks of carrion that lie out upon them, in every flowered cross planted strangely beside them.

Should we hate the highways with a particular hate? Trains are armored to shatter and plow aside errant livestock, whose wet flopping dead weight would otherwise derail even the engine that batters them. Planes in flight devour birds; black humor has a word, *snarge*, for the product. Ships strike whales – even on the whale-roads there is roadkill. To banish the highways would save nothing.

Montaigne counsels us that the fear of death is to be overcome by making it familiar, by not looking away from it, by looking out for it. You need not look far. To live is to kill. Just to eat food that something else might have eaten is to kill. At every level, from breakfast to the evolution of the species, life advances by a rocker arm, pushing one down as it pulls one up. To compete as a lifeform is to obstruct or be obstructed. Either what obstructs kills what is obstructed, limits, confines, and starves it, or what is obstructed kills what obstructs it, tosses it aside, beats it down, or runs it over. Life's accounts do not balance. Life runs a perpetual deficit in the debt of death.

Plant flesh, animal flesh, human flesh, grow, spread, and die, cell by cell. We do not always treat them differently. The bullet passing through wall and occupant and wall again; the parallel logistics of sustenance and deployment, of sanitation and undertaking; the red truth that really is the same under our skins; how easily all gifts and accomplishments are undone by the severing of the narrow threads they hang from – metaphorically, a slip on the stair, a stumble in the shower – literally, the nerve and tendon threads the surgeon loosens with sharp steel; the exact delineation of acceptable and unacceptable probabilities of death or maiming, of acceptable and unacceptable rates of wearing out the body; accident victims, and roadkill.

The most original and apt image in modern fantasy is the car gods with their black gloves and chrome teeth, powerful recipients of more blood sacrifice than all the unclean temples ever sent to Huitzilopochtli. To feed that thirsty god the Aztecs waged wars by appointment and agreement, flower wars to drain the supply of hot-blooded young men. The car gods have a more efficient arrangement.

Every action of government contains a writ of execution. To govern is to uproot, unman, disabuse, starve, poison, and exile. Some people always live at the margins of any way of life. Adjust the limits and they fall off. People die for daylight savings.

There is a courtesy among predators, at least on land. We tend not to eat each other, in part because we are poor nourishment for each other, in part because nature prefers competition to warfare. Competition improves fitness. Warfare is generally won by other means. It is better for the edification of hyena and lion that they compete to kill their prey, not to kill each other. Fighting between them accomplishes nothing – evolution cannot work with winners. Victory ends competition.

Consider how animals die, and how animals react to death – not because our deaths or reactions to death are or should be anything like theirs, but because they show nakedly where and how the boundary lies. They seem to feel and recognize the difference between recoverable sickness and the approach of death, even when the former has the more severe symptoms. They seek solitude to meet it. In others they sometimes attend it with impossible patience, sometimes leave it – what a thing it is to see a cat, for example, approach another cat dying, sniff at it, then simply leave. Yet even cats show anxiety when one of their number is removed by sudden death. Learn the lesson: death has a shadow and a mark. It shadows where it has yet to arrive, it marks what it has yet to claim.

The troubling thing about a dead body is not its emptiness but that its emptiness is not complete. A dead body is never really limp or unresisting. While it is fresh its habits of movement linger until it stiffens wholly. Body language does not shut off when no one is speaking: it goes on in gibberish and static. But then I have felt animals stiffen so quickly after death that it is hard to believe they were not already mostly dead even while they were moving.

The saying goes that human is the only animal that knows it must die. This is absurd if it is understood to mean that animals die blindly. But even then, do we really know? We have a name for something we dread. But who knows what that thing is?

Dying well is no more impressive than holding liquor well. Biology has no discretion. The imperative of survival inflicts itself even on the hopeless in an endocrine frenzy. To withstand those chemicals well is no more or less a quirk of constitution than withstanding any other chemical.

It is unique to human beings to choose death – but do we choose to die, or not to live? Those who choose to die do not choose dying, but dying for, dying in, dying with, dying as – all things you do before you die.

Thinking about death is as futile as thinking about life. If death matches life, then death is as much and as various as life, in comforts and in stings – as uncertain as life, and as surprising. But though one cannot define life, one can say useful things about it. There may be useful things to say about death. But remember that the segment of life that thought can influence is a small one. The substance of life is the same for every human being, and for other animals: individual but not individuated – eating, sleeping, walking, loving, laughing, crying. Likewise most of what it is to die is unoriginal and familiar.

But human deaths are different. The last dinosaur, say, was much a dinosaur as any other had been. The last cat will be a true cat. But the last man will be no such thing. No man abridges mankind. Nature, when it kills us, does not know we are human beings, does not know we are different. It does not consult or consider us in dying any more than in being born. But nature is wrong. Its excuses are inadmissible. Its generalizations are misguided. We are not interchangeable, we cannot be replaced, we are never unjustifiable. Nature does not gather us in; nature runs us down. It ends us and dissolves us, or dissolves us to end us, and we do not slow its wheels.

I wish I could ask after sanity as easily as after religion. Many have their sanity from ritual who do not believe, and many who believe have their sanity from reason. Children are another reliance: better they bury you, than you bury them.

Since as an essayist I cannot bestow belief or children on my readers, I will address reason.

Define the problem: what is reason asked? Reasoning about life tries to show us what power we have when we feel powerless, how to *bear and forbear*. Reasoning about death must show us how powerless we really are, even when we feel we have power. We are strangely able to think like immortals, to ignore death's oncoming, to ignore time's outgoing; able in looking forward to let age creep up on us, in looking backward to let death approach from behind. This is not foolish: too much awareness of death, because we cannot escape it, elides with surrender to it. It is brave to go down and joke with the gravedigger, but someday you must return from England.

And what does the gravedigger have to tell? He will not patronize you; he knows that you know you must die. He asks: do you know you can only have so much life before you die?

We have so much to say. Within ourselves we go on and on in a steady burble of language worn down to smooth unresisting kernels. To express them is a slow, hard cementation that always omits as much as it includes. No practice, no pursuit, no art, no relationship, no devotion can really empty a human being out. The greatest wit, the most indefatigable scribbler, the hack, the genius, the most passionate lover, the most kneeworn worshiper – we all die less than empty.

Some wit observed that the centipede is so called because human beings are too lazy to count to fifteen. But really we are not too lazy to count; we are afraid to count. We use names instead. We speak of character and personality as we speak of centipedes. But though we refuse to count them we die bearing these cruel secret tallies. For the most daring there are only so many victories; for the wisest only so many thoughts; for the most loving, and the most loved, only so many kisses.

The wheels of reason crush all shapes together. What am I? What lives? What is it that will die? Surely I fill out something that outlives me. I am a kind of person; I was not the first and I will not be the last. Or I am unique, I have a claim that outlives me. *Draw thy breath in pain to tell my story.* Either way I have a story that is mine, whether I inherit it or originate it.

This is a comfort I am willing to defend, though not to commit to. This word *story* has become pejorative. Stories are ways of making the inexplicable palatable (as in the neurological concept of confabulation: when the right hand does not know what the left hand is doing, and the left side of the brain [governing the right hand] invents an explanation for the actions of the left, subverting memory to reshape it.) Or stories omit pertinent information from complex events to make them useful, as history told through Great Men omits almost everything that actually happened.

All this sounds very wise, has that bite of wisdom going down in phrases like *we tell ourselves stories* or *the human need for simple stories.*

But just what is it that a story is? Does it supervene on events or inhere in them? The impossibility of proving a story is not a demonstration of its vacuity, but of its irreducibility, its centrality, its coherence.

A story cannot be broken down into simple parts not because it is unreal, but because the idea of a story is perfectly simple – there are no simpler parts. The maturity of twentieth century science discovered that the world is not matter acting mathematically but mathematics acting materially. Likewise it is no more plausible that life is biology acting narratively, than that life is narrative acting biologically.

I do not commit to this because even granting that stories are real and potent there is no reason why that power must be beneficent. If stories are substantial enough to support as a reliance, then they are also substantial enough to construct as a trap. And even stories die – they can die, at least, though they do not have to. They are immortal but not indestructible.

And a story has an end; to speak of the story of a life parallels in death the story's quality of having an end. But to run out of time is not to finish. To stop is not to be over. Even the story of a life too soon ended, or wrongly ended, only assigns the role of death a part in the masque of justice, where we conceal Death in the costume of Crime.

Instinct compels us to live toward something, some legacy of possessions or powers, some residue of belief or meaning; compels us to think of death as the occasion of it. We cannot help but live all our experiences as if we will tell about them. Even if we choose not to tell, we experience that choice as if we will tell how we never told. Even if we do not hope to be heard, we experience that hopelessness as something we will tell.

Then we look at death – we cannot help it – as if it will be the great telling. Even if what is to be told is: "I lived without illusions, without the need for neat satisfying stories."

Story creeps in. Those who would tell God how they lived only require God to be audient to what they already had to say. Even those who would be silent in the Void have somewhere in their minds the thought of telling how the Void absorbed them.

The lapse of this instinct – the feeling, not the thought, that you might never tell – cannot be told; but it does exist.

Science has its particular comforts. Psychology is ready to assure you that once you have learned to live, you have learned to die, because death is not the end of life, but part of it. Neurology is ready to assure you that consciousness is a phenomenon, not a species, that once relieved of memory and embodiment, your share of it is only a repetition of the common pattern; and that you, in recorded memory and the memories of others, in the substance of your DNA, and in the generic phenomenon of consciousness, continue to exist in every sense but that of existing within an individual – you never die, only disband. Biology is ready to assure you that you are only a modification of the one continuous stream of life stretching through the years in their billions – that all you are was always possible, and all you were will remain forever possible. Chemistry is ready to assure you that you are made of starstuff, that in your death you perform a stage of a cycle grander and finer than any that human imagination has feigned to religion or philosophy. Physics is ready to assure you that time is an illusion, that before and after are obsolete, that everything that happens is still happening somewhere, that just because you have lived there will always be something in the universe to which you are still alive.

All these comforts are worth attending. All these comforts are noble and good and fill the mind with melancholy serenity and a musical sense of the harmony and fitness of things. I commend them to those who can rely on them. But I do not feel equal in life to the sum of these posthumous immortalities. Nor is death declawed for me by doctrines that teach I cannot die because I was never alive.

Not existing is as nightly-familiar as dreamless sleep. We die for a few hours before smooth and painless resurrection. If we define consciousness as something material then this death and resurrection are literal. Consciousness is a process; whether the process stops because of a temporary alteration of the state of its medium, or because of the destruction of its medium, is irrelevant. Your computer is no less inactive when it is off than when it is broken.

If we define consciousness as something spiritual and indestructible then dreamless sleep shows that experience, memory, and embodiment are not involved in consciousness, only employed by it. And if we define consciousness as something spiritual and destructible, then there is a power that destroys and resurrects us every day, in promise of doing so again.

The existence of dreamless sleep leaves only these three alternatives. There is no possible view of life in which there is any novelty to death. You have died before, and risen. Perhaps you will die again tonight.

Either life has value or it does not. If it does, then it has value in any quantity. If it does not, then to ask that it continue forever is only to ask that the charade never end. But if life has value, what kind of value does it have? A possession, a loan, a gift? Life cannot be given value by words. Words fail, not because you cannot succeed in speaking, but because you have succeeded just by speaking. The blind circle of words cannot reach life, not because life is beyond words, but because life is inside of words.

Under the laws of nature no one has the right to be born; no one has the right to live. Be grateful! Do not ask to whom; be grateful because you have the capacity for gratitude. Not grateful in principle, not observing the rites of gratitude; be panicked, paralyzed, choked with gratitude. You live, you communicate, you exist – and this infinite improbability, this absolute unjustifiability, outweighs the mere certainty of your death.

But let fear speak. "What should we be grateful for? For other people who have us, people we leave? For the beautiful things we must shut our eyes on, or the beautiful things that fall apart while we watch? For experiences we cannot repeat, for joys we forget, for achievements that either embitter us in failure, or leave us jaded in success? For love we are not strong enough to stay with or save? These are not gifts. These are decoys, lures, the hooks on the lines that jerk us along – no, not even lines, the shaft we fall down. Should we be more thankful for the paintings on the sides of the shaft than we hate what dropped us down it? Don't you know yet what they are painted with? They are painted with the gore of those who have already hit the bottom. Be grateful? What a word you trot out, what a silly little word. Is this it? Is this the word you would hold onto, here of all places, where words make no difference at all, where no words can ever be heard or spoken? Grateful? You profane!"

What can I say? I cannot teach you what to be grateful for. This is work only you can do. You have already begun. It is the reward of good taste, of deep attachment, of the discipline of delight, to know at the last with certainty that some things are good, true, fine, brave, in a way that cannot be diminished – undeniable to the last denial.

Year Four

"Sometimes when a book is lost, something like a world, something like cities and peoples, falls silent."

LITERATURE AND PHILOSOPHY

APRIL 16, 2011   Philosophy needs literature more than literature needs philosophy. Of course literature does not need philosophy at all. In each of the three origins of philosophy – Greek, Indian, and Chinese – literature preceded philosophy, and the first philosophers were so concerned with literature that, in ontogeny, philosophy and literary criticism are difficult to distinguish.

But philosophy's need for literature is more than genealogical. Philosophy is a project of discovery, not invention. A philosopher who only invents something that we could believe about the world and about our place in it is, as a philosopher, a failure. Rather, in order to live, a philosophy must show that it has always been what people believed, though they did not yet know it. For the discovery of such unknown beliefs literature is the only body of evidence.

A philosopher must also account for how false beliefs came to be; again, only literature shows the range of what it is possible to believe, records the means by which false beliefs spread and develop, and preserves the occasion and substance of their error.

Of course, philosophers in the last few centuries have more often taken mathematics or science as their starting point than literature. And I cannot call this is a decline or aberration, because more philosophy has been done in these centuries than had been done in all history before. But the question must be asked: does philosophy, in starting from mathematics or science, receive them as mathematics and science; or does it coerce the statements of mathematics to a literature of mathematics, the statements of science to a literature of science?

We know that philosophy, in relying on mathematics, has sometimes fallen apart when mathematics shifted beneath it – most infamously in Kant's now-embarrassing reliance on Euclidean geometry. Yet philosophers are more often mathematical than scientific. Locke, philosopher, faced with Newton's *Principia*, asked Huygens, mathematician, whether he could trust its proofs implicitly. On Huygens's word Locke, founder of modern philosophy, read the foundational work of modern science by skipping the proofs. This seems representative.

Consider philosophers (and artists too) trying to digest relativity or quantum theory, declaring the advent of a new world, pledging themselves to it, raising its banner – philosophers (and artists) who could not tell Feynman's diagrams from Agrippa's sigils, who think a tensor belongs in a gym or a girdle.

But besides the significance of the results of science is the significance of Science itself. Its attraction for philosophers is obvious. Science can show something has always been true without having been noticed; it can show that what people always believed was simply false, and it need not qualify or blunt its disproof. Fires have always burned by binding oxygen. This is true of every fire that ever burned; it is true of fires that burned before human beings lived; it is true of every fire human beings have ever kindled or set, whatever they looked into it and saw – the fire-god, the image of hell, the liberation of elemental fire, the release of phlogiston. Every fire, always, everywhere, forever, burning. Science can deliver such eternities.

But the carcasses of philosophies based on obsolete science litter the last century. To learn from experience would be to notice that philosophy can learn from science only by expanding the phenomena it must account for – only literarily – and that the attempt to join philosophy to science is at best a balancing act – a stunt.

This is not just because science is subject to shifts – of paradigms among others – but because even subtle drifts in terminology and in the emphasis of education can break – in their natural development they must break – the link between a science and the philosophy supposedly based on it. The positivism that elides with foundations of mathematics is out of date, not because of Gödel or any other shock, but because the interesting work in foundations of mathematics is done and working mathematicians concern themselves with other things.

Philosophers are far harsher with philosophy than scientists would think to be. No would-be bicultural has ever delivered a blow to philosophy like Wittgenstein's sledgehammer. And scientists are far harsher with science than philosophers would dare to be. No would-be deconstructor has ever flensed the scientific method with Feynman's astringency.

For philosophical purposes, science is literature. But are other kinds of literature still relevant to philosophy? How else does philosophy need literature? Ethics is the neediest of philosophical disciplines. Ethics as the study of virtue and vice, of the good life, is inextricably literary, and thus enfeebled by the neglect of literature. Instead we find everywhere in ethics the philosophical misfeasance of the moral paradox.

Moral paradoxes are not just experiments in lesser evils; they are evil experiments. It is absolutely irrelevant how a moral paradox is answered because the idea of a moral paradox is absolutely irrelevant to human beings. A moral paradox is a crisis without room for imagination. But imagination is how human beings do good. It is the only way in which human beings do good. I do not mean that both are evil choices; I mean that choosing is evil. There is absolutely no more good in reasoning about moral paradoxes than in resolving them with dice. Of course moral paradoxes do happen. We are not always strong enough to resist or clever enough to escape them. But the proper treatment for those who would call one choice right and the other choice wrong is not to argue with them, but to beat them with sticks.

Kantian ethics, ethics practiced as pure reasoning, without consulting literature, are as vain, silly, and absurd as Aristotelian physics, physics practiced as pure reasoning, without consulting nature. The resemblance is not an analogy but an identity. Aristotelian physics refused to look outside itself to discover its real tasks, the phenomena it had to explain. Kantian ethics commits the same error.

As with physics, the phenomena for which ethics must account arrive from two sources. One is experiment; one is exploration.

Experimentation in ethics is singularly unreliable, because it must penetrate delusion; and adopting the vaunted methods of cognitive psychology is a mistake, not because there is anything wrong with experimentation or even with cognitive psychology, but because the methods of cognitive psychology are exhausted and their application has become compulsive and rhetorical.

Exploration is easier; it is already done. The reports of the explorers of the mind are stacked as high as the reports of explorers of seas and continents. Yet the map is permitted to remain blank, or it is drawn with some geometrical conceit, subs and supers, ectos and mesos, intros and extros, like old cartographers drawing pizza maps of the world with slices for continents, crust for ocean, and Jerusalem perched in the center holding up the lid.

The cartography of the mind is an empty field; the geodesy that would unravel its tectonic rind, and which would really deserve the name of *evolutionary psychology*, is unthought. Someday the map must be filled; but the work must start as a kind of philosophy, and it must be informed by literature with some more urgent use than illustration.

ENVY

April 23, 2010   Envy is half of love. For the envier, it is the high regard without the goodwill. For the envied it is the attention, without the faith. Thus where there is the appearance of love, but no real connection – there is not love, but envy.

I say this not to diminish love, but to better understand envy. The word has a certain exoticism, a certain dramatic quality, a Biblical or Shakespearean stature. It belongs to Cain and Iago. Who in these diminished latter days is even capable of envy? Modern vices are so bloodless: not wrath, but tantrums; not greed, but CDOs*. What business do we have with envy? I hear it went out with crinolines.

But envy is everywhere; envy reigns. It is the poison we live by, the dilution in our blood: watered enough to be safe, strong enough to be addictive.

Envy is not jealousy. Jealousy is as direct and solid as a bullet. When a man hates his neighbor because he wants that man's wife, he is jealous. Envy is as diffuse and insidious as a gas. When a man hates his neighbor because that man has a wife, he is envious. Jealousy is satisfied with defeat; if our man has the wife, he is indifferent to what may become of the neighbor. Envy demands degradation; if our man accomplishes the humiliation and dispossession of the neighbor, he is indifferent to what may become of the wife.

We are not busybodies; we mind our own business. We are proud; we resent being told that our lives are pointless and our possessions contemptible. Envy – properly diluted – is the only reagent to catalyze us, we indifferent human beings, into a society bound together by commitments and aspirations. Every channel for us to preoccupy ourselves with what cannot concern us, every prize held out as the reward of labor beyond needs – all this is only envy can create and support.

---

*Collateralized Debt Obligations, the time bombs that set off the financial crisis of 2007ff.

But envy is not a link, not a social contraction; envy is a force. It drives the wheel of fortune. It conducts the rise of the great and smites their downfall. In between it propels their blind, scuttling epicycles. Celebrities envy politicians; politicians envy celebrities. Businessmen envy intellectuals; intellectuals envy businessmen. Celebrities pursue politics and curse Washington; politicians deploy celebrities and damn fame. Businessmen quote philosophers and mock professors. Intellectuals abuse capitalism and invest. You stake your envy to enter the game; and those without envy (if they exist) are never seen to win.

True, analogies between matter and society should always be suspect. A reagent causes matter to break down, so the bright moment of commitment and aspiration should be a singular, unrepeatable luminescence. Like a fire, it should burn out. But society is not matter; it is capable of perpetual motions, like insurance, which is a scheme that never collapses, because most of the insured die without payouts. What seemed unsustainable to our grandfathers has been sustained this long and shows no signs of weakness.

PSEUDOSCIENCE

MAY 1, 2010   Because historians do not understand science, scientists write their own history. So when the perimeters of science change – when what appeared to be a science turns out to have been a pseudoscience – the dead or, worse, retired scientists who pursued it are sorted *ex post facto*. The ones who anticipated the change remain scientists; the ones who fell for it turn out to have been pseudoscientists. Of course, they were pseudoscientists all along – everyone knew it – but that media, that irresponsible media, they were the ones who made it seem otherwise – we scientists always knew better; it's your fault for being gullible, you cargo cultists.

You can watch this happening to string theory. In one direction or the other expect to see it in climatology. Let us rehearse the explanations in advance. Someday you may recognize one or the other as a news item or a footnote in history.

Case A:

Despite the overwhelming evidence for the anthropogenic origin of global warming, a movement of so-called skeptics, organized through the resources of corporations and political parties whose interests were threatened by the urgent measures the situation required, were able to delay action until the forces behind climate change had become irreversible. Certain scientists, some through misplaced but sincere conviction, but most because it was convenient and attention-getting, continued to cast doubt on the evidence even after the scientific consensus was incontrovertible. Nonetheless, none of the best scientists failed to see reason, and it is simply false to assert, as some have, that scientists themselves were at fault.

Case B:

In the tense political atmosphere of the early 21st century it was only natural that movements were eager to enlist scientific evidence to support their policies. Given the apocalyptic mood of the time – a quick look at the box-office returns for the first decade of the century will show that the impending end of the world was a cultural commonplace – it is unsurprising that what developed was a superficially scientific vision of the apocalypse. The media too were part of this *zeitgeist*, and they freely exaggerated a concern many scientists had with the unknown effects of carbon dioxide, and certain alarming high-level trends, into a movement complete with speeches, rallies, and platforms. Nonetheless, none of the best scientists failed to see reason, and it is simply false to assert, as some have, that scientists themselves were at fault.

I am not proposing a debate. I am not trying to convince you of anything except the irrelevance of your convictions. Climate change is just a convenient subject.

(For the record my view is: better safe than sorry. The absence of anthropogenic global warming would be harder to explain than its presence; I therefore am in favor of anything short of irreversible geo-engineering.

Though I do admit to disgust for those who condemn "economists' reliance on models" with one fork of their tongues, while the other extols "the proven science of climate change" – as if modeling the economy were any harder than modeling the climate.)

I am sarcastic because I am disgusted. But I am not attacking science. I trust that what has been declared a pseudoscience is so. In this retrospect science is as good as infallible. But I dispute the hypocrisy which would pretend that pseudoscience has never entered the mainstream of science, or that if it ever had, it would have been due to outside meddling.

"No true scientist would have participated in X; therefore any so-called scientist who participated in X was not a true scientist." The whole history of the relation of science and pseudoscience is constructed with this tautology.

True, science is not just a vocation, but also an affiliation, a group, and therefore, like any other group with a purpose, compromised by loyalties and solidarities. But the more acute problem is that science and pseudoscience are not dichotomous. Degrees exist between them.

The world *protoscience* has been advanced for the pre-scientific pursuits that led into sciences – as astrology led into astronomy, as alchemy led into chemistry, as doctoring led into medicine. There may be many more intermediate degrees of this kind, but I propose only one. Some scientific pursuits are neither sciences nor pseudosciences, but *placeholder sciences*. The textbook scientific method expects, within a science, that observation, hypothesis, and theory will follow in order. But in much scientific work the science itself is a hypothesis. The first question is not, "What law governs this phenomenon?" but "Is this a phenomenon at all?"

Most -ologies are not really fields at all, but gambits. In science a field does not arrive and then demand methods, subjects, a center and journals; instead the methods, subjects, the center and the journals are how hopeful scientists attempt to bootstrap a new science into being. In the end the attempt either succeeds as a science, or fails as a pseudoscience; but in the meantime it is neither – it invites a science and clears a space for it, saves it a seat. It is a placeholder.

For scientists of a later generation to judge a placeholder science according to its final result is unfair. The scientists who failed were not cranks; the scientists who succeeded were not visionaries. To suppose they could have known better in advance is to suppose a faculty which, if it did exist, would make actual science superfluous. A scientist can no more know in advance if a science is a pseudoscience than a computer can know in advance if a program will halt.

All sciences begin as gambits. The sooner we recognize this, the sooner we can avoid misplacing the faith due a mature science in its placeholder; but more importantly, the sooner this is recognized, the sooner we can begin, not just accommodating such gambits, but encouraging them.

READING

MAY 14, 2010   We readers – some of us are compelled to seek the true way of reading, the one discipline that suits all books. The attractions are many. There is a sense of belonging in knowing what kind of reader you are; there is confidence in knowing exactly what you will get from a book; there is the general attraction of any discipline in life – the focus that comes from the neglect of any concerns beyond that focus.

But we readers, after all, are people who choose to spend unusual proportions of our time alone. The value of the independence we must have to read at all holds for our choice of how to read. We do not read to rehearse an opinion, but to animate it – to produce some motion in it analogous to the biology of growth, or healing, or even decay. (Sometimes we read not to reinforce our opinions, but to escape them, gradually page by page.) And sometimes a book should produce the same motion in the idea of reading itself.

The value of reading a book for instruction, instead of running a search; the value of reading a book for diversion, instead of participating in the lives of friends – the value is that the writer, in filling up so huge a thing as even a short book is, must call upon and involve their whole experience and sense of the world, must turn themselves inside-out in such a way that someone else can put them on.

If reading is to be creative – and why not let it be, if it can? – then it must be by a parallel inversion, a counterpoint to writing in which reading calls on and involves you as writing does; which must therefore be subject to change as your experience of the world changes. And for a reader, experience must include reading itself.

All of which is to say that I try not to worry about what kind of reader I am or about how I should read. I change with reading, and I do not even know it until I re-read a book after a long interval and discover how different a reader I have become.

COGNITIVE PSYCHOLOGY

MAY 21–25, 2010

I

So pervasive have the claims of cognitive psychology become, so often do I encounter the rhetoric in which the introductory anecdote takes the form of a cognitive psychology experiment, that I find it necessary to decide just what I think of it, and where I stand. I do so best by doing so publicly.

I admire cognitive psychology. It is the most coherent and fruitful paradigm in psychology. The nosology of biases, by itself, might be the greatest act of thinking about thinking since the Greek achievement of logic.

Of course, like logic, the doctrine of biases is subject to misuse – the more so because it is new and we have little experience with its limitations. In logic, the spirit of catching out logical fallacies trivializes itself in the principle of the fallacy of fallacies – the error of assuming that because an argument is fallacious, its conclusion is wrong. Now, because biases are innate, but the recognition of biases is acquired, the use in argument of accusations of bias cannot be closed by a neat "bias of biases"; but something equivalent is required to avoid the error of rejecting conclusions not because they are wrong, but because they are biased – which, in itself, is no argument.

Biases are everywhere. But the very pervasiveness of cognitive psychology risks creating a new bias – a meta-bias, a confusion between *biased* and *wrong*.

II

Before I attempt a reasoned argument I want to sketch some broad points of discomfort with cognitive psychology.

1. It is impossible to pay sustained attention to cognitive psychology without suspecting that the point of many experiments is not the paper, but the press release. When we hear "science writer," we imagine journalists trawling scientific publications for stories with headline appeal.

But this is not how it works. Institutions (with what degree of involvement from researchers I do not know) push press releases to sites like EurekAlert!; journalists may check up on them to add human interest; but the transition between *experiment* and *news item* happens inside the institution. As a regime of incentives, this strikes me as perverse.

2. Cognitive psychology is based on the model of the brain as a computer; but this is a trivial statement, nearly a tautology. It implies that a computer is a kind of machine, another something like a clock or car; a sophisticated machine, certainly, but just a machine; just a machine, and the brain just another example.

Cognitive psychology began when the psychologists of the 1960s saw the first electronic computers and found in them an analogy for the mind. Unfortunately this is still true: cognitive psychology still understands the mind as a computer of the 1960s, complete with fMRI blinkenlights.

But this is not what a computer is. The history of computers is not a history of invention; it is a history of discovery. We did not invent computers; we discovered computation. Computation is an aspect of nature, something like heat or gravity, a property of all sufficiently complex systems. If something is not a computer, it is less than a computer. Of course the brain is a computer; and—?

3. Cognitive psychology and ethics in psychological research are roughly coeval. The obvious suspicion is to wonder: did we discover cognitive psychology because it was the only psychology we could discover ethically? In ages when the human form was held sacred, even after death, anatomy without dissection went badly wrong. Medieval anatomy reflected not the body, but medieval ethics. Does psychology reflect the mind, or does it reflect the ethics that direct our examination of the mind?

III

The textbook scientific method abstracts a discovery from the experiment that made it as early and thoroughly as possible – by suppressing the personalities of the experimenters; by using standardized equipment and methods of analysis; by ensuring reproducibility and undertaking it. All these mechanisms are relatively weak in cognitive psychology. Success results in advancement, experiments are themselves the instruments, and with the expense and inconvenience of recruitment, and the backlog of experiments yet to be done, reproducing experiments is a last resort. But psychology has never worked the formal way – try it, and you get Behaviorism – and this way seems, for the most part, to work.

Cognitive psychology had to fight to free itself from Behaviorism. Here we come to the problem. Behaviorism rejected introspection; cognitive psychology accepts it; but it exchanges uncritical rejection for uncritical acceptance. I think that there is something that cognitive psychology gets fundamentally wrong about introspection: it assumes that our perceptions resemble our perception of our perceptions.

(Nominally cognitive psychology rejects "introspection" but accepts "self-reporting" – I do not understand the difference.)

For example: a form of experiment is to present a list of words on a common theme for memorization. The list omits some particularly obvious entry that could be expected to occur with the rest. When memorizers repeat the list back, they often supply this absent word. The obvious conclusion, the conclusion that cognitive psychology draws, is that the memorizers have perceived the absent word; that a subconscious process – *sub* in the sense of subroutine – inserts the extra word into the memorizer's perception of the list.

But this may not be so. Precisely because the list is simple it obscures the distinction between perception and perception-of-perception. There is another interpretation. What if the memorizers do not perceive the extra word? What if, instead, in reproducing the list, the memorizers perceive their own perception of the list in an incorrect, yet conscious way?

IV

In the laboratory this fine distinction can only split hairs. I should supply a larger example that will bear the division better.

Drawing is self-reporting of a kind. Proposition: if you accept the standards that cognitive psychology uses to judge the self-reporting of perceptions, then you must also accept that people who draw perceive the world as they draw it to be; which is absurd, because they could not survive. When you draw a stick figure, that does not justify the conclusion that stick figures are what you see.

Some objections present themselves.

1. *If drawing is a manual skill, then non-artists may simply lack enough control to make the pencil do what they want.*

There is certainly room for manual skill in drawing; but it is not required. Anyone who can negotiate the angles and curves of the alphabet has all the control required for a sketch.

2. *Non-artists do not perceive the world as they draw it, but the way they draw distorts what they see, the same way memory in general distorts what they experience.*

There is an obvious comparison between how memory and drawing both exaggerate emotionally significant aspects of perception; between how memory artfully fits experience to narrative, and how drawing unartfully fits vision to outline.

Consider outlines. Outlines exist nowhere but in non-artists' drawings. Nature defies outline; vision nowhere finds it. Nonetheless when non-artists draw, invariably they first attempt an outline – even cave painters, who were artists when they drew, still loved to outline their hands on the rock. Outlines are not incompatible with art – the Egyptians made high art of shaded outlines – but they are prior to art. Abstract outlines do not depict anything: their value is that, being abstractions, they preserve the symmetries and topologies of what they anonymize – they are mathematical in character and, for simple shapes, the origin of mathematics in the promise of geometry.

The comparison with memory and narrative is obvious. We need not invoke the world-cone diagrams of physics to understand that in anything that happens, an imponderable diversity of causes conspire, and that for anything that happens, an innumerable diversity of effects result. Every event is part of the fabric of the whole world.

Narrative, like outline, is unreal but useful; patterns of events, like shapes, though potentially infinite in variety, tend to approximate simple forms with predictable properties.

But drawing cannot distort information in the same way as memory. However badly someone draws, they do not ever act as if they see the world that way. To walk or sit, to touch or pick up, proves that a non-artist does not bungle seeing the world in same way as rendering it. Even in dreams no one sees as badly as they draw. The brain does not retouch value into outline before storing it; the reduction to outline is a loss within the brain.

3. *If someone does not draw in a style that resembles Western art, that person*

is not therefore a non-artist. High cultures elevate as art what Westerners might regard as mistakes. Non-artists may not exist. Could it be that everyone distorts their perceptions artistically when they draw, most in more dramatic ways than the subtle ones traditionally valorized in the West?

Western art has its conventions, but to say that photography and the kind of art that obeys the same laws of optics and projection is essentially a cultural convention requires more gall than I have. Human eyes only work one way. The anecdote says that a pygmy brought out of the forest could not tell buffaloes on the horizon from insects. Assume the anecdote is true; what does it prove? It proves that there exists such a thing as a myopic pygmy. Or should we believe that pygmies never look up into the crowns of trees? That they cannot tell that the bird overhead is the same as the bird in the bush? To prize optic validity as artistic quality is cultural; but the validity itself is physiological.

So if for the first 3500 years or so of human history no culture or civilization held the goal of art to be to represent just what was seen, then of course we are readily distracted by other goals, and must be induced by long training to give them up for this one particular goal of realism.

But I am unwilling to credit that the artistic way is ever the easy way. The artists of the cave walls, of Egypt and Sumer, of India and Persia, were no lazier than the artists of Venice, Florence, and Amsterdam. They were not primitive; they were not innocent. Assimilating natural errors to artistic traditions they happen to resemble represents a more ridiculous pedestal for Western art than any academy ever proposed.

Too, perspective and foreshadowing are not utterly alien to the brain; I suspect that even those whose arts reject these values, do in fact dream with them.

V

If all this were true it would have two consequences. First, it would require a strict distinction between what a person reports their perception to be and what that perception actually is. The act of perceiving a perception in order to describe or render it would be understood as a skill, subject to cultivation. What cognitive psychology identifies as a bias of human perception would be no more than an untrained clumsiness. And second, it would regard the ways that cognitive psychology identifies to influence human behavior as weaknesses to be compensated by education, not intrinsic handles to pull in a desirable direction.

All this essaying is futile, I know. Even if I were right, no one would ever call me right, except in retrospect; and I am very likely wrong. In doubting a large field of scientific work I am certain to sound like a crank. I can only note that I am not nailing up theses; and that if I am wrong I am only hurting myself.

Postscript 2014

Since I wrote this essay I have participated, as a subject, in several experiments in cognitive psychology. In consequence, I now regard cognitive psychology as a pseudoscience.

I still think cognitive psychology is interesting. It is philosophically interesting, not because it uses science to cast light on the problems of philosophy, but simply because it is interesting philosophy. Its scientific pretensions are false.

Here is the problem: in order to avoid the appearance of *shirking*, the subject has no choice but to express preferences in the absence of preference and beliefs in the absence of belief. Even without financial stakes, ordinary social conventions compel the subject, in order to be kind to the experimenter, to deceive them.

It goes like this. The experimenter asks, "Does this make me look fat?" The subject says, "No." And the experiment concludes: "Human beings are incapable of accurate estimation of one another's weight." Soon books are written about "cognitive weight bias." "For our ancestors," the press release begins, "underestimating one another's weight was an important survival strategy." This is what cognitive psychology is, and it is all cognitive psychology is: the heedless elaboration of a social solecism.

To put it another way: professors should not experiment on students for the same reasons professors should not date students. (Effectively all cognitive psychology is done by professors experimenting on students; where the subjects are not students, they are still acting in the role of students.) Between professors and students there are power differentials that preclude sexual consent. But someone who cannot give an honest answer to a sexual proposition certainly cannot give an honest answer to a personality inventory. If it is a bad idea for professors to date students, it is a far worse idea for professors to experiment on them.

ART VS. LIFE

MAY 29, 2010   Sometimes art frightens me. Sometimes I wonder what art is taking to match what it gives. Surely talk was faster and more excursive before recording; surely clothing was more splendid and plumed before photography; surely gesture and pose were quicker and more lifelike before movies. Maybe worship was more devoted, before idols and icons; maybe love was stronger, memory keener, regret fiercer before the portrait; maybe voices were softer, birdsong sweeter, before music. Art universalizes particular experience, delivers it across space, time, and language. But what we receive as if transmitted, might only be lost; what we receive as if preserved, might only be embalmed; what we receive as if translated, might only be parodied. How are we, art-shrouded, art-addled, to know any better? When every sense bends to its particular art, do we more watch than see, more listen than hear, more savor than taste? At best art stands between us and life; at worst it supplants our lives. What could Arthur Henry Hallam have done with his life to match *In Memoriam*? — where the use of grief in art prevents us from sharing that grief, we who so value the expression. I fear art and I love it; I fear it as I love it, because love is power given, and power brings abuse of power. So many minds are lost to art, full of images and stories they do not even recognize as art, puppets to old, ingrown art (they call it common sense). I study art, value it, and judge it not to pass life but to save life: because to study, value, and judge art is the only defense against it.

COMMON SENSE

JUNE 4, 2010   I respect common sense only because it is inconsistent. Of course consistency is good; certainly inconsistency is bad; but there is a kind of knowledge which is useful, not *because* it is known to be right, but useful only *until* it is known to be right.

Beginning with what we cannot deny, consistency brings us to what we cannot support. Surprise is a conserved quantity. We can begin with common-sense principles and end with surprising conclusions; or, if we wish to derive common-sense conclusions, in working backward we will arrive at surprising principles. Consistency always incurs surprise – surprise relative to common sense.

This is why I avoid political systems. They begin with, they have as their attraction, common-sense conclusions I could no more disagree with than fail to think of myself. Of course I see, and seeing condemn, the horrors of exploitation, the grotesqueness of consumption; of course I see, and seeing condemn, the incompetence of government, the farce of bureaucracy. But commitment demands consistency, and what begins in the recognition of common sense ends unrecognizably.

Always use common sense; never trust it. Common sense is not wisdom, it is wisdom made fungible. All of its rings true, but none of it agrees with itself. You can no more think with common sense than you can eat money.

HISTORIOGRAPHY

JUNE 11, 2010   Historians are the natural predators of history. History, like entropy, always increases in a closed system. Without historians to control it, history would suffocate us. Whole peoples live today enthralled by history, peoples for whom the dishonors of a thousand years ago require the murders of today – and all because they never had historians to set them free.

History always increases. There are always more artifacts and more events, always more memories binding those artifacts and those events. The natural condition of history is not the absence of history, but absolute history – when commemoration and observance fill every every hour and block every path, until any choice is violation or sacrilege, and any novelty is hubris or corruption.

Of course there are other, uglier ways to fight history than the historian's. But besides its low success rate, fighting history with atrocity is perverse. It is only a way of destroying someone else's history; the winner is still doomed to have their own history written.

The historian is gentler and more effective. In consolidating and concentrating history, in resolving it with narrative, the historian does to history what the distiller does to grain: reduces so many tons of space-consuming, care-intensive material into something stable, compact, and portable. The historian who puts a name and meaning to a period gives us categories of thought that allow us to sort and assess masses of artifacts and memories that would otherwise lay total claim to our attention and devotion.

History is not over. History is still happening. History is still flowing from the invisible meanwhile to the obvious retrospect. But just because we are in history, because we must learn from it – so we must not submit to it, we must not inherit our place in it; we must be free enough of it that we can range over it, that we can examine all of it and it can examine us. Let us look at the past and let it look at us; let us invite the dead to judge the living as their most impartial judges. But first we must be free to take the judgment of the best wherever they are found, not only among our fathers and forebears.

Polyps make coral; trees make wood; human beings make history. Freedom from history is not freedom without history, but freedom for history: the freedom that makes us equal in history with those who have come before us and those who will come after us: not the wreck of the past, not the redeemers of the past, not the seed of the future, not the betrayers of the future, but what we are: the inescapable present.

AMATEURS

JUNE 19, 2010   In the twentieth century, better a professional and wrong than an amateur and right. A lie in the high tower commanded the respect and attention of the world. It shaped the textbooks and the encyclopedias, it directed the cameras and the microphones. A truth in the street had to recruit and organize, had to keep the heat on and blow the lid off.

In the twenty-first century, better an amateur and wrong than a professional and right. A lie in the street finds friends everywhere. It supplies interests and activities, it bonds a community: the less self-supporting, the more room for supporters. A truth in the high tower must patiently plait its proofs until they hang long and thick enough to support the perilous climb down.

The distinction between the amateur and the professional is not necessary or ancient. It is a conclusion of the philosophy of pragmatism, one of pragmatism's dynamic alternatives to the statics of classical philosophy. Everything used to be much more like cooking, where the difference between professionals and amateurs — the difference between livelihood and pastime — is one of better ingredients, better equipment, and wider experience — a difference not of kind but of degree.

The distinction does not divide one scale of practice into the amateur and the professional; it removes professional practice from amateur judgment. Success in all practice had been judged against something prior to practice. There were judges then because there were standards. But the professional, having some arduous qualification, defines the profession as what professionals do. Professionalism is not a standard; professionalism is an alternative to standards. Now there are standards because there are judges. Who are you to tell someone instructed and trained, tested and proven — to tell a doctor, a lawyer, an artist, a scientist — who are you tell them what to be? They are not told; they show. If you must have a system, describe them; but do not expect them to notice. Apes do not care about primatology; scientists do not care about philosophy of science.

We do not recognize this division as pragmatism because it has left pragmatism behind and become, instead of a conclusion, a postulate — no, more than a postulate, it has become its own form of logic. The necessities of professionalism define reality. Professions do not serve purposes; purposes serve professions. Not that professionalism is priestcraft. The professional is not the priest of the god; the professional is the very god, and unanswerable. It is difficult to read Job today except as God the Professional shutting down His critics.

Professionalism won; but professionalism is not self-sustaining. Like nature around technology, amateurism grows up in all the cracks of professionalism, and encloses all of its structures. One of the wonders of the early web was to see, in all its private seriousness, the wider ecosystem of amateurism inside which professionalism lives. Until then professionals, like migrating birds, came from somewhere, somehow, and went somewhere, for something. Now we saw the grave mimicry of the professional manner by which postulants committed themselves; we saw the ingenious criticisms by which they kept themselves involved; we saw how the necropolis of obsolete methods, dead-end theories, and abandoned movements was refurbished and inhabited.

But nature around technology is not just what remains of nature before technology; it is something different. Prey becomes pest; wild becomes weed. Amateurism around professionalism is something different than amateurism before professionalism. Separation from money made it resourceful; separation from recognition made it incorrigible; separation from responsibility made it reckless. These changes cannot be reversed. To let go of professionalism would no more restore Renaissance men, gentleman scientists, scholar-adventurers, or philosopher-legislators to mankind, than to remove mankind would restore to nature the mammoth, the aurochs, or the thylacine. There are lines of descent in human varieties as much as in natural species. With these too, extinction is forever. Sometimes backbreeds and hybridization revive the traits; but without a niche to inhabit the result is only a curiosity. In an ecology, if a niche is extant, something will fill it, and if the niche is gone, some other ecology has displaced it. Effectual amateurism has been re-opened; but what we get from it may as little resemble what we had before, as the kangaroo resembles the deer.

Professionalism is an evident pathology. Its privileges are too tempting for us. All professionalism decays toward the asymptote of the DSM*. But for now, there is no alternative. Professionalism and amateurism have coexisted too long; they require one another for correction. One cannot be right unless the other is wrong; for now, to be right at all, we need them both.

---

*The Diagnostic and Statistical Manual of Mental Disorders, which defines the mental disorders that health insurance will cover.

SCIENTIFIC CHEWING

June 25, 2010   I am not going to tell you to read Upton Sinclair's *The Jungle*. Once you know that Durham's Pure Leaf Lard is people, you grasp the idea. But at the end of the book, after surviving innumerable horrors and humiliations (the only mercy Sinclair allows him is a stint as a migrant worker), the main character falls in with a group of talkative Socialists. Sinclair is artist enough not to make them saints. He makes them almost silly. He wants us not to agree with their solutions, but to respond to the fact of their caring, to respond to their trying to do anything at all. He wants us not to admire them, but to imagine ourselves as one of them. I forget the rest of the projects, but one, mentioned in passing, stuck in my mind. One man proposes "to double the nutritive value of food through the practice of scientific chewing."

My mind has an alarm for absurdity in reforms and projects; *scientific chewing* is the noise it makes. Sometimes I read about a project, and despite its well-designed site, its clever name and cleverer slogan, and the intent, conscientious faces of its young founders – all I hear is *scientific chewing*.

All useful ideas have three life stages: an infancy when they seem ridiculous; an adolescence when they seem all-important; and a maturity when they are present and useful, but limited, and possibly invisible. *Scientific chewing* belongs to the adolescence of the idea of the *scientific*. Those who have only recently learned the benefits of scientific handwashing are susceptible to the idea that chewing might also advance.

The projects that make me think of *scientific chewing* belong to the same stage, the analogous adolescence, of other ideas. Recent examples are many. *Online* has finally achieved its maturity. There are no more projects tantamount to *online chewing*, though their weight once sank the economy. *Social* is in the throes of adolescence; most days some variant of *social chewing* shows up in the news, flush with seed funding. *Crowdsourced* is just settling down; *mobile* is just hitting puberty.

These examples are worth enumerating because we are very fortunate in them. The worst their excesses have done is make fools of us. We have been spared the upheavals and atrocities that accompanied the adolescence of ideas like *the people* or *the nation*, like *society* or *central planning*. The motion of ideas is circular, but not static; a cycloid, not an orbit; but though it moves forward, it moves with wheels that are heavy and iron, and able to run you down.

My interest is not critical but analytic. I want to know where I stand; I want to know when to get out of the way. If ideas really move in a circle, born boosters and born skeptics will both be right sometimes, like stopped clocks. *Scientific chewing* is my cue to stand with the skeptics. I have no equally vivid cue to switch the other way; though I have found that my initial sense that something is pointless and weird reliably predicts its popularity – witness the Internet.

I know this essay is a little miscellaneous; so are the rest of the essays where I try to think about ideas as such. I feel something enormous and terrainous loom in the darkness; when something lights that bulk I observe it as an explorer, and not knowing which features are most important, I cannot omit any.

SOCIALITY

July 6, 2010   Living among animals, you notice there are people – many people – who can handle themselves well with animals, but not with other people. This is strange, because body language and tone of voice are the only channels of commmunication with animals, but body language and tone of voice are where these unfortunates fail with other people – they are oblivious to other people's cues, and when they speak they seem cursed with bodies they do not know what to do with.

I classify this as one kind of overthinking. They believe that there is something special about social interaction, some difference that raises human sociality above animal sociality, some special prospect of human connection in what human beings, and only human beings, share. But when they reach for it, they lean too far, and they grasp only dead air.

They are not wrong about the difference; they are just looking in the wrong place. Our difference lies, not in social interaction, but beyond it. The mechanism of sociality is not how we connect, but how we avoid and regulate connection. In all human beings there is something so tender, so piteous, so kind, so sympathetic and so generous that it would sooner have us, like the heraldic pelican, wound ourselves to issue blood and give it, than see another go thirsty – something more than vulnerable, self-vulning. To survive we must armor and bar this something; so we place it in the same protected center of our instincts where the animal keeps its throat and belly. It will not be exposed to you until you have proven trustworthy, well-intentioned, and undemanding. That you are human does not give you the right to expect others to undress for you, even if you undress for them; to expect this deeper unveiling, even if you go about so deeply unveiled, is deeper folly.

COERCIVE PERCEPTION

JULY 9, 2010   Toward a science of memetics consider the phenomenon I will call *coercive perception*. "That's not a vase, that's an old woman's profile." "That's not a sword, that's a phallic symbol." "She's cheating on you." "That cloud's shaped like a rabbit!" "That's not an idea, that's the false consciousness of the bourgeois." Or, of course, "That's not a belief, that's a meme."

A perception is *coercive* when simply understanding it reorients you. Understanding is sufficient; belief is irrelevant. The coercion is instantaneous, irreversible, and permanent; it is seen and cannot be unseen. You cannot be argued out of it, because you never believed it; but, in the end, you may act as though you believe it, because you cannot forget it.

This sounds terrible in the abstract; but in practice it is something we value and seek out. Reading horror stories will coerce your perception of small quiet backwoods towns, of quiet staring backwoods people, of blackletter books and remote silent wastes, to an atmospheric unity. Being coerced this way is pleasant, despite its unpleasant content.

But then imagine a young girl or boy, and the sort of friend who says cruelly, "Did anyone ever tell you look like ———? Look at this picture – can't you see it?" And of course they see it, they have been coerced to see it, and they will always see it, no matter how absurd and wrong they know it is. They will see it till they die.

This kind of perception is unique to human beings. It is not the substance of human difference, but it might make a good test for human difference – better than the silly Turing test, which even Eliza has passed. So this thing is supposed to be intelligent – can its perceptions be coerced? Does its intelligence close over its perceptions? Correct perception is no test of intelligence. A mirror perceives correctly; what only perceives correctly is no more than a mirror. What cannot misperceive cannot think; what cannot be coerced in its perceptions cannot communicate.

VERSATILITY

JULY 20, 2010   Why is it surprising for someone to be versatile? When the question is (rarely) asked, the usual answer is to blame capital-s Society. Society wants us to specialize; Society wants labor to be divided. Without Society, we would all be versatile. I do not dispute that the state of nature would be one of versatility. But I think it is really small-s society — common friendship, mere company — that keeps versatility rare.

The downside of versatility is that people who admire, or even share, one of your abilities may be contemptuous of the others. "What have you been up to?" An elaborate series of asymmetrical values must be weighed to obtain the answer. It is safe to say *building* to a writer, unsafe to say *writing* to a builder; safe to say *music* to a mathematician, unsafe to say *math* to a musician. The worst is when they assume *day job*, and you have to explain: "No, I care about that too." Being written off is actually something you can feel. It was not said but you still heard it: "Sorry, I thought you were one of us." Better to be a little apart and aloof from the beginning than to walk into that wall. Certainly if versatility were not nearly a religion to me I would have found some more presentable way to live.

Then there is the problem of taking sides. Your friend the writer calls in a technician to fix their computer. Your friend thinks the technician is subhuman; the technician thinks your friend is braindead. Anything you say will either abet arrogance or insult ignorance; and so, precisely because you understand both points of view, you cannot say anything. The gap is larger, the problem worse, when, say, a plumber is called in. Your friend thinks it proves their own education that they cannot talk to plumbers; the plumber thinks your friend is hardly fit to live. How do you stand — are you for the Morlocks or the Eloi?

But the worst problem is communication. Having a broader base of analogy, you understand faster, but often cannot explain why you understand. Your friend has some half-formed idea; you recognize the shape of it from some far-off source; you say, "That's just like…" But whatever you say, your friend hears gibberish. It does not matter that you understand; you have committed an error, you have lowered yourself with a blunder, as if you were the traveler-bore who kills conversations with "When I was in…"

Still I think versatility is natural. I often discover that people are more versatile than they think they are, because they have not allowed themselves to recognize, in themselves, abilities which it would be awkward to have others recognize in them. Society is at fault, but not *our society*; only the fact of society at all.

THE CORAL SHIP

JULY 23, 2010   [In my dialect *water* and *order* do, in fact, rhyme.]

Come, ship, lie down with us;
Come, ship, lie down and rust.
The sand is soft, the coral is kind,
The sun is dim, we softly bind.
Do not be lonely, we remember
While we grow, and grow forever.
Your shape, our hollows; your stuff, our spires
Where silent fish gather in choirs.
Silence is music, stillness is motion
Growing cathedrals by grains of devotion.
Too long apart from water,
Too long outside of order:
Come ship, sink fast;
The sea has let you in at last.

GENIUS

AUGUST 2, 2010   Analogies between intelligence and physical strength are easy to make and often useful. I have used them before and I expect to use them again. But the correspondence is not exact. If to say "genius" is to mean anything, it must do more than name qualities of intelligence that are superior to ignorance in the same way that athleticism is superior to clumsiness. There are such qualities, such matters of degree; but they are not genius.

To use the word *genius* significantly, I would posit that strength is *stable*, but intelligence is *metastable*. These are terms from physics; they have statistical analogs but the terms from physics are more easily illustrated.

Imagine a marble rattling inside a bowl with tall sides. Rest the bowl on flat ground; shake it. Sometimes the marble climbs one side; sometimes another; but always it come to rest on the bottom – and when it falls out, it falls no lower than the bottom. In this bowl the marble's condition is *stable*. (Chart the marble's movements, and you have a bell curve.)

But intelligence is *metastable*. Imagine the same bowl; but this time, instead of resting it on the ground, put it at the summit of a hill. Mostly the marbles rattle inside this bowl as they did in the other; but sometimes a marble overtops the side, and shoots off down the hill on a trajectory we rattling marbles cannot imagine.

I believe in genius – not in geniuses. All of us spend most of our time rattling around in the bowl. But when the right person thinks about the right subject at the right time, a mind can take a trajectory that briefly places it, not just above all others, but above the sum of all others. In a work of genius, however briefly, a brainpower is concentrated that exceeds the combined brainpower of the rest of the human race. (Or, if not the sum, at least the sum of what language could coordinate to be applied along those lines.) Not a bit-for-bit balance of computations – only an unpredictable and incomparable excession.

A work of genius is recognizable because it arrives, even when it is simple in itself, as a characteristic expression of an unknown order of things – the way that the first artifact discovered from a lost civilization stands, the way the first signal from an alien civilization might stand – standing apart from all you know, not because it is overtly different, but because it implies in its negative space, in its outlines and hollows, a system of beliefs and concerns altogether contained in itself, a strangeness that is not a shock but a rich and intricate surprise.

Maybe this is why I feel such desperate pity for lost books. Sometimes when a book is lost, all that is lost is one more thing in the world; but sometimes when a book is lost, something like a world, something like cities and peoples, falls silent.

WEAKMINDEDNESS

AUGUST 8–SEPTEMBER 1, 2010

I

Is intelligence obsolete?

The question is: will the digital technologies of intellectual augmentation make exceptional intelligence obsolete, in the same way that the mechanical technologies of physical augmentation made exceptional strength obsolete? Not, "is the net is making us stupid?" but "does the net make it as impossible to be stupid, as the grid makes it impossible to be powerless?"

The saying goes that any article that asks a question does so in order to answer "no." If they were sure, they wouldn't ask. This is not one of those articles. My answer to the question "is intelligence obsolete?" is *yes* – though with reservations about the concept of obsolescence.

I say *intellectual augmentation* to reference Douglas Engelbart's 1962 *Augmenting Human Intellect*. I will use this book as the scaffold for the first part of my argument. Anyone who has investigated the origins of the net will know Vannevar Bush's 1945 *As We May Think*, a prefiguration of the Internet in light-table and microfilm. *Augmenting Intellect* is explicitly an attempt to show how Bush's vision could be made workable in electronic form. It is not a marginal document; six years after it was published the author, head of the Augmentation Research Center at Stanford, gave what is now known as the "Mother of All Demos," where he débuted, among other things, hypertext, email, and the mouse.

Some of the possibilities that *Augmenting Human Intellect* proposes have been fulfilled; some have been overtaken; some have failed; and some remain untried. The interesting ones are the untried.

The relevant part of *Augmenting Human Intellect* begins with Engelbart's description of the system he used to write the book – edge-notched cards, coded with the book or person from whom the content was derived.

(I say "content" because, as anyone who has attempted to maintain a system of notes organizing small, disparate pieces of information will realize, it is impossible to strictly distinguish thoughts and facts – the very act of selecting a fact for inclusion implies a thought about it.)

Engelbart calls these thought-facts *kernels*. He would arrange his cards into single-subject stacks, or *notedecks*. In the book he summarizes the frustrations of creating a memo using these cards – the lack of a mechanism for making associations (links, that is, but in both directions); the tedium of copying the links out; the confusion of keeping track of what linked to what.

He considers a mechanical system for leaving trails between cards and for copying them, but objects:

> It is plain that even if the equipment (artifacts) appeared on the market tomorrow, a good deal of empirical research would be needed to develop a methodology that would capitalize upon the artifact process capabilities. New concepts need to be conceived and tested relative to the way the "thought kernels" could be knitted together into working structures, and relative to the conceptual presentations which become available and the symbol-manipulation processes which provide these presentations.

He proceeds to further object that by the time some such mechanical system could be perfected, electronics would be better suited to the job. And we're off.

II

Pause, first, to consider Engelbart's concept of the *thought kernel*. Engelbart is explicit that the kernel itself represents a "structure of symbols." Yet, for purposes of inclusion in a larger symbolic structure, the kernel must be treated as smooth and integral. Every symbolic structure is made of smooth kernels – but all kernels are composite. This tension can be dealt with in more than one way.

Ascending levels in the sophistication of search are independent of the internal structure of a kernel. Even the most sophisticated searches now possible, and those not yet possible, are still a matter of *folders* and *contents*. And putting a kernel into one or many folders is not the same as parsing it.

Parsing is an impediment to search, not an aid. Certainly it is good when we search for Edward Teach and are directed to a "Blackbeard" chapter in a book about pirates. For our purpose the book as a whole is a kernel; and the chapter is too – we may print it out, or find the book and photocopy it, or collect it screenshot by screenshot. But how far can we break it down? It may be true that half the chapter is not about Blackbeard at all – this paragraph tells us about the town where he was born, this paragraph tells us about his ship, this paragraph tells us about his competitors – and it may be true that of the paragraphs about him half the sentences are not about him – here is a thought on the nature of brutality, here is a thought about why bearded men are menacing. If you isolate only the sentences that are about Blackbeard specifically, the result is gibberish. You wanted something about Blackbeard? Well, this chapter as a whole is about Blackbeard – but no part of it is actually about *him*.

This is why PIM ("personal information management") is hard: there need not exist any necessary connection between a kernel's internal structure and the folders where it is classified. The relationship is unpredictable. This unpredictability makes PIM hard – *hard* not as in difficult, but *hard* as in *insoluble*, in a way that is revealing of some human limitation. Classification is contingent, irreducibly.

Accordingly PIM is always tendentious, always fallible, and not always comprehensible outside of a specific context, or to any other but a specific person. And the most useful abstract classifications are not the best, but the most conventional – like the Dewey Decimal system, whose only advantage is that it exists.

III

Now I return to Engelbart and his "quick summary of relevant computer technology." It would be tempting to pass over this section of *Augmenting Human Intellect* as pointless. We know computers; we know what they can do. The introductions necessary in 1962 are needless for us. And true, some of it is funny.

> For presenting computer-stored information to the human, techniques have been developed by which a cathode-ray-tube (of which the television picture tube is a familiar example) can be made to present symbols on their screens of quite good brightness, clarity, and with considerable freedom as to the form of the symbol.

But we should look anyway, because *Augmenting Human Intellect* predates a great schism in the design and use of computers. Two sects emerged from that schism. The technologies that Engelbart thought would make augmentation practical largely ended up in the possession of one side of this schism – the losing side.

Engelbart thinks of computers as symbol-manipulating engines. This strikes one in the face when he talks about simulation:

> [T]hey discovered that the symbol structures and the process structures required for such simulation became exceedingly complex, and the burden of organizing these was a terrific impediment to their simulation research. They devised a structuring technique for their symbols that is basically simple but from which stem results that are very elegant. Their basic symbol structure is what they call a "list," a string of substructures that are linked serially in exactly the manner proposed by Bush for the associative trails in his Memex – i.e., each substructure contains the necessary information for locating the next substructure on the list. Here, though, each substructure could also be a list of substructures, and each of these could also, etc. Their standard manner for organizing the data which the computer was to operate upon is thus what they term "list structuring."

This is in reference to IPL-V. A few paragraphs later he writes, with spectacular understatement, "Other languages and techniques for the manipulation of list structures have been described by McCarthy" – followed by eight other names. But McCarthy's is the name to notice; and his language, LISP (LISt Processing) would become the standard tool for this kind of work.

There is a famous essay about the schism, by Richard Gabriel, source of the maxim "Worse is Better." It contrasts two styles of programming: the "MIT style" – the style of the MIT AI Lab, with the "New Jersey style" – the Bell Labs style. Software as we know it – based around the C programming language and the Unix family of operating systems, derives from the New Jersey style. Gabriel's essay actually characterizes the New Jersey style as a virus.

But how does this difference in style relate to the concept of "symbolic structures"? Lisp is focused on the manipulation of symbolic structures; and Lisp is the language best suited for this because Lisp code is in fact itself a symbolic structure. C-like languages are instructions to a compiler or interpreter. The instructions are discrete and serial. The symbolic structure remains implicit.

(Note that the difference is one of tendency, not of possibility. It is an axiom that any program can be written in any programming language that has the property of being Turing-complete – as all these languages are.)

Why C-like languages won may be suggested by a point of jargon. In Lisp-like languages anything besides manipulating symbolic structures – say, writing a file to disk or rendering it to the screen – is called a *side effect*. What are side effects to Lisp programmers are the business of C programmers. So instead of symbols and trails we deal with files and windows and websites, and have to hold the structures they are supposed to fit into in our own heads.

Coincidentally, in construction the quick and dirty style of framing a house is called "New Jersey framing." The standard way is to frame a wall is as a unit – a grid of studs nailed through their ends at right angles – then stand it up and nail it into place. Jersey framing instead maneuvers each stud into its final position before toenailing it in place – that is, hammering nails in at an angle. The standard style is more secure, but involves delay and forethought; New Jersey framing is less secure, but makes constant progress. New Jersey programming has essentially the same advantages and drawbacks.

IV

To make his ideas more tractable Engelbart tells a story of two characters: "You," addressed in the second person, and "Joe," who is experienced with augmentation and is giving You a demonstration.

First Joe shows off his workstation. His desk has two monitors, both mounted at slight angles to the desk – "more like the surface of a drafting table than the near-vertical picture displays you had somehow imagined." He types into a split keyboard, each half flanking a monitor, poising him over his screens as he works.

The ergonomics are impeccable. Consider how tradition forces us into a crick-necked and hunched-shouldered position whenever we sit at keyboard – how it literally constrains us. Judge how much more of the way you work is so ruled.

To introduce the capabilities of the system Joe edits a page of prose. Lo – every keystroke appears instantly onscreen! When he reaches the end of the line, carriage return is automatic! He can delete words and sentences, transpose them, move them around, make them disappear – "able to [e]ffect immediately any of the changes that a proofreader might want to designate with his special marks, only here the proofreader is always looking at clean text as if it had been instantaneously retyped." He can call up definitions, synonyms and antonyms "with a few quick flicks on the keypad." He can define abbreviations for any word or string of words he employs, whenever he wants, and call them up with substrings or keychords.

In short the capabilities of Joe's editor are somewhat above those of a word processor and somewhat below those of a programmer's editor.

Here we find one of the problems with Engelbart's vision. It is hard to augment procedures. If the act of typing a word is just the procedure of hitting a certain sequence of letters, then in the near term, it actually costs energy and time to change to typing the first few letters of a word and letting the editor expand it. It requires you to think of the word as an entity, not a procedure. For most of us, this is difficult.

Consider the abacus. The frictionless operations of mental arithmetic should be easier than the prestidigitation the abacus requires. And the most practiced algorists are indeed faster than the fastest abacists. (Sometimes, as in the famous anecdote of Feynman and the abacist, the algorist's superior knowledge of mathematics will simplify the problem to triviality.) But of course it is easier to learn the abacus than to learn mathematics, and for a fixed amount of practice the average abacist will be much faster than the average algorist.

There are abacus virtuosos who can calculate faster than the abacus can be fingered, who calculate moving their fingers on an empty table, but who cannot calculate at all without moving their fingers – slaves to a skeuomorph.

Skeuomorph is a term from architectural criticism. It names, usually to disapprove, a building's needless imitation of the traces of old-fashioned construction methods and materials it does not itself employ. But skeuomorphs are not always bad – classical architecture, in its system of pillars, pilasters, and entablatures, is a representation in stone of the engineering of wooden buildings.

The experience of using a computer is run through with skeuomorphs – the *typewriter* in the keyboard, the *desktop* in the screen, the *folders* on the hard drive, the *documents* they contain. Through a cultural process they dictate – even to those with little experience of the analog originals – how computers are to be used. In the beginning they let us in; in the end they hold us back.

The dominance of portable devices moves us toward the pole of the abacus – easy for competence, limited for mastery. As they break down walls, they close doors. As they are more and more physical and spatial, they are less and less symbolic.

V

Now we come to the last part of Joe's demonstration, and leave the familiar behind. The talk from here on is of arguments, statements, dependencies, and conceptual structures. Joe explains that he uses his workstation to produce *arguments* from *statements*, arranged sequentially but not serially. Quote:

> This makes you recall dimly the generalizations you had heard previously about process structuring limiting symbol structuring, symbol structuring limiting concept structuring, and concept structuring limiting mental structuring. You nod cautiously, in hopes that he

will proceed in some way that will tie this kind of talk to something from which you can get the "feel" of what it is all about.

He warns you not to expect anything impressive. What he has to show you is the sum of great many little changes. It starts with links: not just links between one document and others, but links within the document – links that break down sentences like grammatical diagrams, links that pin every statement to its antecedents and consequences.

[T]he simple capabilities of being able to establish links between different substructures, and of directing the computer subsequently to display a set of linked substructures with any relative positioning we might designate among the different substructures.

Note that this does not just mean creating links – it means creating *bidirectional* linkages, linkages that have kinds, linkages that can be viewed as structures as well as followed.

Here is a skeuomorph: the index or cross-reference in the hyperlink. The hyperlink are we know it is *hyper* only in the most trivial sense. You cannot even link a particular part of one document to a particular part of another document unless the target is specially prepared with anchors to hold the other end of the link. Except inside of a search engine (and the failed experiment of trackbacks), a link contributes no metadata to its target. The web has no provisions for back-and-forth or one-to-many links, let alone, say, uniquely identified content or transclusions.

These are not particularly exotic or difficult ideas; to understand how they might have worked – what the net might have been – look at Nelson's Xanadu.

The problems of the web – the problems smug commentators vaunt as unpredictable consequences of runaway innovation – these problems were not only thought of, but provided for, before the web existed. The reason we have these problems anyway is the haphazard and commercially-driven way the web came to be. The ways in which the web destroys value – its unsuitability for micropayment, for example – and the profit potentials the web affords – like search – are consequences of its non-architecture. If the web had been designed at all, music, news, writing would be booming in proportion with their pervasiveness. Instead we have Google; instead we have a maze where the only going concern is ads on maps.

Of course the net – the Internet – and the web – the World Wide Web – are different things. The net is the underlying technology, the pipes; the web is one way of using that technology. Email, for example, is part of the net, but not part of web; the same is true of BitTorrent or VoIP. At one level the answer to the question "Is Google making us stupid?" is "No, the web is making us stupid – wiring our brains into the web is just Google's business model."

Certainly it is easy to defend the web against this kind of heckling. "Nothing succeeds like success." The guy in the back of the audience muttering how the guys on stage are doing it wrong is always and rightfully the object of pity. What are we, guitarists? And there is no returning to the whiteboard; the web is, and it is what it is.

But we should remember that it could have been different – if only because, someday, we will have more choices. What has happened was not necessary; what has been predicted is not inevitable.

VI

The way Joe describes the effect of augmented symbol structuring is worth quoting in full:

> I found, when I learned to work with the structures and manipulation processes such as we have outlined, that I got rather impatient if I had to go back to dealing with the serial-statement structuring in books and journals, or other ordinary means of communicating with other workers. It is rather like having to project three-dimensional images onto two-dimensional frames and to work with them there instead of in their natural form.

This is, of course, again recalls the question, this time in its intended meaning: "Is Google making us stupid?" It is not a problem I have, but people do seem to suffer from it, so I can name the tragedy – we have just enough capacity for symbol structuring on the web to break down some people's tolerance for linear argument, but not enough to give them multidimensional ways of constructing arguments. The web is a perfectly bad compromise: it breaks down old patterns without enabling new ones.

Joe moves on from symbol structuring to process structuring. Here the methods resemble those used for symbol structuring – these are links and notes – but they are interpreted differently. A symbol structure yields an argument; a process structure answers the question – "What next?"

And this, of course, recalls the various methods of productivity. Productivity, however, is the abacist approach. Adherents of productivity methods manipulate physical objects or digital metaphors for physical objects – inboxes and to-do lists – and reduce them to next steps. Ultimately this is all any process structure can disclose – "What do I do now?" – and for most tasks something like this is adequate.

If there is a hole in your roof that leaks, the fact of the leak will remind you to fix the hole. The process is self-structuring: you will fix it or get wet. To a lesser extent, the same is true of the letter on your desk. But the email in your inbox – if you expect to answer it, you must find some way to maintain its urgency. But why should this be? Why can't you instruct the computer to be obtrusive? Why can't digital tasks structure themselves?

They can; but they don't, because there is no metaphor for it. The abacist email program has an inbox; following the metaphor, to get something out of the inbox, you must do something with it. More algorist email programs, like Mutt or Gnus, invert the problem – once you have read a message, unless you explicitly retain it, it disappears. This approach is vastly more efficient, but it has no straightforward paperwork metaphor, so it is reserved for the geeks.

Or again: why can't you develop processes in the abstract? Bloggers are forever writing up their own workflows. Why can't your computer analyze your workflow, guide you through it, help you refine it? Why can't it benchmark your activities and let you know which ones absorb the most time for the least return? Why is there no standard notation for workflows? Of course programmers have something like this in their editors and IDEs; but probably you do not.

Augmenting Human Intellect is worth reading but I am done with it. If I have been successful I have disenchanted you with the net – disenchanted literally; broken the spell it casts over minds that should know better. If I have been successful you understand that the net as you know it was not inevitable; that its future is not fixed; that its role is not a given; that is usefulness for any particular purpose is subject to judgment and discretion.

VII

Intelligence has never been in fashion. It has been news for a century that individual intelligence is becoming obsolete and the future belongs to procedures, teams, and institutions. This is a future that is always just about to arrive. The lesson is not that intelligence has always appeared to be on the verge of becoming obsolete (although it has); the lesson is that something in society hates intelligence and wants it to be obsolete – needs to believe that it is becoming obsolete.

Obviously in a commercial society we are always worth more for what we can own (or for being owned) than for what we can do. And it is true, regarding the advantages of teamwork over intelligence, that all the inputs into the economy from outside it involve teams and companies. An industrial army keeps the wells flowing, the mines yielding, the fields fruiting. Naturally the institutions that handle these inputs expect to deal with teams and institutions – an affinity that propagates throughout society.

Society, remember, is not a human invention, but a pattern in nature, a pattern we share with bees and ants and mole rats. It has its own logic, its own dynamics, and its own tendency – a tendency which is always toward the intelligence-free ground state of the hive or colony. For society as such intelligence is an irritant, something to be encapsulated and expelled, like a splinter in the thumb, or cicatrized in place, like a piece of shrapnel.

The greater the intelligence, the more likely it is to destroy its own advantage. Be born with exceptional strength and the best thing you can do with it is to use it yourself. Be born with exceptional intelligence and the best thing you can do with it is to turn it on itself – to figure out how the exceptional part of your intelligence works so you can teach it to others. We all think a little like Einstein now, because we have the maxims he wrought out, the examples he related.

Of course human beings are not ants or bees or mole rats and society cannot turn them into drones. People scheme. This is natural: intelligence atrophies when unused. It is as uncomfortable to be flabby in mind as in body. Nor would society want us to be; the software of society needs human speech to run on. Society does not want or need human beings to speak well, but it does need them to speak well enough.

To perfect this balance, we have the job, which stands in relation to the mind as exercise does to the body: it keeps you from becoming flabby, without fitting you for any particular use. Not that jobs are inherently useless; only that, given a minimal denomination of employment (say 9–5), real work is always padded with makework to fill it out fungibly.

Society's capacity to encapsulate intelligence is limitless but slow to respond. A sudden jump in the efficiency of all workers opens a gap, leaves intelligence idle – this has been called a *cognitive surplus*. In the last two decades we have seen one open up; remarkable things emerged from it – the web, the blogosphere, Wikipedia (more later) – and I think we have begun to see it close, soaked up into streaming video and social networking.

The central role which magazines have resumed in online intellectual life is a sign of intellectual decay. Witness the return of the article, the lowest form of writing, opening with an anecdote and closing with a cop-out. Watch the hopeless imitators of the intellectual thugs of undead ideologies playing intellectual. Could this be all that it comes to? All our work, all our hope? The same sad cycle of toothless posturing vs. splenetic emission, only this time on screens instead of paper, and with *Star Wars* references? Well, we had our chance; now we will see what came of it.

VIII

I began by comparing strength and intelligence and should justify it. This is difficult because silly ideas pass about both. Witlings think smart people quote cube roots the same way weaklings think strong people are musclebound. Smart people do not obsess over mental math, knowledge of trivia, and the size of their IQs; strong people do not obsess over diet, dead lifts, and the size of their biceps.

The parallel stereotypes are collateral results of the same error: if an ability is not economically rewarding, people pretend it does not exist. To account for records of its existence, some such stereotype will be foisted as its modern descendant.

Strength has not ceased to exist; it is even still useful. All the marvelous mechanical contrivances of modern life are lubricated with human sweat. Strength is necessary, but not advantageous. Everywhere, for free, strength is making civilized life possible; but there is nothing strength can do for free that cannot be done without strength for money. The best that strength can do is keep you from failing; you cannot distinguish yourself with it in any but recreational uses. No one earns a profit or a promotion for being strong.

Likewise by intelligence becoming obsolete I do not mean its disappearance, but its insignificance. The intellectual machinery that makes life faster and more brilliant will always need lubrication; but that work will be invisible, underground, and unrewarded. And being taken for granted, it will cease to be believed in.

Of course it is difficult to prove strength in physical teamwork; when working with someone weaker than yourself, you must moderate your own strength to avoid hurting the other person. Say *confuse* for *hurt* and the same applies to intellectual teamwork. If teamwork is expected, if the idea of intelligence is undermined with untestable reductive explanations ("Anyone could do that if they spent ten years learning it" – will you take ten years to find out?) – then intelligence will no longer be thought of, let alone believed in.

For now, intellectual work is still valorized. The gospel of productivity offers to make it accessible to everyone, by debunking its romance, by making it as tractable as "cranking widgets." Somehow intellectual work reduced to cranking widgets comes across more like intellectual work and less like cranking widgets. But this is to be expected.

Twentieth century industry enjoyed the prestige of muscularity, virility, and futurity for decades while it chained generations of children, abused generations of women, and poisoned, wore out, and discarded generations of men. Likewise intellectual work may be expected to enjoy the prestige of thoughtfulness long after thinking has been lost from it.

IX

I cannot get away with referencing the idea of *cognitive surplus* without engaging it. Or more directly: "What about Wikipedia?"

Do consider Wikipedia. But first, forget what you have read about Wikipedia: it is all lies. No one who opines about it understands it. It is almost certain that if you have not participated in it, you not only do not understand it, but are deluded about it.

I should disclose my participation in Wikipedia. I have written two obscure articles and heavily rewritten another. Beside that, my contribu-

338

tions have been limited to weeding vandalism, polishing grammar and expression (the bad to the acceptable; improving the adequate to the excellent would be rude), and filling in gaping omissions – though I do less and less of any of these, partly because there is less and less need, partly because I rarely look up things I already know. I do have the Wikimedia franchise.

I love Wikipedia, esteem it as the best service of the net, and consider it, in the long run, the most important and consequential cultural development of the twenty-first century – much more so than, say, social networking or Google. (Though I acknowledge that the Google-Wikipedia relationship is symbiotic.)

Wikipedia is not collaborative. Collaboration, of course, happens on Wikipedia. I mentioned an article I revised, an article about a place: a few days after the revision a native of the country concerned corrected my misspellings, substituted the native alphabet for my transcriptions, and added details only someone who had been there could know. Wikipedia relies on collaboration; but it is not inherently collaborative. It is often almost perfectly competitive, where free time is money. From the history tab of a hypothetical controversial article click over to the discussion and you will encounter the most bitter discussions the Internet has seen outside of Usenet – worse, sometimes, because Wikipedians, since their contact with each other is largely limited to their controversies, have no contiguous way to make nice or make up. There is a jungle three tabs behind the white sans-serif façades of Wikipedia.

Wikipedia is not spontaneous. The typical Wikipedia article is not a lovely crystal of accretive collaboration. It is a Frankenstein's monster of copy stitched together from a dozen donors, a literary teratoma. Wikipedia as a whole is a ravenous black hole that sucks up endless amounts of copy: the out-of-copyright public domain; the direct to public domain; and the unpublishable. Wikipedia is not just the last encyclopedia; it is the Eschaton of all encyclopedias, the strange attractor drawing them on to the end of their history. Wikipedia is the hundred-hearted shambling biomass to which every encyclopedia ever printed unwittingly willed its organs. Whole articles from Chamber's *Cyclopædia* – the very first encyclopedia – turn up inside it completely undigested. As soon as it was born it ate its parent, the Nupedia, and went about seeking whom it might devour. Its greatest conquest was the celebrated 11th edition of the *Encyclopædia Britannica* – the last great summary deposition of proud imperial European civilization before it passed final judgment on itself. (As the article "Artillery" states: "Massed guns with modern shrapnel would, if allowed to play freely upon the attack, infallibly stop, and probably annihilate, the troops making it.")

If you had heard of Wikipedia but not seen it you might surmise that the kind of people who would edit it would have a technical and contemporary bias, and that trivia would predominate: there exists a band that no one has ever heard; there exists a town in Scotland where nothing has ever happened. And you would be right. But the massive scholarship of the 1911 encyclopedia perfectly counterbalances that bias. The credibility of the Wikipedia as a universal reference was invisibly secured by this massive treasure, excavated as surely and strangely as Schliemann excavated the gold of Troy. Whole articles from the 1911 edition live in Wikipedia, and even where the revision of obsolete information and prejudiced opinion has replaced most of the article, whole paragraphs and sentences remain intact. If while reading an article in Wikipedia you feel at a sudden chill in the air, shiver with a thrill of dry irony or scholarly detachment, feel a thin rope of syntax winding itself around your brain – the ghosts of 1911 are speaking.

(The Britannica itself dispensed with this material during its reinvention in 1974.)

The second source is material that is directly released into the public domain: press releases, government documents, think tank reports. A business has two vital functions: to do something and to let people know what it is doing. The latter provides great opportunities to Wikipedia, which is always looking for new things people might want to know about. Wikipedia has a magpie eye; press releases are very shiny.

(Wikipedia also picks up shiny stuff where it shouldn't – it's always distasteful to click through a reference link and find that the text of the reference, a private website, evidently not in the public domain, has simply been copied – but then again Wikipedia saves some valuable information this way that would otherwise be lost to link rot.)

Beside the brook of business runs the massive river of text thrown off by the military-industrial-governmental complex, large amounts of which (in the US) are explicitly in the public domain, other parts of which are too evidently of public interest to be neglected. Wikipedia soaks up this stuff like a Nevada golf course.

The third source is sophisticated yet unpublishable material. If you have ever been dismayed at the thought of how much intellectual energy goes into a school report, written to be read once by someone who learns nothing from it, know that Wikipedia is there to catch all these efforts. (Or was, before it began to inform them.) I suspect that the preponderance of original articles on Wikipedia were actually executed as assignments or requirements of teachers or employers. Wikipedia strains the plankton from the sea of busywork like the baleen of a whale.

What is Wikipedia? Wikipedia is a sublimely efficient method of avoiding redundant effort. Wikipedia is write once, remember forever. Wikipedia is make do and mend. Wikipedia is reuse and recycle.

X

Don't I know how Socrates condemned writing – how it would give the appearance of wisdom but not the substance – with an Egyptian fable where Thoth presents writing, among other useful inventions, only to have it rejected by the god as harmful?

This little anecdote – a single paragraph of a long dialog, a minor support to a more complex argument, and the least extended of the many fables which adorn the *Phaedrus* – has acquired a reputation and argumentative weight that its duration cannot support. Here it is in full, after Jowett:

At the Egyptian city of Naucratis, there was a famous old god, whose name was Theuth; the bird which is called the Ibis is sacred to him, and he was the inventor of many arts, such as arithmetic and calculation and geometry and astronomy and draughts and dice, but his great discovery was the use of letters. Now in those days the god Thamus was the king of the whole country of Egypt; and he dwelt in that great city of Upper Egypt which the Hellenes call Egyptian Thebes, and the god himself is called by them Ammon. To him came Theuth and showed his inventions, desiring that the other Egyptians might be allowed to have the benefit of them; he enumerated them, and Thamus enquired about their several uses, and praised some of them and censured others, as he approved or disapproved of them.

It would take a long time to repeat all that Thamus said to Theuth in praise or blame of the various arts. But when they came to letters, This, said Theuth, will make the Egyptians wiser and give them better memories; it is a specific both for the memory and for the wit. Thamus replied: O most ingenious Theuth, the parent or inventor of an art is not always the best judge of the utility or inutility of his own inventions to the users of them. And in this instance, you who are the father of letters, from a paternal love of your own children have been led to attribute to them a quality which they cannot have; for this discovery of yours will create forgetfulness in the learners' souls, because they will not use their memories; they will trust to the external written characters and not remember of themselves. The specific which you have discovered is an aid not to memory, but to reminiscence, and you give your disciples not truth, but only the semblance of truth; they will be hearers of many things and will have learned nothing; they will appear to be omniscient and will generally know nothing; they will be tiresome company, having the show of wisdom without the reality.

Its prominence is due more to the names involved than its contents. It is told by Socrates, historical founder of philosophy. It concerns Thoth, mythical founder of esotericism. To Socrates and Plato he was only one Egyptian deity; but intervening tradition crowns him Thrice-Great Hermes, founder of all Western esoteric traditions (excluding of course the Cabala, separately descended from the secret revelation of Moses). Here is the author of the Emerald Tablet, condemned for his vain and foolhardy invention of writing! The irony of the anecdote impresses it in the memory.

But consider the context. I will not rehearse the whole of the *Phaedrus*, only call attention to its last section. It begins when Phaedrus remarks in passing that the politicians of Athens care so little for their speeches that they must be begged to write them down.

Socrates calls him on this absurdity. He contrasts true and false rhetoric – the false rhetoric of politicians, giving set speeches to a lump audience; and the true rhetoric – that is, dialectic: to understand and address your argument to the conditions and abilities of one person. Writing, they come to agree, is a weak thing, because like speechifying it does not accommodate itself to any particular understanding. Like a painting, it has the semblance of life, but remains dumb when questions are asked of it.

Note that a specific kind of writing is meant – persuasive writing – and that a specific fault is diagnosed – generality. Writing that is addressed to a specific person and meant to be replied to, like a letter, is not considered, nor is writing that preserves facts, like histories or treatises. Within the limits of his actual argument Socrates is hard to disagree with. Of course it is better to persuade in person. Of course it is a higher skill to persuade someone in particular than to sway a crowd. But even then Socrates recommends writing to hedge against old age. I would add death and distance. He really has no argument against writing at all; it is merely an occasion to express the difference between rhetoric and dialectic, which is not specific to writing.

But to show that Socrates did not mean what people think he meant is not to show that what people think he meant is wrong. Surely writing impairs memory? Surely writing gives us the voice of wisdom, without the substance?

We wrongly think of mnemonic feats as proper to pre-literate cultures; but the *ars memoriæ* shows that memorization only gained in urgency with the invention of writing. Before writing there was simply less to remember. The feats of illiterate mnemonicists in memorizing long epic poems are rightly impressive. But this means that to be remembered for more than one lifetime, knowledge had to be worked up in poetry – no easier then that is now, whether of the the "Sailor's delight" variety or the "Sing, goddess" variety.

By itself writing lets knowledge persist without being remembered, but does not itself retain knowledge. Yes, the knowledge you want is in a book; but that book is chained up in the next country. You may obtain knowledge through reading; but you must bring it back in your head. What trivialized mnemotechnique was not writing, but printing.

But then may what is said against writing apply to printing? Consider another anecdote about memory and writing, this one from the *Life of Johnson*. It is the source of a quote which has become so familiar that it passes for a cliché or a snowclone. Johnson, on his arrival at a house, surveyed the books there. Joshua Reynolds, painter, quipped that his own art was superior to writing: he could take in all the paintings in the room at a glance, but Johnson could hardly read all the books. Johnson riposted with a distinction:

> Sir, the reason is very plain. Knowledge is of two kinds. We know a subject ourselves, or we know where we can find information upon it. When we enquire into any subject, the first thing we have to do is to know what books have treated of it. This leads us to look at catalogues, and the backs of books in libraries.

Very good, of course; telling; and the standard explanation for the effect of printing: it replaced knowledge of facts with knowledge of the sources of facts. But I am not willing to accept this – I think that Johnson, and we, are wrong.

We need something to compare to language, something else which has gone through the same transition from oral transmission to written form to printing. There is such a comparison in music. Music too underwent transition from aural to written to printed form. Unlike language, its first transition is not prehistoric (as language's tautologically must be); and its unwritten forms have continued to develop, and may be compared to the written forms.

A musician who plays wholly from written music may not be particularly good at memorizing long pieces or at improvisation. But such inability to memorize may be by choice – pianists strictly play from sheet music because they think it better to do so than to memorize – and the ability to improvise arises mostly as a consequence of the feeling for music theory – the theory required (at least implicitly) to understand, play, and compose music. Playing from written music does not prevent a musician from playing with feeling tone, living rhythm, and meaningful phrasing.

True, in principle, one could be able to read music but not to play it – but that would be perverse. It would be like reading without thinking – which is impossible, because written words have no meaning of their own. Their meaning must be reconstructed in the mind of the reader; and this reconstruction is a skill, an ability, an act, like playing music. The skills you must have to read at all, and the skills you must have to play at all, are far more difficult and important than the skills whose necessity reading relieves. They blend in their perfection: memorization from a position of ability, understanding the rules behind the changes, is better than memorization from inability, taking every note on faith.

Do I then excuse the net? Do I consider it as safe as sheet music? If the net were another such step, as from writing to printing, I would.

More than anything else, the net is a machine for exaggerating its own importance. In its function of making information accessible it is not transformative. Comparisons between the net and the invention of printing – even the invention of writing – are commonplace, but absurd. Those who so compare reveal their dependency on inherited thought patterns, on the Whig history of the intellect.

It is comparable to the wrong idea most people have about industry – there was an Industrial Revolution; and since then, more of the same. But of course modern industry is as far from the old mills and factories as they were from cabin piecework. The invention of electric lighting and air conditioning mark transformations of the factory system as profound as mass production and the assembly line. But somehow we do not notice such changes.

Likewise we do not notice the two most important events in the history of the intellect: the public library and the paperback book. Between these two inventions more information has been made available to any human being than any human lifetime could absorb. They changed a world of scarcity into a world of plenty. The net – a change from plenty to plenty – is comparatively insignificant. A thousand or a million times too much is still just too much. (Of course this is not equally true everywhere.)

But the net does have peculiar advantages; the net is different. It is frictionless, instantaneous, ubiquitous – and consequentially so. Consider drink. Spirits were once the only way to preserve surplus harvests, for storage and transport. Intelligence has had the same use: to distill, compact, and preserve masses of information and experience. Now we can move harvests in refrigerated bulk, preserve them as long and transport them as far as we like. Of course people still drink; but now drink serves a recreational purpose. When notes are as accessible as narratives, when eyewitnesses are as accessible as reports, there the exercise of intelligence, though no less useful to sort excess than to defy scarcity, loses its urgency, excusability, and remunerability. The price of the cheapest smartphone is enough to make a "walking encyclopedia."

XI

Everything with an outside has an inside. (Topological curiosities notwith-standing.) If digital augmentation obsoletes intelligence on the outside, what about the inside? Surely, however hard the wind blows against the rest, programmers are safe in the eye of the storm.

So far I have written *intelligence* and *intellect* interchangeably; but there is a distinction. It is best made by an example Jacques Barzun relates in his *House of Intellect*. Consider the alphabet: 52 utterly arbitrary signs (26 uppercase, 26 lowercase), with history but without rationale, which make it possible to record and represent anything that can be said. Millions use it, as Barzun observes, who could not have invented it. Intelligence so crystallized, so made current and bankable, is intellect.

The book itself is remarkable – I recommend it for anyone impressed by *The Closing of the American Mind*, which is tedious, muddled, and dated by comparison. But I will not rehearse his argument. The battle is over, the other side won before I was born. Of course intelligence does not require intellect; but without its tools, fending for itself, it moves slowly and wastefully. Relying on its own resources, it becomes too serious; everything is so costly that it cannot take anything lightly. It loses time.

Programming is the most purely intellectual discipline which human beings have ever created – as it must be, given (Dijkstra observes some-where) that computer programs are the most complicated things human beings have learned to make. Programming cannot be learned, it must be adopted; it is a skill not just of action, but of perception.

Some people wonder if programming is an art or a craft. In seeking humility the usual answer is craft. But this is false. A craftsman works with stubborn materials and gets it right the first time. A carpenter who takes three tries to build a table and throws away the first two is not a craftsman. But three tries at a painting or a program is typical. A craftsman is finished when the work is done; an artist's work must be declared finished. Of course the better the programmer, the larger the chunks of the program that come out right in the first place. But the challenge of programming, its possibilities for flow, lie at the point where it is pursued artistically.

In a small way the early web made this art accessible and meaningful for those who did not think of themselves as programmers. In a small way it brought intellect into lives otherwise unaccommodating of it. The primitive character of the technology and the intrepidity of its early adopters, both required and welcomed intellect. Anyone who accepted the discipline of HTML, who studied literature to write better fanfiction, who studied the fallacies to call them out in forums or newsgroups – they were embracing intellect as they had never before had the freedom to do.

But this is past. You can, of course, study photography toward a better photostream, writing toward a better blog; but the improvement is along a spectrum. Formerly those unwilling to take trouble were absent; now there is no break to differentiate those who take the trouble from those who do not. We are all on the same footing, because we all possess personalities. When all the tools are provided it takes intelligence, but not intellect, to use them well.

The old web promised to change relations, to establish an invisible college; the new web promises to recapitulate existing relations.

(Note that the succession of Web 2 to Web 1 was not gradual or competitive; 9/11 broke Web 1, and something else had to be created to replace it. The relative political tranquility of the time was as important a precondition as the technology; politics, when passionate, is neurotoxic to intellect – a drop in the reservoir makes a reservoir of poison.)

Programming is writing: a very exact kind of writing, for a highly intelligent, totally unsympathetic, viciously literal reader. But here, too, there are fashions. The anarchy of Perl and the onramp of PHP yield to the whiteroom of Python and the velvet rope of Ruby. The hacker, who looks inside everything – with or without permission – yields to the developer, whose job is pasting together blackbox libraries and invoking their "magic." Even MIT has ceded software engineering to Python. The cathedral has fallen on the bazaar; the freedom of free software is not free as in beer or as in speech, but free as in sunlight, air, and other unmetered utilities.

Of course computers failed to deliver artificial intelligence. But machine intelligence need not equal human intelligence to render it obsolete. The assembly line never matched the finesse of the workbench. The progress of transportation was not from meat legs to machine legs, but from legs to wheels. Programmers have their own ways of taking a spin.

XII

New technology has previously made intelligence easier without depriving it of value; why should the net be so dangerous to it? I have considered only the means of its attack, not the cause of its enmity.

In truth there is no intrinsic reason why the technology of the net must oppress intelligence; I use it heavily in that faith. But though the enmity is not intrinsic, it is still inborn, because the net was conceived in the pursuit of efficiency. Efficiency, like society, hates intelligence and wants to destroy it.

What is efficiency? Efficiency means maximum return on minimum effort and minimum expense. But not everything that ensures more return for less done is a measure of efficiency. In the simplest case the efficiency of one technology may be superseded by another technology that is inherently more efficacious – highly efficient systems of horse-powered mail delivery like the English mail coach or the Pony Express were displaced by steam power in its earliest and least efficient forms. The horse's lineage and the rider's tack were the products of millennia of tradition that allowed horse and rider to operate as one animal. Rail, by comparison, was unreliable and unpredictable; intrepid for engineers, opaque for passengers.

If computers were the successors of paper-based information management, as rail was successor to the stagecoach, there would be no problem. The problem is not inherent to computers or to the net at all; it belongs to culture. Technology does not incur, it enables. It is not the fault of the orgasm button that the mouse starves while pressing it. This was always a weakness in the mouse; the button just gave him the chance to destroy himself as he had always been prepared to destroy himself.

We all suspect, most quietly, that the technological developments of the late twentieth century, and of our own time, let down the rapid pace of progress which developed the developed world; everything is sleeker, everything is faster and more brilliant, but little is new. Remember Engelbart débuted the net forty years ago. Progress, once an irresistible force, is now hardly felt; in its place are so many immovable objects, so much foot-dragging, second-guessing, and public relations as the art of excuses.

The most parsimonious explanation of this state of affairs is that after decades of focus on efficiency, there is no more room left for innovation – not even on the scale of the refrigerator, let alone the scale of the jet engine. Standards for return on capital have become so high that there is no indulgence left for the expensive and unrewarding infancy of really new technology.

But this is too limited an example. The idea is more general, and more familiar; we carry the lesson in the very frame of our bodies. Human beings are terribly inefficient at moving around. We traded the gait of the quadruped, even the lope of the knuckledragger, for the endless high-wire act of the biped. For most of our lives we leave two limbs – two perfectly good forelimbs – hanging unused by our sides while our hind limbs waddle precariously. Through idleness and inefficiency we trade forelimbs for arms and hands, and all that hands can do.

Consider Aristotle: "Civilization begins in leisure." The phrase passes on Aristotle's credit; but in itself it ought to be shocking, if not absurd. Who believes in leisure? We have psychology; and whatever the school all psychology is one in its unwillingness to cede the possibility of leisure. If there is such a thing as leisure, psychology is impossible just as, if there are such things as miracles, physics is impossible. Everything we do must serve some urgent purpose of the unconscious or of the genes.

The paradox is curious: we have the most refined instruments of leisure ever devised, but we will not believe in it. We admit to resting, relaxing, blowing off steam, unwinding, recharging, renewing; we admit to solace, consolation, distraction, and escape – but we do not admit to leisure. We suspend work to work more. For this god we admit no counterpart.

There is so much to do, and so little time. There are only so many open slots; no matter how efficiently you pack, at some point every new claim on your time pushes an old one off into oblivion. Productivity systems in general strike me as perverse, because they keep the least worthwhile, most predictable claims uppermost, and push the more interesting, amorphous claims down and finally off the edge. It is life laid out in line, without recurrence, without themes, without center. It is the final victory of school over life, when last year's projects are as irrelevant as last year's homework.

But we are tired. Enough of the open-ended, the uncertain, the un-known. There is something to be said for life that is modest in its ambitions, confident within its limits, at home with itself – at least by way of *amor fati*, since it is trivially true that the ordinary life cannot be extraordinary. We are so tired, and the world is so old. There are so many big ideas; do we really need more? Let the scholars publish and perish; at least it keeps them too busy to preach. And politics – after so much politics nothing is settled, nothing is certain – let those who can do nothing else devote themselves to it. Do not trouble us with that frenzy – whoever the people are, we are not they. "This is a sweet, comfortable thing; by what right do you condemn the consoling scent of the lotus, and bid us onto the open sea?" By no right; only because I am arrogant – arrogant enough to believe that if the sea calls to me, it must call to others.

XIII

What is obsolescence? Plainly the concept is partly technological, partly social. Cars made draft horses and buggy whips obsolete, but there are still mounted police, and buggy whip manufacturers made a smooth transition to manufacturing car parts. (Capital finds its level.) A technology that displaces another never does so completely; no technology is completely interchangeable with another. They all imply their own particular scale of values. Too, there is an index of obsolesciveness, a function of complexity: the ax survived the chainsaw, because it is simple, but the vacuum tube did not survive the transistor, because it is complex. But even these technologies sometimes linger. Investment has inertia, nobody likes to close a factory, and what's so bad about COBOL after all?

Obsolescence happens, it is a real force; but it is over-billed. Nothing disappears, nothing ceases to function the day it becomes obsolete. Obsolescence is something that happens to technologies, but it is not the chief or limiting condition of their existence.

Real obsolescence is the opposite, not of progress, but of simplicity. This is vividly, though shrilly, argued in an interesting but flawed book, *The Shock of the Old* – shrilly, because a cogent case against the doctrine of obsolescence would have to consider not just products but production methods. The author writes as if the ax of 2010 were the same as the ax of 1910 or 1810 – as if there were an equivalence between the product of a blacksmith, an assembly line, and a laser-guided CNC machine. He adduces shipbreakers tearing down the most massive artifacts of industrial civilization with muscle and hand tools, but passes over the fact that this manpower is fed by the high technology of the Green Revolution.

So what do I mean when I say "intelligence is obsolete"? Is its obsolescence real or doctrinal? I think it is doctrinal because, as I said before, intelligence cannot just disappear.

But this sounds circular. What is obsolete? Intelligence is obsolete. What judges obsolescence? Intelligence judges obsolescence — even granting some part of the emotional repulsion of obsolescence to distaste for the unfashionable, still the idea operates too broadly not to imply judgment, intelligence, and intellect.

It is this circle one sees, I think, in the odd paradoxes pronounced by the boosters of technology-as-magic, which would solve the bewilderment of technology with more technology, who would loosen the constraints of technology with more constraints, and who would make technology less demanding by ensuring that it follows you everywhere. They recognize technology as something enabling choice and critical judgment in everything except technology; technology as something solvent to ignorance, helplessness, and herd behavior in everything except technology. But I see nothing that makes technology such a fixed point; it seems to me as unstable, as potentially a topic for deliberation, as it encourages everything else to be.

I have heard it argued that technology — be straight, computers — is becoming more like cars — devices practically magical, in that they are operated more through ritual then understanding. This cuts me a little because in fact I understand very little about cars. But why do I know so little about cars? Not lack of curiosity, but lack of opportunity. I have never been in a position where a car was something I could afford to break — not to mention putting life and limb in hazard. But the evident trend of computers is towards commodification; everything done to de-commodify computing devices is ultimately doomed. Once I had one computer, heavy metal taking up desk space, and that was a serious investment in hardware; now I have several computers, and the most valuable thing about them is the peculiar configuration of each one. But, increasingly, anywhere I can check out a few repositories, I am at home. It is this possibility, the chance to evolve your own peculiar relationship with technology, one that is cumulative, personal, and free; one that you own and control; one that is a slow growth of the mind into the possibilities afforded by intellectual augmentation, not an accommodation of the mind to the tools and metaphors dictated to you – this possibility which allows intelligence to employ technology, not serve it.

In finding intelligence obsolete the doctrine of obsolescence obsolesces itself. A replacement is in order; some new view of technology is required; maybe something like the idea of a technosphere; if not that, certainly something of equal scope. But then I am hasty. So obsolescence obsoletes itself; so there is a contradiction, so what? A dissonance implies a resolution but nothing says that it has to resolve. Self-contradiction may even strengthen an idea, by imbuing its holders with faith.

Intelligence is obsolete. Obsolescence is obsolete. Somewhere between these poles our future lies: either a course closer to one than the other, or a circle trapped between them.

THE GOLDEN DISK

SEPTEMBER 4, 2010   They came from the sky in disks of gold and told us we were not alone. When they walked, they walked like us. When they spoke, they spoke like us. They said they had found our golden disk, our message of music, and they had accepted it. They had come for our Bach, to crown him with glory, to admit him to the fellowship of the music masters of a million worlds. We told them he was dead and they asked us what that meant. When we could no longer bear the pity in their so human faces we asked them to leave and they went. You call my silence a conspiracy. But I have no words.

SHORT STORIES

SEPTEMBER 12, 2010   There are too many short stories in the world. For all x, where x is heartbreaking or horrifying, mystifying or magnificent, pitiful or precious, agonizing or astonishing – some short story already satisfies it perfectly.

There is always room for another novel. Novels are too long for perfection. All novels do something wrong, leave some promise unfulfilled. There is always room in the gaps. The novel is fractal; from the right perspective we could see every novel growing out of another – see *Don Quijote* as the Mandelbrot set, dark among halos.

There is always room for another movie. I suspect good directors become so by watching bad movies. Every bad movie has one good character, one good scene, one good shot, one good line. Watch enough of them and these scattered goods add up to the shadow of a great but unmade movie.

But short stories can be perfect. Pry open the novelist and you find a frustrated reader of novels; pry open the director and you find a frustrated watcher of movies. But pry open a short story writer and you find delight and devotion. This is strange. Perfection is so high and so cold a thing; it should quell and silence us, it should make us prefer some open field. What could inspire us to imitate what we cannot rival?

(There is of course an analogy in music – old Bach is perfect, yet inspires composers – but that is only a parallel mystery.)

The point of fiction is its process. No work of fiction worth writing is fully planned. Not that fiction must be unplanned or shapeless; only that, for the writer, fiction is as much discovery as design – a revelation that may be determined, but cannot be predicted.

Imagine a pantograph mounted to a drafting table. Some points are fixed, some points are free. As the draftsman moves the arms the fixed points determine, as translated by the configuration of the machine, the shape traced out by the free points.

We only see the shape traced out when the drawing is done; but every work of fiction starts with something fixed and something free. Fiction is always experiment. The writer fixes certain points. Given the machine that the writer's knowledge and sympathy are, what shape will be traced?

In the novel the apparatus is somewhat flexible. Time and tedium, research and tendency, blur the resulting image. But in the short story the apparatus is rigid and quick. The shape is distinct. For the writer, the short story is an experiment; for the reader, the short story is a demonstration.

If the point of fiction were for us to tell what we know about the world – to put on masks and do impersonations, to manipulate puppets and cast our voices into their mouths – then fiction would not be worth writing. Essays and treatises can tell more easily, completely, and comprehensibly.

We waste our powers when we exercise them only in being ourselves. To observe is to imitate; to sympathize is to become. We all do this; we simply call it knowing a person – knowing how they look at things, knowing what they would say, how they would say it. This is a basic human faculty, something we take pleasure in doing and cultivating for its own sake. We build music on hearing, art on seeing; we build fiction on knowing.

THEORIES

SEPTEMBER 24, 2010   I look at the sky and see nuclear furnaces and transcendental distance. I look at an apple and see molecules, atoms, quanta of energy and motion. I look at a bird and see evolution, metabolism, aerodynamics. Yet looking at the same things others have seen a sphere of fixed stars, an apple-substance, and upholding angels. Some wit observed of the Ptolemaic cosmos: "If they had been right, what would the world have looked like?" The answer, of course, is that without a telescope it would look the same. Most experience is theory-neutral; we can get by believing almost anything about inner workings and ultimate origins. Even in the part of experience that science enables, people can get by without seeing scientifically. (I recall the moment of horror when I was learning to drive and realized there were people with driver's licenses and Aristotelian intuitions about motion.)

Thus I try from time to time to put on wrong theories. I try to see Ptolemy's sky spin or Newton's sky tick, to see elemental matter with Aristotle or vortical matter with Descartes – to grasp and hold the view as long as I can. It interests me that this can be done at all, but properly the interest is in the consequences. The longer I can hold the view, the more I accommodate it. I feel the possibility of otherwise unknown moods; I feel a derangement in my scale of values; I feel a shift in my physical bearing – somehow how much of the universe is above my head matters to how I hold it; somehow the composition of dirt matters to how I stand on it.

The same life, the same world, but in a different key: the names, the patterns, the movements are the same, yet the overall effect is different. I wonder if this was what it was like to live through Einstein. I think of Feynman's melancholy observation that science is not an infinite project, that it is at last doomed to run out of nontrivia to discover. I think of the commonplace that schools in art and philosophy sometimes end simply because they are too developed, because they require too much time to catch up with, foreclose too many possibilities. But there is no such escape from truth.

SURVIVORS

OCTOBER 3, 2010   Reading in another language poses a recurring doubt. An image, a turn of phrase, an expression pleases you. Is it original to the author, or is it a commonplace of an unfamiliar tradition? Corollary: a minor writer within a tradition may be a major writer in literature generally, if there are no other survivors. (Even the first entrant to the mainstream from some tributary looms as better writers within that tributary never can.) No novel so trashy, no polemic so petty, no puff so creepy, that if some cataclysm obliterated the rest of the accomplishments of our civilization, it would not impress itself on our posterity. In any living literature there is something in common that counts for nothing from within, and everything from without. Lemma: greatness in writing requires you either to enlist an otherwise hidden tradition and impinge with it, or to imply the presence of an alien tradition, to bring some hidden weight to bear behind the cutting edge.

THE SOUTH

OCTOBER 18, 2010   In order, my first observations of the South. The stupendous clouds, like levitating icebergs. The jumble of wealth and poverty. I had seen mansions and hovels, but I had never seen a mansion, a hovel, and a clipped suburban lawn, all along the same mile of highway. The rarity of winter clothing – at temperatures when Northeners would bundle up, Southerners persevered in shorts and T-shirts, as if taking notice of the cold would only encourage it.

I have not gone much farther. I have become a Louisianan, but not really a Southerner. Of course being a Rodriguez helps with that. Here I pass for native unless I bother to deny it; but of course Rodriguez is not so happy a name in the rest of Dixie.

Comparing Louisiana with the South is tricky. Which Louisiana do you mean? Broadly speaking, all Louisiana is divided into four parts. The northwest, the watershed of the Red River, was settled by Americans of the same Scotch-Irish stock as the rest of the South. It is something like East Texas. This is where rock and roll happened. In the less south southeast, the Florida Parishes (Percy's Feliciana) were settled by the English, and are something like Mississippi. This has been at times the most violent area in the US, host to multigenerational blood feuds. In the southwest, Acadiana was settled by Germans and Acadians; and in the very south southeast, Barataria (including New Orleans) was settled by the French and Spanish. (This is where jazz happened.) These last two regions are both culturally unique to Louisiana and very different from one another. Chances are, when you think of Louisiana, you are thinking of them: aristocatholic decadence and europeasant uninhibition.

But even allowing for regional variation, the interests of Louisiana were never quite the interests of the South. Again and again Louisiana has sacrificed for the South, and the South has taken. In the long view the relationship between Louisiana and the South has the shape of an unhealthy marriage: on Louisiana's side, all passion and devotion; on the South's side, something between tolerance and contempt.

In 1861 Louisiana was the wealthiest, most splendid state in the Union; four years later it was the poorest and most desperate, forever. "Often rebuked, but always back returning." Mississippi, for example, resents Louisiana for stealing the spotlight during Katrina. When they talk about it there is a subtext something like this: *We had it bad too, but we didn't squeal on national television. We hearty salt-of-the-earth goodmen took our knocks, gritted our teeth, and rebuilt while those weirdo slacker heathens whined and sat on their thumbs.* One might object something about the different challenges of rebuilding neighborhoods that were swept away in a night vs. rebuilding neighborhoods where the very ground spent weeks steeping in poison; but who can fight myth?

The Civil War is history to Northerners, yesterday to Southerners; something northerners learn about in school, something Southerners learn about at home.

In this respect I am an atypical Northener. As a child my best friend's father was a Civil War re-enactor. I know the smells of campfire and canvas, of wet wool and black powder. I think "Battle Hymn of the Republic" was the first song I ever memorized. I am reflexively blue the way Southerners are reflexively gray.

The contradiction in my feelings about Louisiana and about the South is clearest when I look at the war. I have no quarrel with Sherman, the bugbear of the South in general; but I personally dislike Butler. True, the war was particularly bad here – things went on in the Florida Parishes under Butler's blind eye that read more like *Apocalypse Now* than *Gone With the Wind* – but there is no real basis for this distinction; it is simply emotional.

Still, I am not a Louisianan by birth. As an outsider I have to recognize that Louisiana is part of the South. The distinctions are many, but they are only distinctions, not differences. If I want to understand Louisiana I should understand the South better.

REGRET

OCTOBER 25, 2010   Evil is the bad things that happened. Regret is the good things that did not happen. Regret troubles us more. Evil is bad in itself, not because of the things that did not happen instead; but we value what might have been more than what was as absolutely as we value the lives of children over the lives of adults. What happened is finite. What did not happen is infinite.

If harboring regret is weak then we are all weak. We shame regret in others, because we have no way to defy it in ourselves. Meanwhile regret reigns. Dreams beguile hope; fantasies beguile regret. The distinction matters because regret is stronger than hope – hope is finite. Love or money always come into it somehow. But less often as, "This will get me rich" or "This will get me laid" than as "It is not too late to succeed" or "It is not too late to be loved." This is nontrivial. Hope only wants; regret has something to prove.

There is something heart-softening, something miraculous, about the repair of a regret, about a second chance. We stand naked before these incidents. Forget cures and escapes. A miracle is whatever repairs regret. And even then, even with the miracle, regret can still win. Too much time has been lost. It is too late anyway.

There is a poignancy to cosmologies which transcend regret – say, reincarnation, or the quantum theory of many worlds. We could be born again. We could have been born before. All the connections and chances we recognized but did not make, did not take, they were real – we missed them this time around, but we have made them before, we may take them again. There could be more than one of each of us, flickering above neighboring peaks in one eternal unresolved chord, near as the backs of one another's mirrors – all arrayed, some strangely better, some strangely worse, some only strangers – but at least one, surely at least one, who was lucky, who was helped, who did not have to, who found a way.

But regret is not for escaping. The worst man is the man without regret. As far as philosophy purges regret, philosophy is bad. Ancient philosophy, the kind that would have us make philosophers of ourselves, is moving and useful, yet there is something in it not quite worthy, even somehow seedy: and this is because it does not recognize or accommodate regret. Here is Polonius. Here is a man learned, wise, crafty, with good taste in poetry – but he lacks regret, and this is enough to make him ridiculous.

Regrets are the broken circuits of actions. There they lie, loose and fatal as wrecks of power lines after a storm wind, still electric. Think of actors, finding in themselves the other people they might have been, getting to know them, putting them on. Think of music – music, after rhythm, runs on regret. (Thus the ancient enmity of music and philosophy.)

Regret is a shadow theodicy with an unknown god. Heaven, the very most that can be hoped for, promises to unite you with your loved ones; but not with the ones you should have loved, not with the ones who should have loved you. Regret is too large a part of this world to be salved by another. The veiled being who afflicted us with regret remains silent. Without evil we could still be ourselves. We are made of regret.

THREE HORROR STORIES

HALLOWEEN, 2010

I

"I'm sorry, sir. You can't leave. The building is under quarantine."

"Quarantine? For what? I feel fine. Just calm down. You don't have to point guns at me. What is the welding equipment for?"

II

"Honey! I'm home!"

"Honey. I'm home."
"Very funny. What's for dinner?"
"Very funny. What's for dinner."
"Honey, is something wrong?"
"Honey is something wrong."
"Stop it! Jesus, honey, stop it!"
"Stop it. Jesus honey stop it."
"Look at me! Honey, I'm right here. Look at me."
"Look at me. Honey I'm right here. Look at me."
"Stop it! Stop it, stop it, stop it!"
"Stop it. Stop it stop it stop it."
"What's wrong with you?"
"What's wrong with you."
"Honey, where are the kids?"

III

"Thank God I found you. I don't know what's happening. All my things are gone. My keys don't work. Let's get out of here. Let's go home."

"I'm sorry. I think you've mistaken me for someone else."

DESCENT

NOVEMBER 7, 2010   I play few computer games and no video games. But when Windows was wondrous, the Internet was a rumor, and time spent with the miracle machine was its own justification, I spent far too much time at it.

I played two more than any others: Civilization and Descent. Civilization was and is a popular game; I have nothing new to say about it. But I cannot assume that anyone remembers Descent. It did have sequels; it was a plausible rival to Doom, making it Lilith to Doom's Eve in the ancestry of first-person shooters. Descent was also an FPS: but an FPS with a difference.

Here is the boilerplate. An all-powerful corporation operates off-world mines crewed with robots. In some of these mines the robots have gone wrong – suffered some infection. They have massacred or imprisoned the human staff. You have a heavily armed one-man ship. In one mine after another you must fight your way to the power core, destroy it, and get out before the mine goes up. If you should rescue any hostages along the way, that would be appreciated, but is not required.

None of this hints how strange and intense playing Descent is.

All your opponents are robots; the hostages wear helmets; except in cutscenes, nothing like a human face is seen. You are alone from beginning to end.

The mines are not just underground spaces; they are warrens, tangled nests of open and hidden tunnels, labyrinths in three dimensions and zero gravity.

The Wright brothers deserve their fame, not because they were the first to lob a glider into the air with an engine strapped to it, but because they were the first to wrap their heads around the fact that a plane must be controlled in three degrees of freedom – roll, pitch, and yaw. It took about fifty years from the first experiments in powered flight for earthbound minds to make that leap.

In Descent your ship has six degrees of freedom: roll, pitch, yaw, heave, surge, and sway – the combined maneuverability of an airplane, a car, a submarine, and a dream.

This is a puzzle in interface design. Playing Descent with standard gaming equipment is impossible. The default compromise puts two degrees of freedom – pitch and yaw – under the right hand, on the mouse or joystick, and distributes the rest somewhat haphazardly on the keyboard. A good player will change the keybindings to bring all the controls under the left hand, coordinating patterns of motion like musical chords.

(Note that the ship behaves as if it had six separate engines, not one engine with six separate nozzles. With six engines simultaneous motion along multiple axes is a vector sum – which means that to achieve top speed you must move the ship simultaneously along three axes, triangulating your direction. This is called *trichording*, and mastering it is the only way to actually win the game.)

Just learning to play the game is mind-expanding; but that is not the intense thing about it. The game is claustrophobic. You fly at high speed down tortuous tunnels not much wider than your ship, whirling like a cell in the bloodstream – in a hostile bloodstream. As you thread each level, you map it; but the map must be presented as a model, not a projection – there is no two-dimensional way to make sense of a level in Descent. If you play for more than an hour I guarantee you will dream of those tunnels. You will see them when you shut your eyes.

Descent is unique for good reason. It has the steep learning curve a game could only get away with when there were few other choices. And some people physically cannot play the game; just being in the same room with someone playing Descent can cause motion sickness. (Really, Descent has seven degrees of freedom – roll, pitch, yaw, heave, surge, sway, and puke.)

The question has been raised: "Can video games be art?" Inclusively of video and computer games, I say no. Games can contain art, but the game itself is no more art than a museum is art. Games cannot be art to the satisfaction of genteel tradition. They are not art, but they are something. It is arrogant of me to dictate to a genre I do not participate in, but what I want in a game is not a movie or a novel – old wine in new skins. I want something to rewire my brain; I want something to infest my dreams.

NONTRIVIA

NOVEMBER 13, 2010   People do not mean what they say; they say what they mean. Taking things literally is the lowest conversational gambit. Conversation is not mathematics. *Reductio ad absurdum* is a dead end. "Nobody really…" "There is no true…" "Strictly speaking…" – all true, but trivial. Say something nontrivial. The solipsistic machine of logic never surprises. Inhabit a world that you share. See words as things – stubborn stuff, taking effort, substantial even when they are senseless. If you hear only what was said, not what was meant, you have not heard at all. Judging human things on other than human scales is a disease of the mind. Everything is footnoted with mortality and futility. Everything is perishing. Of course the play looks absurd when you watch it from backstage. But the absurdity is not in the play; it is in you. You are watching from the wrong angle.

STOICISM

NOVEMBER 22, 2010   Colloquial stoicism – the stony stoic temperament – is a vice, inevitably compounded with sullenness, passive aggression, brooding, and envy. Stoicism as a school of thought – Zeno to Aurelius – has nothing in common with it. The big-S Stoics knew how to be happy and how to weep. But though I may be a Stoic myself I think the real thing has its own vices.

Necessity is called the mother of invention. Therefore inventors must be necessitous: the inventor is the obverse of the whiner. Stoicism forbids us to dwell on what we cannot change; but if the inability is only temporary, premature acceptance risks making a temporary difficult permanent.

Asking for help is hard to do. We ask for help only when we must; the sting is the prod. We are each pricked with our own miseries, but suffering reaches its maximum when everyone keeps their troubles to themselves. Nature has usefully given us signals of suffering that compel attention: acutely, to cry, cry out, go off; chronically, depression, distraction, misjudgment. Telling your sad story with tears can get you help when telling it plainly would only get commiseration – or worse, some reciprocal confession. Tell another's sad story with tears and it sounds like bad news; tell it plainly and it sounds like a joke. We hear, *the squeaky wheel gets the grease*; we should also hear that the silent wheel gives no warning before it breaks.

Suffering is a kind of work. A certain amount of the bad demands a certain amount of sorrow. And, like work, it can be divided. If someone else joins in, it feels like half the work is done. Maybe your arguments will chip away at the bulk of sorrow, someone else's or your own; but by sharing that sorrow, or sharing in it, you cleave it instantly.

Stoicism is strong medicine. Like any strong medicine, it has side effects. Sometimes invention, consolation, and the power of sympathy are helpless; but Stoicism should not be prescribed for lesser evils.

DESIGNISM

mall caps">December 1, 2010</small> This needs naming. The ists are easy to recognize: designists are to designers as jocks are to athletes. Most athletes are not jocks; most jocks are not athletes; but jocks worship athletes. Likewise, designists worship designers. The ism is also simple: its creed being that design is *necessary* and *sufficient*.

This ism is objectionable on three grounds.

It is irresponsible: the designist holds the designer to no responsibilities, even to design – what would it would even mean for a designer to sell out? It is amoral: designists respond shamelessly to good design in the service of Soviet propaganda, and the response is more convincing than the shame where Nazi hardware is concerned. And it is brutal: good design is like good aim. To praise the shot without asking who got shot, and why, defines brutality.

Designism is dogmatic mediocrity.

Designers must be dogmatic, because they are responsible for just the part of a thing with the least, or without any, constraints. It is the job of a designer to deflate possibility with orthodoxy, to halve the possible into the good and the gauche, and halve it again until it contracts to the practicable. (Water cannot boil in a perfectly clean pot; some grain must be present for the bubbles to coalesce around. Likewise, without grains of dogma, there is no inspiration.)

Designers must be mediocre, because design targets the masses, in possession or in aspiration. Designers must be able to trust that their own reactions represent the average reaction. Skilled as they may become, designers cannot design unless they remain mediocre in their souls.

Designers are dogmatic and mediocre, but they are not therefore dogmatic about mediocrity. That is the extra step that makes the ism. Review the creed. If design is *necessary*, then what is not deduced from the dogmas of design cannot be good. If design is *sufficient*, then what does not appeal to mediocrity must be a mistake.

Nobody defends bad design; not even I do. But I do not trust design. Bad design irritates, but good design sedates. Design harmonizes the things that are intruded into our lives with the patterns of our perception and attention, makes them blend in or fit in. Design camouflages; design encysts.

Of course it is the intrusion, not the design, that is good or bad. Design is analgesic. Analgesics make life better, they give us control over pain; but when the leech injects them, we are bled without noticing the loss. Designism confuses the mechanism with the thing that uses the mechanism, and applies more leeches for a deeper cure.

GENDER NEUTRALITY

DECEMBER 10, 2010   When I took up writing essays I learned that writing is best when it is gender-neutral. Tradition told me that *he* is an adequate contraction for *he or she*. Languages where gender is obligatory have no problem with it. But as soon as I tried it, I saw that tradition was wrong. In English at least, gender neutrality is simply better than gender conflation, for three reasons.

1. You cannot be gender-specific when you want to be unless you are first gender-neutral. There is no way to gracefully modulate from equating *male* and *human* to discussing men and women separately. Try it: *If he is male… If he is a she… The man who, as a male… The man who, as a woman…*

Of course confusing *men* and *human beings* may be evil, when it hides women; but even when it is not evil, it is still silly, because it will not let you say anything about the difference.

2. Gender-neutral writing is more forcible. True, formulas like *he or she* and *men and women* are tiresome. Interpolating a piece of gender-conflating writing into gender neutrality neuters it. But expressions originally conceived in gender neutrality are more direct and vivid than those that conflate genders.

Some people find *men and women* or *human beings* or *people* intolerably awkward expressions; they would rather say, with Germanic inclusiveness, *men*. Now I like *human beings* – it asserts biological solidarity without anthropocentrism. But if you want to address the human condition, why not say *we*?

For the most part, gender neutrality is only a problem because English overloads the third person. Balance the load and you avoid the problem. Are you talking about yourself? Stand up; say *I*. Are you addressing your readers directly? Look me in the eye; say *you*.

Not all gender-neutral expressions are more forcible; but those that are gain so much that they justify the rest.

3. Gender-neutral writing is underdeveloped. Someone who becomes a writer in admiration of great but gender-conflating works of literature will understandably suspect gender neutrality as a subtle form of philistinism. So it can be, as gender-conflation can be a subtle form of misogyny. But the strongest argument for gender neutrality is literary.

It was a favorite technique of the twentieth century to escape the weight of literary history by subjecting writing to constraints. Someone wrote a book without the letter *e*; which is remarkable, but trivial. Gender neutrality is a nontrivial constraint. Literature is desperately overcrowded, hopelessly competitive. Everything has been done before and done better. But gender neutrality opens a new world, with space, horizons, elbow room.

THE YEAR OF TEMPTATION: FIVE SONNETS

DECEMBER 18, 2010   [Somewhere I read how a Teutonic Knight, to prove his chastity, chose a beautiful woman and lay beside her every night for a year without touching her.]

I

The night she lay beside him first was dark;
But now the moon slips through the arrow loop.
The blade of moonlight finds a fatal mark
Only the hair that has shed its raveling loop.
A child will watch the clouds before the storm
And thrill to thunder's footsteps in his bones
While strength and wisdom huddle safe from harm.
Her hair uncoils. He watches back to stone.
Her hair is silvered wire where each strand is loose,
The sheets as white and hot as steel in coals:
All winter's breath and summer's clouds reduce
To floating, knotless waves and shining shoals.

The knight has never touched the lady's hair;
But he is wound about and captured there.

II

He left to preach for Christ with sword and lance.
In the way he saw her shadow stand demure,
As soldiers still await the hostile advance
As hoodless hawks await the word to soar.
Behind him sun, before her blinded gaze.
He watched her hope all down the faceless file
The scrim that furled before the morning haze.
The heat of her eyes on his back did not fade with the miles.
He felt no fear before the howling rush,
No fury when he swung his fist to kill,
No pain to bear a pagan's lucky touch.
Half-out the door of death his heart was still.
  If he put out his hand in the dark and pulled her close beside
  Her flesh could not heal the wound of the love in her eyes.

III

Her breath is like the voice of steady rain;
Now hard, now soft, while clouds conceal the sky.
Rain is the prayer of farmers' life and gain;
But rain brings mud where knights must walk and die
In the wooded valley twilight. The path is lost,
The pagan voices speak with tongues of rain
The pagan wailing echoes under frost
The wordless speech of frozen rain and pain.
The ancient sacred words of monks and priests,
The paters counted over knots and beads,
The wordless howling passed from beast to beast,
The wind a breath that whispers in the reeds:
  Her breath is like some strange and secret speech
  Which none shall learn when none remains to teach.

IV

She swore, before the priest would give his leave,
Never to touch and never a touch to allow.
Sometimes she pulls her arms in through her sleeves
And sleeping winds herself inside a shroud.
The narrow cell is narrower every night.
He sleeps in belt and boots and wrapped in wool.
He flees the bed once the sky is gray with light,
To charge the field like the heavy, heedless bull.
How could the knight who always won before
By force and strength, the first to leave the castle,
Have known that he already lost the war
Only when he gave a needless battle?
    They were no friends who led him to this oath:
    "A year to prove you bravest and purest both."

V

Her skin is still as smooth as banner silk
Streaming over the tents of Tartar kings,
Still pale as ice when rivers turn to milk,
Still somehow like all rare and precious things.
The knight has learned with steel that skin's a lie,
The lie of life that covers death within.
The strongest knights, like oaks so broad, so high
Still rot, still fall, from the smallest scratch of skin.
He knows how soon her skin will fail the lady.
The priests have taught him all that age can do.
He knows the painting already is fading
And only memory is always new.
    His blood had yearned for the touch of painted saints:
    But he turns from the taint of blood beneath the paint.

AUDIENCE

January 3, 2011   All writing has a sense of audience. The sense may be latent or explicit, attenuated or definite, but it is always there. The more explicit and definite this sense, the fewer the choices the writer must make, and the better-informed those choices are. To have a public is to have it easy. A circle of the likeminded, something the writer can be a member of, is also helpful. But the audience does not have to be real to be sensed. Just to have something to prove and someone to prove it to – whether or not they are paying attention – is a great help. Even the voice in the wilderness has the wicked world to harangue.

The writers of the Dark Ages read the classical authors and tried to do what they did; but they lacked the classical audience. Their work has a feral, furtive quality. No matter how they tried – and some of them were brilliant, had great minds – something was always missing, always off-key. You do not know their names because their work has little value in itself. The interest it keeps is in tokening what might been – without the thrall of priestcraft, without the isolation of monkhood. I think of them often, and with sympathy.

Still, failing all others, there is a true audience, the true one because it is the only inevitable one – yourself, plus time. The hardest and therefore the worthiest thing to write is the thing you can reread – now, later, ten years later – without embarrassment or frustration.

Of course you hope to improve, and improving to see flaws that were invisible to you before. But the visible flaws are enough. The audience you write for may not notice your omissions and exaggerations. You may get them on your side. They may forgive you for being glib or hasty. You may learn the tone of their voices so well that in your head you can hear them defending you even as you cut the corner. Audience excuses a lower standard. But just because you can write does not mean you should. You will never stop seeing the flaws. They will always be there; they will accuse you forever. Anticipating your own retrospect is the only antidote to so attractive a complacency.

I built a shed over the summer. It is easily the largest thing I have ever built. Naturally I made mistakes, and naturally I learned from them. Having built one shed, I could build a much better one. But a shed is a physical object. Because I am not willing to waste the materials I used, because it works well enough that I cannot justify the effort and expense to replace it, I am stuck with all its crooks and gaps and rough edges.

As a writer you do not have to compromise. You can learn by doing and apply the lessons to what you have done, without losing anything. Style is only the quality obtained by this adaptation of means and ends. The vaunted ability to write without reading, to get it right the first time and let it go, to write altogether efferently, to remove yourself from your audience: this is nothing to be proud of; this is missing the point.

True, self-criticism is a dangerous habit. You know where all the knives are in, and how to twist them. And there is a deadness to self-inspection that deceives. The worst you will ever look is to yourself in the mirror. But I am not talking about criticism. There is always something to criticize, something to change. I am talking about recognition and responsibility: about being able to say, without hesitation or qualification: "Yes, that is mine."

STUPIDITY

FEBRUARY 1, 2011   "People are stupid" is a non-answer, like "God made it so." It is a dead end. What are you missing? You misunderstand what they are trying to do. You overestimate the resources available to them, or you underestimate how hard the things you take for granted are for them. They are not deluded, but deceived; or you are deceived. They choose not to see what they cannot bear to see; or you are choosing not to see something unbearable. The system in which they are caught perversely rewards stupidity; or the system is not perverse, but malicious. Or they just made a mistake. Assume people are not stupid and you may learn something; assume people are stupid and you will never learn anything. Of course stupidity is real. But truly stupid people do not lack intelligence: they reject it. True stupidity is a skill: a kind of aikido that deftly unbalances the most powerful arguments and sends them sprawling on their faces.

EBOOKS

February 11, 2011   I just spent five days in the hospital; I beguiled them by reading ebooks. I bought a Kindle recently. I had the chance to try one, and was immediately taken with the idea that if I could transfer the reading I do onscreen to the device, my eyes would have an easier life. Once I confirmed this was possible, I bought it.

It immediately paid for itself in canceled magazine subscriptions. With exceptions, I dislike magazines as physical objects: glary, bulky, ad-ridden. Why pay for the piles, when I could get what I want for free, in a more legible form? And I soon relieved my perennial browser session of all the things I kept open to read in fragments. Besides articles and posts, I had also been thinking of books that were unavailable or exorbitant in print (or only available in those dubious POD reprints with the generic covers) but free on the net. I found myself pilfering the treasure-house of Project Gutenberg.

I have a history with ebooks. I was an enthusiast in the false dawn of ebooks, about ten years ago. Back then the idea was not to save publishers, but to destroy and replace them: to behead the behemoths of New York, to throw open the gates and welcome the multitudes in, to replace the stagnant world of editors and exploitation with something brighter and more breathable. This was the mission of the ebook publishers. For a time I seriously meant to become one. This ambition was twice cured. I assisted a judge in an ebook contest; this was my first contact with the slush pile, and it has never washed off. And I realized I spent far more time reading about ebooks than I did reading ebooks. I excused my disaffection with the argument that ebooks would never be practical without the then-speculative technology of e-ink. By the time e-ink showed up, disaffection had become distaste.

But in the hospital, while I was too weak to hold a paper book open, I read ebooks, and was engrossed. Or, better, I was not reading ebooks; I was reading.

I am not a convert. I will always shun anyone who thinks paper is just dead trees. But I must recant a witticism I was formerly proud of. "I cannot remember who said, 'The world exists to end up in a book'*; but I

---

*Mallarmé

am sure no one will ever say, 'The world exists to end up in an ebook."
The world exists to be written and read; what we read it on is no more
decisive than what we write it on.

IVORY TOWER

FEBRUARY 25, 2011

So here we lie at last, having arrived,
Upturned, unraveled, undisturbed.
Here we lie where there is no more hurry,
Here we lie where there is plenty of time.
No more alarms, never early or late,
No more errands, nothing to muddle our thoughts.
Free between earth and sky, picked men,
Sweetly discoursing, attended by nodding birds.
And what is soft and dark in us must fly,
But what is hard and bright in us can stay.
For here in the tower of ivory, brilliant and bare
We are the men of ivory, with nothing to fear.

GENERATIONS

MARCH 4, 2011   Why should generations be interesting? There are
two questions here, because generations have two kinds of interest. They
have historical interest: a succession of generations from Lost to Greatest
to Silent to Boomer to X to Millennial. And they have personal interest:
the generation in the first person, what separates us from our parents and
divides us from our children – "my generation," "our generation."

As a unit of historical analysis the generation is worse than useless. The
biologist's refutation of race applies: since variability within a generation
equals or exceeds the variation supposed to divide generations, generations
are supposititious.

Of course generations really are different. Every generation has its
own distinctive patterns of behavior – but *distinctive* is not the same as
characteristic. Nothing is more distinctive of a generation than its common

names – but, remember, the fact that some names are common does not mean that most people have common names.

The generation is unreal, but unreal is not absurd; unreal things can exist formally, like lines on a map. The generation is likewise formal: consensual, not demonstrable. But why this consensus?

It is a pleasure to be sorted into a particular generation because being sorted, if it is not discriminatory, is inherently pleasant. Advertisers know this. They know that offering to tell you "Which x are you?" or "What kind of x are you?" tempts you, for all x.

And something loves to displace the faults of human nature to contingent aspects of it. Sentences that begin by naming "these days," "this country," or "our society," generally become intelligible only once they are universalized, and referred to human beings as such. The generation provides another means for such displacements. Then such awful questions as "Why are we here?" can be rephrased in cozier terms like "My generation has no sense of purpose."

What is it that we share when we share a generation?

Sharing a generation is the least two people can have in common (who have anything in common at all): thus we are most attached to our generation when we have few other attachments. Those who have something more definite to be loyal to – nation, religion, community, cause – they would never number their generation among the things that define them. And, inversely, those who expect their generation to define them tend to lack particular loyalties.

Sharing a generation is the weakest hold two people can have on each other, who have any hold on each other at all. It is because it is so weak that is so hard to shake off. Say: my generation is my blind spot. I think there is nothing so utterly mysterious to me as my own generation. Because I must draw lovers and friends from it, I want to believe it is better than it is, and when it disappoints me, I see mystery instead of accepting the fact of disappointment.

If it is to take hold at all, generational solidarity takes hold in childhood. Sometimes I would have to explain and defend to adults the things that I and my friends did – defend them to members of other generations. At those times I did not feel as if I were speaking for myself: I felt like an ambassador, charged with a heavy responsibility and answerable to my peers. Suddenly I was not only included, but important. Under threat of scorn from another generation people who would not otherwise speak to me leaped to my defense; people who hardly spoke at all surprised me with the capacity to form complete, reasonable, and persuasive sentences on my behalf.

To embrace the undemanding solidarity of the generation, to build life and work around this experience of inclusion and importance, is understandable. We writers are most susceptible. The generation is our fallback – once we have, for fear of prejudice, abstained from everything else. The temptation is always present: why speak for yourself, when you can speak for your generation? Why stand alone, when you can recruit their implicit support behind everything you say, or make, or do? Why be objective when at last, after everything, you could have them all on your side?

ANIMALS

MARCH 11, 2011   The facts of life cannot be hidden from people whom live among animals. Birth and death are as open and current among them as weather. Human beings cannot learn much from one another; we conceal too much in shame and pride. The short and unreserved lives of animals are the true parables. They enact life back to us on a scale we can grasp. The horse, the cow, the dog, the cat, the chicken (like the llama, the camel, and others) – these are the truly ancient sages.

Sometime in the nineteenth century it became possible for masses of people to live away from animals. Deprived of its foundation in the shared witness of animal life – left untethered – culture became a castle in air.

Victorian prudery came first. Bowdler only becomes possible once he may suppose readers who do not know the way of a dog with a bitch. But his overthrowers were equally unworldly. Freud could only have lived in the city. (Animals, despite their undivided minds, are as neurotic as people.)

But Freud's city was still a city of horses. When the automobile replaced the horse and left animals with zoos and field trips for their habitats, pathology became derangement. It was the analogies that the observation of animals implicitly afforded us that made reasoning about life possible.

We have lost the animals, but we still need the analogies; so we grub them where we can. The machine served until it threatened to master — to remake us in its image, machines, not people. The net may yet make nodes of us.

(Of course analogy is not explanation, but a real explanation would have to explain us all, human and animal: developing a theory of human nature and trying to work animals into it parenthetically is a dead end every time.)

I invite the accusation of anthropomorphism; so be it. The dangers of anthropomorphism are abstract; the dangers of anthropocentrism are practical. It is not a question of dominion; it is a question of definition. We are the rule, not the exception: since we can no longer learn it by observation, we must be told, and trust.

KNOTS

MARCH 18, 2011   Are knots technology? Knots were never invented: like fires, knots happen naturally. But unlike fire they cannot not be made useful by propagation: they have to be translated. Like language, knots are immaterial, passed on by example and subject to regional variation. Unlike language, knots are finite — there are only so many — and eternal — the same knots recur worlds and ages apart.

Like tools, knots are useful and increase our power over nature; but unlike tools, we carry them in our heads, not our hands. When they parallel tools, it is on a different level of abstraction. The trucker's hitch is an image in cord of a block and tackle. It is no more a tool than a picture of a tool is — and yet it has the power of a tool.

Knots are a form of mathematics, but math with a difference. Arithmetic has a history of progress: but before history began, knots already embodied the highest level of mathematical abstraction. Knot theory is a twentieth century invention. Only in the twentieth century, only after thousands of years of development, did exoteric mathematics finally equal the mathematics esoteric in knots.

Knots are magic. With a piece of cord and a sequence of gestures we produce direct results in matter. "The rabbit jumps out of the hole, runs around the tree, and jumps back down the hole": what is this but an incantation? Reasoning from knots, we get magic; reasoning from tools, we get technology. Technology works, magic doesn't; nonetheless, the existence of knots violates the order of nature that technology presumes.

ARGUMENT

MARCH 27, 2011   Argument has rules. Argument is not a game – the rules are more in spirit than in letter – but there are rules. Certain moves – certain appeals – appeals to personal experience, to scripture, to studies and statistics, even to logic – break the rules and make argument impossible. Of course these are all useful instruments of judgment. But judgment and argument are different things. Judgment ends argument, but arguments do not want to end.

"Arguments want?" Arguments want what we want. Sometimes we argue selfishly, to win. Sometimes we argue selflessly, to keep the conversation going. But mostly we argue precisely to prevent judgment: to reassure ourselves that some matter is open to question, that equivocation is not irresponsible.

Argument has rules, but agreeing to definitions is not one of them. That is putting the cart before the horse. Definitions are liquid: when they meet, they mix. These triboluminescent encounters are what argument is for. All the valid moves in argument – making a distinction, putting in context, elaborating, unpacking – these are all ways to make definitions meet, merge, and mature. Definitions are always at the center of arguments because shaping definitions is what arguments are for.

Argument is harder than it looks. In large part this is because, while contradictions, fallacies, and biases break the rules, pointing them out is a far worse offense. Argument at the level of fallacies and biases is boring. Argument about argument is not argument. Whatever the point at stake, the opponents are in the same old ring, trading the same old jabs and blocks.

Argument is not a way of deciding. It is a way of not deciding, of doing something else instead: learning, wondering, waiting. You know it is the real thing when it is unpredictable – irreducible – and, therefore, nontrivial. Argument wants; and more than anything else, argument wants surprise.

ALL THE LONELY PEOPLE

April 2, 2011   "But tell us, why would you stay?"

"This is my home," he said, glancing around the café at empty tables, seeing the man with an open computer and the pretty-plain barista who were eloquently ignoring each other. "I may be the only one who knows it, but this is my home."

He sat at his little round table. (What he let himself think of, sometimes, as his table.) He sat with a man and a woman, his guests. They did not look like people who belonged at his table. They did not look like people who belonged anywhere, except in magazines. They were too well-dressed, too well-coiffed. Everything they wore was contemporary, everything in the latest style – walking fashions. When they first walked in, they reminded him somehow of actors in a costume drama.

On the table, centered between three coffees – two of them cold and untouched – his laptop sat closed, fan blowing softly. If he opened it now, he knew, he would see nothing – nothing but the winter-scene desktop and the carefully arranged dock. He would not see again what they had shown him there, a few minutes ago, stealing his screen with a snap of the fingers. He would not see this city as it would look ten thousand years from now, under its dome, its old buildings stasis-locked beyond decay, its new buildings smooth, swooping, imperishable. He would not see the thin ribbons of dark green park that had once been streets. He would not see The War. They called it that – just The War, against The Enemy, waging ten thousands years from now.

"We don't like to let it come to this," said the man, "but you need to understand. Our records are very detailed. We know all about you. We know what happened to your parents. We know about the divorce. We can read your emails. We have your instant messages laid down in diamond dust. Your friends were her friends. They took her side. Nothing is holding you here."

"So what? So I should give up? Run away? Run ten thousands years away to fight for people I have nothing in common with against an enemy who never did anything to me. This is my time. This is where I belong."

Now it was the woman's turn. "Understand, we know. We know everything that happened to you from the day you were born to the day you died. It is a matter of historical record that your life was meaningless.

From now you will always be alone. You will never love, you never be loved. You will never meet anyone, you will never make a friend. You will never go anywhere. You will never accomplish anything. There was a phrase we learned in orientation…"

"'Waste of space,'" the man supplied.

"That was it. Yes." She drawled it. "Waste of space. You were a waste of space."

He grabbed his laptop and stood up. "Fuck you. Fuck you both. Fuck your war and fuck your human race. I hope—"

"We're not finished," the man said, and snapped his fingers.

His legs went numb under him. He flopped back into the chair and hugged the laptop to himself.

"Now, here, you are worthless," the man said. "But you are invaluable to us."

"Valuable," the woman said. "He means you're very valuable."

"They mean the same thing, I think," the man said. "Invaluable and valuable. Like inflammable."

The woman shrugged.

"We're recruiters," he said. "You know that already. But only certain very special people meet our standards. We need people who will not be missed. We mostly used to do corpse shuffling. Take a genetic sample, send it downstream, get a body back, swap it out for the original moments before an accident. But that's not as easy as it sounds. Too many people come into contact with the bodies. It's only safe when the injuries are too gruesome or the body count is too high. And then some of them say no, even after we save their lives. All our efforts go to waste. I spent—"

The woman interrupted. "We found a better way. It turns out that people like you are more common than we thought. People who at a certain point in their lives just give up, shut off. People who can be lifted out of history without affecting anything. We come to them and we make an offer. Come with us, ten thousand years downstream, and we will give you a purpose. We will give your life meaning. Ten thousand years from now all the silent and lonely people who ever fell through the cracks of history are gathering to fight the last battle of the last war. All you have to do is say yes."

"I won't say yes. Why don't you just take me? Snap your fingers?"

"Your weapon needs your consent. All you have to do is say yes and it will take you where you need to go. It will teach you what you need to know. It has been prepared especially for you. No one else can use it. It was made with your records. It knows you more completely than anyone has ever known you. It loves you perfectly and unconditionally. It is totally devoted and infinitely patient. It lives to wait for your answer."

The man took over. "You don't have to answer now. You don't have to answer this week or this month or this year. Our devices are watching you. They will watch you for the rest of your life. From now on, all you have to do is say yes, and wherever you are, whatever you're doing, your weapon will come for you. Like she said, your weapon is patient. Say yes tomorrow. Say yes thirty years from now. Say yes on your deathbed. Your weapon will come and restore you and bring you to the fight."

The man stood up. The woman too. On the way out the woman snapped her fingers and he gasped at the pins and needles prickling his awakening legs. He held onto his laptop. The heat from its racing chips burned his stomach.

"Hey, are you all right?" It was the girl, the pretty-plain barista. "Are you OK? Mr. – I'm sorry, I know your face, but I don't know your name." The boy with the laptop looked up, looked away, typed furiously.

A man left his home, and in the silence that came after he left, he was not missed.

APRIL FOOLS

APRIL 9, 2011   On the net, an effective April Fools' joke works like contrast dye – you discover, by following its path, who does and does not read the stories they pass along. April 2nd is a good day to unsubscribe, unfollow, and defriend. We owe to April Fools' Day some great moments: say, table syrup or the spaghetti harvest.* But surely there is already enough deceit and treachery in the world. Why dedicate a holiday to it? It has the significance of certain seeming-perverse religious performances, honoring the hostile gods of death and ruin, recognizing them in turn lest they obtrude themselves out of turn. If we must be fools, if some god of fools will not be spurned, then let us dedicate a day to his

*From NPR and the BBC, respectively.

honor. And the holiday inoculates us: being an April fool is painful, but it forearms us for when we are made fools out of season.

Year Five

"Even the sky is haunted."

PATHS

APRIL 16, 2011   The far-voyaging French explorers of North America kept running into one another. One explorer could hardly enter a village without finding another in residence or having just left. They could leave one another letters and expect them to be delivered. In Paris a man could disappear; in the wilderness he had to guard his reputation.

Think of traffic as a force. The canal is the artificial version of something natural – the river; likewise, the road is the artificial version of the path. Roads are permanent; paths, unless anchored by permanent settlements or fenced off by property lines, shift freely. The paradox of the wilderness is that the more open and unobstructed it is, the more traffic converges along optima conditioned by the difficulty of the terrain, the availability of resources, and the use of waterways. In the wilderness all ways are highways.

When we consider ancient or prehistoric peoples and their connections we should not imagine of a web of short links between evenly spaced nodes, news and goods moseying from village to village; we should imagine them swept up into a handful of gigantic, continental paths: stable in their broad geographic sweep, changeful in their fine, local structure. Call them fractal: at ten thousand feet, there is one path; lower there are ten paths; on the ground there are hundreds of paths, routes and reroutes circumventing any obstacle with the ingenuity of flowing water.

The existence of paths on a continental scale does not imply a continental consciousness. In their scale these great paths would have been invisible to those who used them: like the Silk Road (the last great path), each path would have been cut up by jealous middlemen, until one end of the road was a myth to the other.

One can imagine, if not document, a vision of universal history hanging on a set of Great Paths, where it is not migrations that leave paths behind them, but paths that guide migrations. Paths have always been before us: from our beginning, the human race spread not by spilling over from one valley to the next, but by processes that, scaling the lines of least resistance, became the salients of our advance. The ascent of man was not just something that happened; it was a single phenomenon, having its own structure – structured in paths.

DREAM PLACES

APRIL 22, 2011   There are some things we can trust, even in dreams. One of them is the dream version of a real place. Little as they resemble the places they represent, in the dream we recognize them, and across dreams we return to them, and find them as we left them. Often they are on a larger scale than their models. For places known in childhood this is explicable. Imagination magnifies and interpolates the facts until they match the impression we retain from when we were small in a place and looked up to it. But all my dream places are magnified, whenever I knew them. Perhaps cinematography is to blame. Many who grow up watching black and white dream in shades of gray; my dreams are wound up to the geographical key of New Zealand. True, I return to dream places which are born of dream stuff, and have no anchor in experience; but dream places, when they are born of real places, retain a cord of connection with them. The change that a place undergoes in becoming a dream place is not lawless: there is a topology, with invariants. The shape of a coast or the path of a river may change, but the waters remain. The dream place has the same palette as its model; no new colors appear. Trees never appear singly, always in stands. New buildings are found, and new features of old buildings, but always of the same stuff as the real ones. Roads widen and narrow, but never change their course, nor whether they turn or go straight. In order of instability the elements of dreams are events, things, people, and places. This is a lesson in the mechanics of imagination: even when anything can happen to anyone at any time, it must still happen somewhere.

GENTEEL TRADITION

MAY 1, 2011   In 1911 Santayana was ready to leave the United States. In California (already liminal America), he said what he could not say in Boston:

> The truth is that one-half of the American mind, that not occupied intensely in practical affairs, has remained, I will not say high-and-dry, but slightly becalmed; it has floated gently in the backwater, while, alongside, in invention and industry and social organization

the other half of the mind was leaping down a sort of Niagara Rapids. This division may be found symbolized in American architecture: a neat reproduction of the colonial mansion – with some modern comforts introduced surreptitiously – stands beside the sky-scraper. The American Will inhabits the sky-scraper; the American Intellect inhabits the colonial mansion. The one is the sphere of the American man; the other, at least predominantly, of the American woman. The one is all aggressive enterprise; the other is all genteel tradition.

This phrase, "genteel tradition," became the weapon of choice for the Mencken gang. They carried it in their hip pockets like a flask of violet perfume, ready to dash over an opponent's head. And once the scent was on you, whatever you had to say, all anyone heard was the calico whine of a high-minded Protestant spinster.

But what did Santayana mean by it? He defines the genteel tradition as a form of anthropocentrism: an anthropocentrism that emulsifies transcendentalism – the sense that the world is your creation – with Calvinism – the sense that the world is your fault. Historically he traces it to the seventeenth century and the renewal of orthodoxy.

That is where it comes from; but what is it?

The genteel tradition opposes education to life. It wants things to be done the right way, openly, and for the right reasons, or not done at all. It requires play to be exercise; thinking to be persuasion; learning to be study. It wants us to be unfettered and spontaneous, but not to run in the halls. It does not care what is avoided, unless it approves of what is done instead. Just avoiding apathy, boredom, ignorance, prejudice, and stupidity – in the judgment of genteel tradition, avoiding them is only permissible when they are avoided properly.

Wealth, learning, and beneficence, even on a grand scale, must leave them cold, or positively alarm them, if these fine things are not tightly controlled and meted out according to some revealed absolute standard.

This should sound familiar; this is our world. Santayana thought the genteel tradition was dying; instead it enjoys absolute victory. It has coopted or outlasted every challenge made to it. How did this coffin case recover and reconquer?

In his speech Santayana names Whitman and William James as models of what was to come after the passing of the genteel tradition. How badly his prophecy failed shows in how unthinkable either man is as our contemporary.

Whitman's generous sympathies would wither in our frost. How dare such a creature of privilege – white, male, educated – presume to contain us? His faith in active humanity – in discoverers, settlers, builders, farmers – is embarrassing. He accepts where we require indignation; he holds faith where we require doubt.

Whitman is an outcast, but James is worse off. He has been brought as low as a dead thinker can be brought. We say he *anticipated recent discoveries* – "now that we know everything, we can admit he was right all along." And this is safe to say, because he has no heirs. Our psychology is blithely built on the compulsive, thoughtless quantification that he travestied.

We shelve pragmatism beside hypocrisy. A judgment that can be changed is a judgment that was never held properly. The impulse of the genteel tradition is theocratic: it will have you only hot or cold, never lukewarm.

Santayana's examples have aged badly. Aggressive enterprise has been outsourced; skyscrapers turned out to be a gimmick, not half so efficient as the anomie of the exurban office park; the colonial mansion was not reproduced, but renovated.

More importantly, women made their own claim on the future: not just assuming male roles, but dignifying female ones. Gender is the worm in the apple of Santayana's thought. Even for his period he is obtuse about it.

The American intellect is shy and feminine; it paints nature in water-colours; whereas the sharp masculine eye sees the world as a moving-picture – rapid, dramatic, vulgar, to be glanced at and used merely as a sign of what is going to happen next.

Santayana underrated women – women as people, and women as a subject. He observes a divide down the middle of humanity, and assumes that one side mirrors the other: one left, one right; one weak, one strong; one shy, one brash; one sentimental, one enterprising.

(In *The Sense of Beauty*, for example, while investigating the mutuality of sex and aesthetics, he infers that, because women are the most interesting thing in the world to men, men must be the most interesting thing in the world to women; whereas [aesthetically speaking] women are the most interesting thing in the world to men and women both.)

When Santayana made this metaphor – *the genteel tradition is female, modernism is male* – he corrupted his view of one dilemma with the quality of caricature that spoiled his view of the other. Thus he sketches both the genteel tradition and modernism (as he names its opposite) clownishly, in greasepaint. If the genteel tradition is feminine, retiring, domestic, careful, then the opposite must be masculine, daring, upthrusting, public. On these terms there is only one complete escapee from the genteel tradition in American letters: Ayn Rand. Ask a silly question, get a silly answer; posit the genteel tradition in Santayana's playground terms and you get Objectivism.

Every form of modernism is tantamount to testosterism. It is the one thing every species of modernism had in common, the weakness they all shared; so when the thing happened that no one expected, they were all susceptible to it, and the genus went extinct.

(I cannot say how far Santayana himself is to blame; but even if others made the same mistake, it is still the same mistake, and bears the same analysis.)

The kind of thinking that modernism valued was the kind of thinking that felt most like work: laborious, therefore masculine, straightforward without the effeminate detours of inspiration or insight, muscular and tense, measurable in foot-pounds and horsepower.

So what happened? This is hard to see because Santayana's future is our past. It belongs to the middle distance; we cannot see it for our own shadow.

What no one expected was the computer. Suddenly, there appeared the machine that proves there is no connection between how hard thinking feels and what it is worth. The labor theory of value does not apply. Thinking feels hardest when it is most trivial. Calculation is effortful, but not difficult – even a computer can do it.

Somehow we still admire feats of memorization and calculation. What computers prove is that these feats are dead ends. Mental mathematics, total recall, musical prodigality, are not signs of a powerful mind, but of a mind that has plenty of room because nothing else is going on inside it.

In this way the computer refutes modernism. Consider painting. Look across, from the first half of the twenty-first century, to the first half of the twentieth. What do we see there? We see nothing worth doing. There are no more Pointillists, Impressionists, Cubists, because Photoshop trivializes them. There is no more Abstract Expressionism, no more Suprematism, because the possibilities of these schools are exhausted by the screensaver.

"No," I hear, "the computer no more refutes abstraction than the camera refutes representation." But a painting is different from a photograph: one cannot see a photograph as a painting that could have been made, but wasn't. But a work of modernism is always something that could have been generated by computer, but happened to be made by a human being.

(This definition applies to more than painting – Serialism, Brutalism, Oulipo – but less than everything that has been called modernist. I draw the line here.)

If we mute the caricature – if we correct for Santayana's error – what is left then? The idea of a genteel tradition will stand. But what of the accompanying diagnosis? Do we have that divided mind? Certainly we have inherited the division as Santayana made it, and as others elaborated it: we find ourselves obscurely constrained to destroy the genteel – even under other names, like *pretentious* or *inauthentic* – wherever we encounter it, like the tribe of Amalek.

But the things the genteel tradition wants and provides are good in themselves. There is sufficiency and even bounty in it. It preserves what might be lost, incubates what might be stillborn. But for the sake of these good things the genteel tradition sacrifices things that may be better. It smothers everything it touches with an anxious sobriety: it would leave us in marmoreal disgust before it let us enjoy too meltingly. This I oppose. I side with ecstasy, rhapsody, and multitude, if only from a distance.

LAIKA

MAY 10, 2011   How fitting that a dog went first, and that, for a time, she was between us and darkness. All our proud rockets, all our brave pioneers, and we entered space as a child might enter a basement, holding onto a dog's tail. She was a Moscow stray. A stray, and therefore nobody's dog, or everybody's – yours and mine, even. A Moscow stray, distant aunt to that remarkable unbreed of hustlers and idlers – Russia's last aristocrats.

Strays live by the old covenant. Dogs never needed us. The deadliest hunter of the African plains is not the lion but the wild dog, whose kills are efficient, coordinated, and relentless. And they chose to throw in their lot with us. What honor! And what responsibility! There is a play (a radio play by Dunsany) where mankind is put on trial. One by one the animals testify against us; only the dog speaks in our defense, with such praise as is, in its way, worse than accusation:

He is man: that is enough. More is not needed. More could not be needed. All wisdom is in him. All his acts are just; terrible sometimes, but always just.

Bacon writes (against atheism) that men are better for having a god as dogs are better for having a master: a strange and improper argument. But if our faith is as heavy as the faith of dogs is to us, we can have a sort of sympathy, and imagine how gods might know shame.

Muhammad relates that a woman was forgiven a lifetime of sin for giving a thirsty dog a drink of water. Consider how the balance is weighed; what does it mean to harm a dog? "Who could eat a dog?" is really the same question as, "Who could eat a man?" Traditionally, nobody eats a dog for its meat; men eat dogs like men eat men: to absorb their power. It is at least respectful. When dogs are twisted into brutality, neglected into savagery, beaten into helplessness, there is no respect; better to be eaten. And yet each new puppy is a fresh expression of absolute trust, never diminished. Our terrible debt vanishes in that unquenchable devotion.

In his last years, isolated in deafness, Goya gave up canvas and impasted the walls of his own house with a series of alien images, primordial and apocalyptic at once. A lone dog – all alone – sinks below the horizon, howling as she recedes over the edge of the world. We sent Laika to die; we sacrificed her. She died within hours. And then for five months, dead, in her dark, silent capsule, she circled our bright world, falling and falling as the horizon slipped away beneath her, one dead dog keeping solitary watch over the billions. Then she fell as a star falls, a burnt offering, trailing fire, scattering earth and sea with her ashes.

Even the sky is haunted.

CAUSES

MAY 17, 2011   The axiom of finance is that having something now is better than having the same thing tomorrow. One who calculates by how much is said to discount. The same axiom holds elsewhere, but no one wants to do the math. The sacrifice that would be saintly if it were selfless is too often only thoughtless.

Take someone who refuses a dish because of ethical objections about how it is now made. Someone who abstains from *foie gras* has made a permanent stand against an inherent evil, and means it. But someone whose argument begins "Do you know what kind of—" may not have weighed their position. You will not live forever. You are not guaranteed the ability to enjoy food even as long as you live. While you could still enjoy food, your health may forbid it. Whether or not you have bothered to count, at the end of your life there will have been only so many meals and far fewer good ones; are you certain you want to subtract this one?

Anyone who proposes to change the world needs to be asked: "If the world were as you want it to be, what would you do with yourself? Could you be doing it now? Why don't you?" Perhaps the answer would deprive a worthy cause of a capable supporter; but if there is nothing good or worthwhile in the world except making what is worst in it less bad, then there is nothing good or worthwhile in the world at all.

(Besides, the most dangerous people in the world are the ones who try to change it without having learned how to live in it. Danton on Robespierre: *Cet homme-la ne saurait pas cuire des oeufs dur*: "That man couldn't hard-boil an egg." A man might become a monster only because he was good for nothing else.)

The taste for causes can be a jaded one. Helping people is one way of hiding from them. Trying to save the world is one way of giving up on it. Devoting your life is one way of throwing it away. You say the fruits justify the tree; but who would eat of it, if they knew how it grew?

SELF-DEPRECATION

MAY 23, 2011   Self-deprecation may be a gesture of meekness, like a dog that shows its belly: a sign that you mean no harm, or are not worth harming. It may be calculated to lower expectations: whether out of discretion, not to disappoint them, or by design, to surprise them. Or it may be an indulgence, extorting praise by threatening self-harm.

(In this way self-deprecation helps define friendship: what is a friend but someone who praises you for what you regret, someone who finds unthinkable the things you fear may be true? These precious offices can only be performed when self-deprecation occasions them.)

It may be a way to evade responsibility. "I couldn't *x* to save my life" is a polite way to say no when it was wrong to ask. And it avoids embarrassment: of course you could *x*, if you put your mind to it, but when there is nothing to gain, why risk failure when you can excuse abstention?

Of course self-deprecation is not always serious. It may be an indirect boast. "All censure of a man's self is oblique praise. It is in order to show how much he can spare." Which is harmless in moderation. Or it may be a provocation. Montaigne appalled his friends by insisting that he had no memory. In the French of the time *memory* stood for *intelligence*: but Montaigne made the distinction, and the very absurdity of his self-deprecation enforced it.

All these uses are legitimate, but none of them can excuse the habit of self-deprecation. If you expect others to take you seriously, you should try it for yourself. Tell me often enough how stupid and useless you are and I may begin to believe you; apologize for yourself often enough and I will begin to believe you have something to be sorry for.

Of course some lives are just that lost, some people are just that broken; if patience can help them, they have a right to it. But I have no patience for people who fear being resented more than they fear being despised. It doesn't even work.

You may resent people for having things you could never have; but the people you hate are the ones who have the things you could never have – and despise them.

Aristocracy was invulnerable as long as aristocrats took pains to enjoy, and be seen to enjoy, their wealth and privilege; but the moment they started to doubt themselves the masses rose up and devoured them and raised the clear conscience of plutocracy in their place.

All persuasion begins in confidence. And since respect will be given, if those who deserve it cannot stand by their words, deeds, and lives, others will receive it undeservingly.

STOCK MARKET

JUNE 6, 2011   The stock market exists to discharge the gap between capitalism and reality. To a greater extent than capitalism's most dedicated enemies imagine, whether a company is in the red or in the black, whether it is getting by or flourishing, is a matter of convention. The bottom line is like the horizon: exact, but it changes with your perspective. Accounting is an etiquette, not a science: the principles of accounting are accepted, not discovered. And because (in the short definition of capitalism) business can run as well on credit as cash, any large aggregation of capital that is not openly burning money remains viable as long as it remains credible.

The purpose of the stock market is to assign, to the companies that submit to its judgment, another value besides the one that stands on paper: one that answers not the accountant's abstract question, "What is it worth?" but the more cogent and interested question, "What is it worth to me?"

Capitalism did not invent the bubble. Sri Lanka, I have just been reading, is covered in the massive ruins of an ancient irrigation network that was abandoned just as it was finished. The most parsimonious explanation is that ancient Sri Lanka had a bubble in aqueducts. Perhaps the answer to why the Maya built so many splendid cities, and then abandoned them, is a bubble in the building of splendid cities. Egypt had a bubble in tombs; Rome had a bubble in conquest; Europe had a bubble in chivalry. Bubbles are a human failing; capitalism is unique because it pops them.

The stock market is this sensitive needle. Its ticks transcribe the quick ebb and flow of an argument conducted in the binary code of short and long, buy and sell. And this is an argument to which we are all parties. Whenever you spend money or time you express an opinion about the economy. Buying a car is saying "Car prices are fair." Getting an education is saying "My prospects are good." Planting a food garden is saying "Food prices are too high." (Of course you may have other motives, but the economy is touchy and takes everything personally.) The stock market is the great bookie who takes these opinions about the economy and turns them into bets.

To put it another way: the stock market is an arrangement that pays people for being right about the future. This is unusual. Elsewhere in life, being right about the future is punished twice: before, with contempt; after, with hatred. But with the stock market, the more unlikely the prediction – the longer the odds – the greater the payout. Thus, as the belief behind a bubble becomes more unquestionable, the reward for questioning it grows. 1929 was the year it became worthwhile to wonder if an upward trend in earnings really meant endless future growth; 2007 was the year it became worthwhile to wonder whether the housing market really could continue to grow forever without ever slowing down.

Crude as it is, this mechanism of homeostasis is unique; and it is what makes the gross, awkward, grasping, adolescent behemoth of capitalism fecund and invulnerable.

THE LOCOMOTIVE

JUNE 12, 2011   [On viewing a restored locomotive displayed in a pavilion.]

Black beast, gnarled in heavy sleep
Red sun thaws cold iron.
Slack boiler swells, remembering steam.
Fused wheels flex, grasping the rails.
Scraps of shadow pour from the cold chimney
Silent shrieks rattle the mute whistle.
Face to the sun, I borrow a flush of hope.
Back to the sun, I tread a path of shadow.

TECHNIQUE

June 21, 2011

I

Technique is the thing that takes the human body, formed by a million years of fight and flight, and turns it to ends nature never proposed. And it is one thing, beneath the conventional distinctions that hide its scope. The fingers of the musician and the body of the athlete are both natural means turned to unnatural ends. What does the turning is technique.

We do not know what our bodies may do. Biology, remember, is made of physics. All our movements only permute the universal grammar of simple machines. The body is a vocabulary: its material is limited, but its combinations are inexhaustible.

II

Technique is paradoxical. Physiology maps the body's range, extension, and advantage, but the means by which we use them in concert, our techniques, either ignore physiology, or imply a false one. We control our bodies only as gestalt.

Consider relaxation. The perfect balance of loose and tight for a muscle is the same as for a knot – not so loose that it slips, not so tight that it binds. But we cannot calibrate this balance by feeling it, because the real action of the muscles is the sum of the voluntary tension we perceive and the involuntary tonus we do not. We have to think of relaxing just to prevent the mistake of bracing. It helps to be told to relax, it helps to try to relax; but if you actually relaxed, you would sacrifice control over the good alignment of your joints, and destroy your body as you used it.

III

Technique is not usually the product of research. Of course physiology is relevant to technique. Duelists applied the discoveries of anatomy in the fencing hall almost as soon as they were exposed on the dissecting table. But fencing survives as technique, not theory.

And research may be an impediment to technique. Techniques are of two kinds. Some techniques amplify our powers, improving what we would do anyway – jump, run, hit. Research helps here by aligning the technique with the underlying complex of mechanism and instinct. But other techniques more enable than help: they let us do new things. Here research may be a mistake. Science invented the triangular pen to make it easier to write with the fingers; but in the technique of the penman* the fingers are not used at all, only the arm.

Techniques like these, though not analytic, are not arbitrary; they have their own logic and converge across centuries, and civilizations. Modulo certain constraints of metallurgy, the knights of Christendom and the samurai of Japan worked out the same technique for the two-handed sword. Or, returning to calligraphy, the peculiar penhold used in Eastern brush painting is paralleled exactly in the technique of flourishing with the pointed pen.

IV

All techniques belong to one of three patterns: cues, checks, or controls.

Cues belong to the mind. If we could see athletes and performers as they imagine themselves we would behold the strangest beasts, like the boxer with the wings of a butterfly and the stinger of a bee. Every discipline has its own imagery of this sort, which is part of its mystery, consecrating its pursuit as a shamanic ecstasy of communion with totemic essences.

Checks are miniature acts: the things you do before and after the main act, how you get ready and make sure. A check may be as formal as a routine or as spontaneous as a wind-up.

Checks are mostly important to the learner. Techniques are not behaviors; they cannot be shaped, in the behaviorist sense – perfected through approximation. Wrong practice just reinforces the mistake. Checks splint the fragmentary elements of technique so they knit together true. Half of knowing how to move is knowing how to stand; half of knowing how to use a tool is knowing how to hold it.

Controls are what prevail, the meanwhiles and the durings. They are the simple things that take time to master, the first things you learn and you

*A penman is a master of penmanship.

always remember: "keep your eye on the ball" or "keep your weight on the balls of your feet." A control is a sort of lever: it is easy, because all you have to do is pull, but it is slow, because by pulling on it you are moving everything else. Controls, as we turn them on and off, almost seem to let us switch between different bodies, adapted for different purposes.

V

Technique has many enemies.

Strength is an enemy of technique.

Of course brutish, blundering strength is the opposite of technique. But feats of strength have their own technique; the strongman is an athlete, not a species. He uses more sense than muscle.

Strength is problematic because it hides bad technique. With enough strength you cannot feel for yourself the difference between the right and wrong ways of doing something. The wrong way may even feel better: what feels more effortful often seems more effective. Jumping in and slugging through feels good, feels like something to be proud of, in a way that taking your time and doing it right cannot. And strength hides not only bad techniques, but even harmful ones: keeping the harm silent until it is irreversible.

Instinct is an enemy of technique.

Instinct and technique are not at odds. In the end, as in the beginning, technique is instinct refined and repurposed. The problem with instinct is that we do not have all the same instincts. Sometimes what is instinctive for others is a mystery to us. If we give up, this is usually why: there is a gap in our instincts – something no one will teach us, because no one teaches it, because it seems impossible not to know. This is when perseverance is hardest, but also when perseverance is most valuable – because in bridging the gap in our instincts we earn an awareness others lack.

Instinct is also problematic for masters. Masters always want to stream-line their technique – to do more with less. But in doing so they risk omitting something essential they did not know was there, because it was never named to them; something they may find it difficult to regain.

Skill is an enemy of technique.

Masters are rarely good teachers. They may be impatient – *ars longa*. Even if they are patient, they may be unsympathetic – "Was I ever such a...?" Even if they are patient and sympathetic, what they teach may be not what they do now, but what they did when they still had to think about it.

And even if they are patient, sympathetic, and self-aware, they may teach the wrong things. Techniques feel different when they are new. The gestalt that mastery experiences is not raw but cooked. Sometimes it cannot be taught in its finished form; sometimes it must be arrived at.

Moreover teaching is a rare and demanding ability; few masters are good teachers, and even fewer have time for it.

And skill has a different use for technique than ignorance has. Ignorance has only two outcomes: getting it wrong or getting it right. Skill has many outcomes. Subtle adjustments and accomodations imperceptible to the ignorant produce wide divergences for complicated ends. The techniques the skilled pay attention to are thus ones the ignorant have no use for. Trying to teach them is pointless.

Of course, bad technique is an enemy of technique.

Techniques link to one another; a bad technique unchains those that depend on it. (To invert: when a generally accepted technique fails to work for you, it usually means you have a deeper problem.)

But good technique is also an enemy of technique.

Technique is its own enemy because the better you become, the harder it is to tell what works. When you are used to bearing a technique in mind, as your muscles learn to perform it on their own, your consciousness of it becomes redundant and may gradually exaggerate means into mannerism.

It becomes harder to test a technique; any change feels like an improvement when its rests tired muscles and favors rested ones.

And, once you have assimilated good technique, the body's mechanisms for self-protection have been disarmed. You could run with bad technique your whole life and never suffer more than an ache, but once you run well you might misstep once and never run again. All the safeties are off.

VI

What we learn when we learn is not just what we learn but how we learn. Sometimes we can reuse that knowledge. Obviously your third language is easier than your second. But this head start is not free. For languages, the work has already been done. There are languages with grammars, and there is grammar itself, as an abstraction. But technique as an abstraction does not yet exist, except in name. Between the snobbery of the gracile, to whom all strength is brutality, and the pride of the robust, to whom all delicacy is weakness, it has gone unseen.

I am no hellenizer. *Mens sana in corpore sano* is a good thing, but only because it is the sum of two good things. Of course the mind and the body benefit each other: a feeble body usually means a confused brain as a feeble mind usually means a clumsy body. But the one may be excellent while the other is only adequate, and when both are excellent it is just a case of two kinds of excellence.

Technique is of course how we build on nature. But technique is also how we find nature. Technique is human instinct: the cue in the totem, the check in the ritual, the control in the talisman.

The human form is caught between nature and culture. Before nature finished standing us on our feet, culture pulled us, still rough, out of the tumbler of tooth and claw. We are neither one thing nor the other. Our bodies depend on our minds as much as our minds depend on our bodies; half the human digestive system is in the oven.

Technique is another such supplement. Under the poorly fitted jacket of flesh and bone that lies heavy on our shoulders we are as far from the grace of the beasts of the field as from that of the beasts of the air. The easy and spontaneous embodiment the rest of nature inherits as its right is, for us, only possible through technique.

THE MISER

JULY 5, 2011   [New feature; the idea is something between Theophrastus and Browning, like the "letters" in the periodical essay series without the framing device.]

"I learned something very early on. I saw that you can survive without friends, and you can survive without money, but it has to be one or the other. And I turned out to be much better at making money than I was at making friends.

"I don't have anything against people who go the other way. Everybody wants to give you a hand – great! Nobody ever gave me a hand. They wanted me to beg and I wouldn't beg. So I did it on my own, and then – it's true – I rubbed their noses in it. That's only natural, if you don't take it too far.

"I'm not happy; who's happy? I know money isn't happiness; I'm not stupid. But I don't have any regrets because I never had a choice. I wish you people understood that. I wish you people didn't look at me like I'd gone over to the dark side.

"I know what it is. It's because you need me and you don't want to admit it. It's resentment. Your friends can't do anything for you unless they have money, and when you follow the money what do you find? You find me. If I tagged my money the way they tag migrating birds, you'd be amazed how far it goes.

"Miser? I'm the most generous guy in the world. In fact I'm the only generous guy in the world, because it's my money to start with. It doesn't count when it's somebody else's money."

ON QUIRK

JULY 17, 2011   Quirky is what breezy was: the style of the writer who writes not as a maker, but as a performer. It may be interesting to compare the two. Breezy and quirky are both inexhaustible. When you lay two breezy or quirky pieces by the same author end-to-end, the grain matches up where the word count cuts off. They are as reliable and predictable as utilities and readers love them for it: the breezy or quirky writer who is not absolutely incompetent can expect their following, however small, to be loyal and loud.

Breezy and quirky do the same job, but in different ways. Breezy is world-wise and wide-awake; quirky is innocent and dreamy. Breezy is suspicious and confrontational; quirky is trusting and fragile. Both are overbearing, but breezy is pushy where quirky is cloying. Breezy is cool and takes things in stride; quirky is breathless and labile. Breezy is a mover, in constant, purposeful coming and going; quirky is a dweller, a home-body. Even when quirky travels, it settles. (Corollary: breezy and quirky both value living light, but for different reasons: breezy streamlines where quirky simplifies.) Breezy and quirky are both fun, but both under false pretenses: breezy is fun because it pretends to be ignorant; quirky is fun because it pretends to be crazy. Of course since real insanity (like real ignorance) is no fun at all, the insanity is aspirational: boredom becomes ADHD, neatness becomes OCD, absentmindedness becomes Alzheimer's.

Both are ridiculous, but neither deserves mockery. True, breezy and quirky both talk about themselves, endlessly, but neither is narcissistic or needy. They claim interest vicariously, by representing something: whenever they are an *x* they are just another *x*. True, breezy and quirky are both indiscreet; but though they are highly personal they are totally unrevealing – a sacrificial persona intervenes between merely human writer and insatiable audience like a patronus.

Of course neither is bad in itself. Archie Goodwin should be breezy; Amélie Poulain should be quirky. For the writer, breezy and quirky are both shams, but shams have their uses. Someone who demands that you *be yourself* deserves the same reaction as someone who demands that you go naked. Still, when they go wrong, breezy is very bad, but quirky is worse. Breeziness is at least an adult sham; but quirkiness is falsely childlike in the fairy-friendly way that only fools adults who have forgotten being children, when they would have caught fairies to pull their wings off.

NAMES

July 26, 2011   To say something unusual in specialized language is easy. A few formulas may unmistakably express a new worldview. To say something unusual in everyday language is very hard. You must choose your words not only to say what you mean, but to refuse to say what the hearer expects. Names alone cannot do it; it takes sentences.

Consider how advanced ideas become basic ones. The joke goes that in 1919, when Eddington was asked whether it was true that only three people understood general relativity, he hesitated and finally excused himself: "I was wondering who the third one might be!" Now undergraduates study it. Postulate that our undergraduates are not smarter than the best minds of 1919. Consider musicians: the violinist's vibrato, the guitarist's tremolo, were once the distinctive techniques of particular virtuosi; now they are part of mere competence. Nobody could play Liszt but Liszt until everybody had to play Liszt. What were once expeditions are now vacations.

This is more than a pattern; it is a phenomenon. What happens is naming: giving something a name is the first step in its domestication. The wild equations of general relativity were tamed by the associations that gathered around the name: the bowling ball on the rubber sheet; the paradoxical twins; the absentminded professor; the starship *Enterprise*. Any whale can be handled once it has enough harpoons in it.

There is a tension between thinking in names and thinking in sentences. Math and science work with names; verbs only participate syntacitly. This is an envied state. Whenever we see a field of study on the make we see it embracing gerunds, copulation, and anaphor. The textbooks always show the development from sententious thinkers to name-wielding scientists as the axis of progress.

But something is suspicious here. To be useful names must be unlike other words: they must have definitions, and there must be some procedure to ascertain that two definitions refer to the same thing. Otherwise a name is not a name at all; it is just another word.

The decline of Freudianism comes to mind. Freud gave names — *ego*, *id*, *repression*, *neurosis* — with a certain drama between them. The names and the drama were then taken up by a series of schools. Each school recast the roles with new definitions, or rewrote the old roles into a new drama, until finally the names, because they meant everything, no longer meant anything in particular, and were heard no more.

This matters. How many brilliant thinkers, who might have enriched the study of the mind if only they had been content to write sentences, went to waste following a dumb faith in names? They should have been warned that mere sentences are never wasted: good writing is always good thinking. It can be translated into whatever names are current, and lasts when names fail.

THE EARLY ADOPTER

JULY 30, 2011   "People are afraid of the future. I can understand that. The one thing we know for sure about the future is that everything's going to go wrong, am I right? You're going to get older, and your marriage will fall apart, and your kids will speak a different language and listen to bad music.

"But I'm in love with the future, because while I'm getting older, and getting shaky and confused, something else is happening. Technology is accelerating so fast that even as I'm coming apart the space of what I can do gets bigger and bigger.

"I may need thicker glasses, but I can talk to somebody in China on a video phone. I may be out of shape, but I can carry a thousand books in my pocket. My hearing, maybe, isn't as good as it used to be, but I have my own personal pocket radio station that plays all my favorites and follows me everywhere.

"So, sure, it's true. Maybe if I wait a year the next model will be better and cheaper and they'll have the bugs worked out and that thing everybody hates, they'll have changed that. But I'm not getting any younger in the meantime.

"You be sensible. What's one more year of circling the drain? Mine's on pre-order."

CELL INTELLIGENCE

AUGUST 17, 2011   Before we live by ideas, we seem to live among them. Nothing goes unprophesied. The shadows of ideas fall ahead of them and mark out the shape of things to come for those who care to trace it. The prophecies of science fiction writers are an obvious example: I nominate *Looking Backward*. In 1887 Bellamy felt the shadow of the radio and colored in the pattern of affordances he traced from prophecy.

> There are a number of music rooms in the city, perfectly adapted acoustically to the different sorts of music. These halls are connected by telephone with all the houses of the city whose people care to pay the small fee, and there are none, you may be sure, who do not. The corps of musicians attached to each hall is so large that, although

no individual performer, or group of performers, has more than
a brief part, each day's programme lasts through the twenty-four
hours. There are on that card for to-day, as you will see if you observe closely, distinct programmes of four of these concerts, each
of a different order of music from the others, being now simultaneously performed, and any one of the four pieces now going on
that you prefer, you can hear by merely pressing the button which
will connect your house-wire with the hall where it is being ren-
dered. The programmes are so coordinated that the pieces at any one
time simultaneously proceeding in the different halls usually offer
a choice, not only between instrumental and vocal, and between
different sorts of instruments; but also between different motives
from grave to gay, so that all tastes and moods can be suited.

Contrast this prophecy, made in the heat of fiction, with another made
in earnest. I own a book – a curiosity – entitled *Cell Intelligence*, self-
published 1916 by one Nels Quevli: registered pharmacist, bachelor of
law, and flaming eccentric. The argument of the book is encapsulated in
its full title:

Cell Intelligence the Cause of Growth, Heredity, and Instinctive
Actions, Illustrating that the Cell is a Conscious, Intelligent Being,
and, by Reason Thereof, Plans and Builds all Plants and Animals
in the Same Manner that Man Constructs Houses, Railroads, and
Other Structures

This sounds stranger than it is; try *The Selfish Cell*. Quevli in 1916 maps
to Dawkins in 1976. Both Quevli and Dawkins conclude that life does not
fall out of any equation, and that since it is not a force or a property of
matter, its existence at all is contingent, and its forms must be historical.

There are two main theories by which the growth and development
of plants and animals in life are explained: First, chemical and mechanical forces; second, Intelligence or a Divine Being. However,
so far no one has yet ventured the proposition or statement that the
intelligence that has caused the production of all these structures we
see, such as plants and animals, was the property of the cell.

And since it is not determined, it must be intelligent (or selfish) because its survival and ramification imply something equivalent to memory.

I do not pretend to know what intelligence is, nor what memory is, but I want to show that the cell is a being possessed of that something, whatever it is. If man is intelligent the cell must be.

Both are asserting that cell intelligence and human intelligence are the same. The difference is whether we follow Quevli in applying the vocabulary of human intelligence to the cell, or Dawkins in applying the vocabulary of the gene to human intelligence.

Bellamy's prophecy is interesting, but after Bellamy radio still had to be invented. But Quevli in 1916 knew what Dawkins knew in 1976. Ideas are autologous: the description of an idea, is an idea. To predict it is to bring it about; to imagine it is to create it.

This property of ideas leads to certain perversities. Everywhere we find that the longest training, the deepest commitment, the finest specialization yield ideas that could just as easily have been dreamed up on a long walk or talked out in a bull session. The difference is the imprimatur.

But if specialization does not yield better ideas – if it only makes them more persuasive – then someone who is more interested in understanding than persuasion might ask whether it would be better not to specialize, and cultivate the faculty of having ideas directly?

The case could be made that the person who has one idea, and devotes their life to advancing it, is wasting their life: settling for an idea that, being their first attempt, probably isn't even very good. The case could also be made that intellectual monogamy ought to be the goal of anyone who takes ideas seriously, and that though essayistic dalliance with a series of ideas may be charming in the exuberance of youth, it becomes absurd and pitiable if protracted into maturity.

This tangle recalls others. Being one person – having one personality – is enough for most of us; yet we see writers and actors contain multitudes where each member, whether absorbed from life or condensed from fancy, is as much a person as the person who contains them, having virtues and vices of their own they do not pass on to their host. If myself is something virtualizable, am I wasting myself in being only myself?

But writers and actors are not the best people; what they contain they do not combine. The conversation of Shakespeare was surely intense, but less than Hamlet times Falstaff times Rosalind. And actors especially may owe their multiplicity to nothing but the quality that Borges imputes to Shakespeare (who was also, remember, an actor): they can become anybody only because they are nobody.

The *homuncular fallacy* is not a real fallacy. It could turn out to be part of the definition of consciousness that it is built from what is also conscious, a potential infinity like two facing mirrors. We contain cells, cells abridge us; we are people with personalities and yet we contain people with personalities. Sometimes it seems that everything is recursive, that even reality only represents itself: considering Robertson's Titan, for example, I cannot help suspecting that the world, too, only serves to perform what has already been anticipated in imagination.

THE ENTREPRENEUR

AUGUST 26, 2011   "Did I ever tell you about my grandfather? Of course I didn't. He was nobody. He spent his whole life at the factory, retired, boom, dropped dead. That's the one thing I've been afraid of my whole life, turning out like him, a nobody with nothing to show for himself, nothing to show he ever existed except for a chip of stone at the veterans' cemetery. Which one? I don't know. I have his medals around here somewhere.

"After I'm gone, people need to know I was here. They need to know my name, and remember me. I want to be up there with the greats. I want to leave a legacy. For all he did with his life my grandfather might as well never have been born. My life has to mean something. The world has to be different because I lived in it. So thanks for your concern, but I'm fine. And I kind of have to get back to work, so if that's all..."

PYTHAGORAS

Notes repeat themselves, higher or lower, at the interval we now call an octave. Double or halve the speed at which a string vibrates and the sound, in some sense which is as undeniable as it is gratuitous, remains the same. And between notes in simple ratios, most of all the interval we call the fifth, there is a sweetness sweeter and more dizzying than wine.

Between the octave and the fifth, the world almost seems made for us. This appearance is deceiving. The world is not just unfair, but rigged. Chances are you know what it is to pick up part A, and part B, never having doubted they went together, only to find that they don't quite fit. The world is like that. Between the octave and the fifth there is a small but shattering discrepancy we call the Pythagorean comma.

The comma of Pythagoras is as bad as the flaming sword. It means that music, even music, must always be compromised, whether by a diet of a few safe notes, or an intricate microtonal dissection of the octave, or a distortion of the fifth.

This distortion (the Western approach) goes by the name of temperament. Since the Middle Ages the West has known and used several exquisite systems of temperament for particular purposes, but in the last century they gave way to a single system brutal in its simplicity. Equal temperament deals with the Pythagorean comma the way the senators dealt with Romulus, when they caught him in a sudden fog, hacked him to pieces and, walking away with the pieces hidden under their togas, called it apotheosis.

(Are the jitters of the West, its frantic days and restless nights, the symptoms of our addiction to this uneasy music, the Pythagorean comma working its way deeper and deeper under our skins?)

Of all things with value, music is the purest, the most abstract. If even music must compromise, what hope is there for anything else? None at all; but do not take it too hard. Consider poor Pythagoras, twice betrayed, once by music, once by math. Traumatic as Gödel, Turing, Russell, and Tarski were for us, how much worse was it for him, the philosopher who thought number was truth and music was beauty, only to find that numbers could be irrational and music sheltered wolves.

The last century was not, as it boasted, the moment when thought ran up against the limits of certainty and perfectibility. From the very beginning, the whole arc from faith to doubt, from certainty to anxiety, has always been with us in Pythagoras and his comma.

THE TRAVELER

SEPTEMBER 11, 2011   "You haven't gone yet? You should go. It's the right time of year. It's wonderful with all that space, and those views, and not a tourist in sight. I wish everybody could go.

"What? What did I...? Oh. That's an oxymoron, isn't it? Like 'nobody goes there anymore, it's too crowded.' But that really is how it goes. Whenever we find something that's really a jewel, people just descend on it until they suffocate it. I can't even go to Venice anymore. I swear it's sinking out of embarrassment.

"If we were smart, really smart, we wouldn't blab about things like that. We'd organize a guild or a secret society. We'd have apprenticeships and an initiation. Seven years of studying languages, and etiquette, and survival skills to become an Honorable Traveler with the right to visit. Plus another ten years of study before you get to take a camera.

"Instead, we love it so much we have to tell somebody about it. And they have to tell somebody and we all love it to death.

"Maybe that's too harsh. I don't want to seem elitist. The fact is I pity the tourists even more than I pity the places they ruin. They have no way out. They cross oceans and continents but they pack their boredom, and ignorance, and petulance.

"I don't know why they bother, unless it's because they still have that instinct that tells them growing up means leaving home. But no matter how far they go, they drag home along behind. It's not even travel; it's just a change of venue."

LOSERS

SEPTEMBER 26, 2011   What makes a loser? There is nothing special about him. Being dull, awkward, foolish, and feckless only makes him unlucky, and being unlucky is not enough to make a loser. What makes him a loser is not that he loses, but that he does not know why he loses.

Losers have always been with us, since Thersites at least, but of course they are rare in hierarchical societies, where everyone is born with a part to play, where every kind of failure is keyed by coordinates of folly and vice. Being a loser is idiopathic, because losers are inconsequential; they do not even have anyone to let down.

He may have abilities, even remarkable ones, but he spoils them. He stops too soon, or he goes too far, and all his good intentions, all his hard work, come to nothing. Worse, just by being the one who has them, he makes his own abilities ridiculous. For his skills, we call him a geek; for his wealth, we call him vulgar; for his commitments, we call him pretentious. He is not a loser because he never wins; he is a loser because even when he wins, he loses.

What makes him a loser are not his mistakes but how he doubles them. Defying logic, he spans the extremes without ever touching the center, impaling himself on both horns of every dilemma, robbing Scylla to pay Charybdis.

He is the one who has nothing to say, and never gets to the point; the one who can't take a hint, and can't take a joke; the one who never learns, and the one who never gets over it; the one who can't talk around girls, and babbles around women; the one who can't express himself, and the one who gives everything away; the one who never takes a chance until he throws everything away.

In short the loser is a bad actor playing himself. Nothing feels real to him unless he is playing to the balcony. In the beginning, he tries too hard; and every time someone leaves, he tries a little harder. In the end the seats are empty and there he is, alone on the stage, the singularity where tragedy and comedy meet: the clown who does not know he is a clown.

HIROSHIMA

OCTOBER 17, 2011   Every year we made a day trip to visit my great-uncle Denny. He lived with his wife in the backwoods of Pennsylvania, in a house older than the United States with wine-dark rafters and a cellar like a cave. The water cycle ran from pitcher pump to outhouse. The old house stood on a rambling property, all deep green, crossed by an abandoned and overgrown railroad.

Denny was an old man, a veteran of Iwo Jima with a steel plate in his head. If I understood his stories correctly he was one of those who raised the first flag there, the little one. Of the second flag, he said "If we'd known, we all would have gone up."

He had no interest in children. Was I oblivious? Was I annoyed at being ignored? When the subject of WWII came up, somehow, I parroted what I had been taught in school, where we had social studies instead of history: that the bombing of Hiroshima was a needless atrocity, only compounded by the spiteful destruction of Nagasaki – all typically American brutality.

That got his attention. He informed me that the only reason he was alive was because of the bomb. Had the war continued he would have been among the first on the beaches of Japan. He would surely have died. He thanked God for Truman and his bomb.

Of course I shut up, but I was more confused than enlightened. We can number the dead and number the saved, but these numbers are not like other numbers. We can count them, but we cannot calculate with them.

Ask: who, exactly, died to save whom? If this were a question of math there would be proportions to work out. "You, lover, your man died to save ten lives. You, father, your daughter died to save three and a half lives. You, mother, your baby died to save half a life. You, child, your dog died to save one twentieth of a life."

And there would be responsibility to assign, givers to match with receivers. "You, survivor, see the face, read the name, of the man who lost his life to save your life and five other lives. Now you must remember him."

But there are no such calculations. These numbers only look like numbers. They are lives. They are incommensurable.

It is true but trivial that I cannot put myself in Truman's place; if I were Truman himself, I would have done as Truman did, and if Truman were someone else, he would have faced someone else's choice, not Truman's. But looking at the numbers we must remember that this is not an equation; there are no factors. These numbers only look like numbers. Nothing cancels out. There is no algebra of forgiveness, no solution for innocence.

DARKNESS

OCTOBER 26, 2011   Darkness is shadow. The golden shadow of the incandescent bulb; the stainless shadow of the fluorescent; the quivering shadow of the gaslight (seek it where it lives yet; deep down in the oven, the pilot flame is the last gaslight). The footlight, the searchlight, live to dazzle, are stingy with shadows; but most generous of all is firelight, flicker and blaze, casting long shadows that strut and stride, the shadow players whose performance has never been commanded.

You will read that, for our ancestors, the succession of the long, dark nights of winter, solaced only by the wavering fire, relieved only by brief treks through a twilight world stifled with snow, gave on to a kind of trance, and that it is to the visions of the long winter that all superstitions may be traced. Now, the tropics have their own superstitions, but certainly the mind abhors a vacuum, and where there is nothing to be perceived, something will be imagined. Night by night, they overlaid the everburning stars with bold constellations.

Darkness is night. Morning and evening circle, glooming and gloaming, matutinal rise intersecting crepuscular fall at the liminal coordinate where the spectrum unfolds. Twilight that never ends while the night lights burn: mercurial moonlight over the fields, mercury vapor skyglow over the cities, and the noctilucent auroboros rattling the northern sky, over forests quiet and umbrageous as the shadow lands. The stones under your feet strike triboluminescent sparks. Fireflies constellate with the stars. Far ahead a porchlight shines, generous intent as harborless as a lighthouse.

Darkness is night, darkness is shadow; the one thing darkness is not is the absence of light. The retina is stretched like a drumhead, strung with tense nerves that toll every photon, an inchoate kaleidoscope so sensitive that it need only be pressed behind closed eyes to coruscate with phosphenes like the scintillas of cold light that kindle the eddies of the troubled sea. What light conceals from us, what we see in caves and face-down on the pillow is not darkness but *eigengrau*, the eyes' gray, lightened by the twitches of our dreaming nerves. Seeing eyes have never seen full dark. Darkness is not even the opposite of light; it is only a mood of light.

VICTORY GARDEN

HALLOWEEN, 2011   "No, I'm happy for both of you. It's a great find and once the work is done, it'll be home sweet home.

"The thing is, it's not just water damage, or termites, or things like that you have to watch out for. You find things in these old houses. Think about people in the old days. No Internet, no TV: it was either stay drunk or go nuts. Did I ever tell you about the cans we found when we started working on our place?

"The whole cellar was full of these old cans. Canning jars, I mean, you know, the glass ones with the metal tops. Shelves and shelves full of them, absolutely covered in dust. Some of them had labels on them. Let me see, there were beets, tomatoes, avocados, beans, pears, peas, everything. I want to say groats. Are those even a real thing, groats? But it doesn't matter; you couldn't tell one from the other.

"The old lady we bought the house from told us it was all stuff her mother grew in her victory garden. You know about victory gardens, right? Back in WWII it was a big deal for people to grow their own food so there'd be more for the troops fighting overseas. People plowed up their backyards and turned them into these little farms and they called them victory gardens. The original urban agriculture.

"Her mom put all these jars up right after dad went off to war. Keeping herself busy, you know? But dad never came home, so she just shut the pantry and never looked back. Out of sight, out of mind, all these years, and now it was our problem.

"You two are the same way about recycling. She wouldn't let me throw all that perfectly good glass away any more than you would. So down I go to this pantry in the cellar, and I start taking these jars up to the kitchen sink, one file box full at a time.

"You can image how creepy it was, looking down at the jars with the bleached shapes swimming around in them. It reminded me of the specimens in the lab, and you know how I felt about that.

"I had some WD-40 so I could get the lids off. With these big gloves on, I twist them open, one after another, and I dump them down the drain. I had a mask out but I never put it on. There was no smell at all. This stuff was practically embalmed.

"Now, understand, I don't have any proof. Everything that came out of those jars sort of melted. But I'm telling you, once I got through the ones in front there was something else in those jars.

"I had this jar of beets. I dump it, and there's a couple of them stuck at the bottom. I take a knife and stick it in there, scrape them loose and then, it's just a reflex, I dump them into my hand. I'm looking at my hand, and just for a second, before they melted away, I could have sworn what I was holding were a pair of human eyes.

"I know, it sounds crazy. It seemed crazy when it was happening. I decided it was my mind playing tricks on me and got back to work. I dumped all the jars, washed them out, and rinsed everything down the drain. But then when I went to wash the sink there were these little scales clinging to the bottom. They were these brittle little yellowish scales about the size of dimes. I wiped them out and threw them away.

"I put it out of my mind until the next morning. She went to use the InSinkErator and it jammed. So she calls the plumber and here I am, with this sinking feeling in my gut.

"I stood right there and watched with my guts getting tighter and tighter. And you know, I was right. The plumber's under the sink, and I can't see his face, but there's this moment when he just freezes. Perfectly still. He backs out and he's got something in his hand.

"I ask him what the problem was and he starts mumbling in Spanish. I ask him again and he just holds out his hand and there it is. He's got a hand full of human teeth. That was the moment I realized what those scales were. They were fingernails.

"What could I do? I just picked the teeth out of his hand, like loose change. I actually thanked him for finding them. So he left. He left in a hurry; we never even got a bill. I guess he figured us for a couple of serial killers.

"I've never told her about any of it. You know how much she loves that house. Why ruin it for her? And maybe they weren't teeth at all, you know? I'm not a farmer. Maybe there's some nut that looks just like a human tooth when you leave it in a jar for sixty years. How should I know?

"I'll you what I think, though. I think the daughter had it right. I think mom had her own personal victory garden. For her own personal victories."

FINIS

DECEMBER 2, 2011   The ending is the most important part. Not in all arts: pictures are endless. Not even in music, where skipping ahead is bad faith. But in writing the ending is definitive. You do not know how a sentence is meant, whether you are being told or being asked, until you reach the end.

The problem with endings is that they are all a kind of punctuation, artificial because the criteria of a good ending are abstract. A speech sums up; a sonnet turns; a story rounds off when something recurs. The key determines the cadence.

I have good reasons to prolong the Ruricolist; I feel how much I owe to it. But I must admit that the Ruricolist is over. The essay series has its natural term. These have been long years and I am different from the man I was when I began. His clothes no longer fit.

In conversation we are improvisers. For our improvisation to succeed, we must be willing to take whatever comes, trusting the outcome as we trust one another. We never say all we meant to say, or everything we think of, but that is the point: as much as we spend, we leave enriched. Now, at the end, I can affirm what I wrote at the beginning: I wrote for myself — not for friends, not for followers, not for an audience, not for posterity. This was my end of a conversation. And since this was a conversation, it must end as all conversations do, with a kind of aposiopesis, when the bill arrives, the sun comes up, the car stops, and suddenly we part.

Nondefinitions

Nondefinitions

Accounting. One of our most popular courses. In the periods (18th–21st centuries) when the profession existed, it was one of the most efficient conversation deflectors, comparable only with undertaking, but much less likely to serve as a conversation-ender and thus dilute the overall quality of the experience. In fact, accounting is our recommendation for all time travelers targeting that period who do not require geographically specialized training.

Acronyms. Once: a proud technical civilization with an awkwardly written language, which solved the problem by resort to acronyms and abbreviations. Near the end, did some sage warn how many the acronyms had become? How they were combining to breed new acronyms? Even as they prepared for their greatest triumph, their language had become utterly confused. None were found now who knew all the acronyms of another. They scattered abroad, forming peoples who shared just enough acronyms to begin to form a basic common vocabulary. Abandoned and untended, Atlantis fell. Some of these groups are known to us: Proto-Indo-Europeans, for example, or Hamito-Semites, or Sino-Tibetans.

Alchemists. To alchemists, fools and frauds, we owe the glorious and world-changing science of chemistry. No one could have invented chemistry on purpose; the wonders we expect from it daily were never unattainable, only unthinkable – except at the miraculous hands of the saints. It had to be stumbled on; we had to overreach to measure our grasp. We are proud of our sciences, and rightly so; but if there are sciences we have not yet imagined, they will not be born in the laboratories and institutes; look, rather, to the workshops and retreats, the lectures, the hyphenated works, to California; look to where the fools and frauds are steadily conceiving new ambitions.

Ball bearings. What is the power in perfection? A perfect day, not much better than a good day, justifies a life; a perfect face, not much better than a good face, launches a thousand ships; and a perfect little metal sphere, not much rounder than a toy marble, allows us to remake the world. If we can but learn to make a perfect sphere of hydrogen, rounder than round by an invisible increment, we can have our power from tame stars. Sometimes striving for perfection is foolish, *the enemy of the good*; but perfection itself should not be despised – when the key fits, doors open.

Blind spot. The hiatus in the visual field imposed by the presence of the optic nerve. We are not aware of the blind spot because the brain fills it in. I would not try to perpetrate another use of this analogy. We all have blind spots – whenever we connect, the line of connection eclipses the thing connected to, and we only think we see it. Very well. But now that we have blind spots everywhere – what did we have before we had blind spots? Prejudices, fondness? Certainly; but "blind spot" says more than either of these. This simple analogy – "blind spot" – changes the very way you think. To have made such an analogy – that would be enough to justify a life.

Brain. An appliance invented by nineteenth-century German philosophers to remove the drudgery from thought experiments. Pity the situation of the medieval Arabic philosophers who had ask God to specially create a *flying man* – separated from all his parts, falling forever through lightless infinity – merely in order to raise the problems which any modern philosopher can confront by borrowing a mad scientist's brain in a vat.

Clouds. Going south from the land of the Yankees, the first thing you notice (if you look up) is that the clouds are growing. Even the smallest southern clouds, on the clearest days, are piled up like northern stormheads. Near the Gulf, there is a constant traffic of mountains overhead. Majestic as these are, they make me worry for children and lovers. They are big, but dumb – mute – I cannot see anything at all in them.

Doors. Devices which, on all civilized planets, remove themselves from the path of people moving from one room to another. Some swish aside, some rush up and down, some dilate, some simply disengage. There are still, alas, backward planets where people must employ their manipulatory appendages to open doors. Such primitive doors, being dangerous disease vectors and traffic choke-points, and reinforcing inequalities with elaborate conventions of who opens for whom, hold back planetary economic and cultural development. When we find such a planet, tragically barred from further progress by its doorknobs, then it is our clear duty to invade and conquer, in order to civilize them.

Eer. A bodiless, malevolent supernatural being. The eer must not be confused with the ghost: a ghost is a remnant of a human being; an eer never was alive. Formerly, cities were inhabited weirdly by ghosts; but since the beginning of urban sprawl, deprived of their natural habitats in wastes, wilds, and deserts, eers have become common in cities, where their prolific breeding has displaced the native population of ghosts. Many young people today have never experienced a real ghostly whisper or flicker in the corner of the eye; sadly, they take it for granted that all silence and dimness is eerie.

Fences. "Good fences make good neighbors" is the famous quotation, and would have made a good motto for a New England confederacy, had they chosen to secede. But the principle has many other extensions, for fences *determine* neighbors. Barbed wire makes neighbors prickly, tense – even wiry. Wrought iron gives neighbors easily overwrought; cast iron, neighbors who are often overcast or downcast – sometimes even cast out or cast-off; and both, neighbors prone to irony. Stones, of course, are unpredictable: sometimes, they cause stony taciturnity and stone-coldness; sometimes they give you neighbors who rock; but most of the time, stones attract stoners. (Fortunately, concrete attracts them as well; if you must build a stone fence, try to make sure of an abandoned building between you and any population center.) You can never be sure what to expect from a wood fence. Such neighbors (especially if they have not been pressure-treated) are known to split, flake off, come loose, snap, rot out – even catch fire. Vinyl fences are very reliable: they draw neighbors who are low-maintenance, low-interest, and of uniform color. And predictably, people who grow their own fences put down roots. Now, though fence analysis is a young science, is is a very exciting one. If you'd like to help, the new Endower Institute Center for Fensive Studies is ready to accept your donations.

Gold. A soft, malleable, non-corroding metal; a primitive form of aluminum. Gold foil is called *leaf*; gold cans were called *goblets*; gold tokens were called *coins*. Gold is very heavy, and so cannot be used to construct monocoque aircraft; an inconvenience which held back aeronautics for centuries.

Guitar. The occult instrument: not played, but addressed with secret hand-signs, transient hieroglyphs of a Mystery whose hieratic rites are carried out before audiences; one hand for Apollo, quiet, smooth, rapid, precise; and one hand for Dionysus, simple, restless, free and frantic; and the whole portable, companionable as a familiar, the conjurer's circle wherein the shade of the ideal orchestra is called up and given voice to tell its secret.

Lachrymatory. In the Victorian period, a small glass bottle used to catch and preserve tears of mourning. Today, tear bottles are made of plastic, pre-filled to be dropped in dry eyes (as of contact wearers), and manufactured in the third world (presumably under third-world conditions). How they fill these bottles, it were better not to ask.

Lawns. Lawns and hair show an obvious resemblance, and many of the tools used for one have equivalents used for the other. There could be an opportunity here for entrepreneurs: where is lawn dye? Mix pigment with fertilizer to drape the cities in technicolor suburban quilts and diversify golf courses (black grass shows up the ball, but hides the terrain; white grass lets you play by moonlight). And what of verbs? If we can *scalp* our enemies, why not *lawn* properties – gleefully tear up pampered, insatiable grass – "Yes, I was the one, I lawned that house – the one just up the hill, where the wildflowers are growing."

Lighthouse. They built the lighthouse where no ships came. Later, they lied to their children – told them that the ships had come first. They chose not to think about how sometimes the spices from the ships needed names, the hides needed scaling, the dolls needed pruning. So they prospered in their lie, until a storm broke the lighthouse. Only its coiled iron stairs remained. The warehouses emptied, and still the ships did not come. So the old men told the young men, who had been children, how they had lied. Some fled; some stayed, and helped rebuild. The sea has long since moved away. In the tower, where once was a lamp, now are bells. But whether the god came first, or the bells, no worshiper now remembers.

Magnolia. A fragrant, flowering tree. A lying tree, frequently found conspiring with moonlight. In combination with sultry summers may bring on political Reaction, with acute fervor.

Mandarin. A kind of orange. In Imperial China these oranges, planted at the proper time of year, under special conditions including a constant supply of cool dry, air and the absence of sunlight, were used to grow bureaucrats. Within a week of proper planting the orange splits open to reveal a small, correctly proportioned man (a trade was carried on in "figurines" of this kind), with roots growing from the soles of his feet.

Mandarin farms would allow the bureaucrat to reach an approximately human size before cutting it free. Bureaucrats grown in this way have an affinity for conditions resembling those they were grown under. Apparently the Portuguese who used the same name for the oranges and the bureaucrats had heard some hint of this; otherwise, it was a well-kept secret, until acquired by other European invaders. This technique is still in extensive use around the world. The roots remain tender; beware bureaucrats in sensible shoes, and never try to reason with one who seems to be having foot trouble.

Mangel-wurzel. (Not to be confused with the Wurzel mangle, formerly a kind of laundry machine, or manglewurz, the condition in workers now and then emerged from the Wurzel mangle.) A kind of gigantic beet, resembling a turnip, formerly much used for livestock feed. As watermelons are to bullets, so mangel-wurzels once were to swords: a vegetable stand-in for a human enemy. And as the watermelon blown to bits is a promise to our enemies, so the mangel-wurzel neatly sliced in two by a stroke (or draw cut) of the saber was (some of) our ancestors' promise to their own enemies. Which raises three questions. One: do all warlike peoples have their particular enemy fruit or vegetable? Did the Romans learn their ferocity in the fight against cabbage? Was the battle of Waterloo won in the pumpkin fields of Surrey? Two: are these fruits merely convenient objects, or do we have some inborn fear of them to work out – were our ancestors the victims of shambling, formless, boneless things – is every watermelon we execute an instinctual way of exorcising the memory of Shoggoths? Three, does every fruit have its associated weapon? Does the tomato sleep on the shelf through nightmares of the day when the raygun will find its fated victim?

Moral paradox. "Can I talk to you a minute? The cops say you were the last guy to see my brother – I mean, he was my brother, you were up there on the bridge with him. Did he, like, say anything to you? I wish I knew what he was thinking. I mean, everybody knew he was depressed – ever since the infection he just kept putting on weight, his glands don't work right – but he said he was OK with the operation, we thought there was some hope finally. I just don't get it. Right in front of the trolley. Do you think – somebody said to me maybe he thought he could stop the trolley – no, never mind. That's stupid. I mean, he was an engineer – he would have known, tons of metal, the trolley would go right through him and hit the other people anyway. Oh, I'm sorry, man, I'm rambling, you had to see that, all those people, I get it, you can't talk right now. Thanks for listening. Look, let me give you my number. If you ever need to talk, I'm here for you. OK, we'll talk later. Thanks. You're a great guy."

Obnoxious. Adj. Persistently or incorrigibly annoying after the manner of an obnox. The obnox (from German *oppnochs*) is an extinct species of Bovidae. Obnoxen were quite small (the size of a small pony or large dog), and had horns which pointed, neither to the sides like modern cows, nor forwards like the aurochs, but backwards. Some scientists speculate that obnoxen originally evolved to live in tropical swamps: their size made them efficient radiators of heat, and their horns were well-adapted for backscratching and fly-swatting; but by the beginning of history they were only found in Europe. Furthermore, obnoxen were congenitally afflicted with bad eyesight. Accordingly, the defensive strategy of the obnox was an unusual one. Rather than violently charging, the obnox who detected a violation of his territory (that is, once he had been struck) emitted a series of alternating low and high-pitched moos to summon any other obnoxen in the area. It should be noted that this gathering would take some time – the soft feet of the obnox, well adapted to muddy marshes, limited them to extremely slow speeds on dry ground. Once assembled, the obnoxen would surround the intruder and begin the counterattack. As they were small, incapable of sure footing, and weaponless – even their teeth were incurved and could not take hold – the attack was limited to a soft, repeated, mass nudging, carried on in absolute silence and accompanied by a relentless cow-eyed stare. By all accounts, no animal, however fierce, having been once been attacked by obnoxen, would ever go near them again. Indeed, the original use of the word *oppnochsisch* was to describe, not likeness to the animals' behavior, but the glassy stares and melancholy reveries that victims of obnox attacks were thereafter wont to fall into. The obnox was systematically exterminated during the wars of the seventeenth, eighteenth, and early nineteenth centuries – for the appearance of a herd of obnoxen in the midst of a battle was known to set even the most hardened warriors to flight.

Relativity. Time (said some fool) is nature's way of keeping everything from happening at once. Relativity, to the contrary, demonstrates that for anything to happen, there must be a perspective from which everything happens at once; and, conversely, that no two things actually happen at the same time, except as they happen to someone or something. If something has happened, then everything has already happened, and nothing has happened yet. If that confuses you, wait: it will make sense in time. It already has.

Scarecrows. Surely scarecrows should have a larger place in psychology. At times they have been the most common and accessible form of sculpture, a distinct branch of folk artistry. Besides their origin, consider their purpose: they are mankind's most honest self-portrait, being made not for human eyes with intention to influence or impress, but for animal eyes with intention to seem human as they judge what that is. Is this really what we think of ourselves? Slouched, awkward, attired in rags and tatters (changing our posture and dress from time to time to keep our enemies from getting used to us), always on the point of falling apart, alone, silent, exposed to sun and rain; yet still standing, still guarding something worth guarding.

Sharks. The shark is no pilgrim: half as old as life, streamlined by a million generations bent on the same restless, uncompromised purpose, he has never yet doubted. He has an ancestry but it does not matter. Once hunger met water the shark was inevitable. He is written into the laws of physics between the ratios of buoyancy and the equations of flow and drag. He belongs utterly. When he dies he leaves no bones to protest it. They say that deep enough there is no more up or down, but they should know better. The shark is down. The moment your blood enters the water, you start to fall. In the whole wide ocean there is nothing to catch you. First he smells you; then he hears you; then he sees you; then he feels the current switching in your muscles as you try not to breathe. But you have nothing to be ashamed of. The hunger you feed is not a vain hunger like the lion's, not a grubby hunger like the worm's, but perfect hunger: unhurried, impartial, and pure.

Shoehorns. A small strip of metal used to force feet into too-small shoes. Here is a device whose near-ubiquity tells you something basic and easy to overlook about the past. Look at old pictures and the looks on people's faces and think: shoehorns. Look at old news and the things people said and did and voted for and think: shoehorns. The next time something about the twentieth century perplexes you, ask yourself: if I had to start every day of my life by levering my feet into stiff, hard-soled shoes, might I be as crazy?

Side effects. Diseases due to cures. The progress of medicine, as it delivers us each newer, more powerful cure, also seems to delivers newer, more powerful side effects. Perhaps the notion of cures is outdated; perhaps the right a patient ought to be asking for is the right of disease choice. "You have disease X? Wouldn't you rather have disease Y or Z?" Trade your disease for another; get tired of it; trade it for yet another. And if the maxim of the greener grass holds, the final achievement of medicine will be to allow one half of humanity to trade its diseases with the other.

Socks. Here is one way the world could end. Not too long from now, when video cameras and wireless transmitters have become so cheap as to be effectively disposable, so tiny as to be unnoticeable, some clever young fellow will get the idea to discover where his socks vanish to, and clip tiny camera-transmitters to each one. Once a few have disappeared he will sit down at his computer, pick up his slice of pizza, click the video feed open, and see—

Solipsism.

Are "you" Happy? Do you "want" to be Happy? Then you need to "know" about JOHN TEMPLE, the "One" you've been waiting for! In 1998 JOHN TEMPLE made discovery while reading Philosophy of "only" completely TRUE religion Solipsism. JOHN TEMPLE discovers that himself, JOHN TEMPLE, is Only "Real" Being in "Universe"! Since then JOHN TEMPLE has made 100's of people "happy" just by "thinking" about them and making them "real". Being real is "only" TRUE HAPPINESS. You too can be "happy"!! Just send name and picture to JOHN TEMPLE and he will make you "happy" by thinking about YOU for FIVE MINUTES!! Only $20 for five minutes of "HAPPINESS"! You too can be "happy"!! JOHN TEMPLE - IS THE "TEMPLE" OF HAPPINESS!

Sticks and stones. An island in the South Pacific; an adventurous anthropologist; and recorded in his journals (found decades later in the proverbial Hong Kong stall) his preliminary observations of a tribe of bone-eaters who never wielded stick or stone – who, prizing even the hyoid, used no violence at all – only tied their victim out in the square and taunted him to death.

424

These days. These days, in our culture, it is generally agreed that (in most cases) in our society, for us today, we can certainly say that, from a modern perspective – as studies have shown – everyone knows, as a matter of common sense – even the other side must see it by now – that anyone who looks into the problem (and this is well-known) has grasped the obvious. It's a matter of record. Also note that polls have shown that most people, across all backgrounds, know very well (whatever they may say) that it's as plain as day. If you can believe that, what's next? I hate to be alarmist, but the sad fact is that, barring some unforeseen catastrophe, at this moment, facing a crisis (somebody has to say it) we need to understand what we're up against. The fact of the matter, and I hate to have to say this, is that what is comes down to, in our culture, is that in the end that's what we have to learn to live with in our society these days.

Think tanks. The distinctive institutions that make modern life modern; the jewels in the watch case – all-important, but self-contained. Most of your rhetorical questions, the ones you let slide with a sigh, staring out the window – "How did we get here?" or "What were we thinking?" or "Whose bright idea was that?" – they do, in fact, have an answer: think tanks. Thinks tanks are to secret societies as airplanes are to railroads – smaller, with less tonnage; faster and entirely out of reach.

Wallet. "In the time of the first Pax Americana," – saith the chronicler, but who believes the old stories? – "every man of age was required to carry at all times a scrap of cow-leather in a fold in the cloth of his garments; and except that he showed this Wallet on demand, no merchant would sell to him, and a judge might throw him in jail only because he was without his Wallet. The word comes from the old *wall*, for the sides of a room; and this because each Wallet was like a key to the Wall, wherein law-abiders dwell."

Yarn. A miniature sacred grove of Ouroboros; an anagogical prefiguration of the Eternal Return; a mystery beyond mathematics, what had once end and beginning yet traps endlessness and eternity in its folds; a kind of life, defying entropy, growing neater and tighter the more energy is spent in its unraveling.

Index of Titles

THIS book is set in MONOTYPE BEMBO
BOOK, using LuaLATEX. ¶ The font
BEMBO BOOK is a revised digitization of a
font originally cut for the Aldine Press and
used to set Pietro Bembo's *De Ætna* as well
as the famous *Many-Lover's Strife of Love in
a Dream.* ¶ The typesetting system LuaLATEX
adds support for OpenType fonts and Uni-
code characters to Donald Knuth's TEX typesetting system as extended by LATEX – the
standard system used for typesetting scientific papers and monographs due to its precision, flexibility, and beauty.

Printed in Great Britain
by Amazon